Guitar Atlas
Guitar Styles from Around the World

Alfred, the leader in educational music publishing, and the National Guitar Workshop, one of America's finest guitar schools, have joined forces to bring you the best, most progressive educational tools possible. We hope you will enjoy this book and encourage you to look for other fine products from Alfred and the National Guitar Workshop.

Contents

Introduction 2

Jamaica 3

Cuba 51

Celtic 99

Flamenco 147

China 195

Russia 241

Alfred Music Publishing Co., Inc.
P.O. Box 10003
Van Nuys, CA 91410-0003
alfred.com

Copyright © MMIX by Alfred Music Publishing Co., Inc.
All rights reserved. Printed in USA.

ISBN-10: 0-7390-6344-8 (Book & CD)
ISBN-13: 978-0-7390-6344-6 (Book & CD)

Cover photographs:
Distressed Asiatic Grunge Frames: © istockphoto.com / albertc111
Earth Model Atlantic View: © istockphoto.com / janrysavy
Guitar courtesy of Martin Guitars.

Introduction

Guitar Atlas: Volume 2, when combined with *Guitar Atlas: Volume 1*, is possibly the most comprehensive and diverse collection of world music available for guitar. These books are designed to introduce you to the music of various cultures and provide you with new and exciting pieces for your repertoire. In addition, new doors will open for your playing style and technique.

In this volume, you will be introduced to the music of Jamaica, Cuba, China, Russia, Spain (Flamenco), and Ireland and Scotland (Celtic). You will learn new and interesting techniques, exotic scales and rhythms, and alternate tunings adapted from traditional ethnic instruments. The music of the world is a wonderful resource upon which to draw when composing and performing. By immersing yourself in this music, you will give your own music a diversity and depth that, otherwise, you may not have thought possible.

Guitar Atlas: Jamaica features an overview of styles such as mento, ska, rocksteady, and reggae.

Guitar Atlas: Cuba introduces you to the diverse musical styles of son, mambo, guaguancó, bolero, changüí, guajira, and danzón.

Guitar Atlas: Celtic features the music of Ireland and Scotland, and it includes jigs, reels, slow airs and laments, hornpipes, strathspeys, and traditional songs by harpist/composer Turlough O'Carolan.

Guitar Atlas: Flamenco teaches you rhythms and techniques such as soleares, llamada, bulerías, alzapúa, alegrías, rasgueado, and tremolo.

Major genres of Chinese music are covered in *Guitar Atlas: China,* including blowing and hitting music, silk and bamboo music, guqin and the Literati Scholar tradition, kunqu and Peking opera, Yi courtship music, and Tibetan folk music.

Guitar Atlas: Russia includes an overview of balalaika music, the ancient tones and chants of the Russian Orthodox Church, music of the Russian seven-string guitar, and traditional village music.

Look for *Guitar Atlas: Volume 1* (if you do not have it already), which features the music of Africa, Brazil, India, Italy, Japan, and the Middle East.

We hope you enjoy these books as much as we have enjoyed bringing you the *Guitar Atlas Series.*

An MP3 CD is included with this book to make learning easier and more enjoyable. The symbol shown at bottom left appears next to every example in the book that features an MP3 track. Use the MP3s to ensure you're capturing the feel of the examples and interpreting the rhythms correctly. The track number below the symbol corresponds directly to the example you want to hear (example numbers are above the icon). All the track numbers are unique to each "book" within this volume, meaning every book has its own Track 1, Track 2, and so on. (For example, *Jamaica* starts with Track 1, as does *Cuba, Celtic,* etc.) Track 1 for each book will help you tune your guitar.

To access the MP3s on the CD, place the CD in your computer's CD-ROM drive. In Windows, double-click on My Computer, then right-click on the CD icon labeled "MP3 Files" and select Explore to view the files and copy them to your hard drive. For Mac, double-click on the CD icon on your desktop labeled "MP3 Files" to view the files and copy them to your hard drive.

Jamaica

Raleigh Green

*Guitar Styles
from Around the World*

This book was acquired, edited, and produced
by Workshop Arts, Inc., the publishing arm of
the National Guitar Workshop.
Nathaniel Gunod, acquisitions, managing editor
Burgess Speed, acquisitions, senior editor
Timothy Phelps, interior design
Ante Gelo, music typesetter
Barbara Smolover, interior illustrations
CD recorded and mastered by Collin Tilton at Bar None Studio, Northford, CT
Raleigh Green (guitar), Matthew Liston (bass), Pete Sweeney (drums)

Contents

ABOUT THE AUTHOR 5
   Acknowledgements 5
   Notation Guide 5

INTRODUCTION 6
   Jamaican History 6
   Jamaican Music Overview 6

CHAPTER 1—Mento 7
   History of Mento 7
   Mento Strumming 8
      Lord of the Fleas 8
      Mento Mama 9
   Mento Lead Melodies 9
      Facing Forward 10
      Check Your Pockets 11
      Papaya Paradise 12
   Mento-Calypso 14
      Color Me Calypso 15

CHAPTER 2—Ska 16
   The Beginnings of Ska 16
      Jamaican Lady 16
   The Skank 17
      Straight Ahead 18
      Fountain of Youth 19
   Ska Horn Lines 20
      Strum It Up 20
      Tie the Knot 21
   The Skatalites 22
      Skanks for the Memories 22

CHAPTER 3—Rocksteady 24
   History of Rocksteady 24
   Slow It Down 24
      Rude Boyfriend 25
      Slow Skank 26
   Keep It Muted 27
      Chill Out Rude Boy 27
   Steady Sixteenths 28
      Stay Steady 28
      Alphabet Soup 30

CHAPTER 4—Reggae 32
   Early Reggae 32
      Jamaican Peach 32
      Roll with the Punches 33
      All Aboard 34
   The Rastafari Movement and Roots Reggae 35
   The "Bubble" 35
      Never Forget 36
      African Riddim 37
   Reggae Rhythm Embellishment 38
      Back Alley Dreadlock 38
   Dub-Style Effects 39
      The Question 40

CHAPTER 5—Bob Marley 41
   In the Style of "Stir It Up" 41
      Natty Dreadlock 41
   In the Style of "Rasta Man Chant" 42
      Nyabinghi Beat 42
   In the Style of "I Shot the Sheriff" 42
      Dread Man Walking 43
   In the Style of "Exodus" 44
      On the Run 44
   In the Style of "Redemption Song" 45
      Rasta Farewell 46

CHAPTER 6—Ernest Ranglin 47
   The Journey Begins 48

FINAL WORD 50

Track 1

A compact disc is included with this book. Using it with the book can make learning easier and more enjoyable. The symbol shown at the left appears next to every example that is on the CD. Use the CD to help ensure that you're capturing the feel of the examples and interpreting the rhythms correctly. The track number below the symbol corresponds directly to the example you want to hear. Track 1 will help you tune to this CD. Enjoy!

About the Author

Raleigh Green, based in the Boston area, is known for his versatility as a guitarist and his expertise as a music educator. Proficient in many styles of music, Raleigh is the author of *The Versatile Guitarist* (Alfred/National Guitar Workshop #28243). He teaches guitar at Phillips Academy in Andover, Massachusetts and is a long-time instructor for the National Guitar Workshop and DayJams. Raleigh teaches online guitar lessons at WorkshopLive.com and is endorsed by D'Addario strings. After receiving a B.F.A. from the University of Missouri with a concentration in art and computer-aided multimedia, Raleigh attended the Berklee College of Music where he graduated *summa cum laude* and was awarded both the Quincy Jones Award and the Professional Music Achievement Award. Raleigh lives in Medford, Massachusetts with his wife, Laura, their son Cole, and an Australian cattle dog named Max.

ACKNOWLEDGEMENTS

Very special thanks to Laura and Cole, Ken and Linda Green, the Breretons, and all of my friends, students, and colleagues at Phillips Andover Academy; David, Barbara, and Jesse Smolover; Burgess Speed, and everyone else in the Workshop family. Also thanks to Kevin "K-Don" Michaels, Wayne Marshall, and Carl Johnson for research assistance; D'Addario & Co.; and Pete Sweeney and Matthew Liston for playing great music on the CD.

This book is dedicated to Cole Leven Brereton-Green.

NOTATION GUIDE

H = Hammer-on.

P = Pull-off.

SL = Ascending slide.

SL = Descending slide.

P.M. = Palm Mute.

⌒ = *Fermata*. Pause, or hold note longer than its indicated duration.

> = *Accent*. Emphasize the note or chord.

= *Staccato*. Make note shorter than its indicated duration.

= *Chuck*. Muted, percussive, unpitched note.

p, i, m, a = The right-hand fingers starting with the thumb.

1, 2, 3, 4, 0 = The left-hand fingers starting with the index finger; 0 = open string. The left-hand fingers are indicated under the TAB.

rit. = Abbreviation for ritardando. Become gradually slower.

Swing 8ths = Eighth notes written like straight eighth notes, but played with a long-short rhythm that produces the shuffle feel. When *Swing 8ths* appears at the beginning of a piece, eighth notes are played like triplets with the first two eighth notes tied.

♩ = 185 = Tempo marking. In this case, there are 185 quarter notes, or beats, per minute. (If you have a metronome, set it to 185).

4x = Play four times.

D.S. al Fine = *Dal Segno al Fine*. Go back to the symbol 𝄋 and play to the **Fine**, which is the end of the piece.

‖: :‖ = *Repeat signs*. Repeat music between the two symbols. When only the end repeat sign is present, repeat music from the beginning.

Guitar Atlas: Jamaica

Introduction

Guitar Atlas: Jamaica is an introduction to the rich musical tradition of Jamaica. From a guitarist's perspective, there is much to love in Jamaican music, especially the guitar-centric styles of mento, ska, rocksteady, and reggae. In this book, the most important Jamaican musicians, guitarists, styles, and techniques are demonstrated through numerous musical examples. Most of these examples are meant to be played with a pick, although there is some fingerpicking as well. You will get the most from this book if you have experience reading standard music notation and/or TAB, as well as some experience with common open chords, barre chords, and basic guitar technique. The Notation Guide on page 5 should help you with any unfamiliar notation. Welcome to *Guitar Atlas: Jamaica,* and let's begin our journey!

JAMAICAN HISTORY

The island of Jamaica is located in the Caribbean Sea. It is situated 90 miles south of Cuba and is a part of the Greater Antilles, a group of islands that also includes Puerto Rico and Hispaniola. With a tumultuous history of slavery, war, poverty, and natural disasters, Jamaica is a true melting pot of mixed ethnicities. Jamaica is smaller than the state of Connecticut, however, the global impact that this Caribbean island has had on the rest of the world is enormous.

When Christopher Columbus first arrived to Jamaica in 1494, the native Arawak people (also known as Taino Indians) had already been there since 650 A.D. Sadly, soon after Spain's occupation of the country began in 1509, the indigenous population was wiped out by slavery, disease, and war. By 1655, Britain seized Jamaica and soon, through intense colonization and a booming slave trade, Jamaica became the largest producer of sugar in the world. After many uprisings, slavery was abolished in 1838. In 1872, Kingston became the capitol, and in 1962, Jamaica became an independent nation.

JAMAICAN MUSIC OVERVIEW

In the early 19th century, when the percussive musical traditions brought over by West African slaves mixed with the music of the European *quadrille* (a precursor to the square dance), the Jamaican folk music style called *mento* was born. Mento was Jamaica's most popular music throughout the 1930s and 1940s; however, during this period, American jazz also became immensely popular in Jamaica. By the 1950s, mento was still alive, but American R&B had largely taken hold of the Jamaican popular music scene. In the 1960s, all of these various influences came together to create a unique Jamaican musical style called *ska*.

The quick tempo of ska was a reflection of the upbeat mood in Jamaica after gaining independence in 1962. Jamaicans soon observed, however, that serious social problems remained, and in 1966, the music changed with the mood. A new style called *rocksteady* emerged, replacing the upbeat pace of ska with a much slower feel. A short-lived movement, rocksteady was only around for two years when Jamaica's most famous musical style, *reggae,* was born. From the late 1960s to the mid-1980s, reggae became a worldwide sensation. During this time period, the *Rastafari* (those belonging to the religious and cultural *Rastafari movement* covered on page 35) garnered a strong association with reggae due to the international fame of Bob Marley and others. English bands like The Clash and The Police started to incorporate reggae sounds into their own music. By the latter half of the 20th century, a wide array of reggae subgenres developed, including *dancehall, toasting, dub, raggamuffin, reggaeton, 2-tone,* and *lovers rock,* just to name a few. Despite being a small island, Jamaica and its varied musical traditions have greatly inspired and influenced musicians and music lovers throughout the world.

Chapter 1: MENTO

HISTORY OF MENTO

In 19th century Jamaica, African and European musical traditions merged to create a unique style of Jamaican folk music called mento. Up until the 1950s, this was Jamaica's most popular music style. Mento bands came in many flavors, some with a folksy, rural sound and some with more of a jazzy, dance-band style.

The rural mento musicians played Jamaican country music, using acoustic instruments such as the banjo on lead and rhythm, acoustic guitar on rhythm, homemade bamboo saxophone (see illustration below), hand percussion, and a rumba box (see below) playing the bass notes. The more polished urban mento style was influenced by 1920s Caribbean jazz bands; instead of homemade instruments, professional saxophones and upright basses were favored, along with piano and electric guitar.

In 1951, thanks to recording pioneer Stanley Motta, the Jamaican music industry was born with the creation of the first mento record, a medley of mento songs by Bertie Lyons (also known as Lord Fly). During this period, many recordings of rural and urban mento music were produced. However, *calypso* (an Afro-Caribbean musical style from Trinidad) was the Caribbean's main musical export, so even though mento and calypso are distinct styles, the early mento recordings were sometimes called "calypsos" in order to appeal to the international music market. As the Jamaican recording industry developed, mento artists gained new exposure, riding on the wave of singer Harry Belafonte's calypso craze. The 1950s were often considered mento's "golden age," partially because of this association with calypso music, but also because of the increase in recording during that decade. This chapter takes a look at the styles of a few of the main contributors to these classic mento recordings.

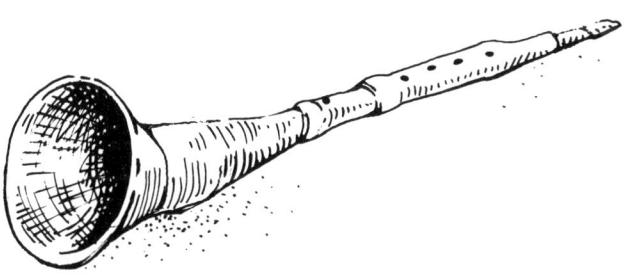

Homemade bamboo saxophone.

Rumba box.

Guitar Atlas: Jamaica

MENTO STRUMMING

This first example is written in the style of a classic mento tune called "Naughty Little Flea." The original song was composed and recorded in the late 1950s by the internationally renowned singer, composer, dancer, and guitarist Lord Flea. Born Norman Thomas in Kingston, Jamaica in 1932, Lord Flea was sometimes called the "Calypso King of Jamaica." The arrangement below demonstrates a common mento rhythm guitar part, featuring downstrums (⊓), alternate strums (⊓ V), and common open chords. "Naughty Little Flea" went on to be covered by numerous artists, most notably Miriam Makeba and Calypso legend Harry Belafonte. (Notice on the CD the guitar is panned to the left. By turning your balance control to the right, you can eliminate the guitar part and play along with the backing band. On the CD, all examples with just one guitar are mixed this way.)

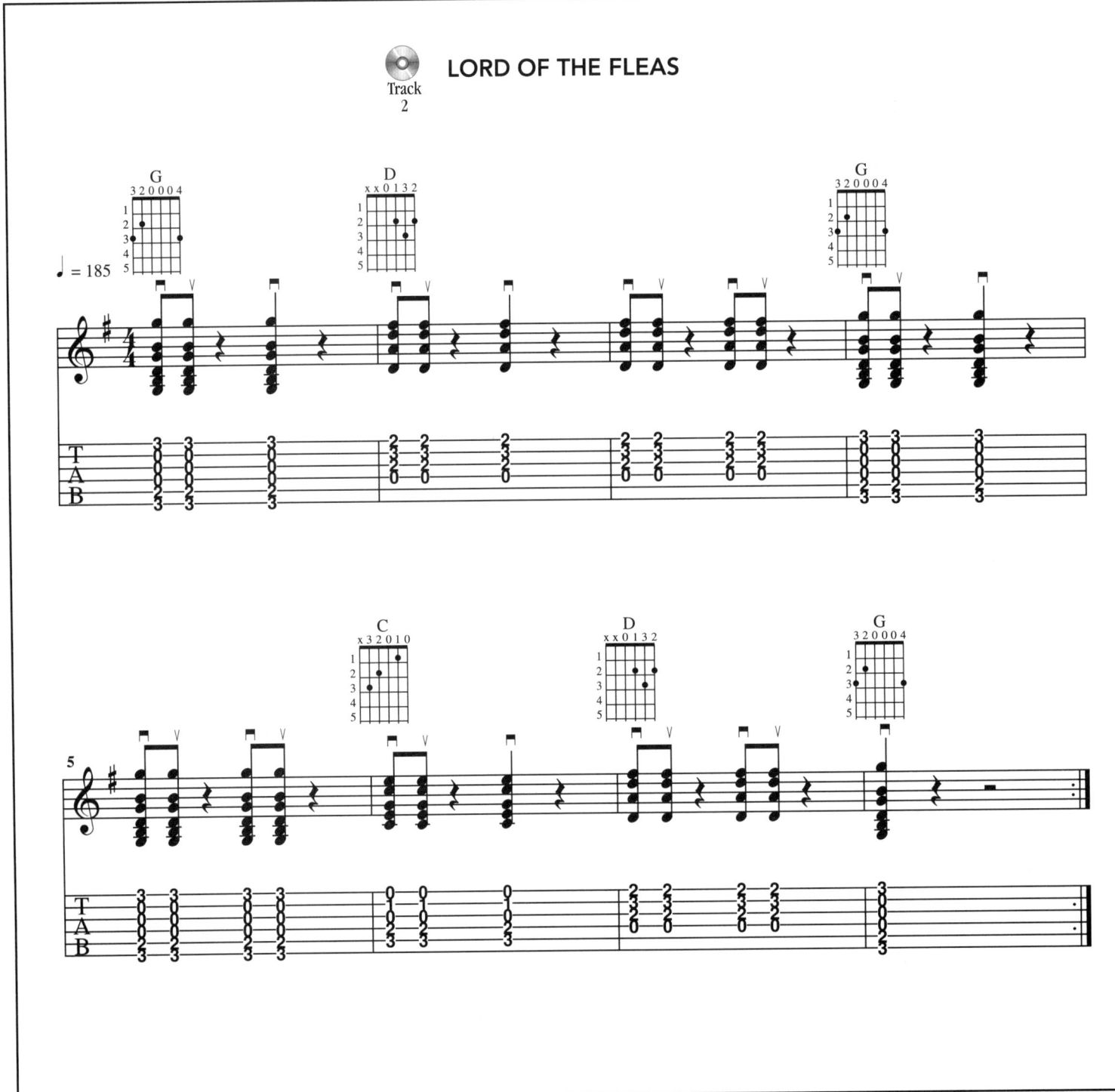

LORD OF THE FLEAS
Track 2

The next example from the golden age of mento is in the style of "Glamour Gal" by Harold Richardson and The Ticklers. "Glamour Gal" was one of the first mento records ever recorded, featuring only guitar, hand percussion, and vocals. Notice in the strumming pattern the emphasis placed on beats 2 and 4; this rhythmic pulse laid the foundation for ska, rocksteady, and reggae.

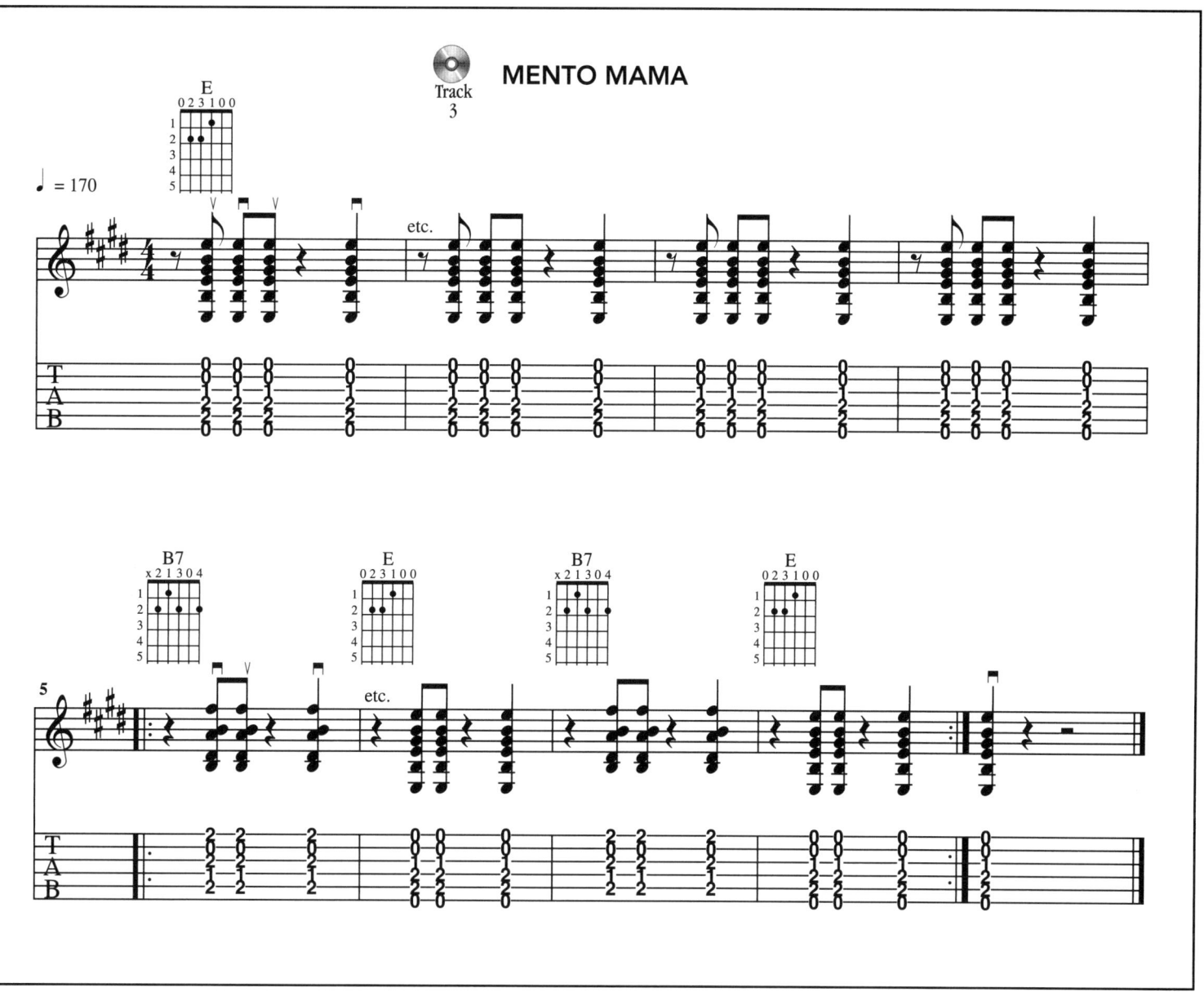

MENTO LEAD MELODIES

The Jolly Boys are one of the most notable and enduring mento bands. Although their personnel has changed numerous times throughout the years, they have been going strong from the 1940s to today. "Facing Forward" (next page) is an early mento tune in the style of "Back to Back" by The Jolly Boys. In mento, the banjo often has the role of a lead instrument due to its volume and sharp timbre (tone), which allows it to easily cut through the band. In "Facing Forward," the interplay between the acoustic rhythm guitar and the banjo (arranged as a guitar part) is illustrated. The lead melody (Guitar 1) consists of *arpeggios* (an arpeggio is the notes of a chord played separately) that alternate between eighth notes and quarter-note triplets. The rhythm guitar strumming pattern (Guitar 2) features alternate strums exclusively. (On the CD, Guitar 1 is panned to the left and Guitar 2 is panned to the right. Turn your balance control all the way left or right to isolate either part and play along with the recording. All examples with two guitars are mixed this way.)

Guitar Atlas: Jamaica

FACING FORWARD

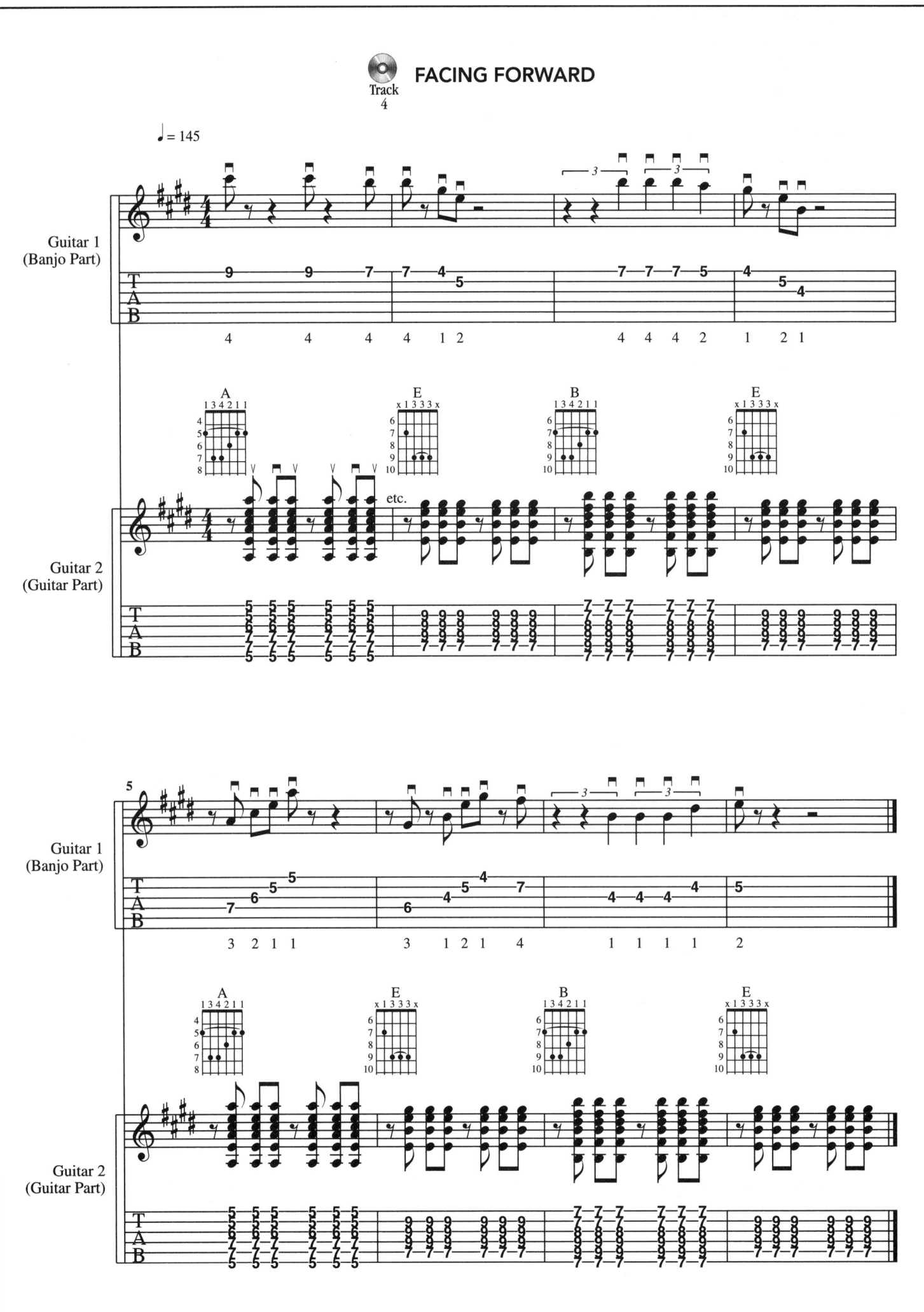

The next two examples are in the style of Count Lasher (born Terence Parkins). Count Lasher was one of the most popular and talented golden age mento stars, rivaled only by Lord Flea. He was also one of the most prolific artists, making at least 50 recordings throughout the 1950s, '60s, and '70s. The tune below is written in the style of "Samfi Man" (a "samfi man" is a con artist). Like the previous example, the banjo part (Guitar 1) plays an arpeggio-based melody, while the acoustic guitar (Guitar 2) plays a common mento strumming pattern. Remember, like all of the two- and three-part examples in this book, you can adjust your balance control and play along with either part on your CD.

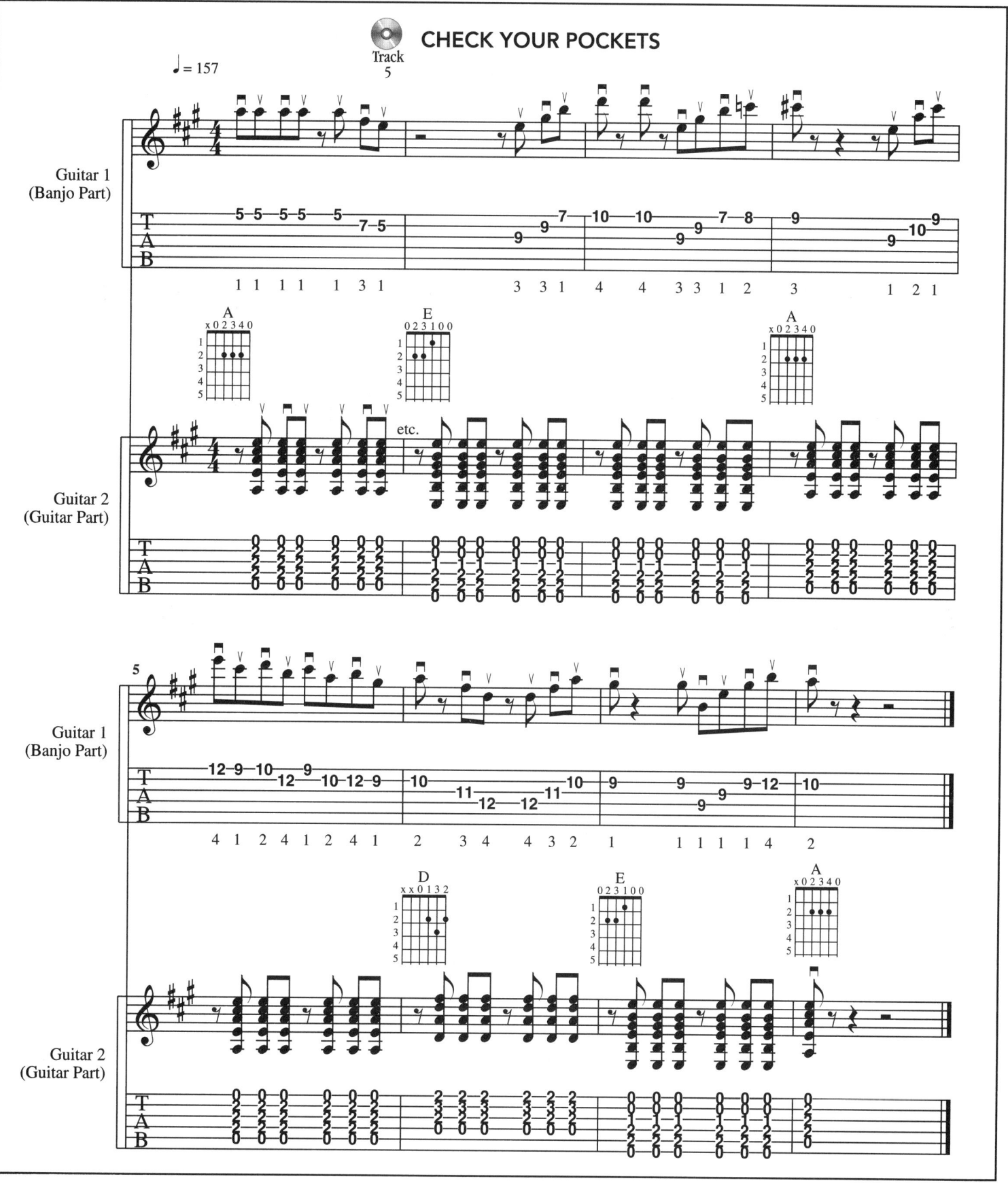

Following is an example based on Count Lasher's rural mento classic "Mango Time." It features a longer song form with a fingerstyle acoustic guitar intro (Guitar 2). After playing the intro, Guitar 2 switches to a mento strumming pattern that, decades later, would become an essential reggae strumming pattern (see pages 38 and 41). Since the intro is played fingerstyle, it will be necessary to strum the following rhythm patterns with either your thumb or fingers, rather than with a pick.

The lead melody (Guitar 1) is a guitar arrangement in the style of what was played on a homemade bamboo saxophone on the original recording. Notice the last phrase of this lead line, which consists entirely of quarter-note triplets. When played along with the strumming pattern based on eighth notes, this quarter-note triplet rhythm creates a compelling polyrhythmic effect that is common in mento music. (A *polyrhythm* consists of two or more independent rhythms played simultaneously.)

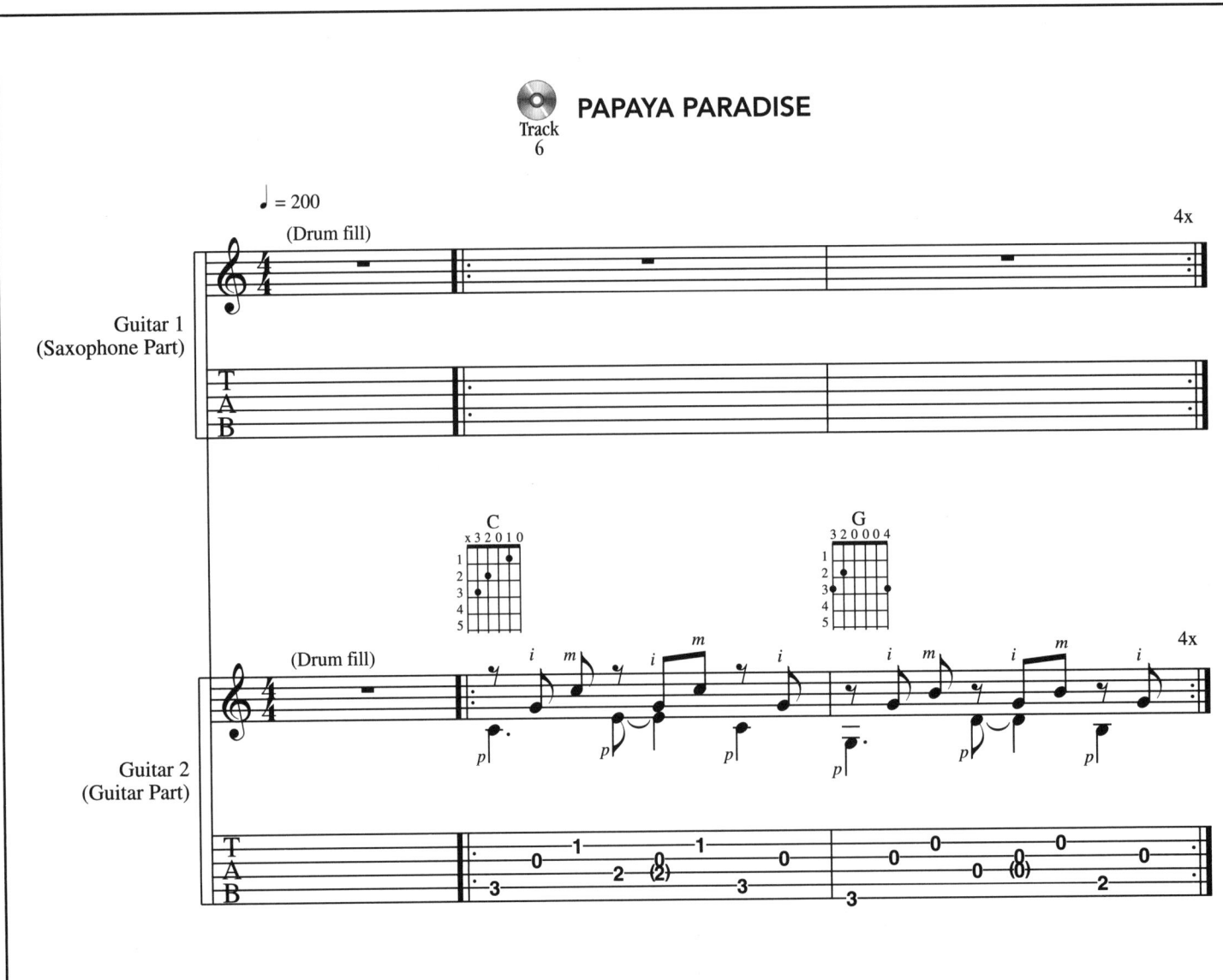

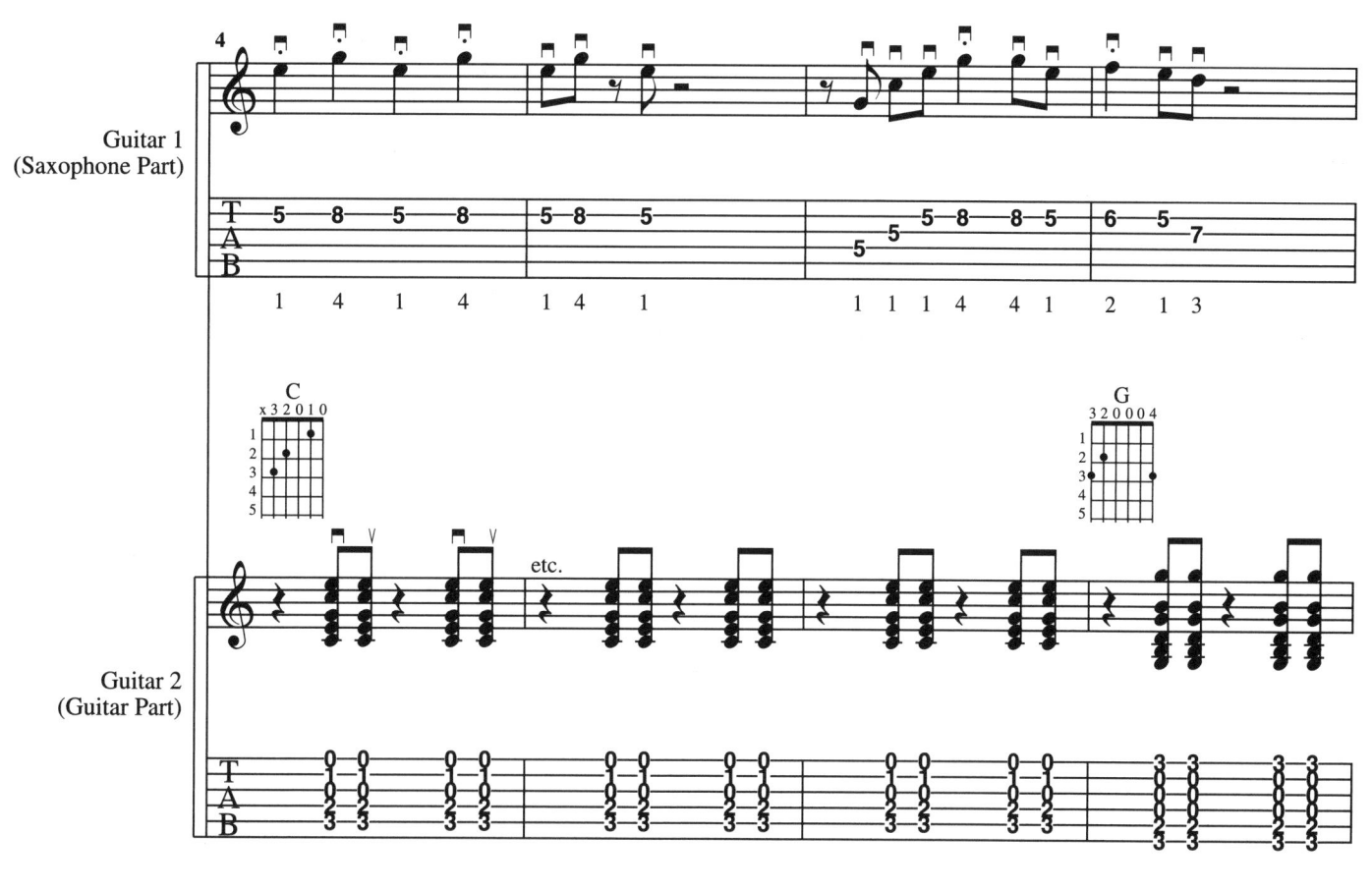

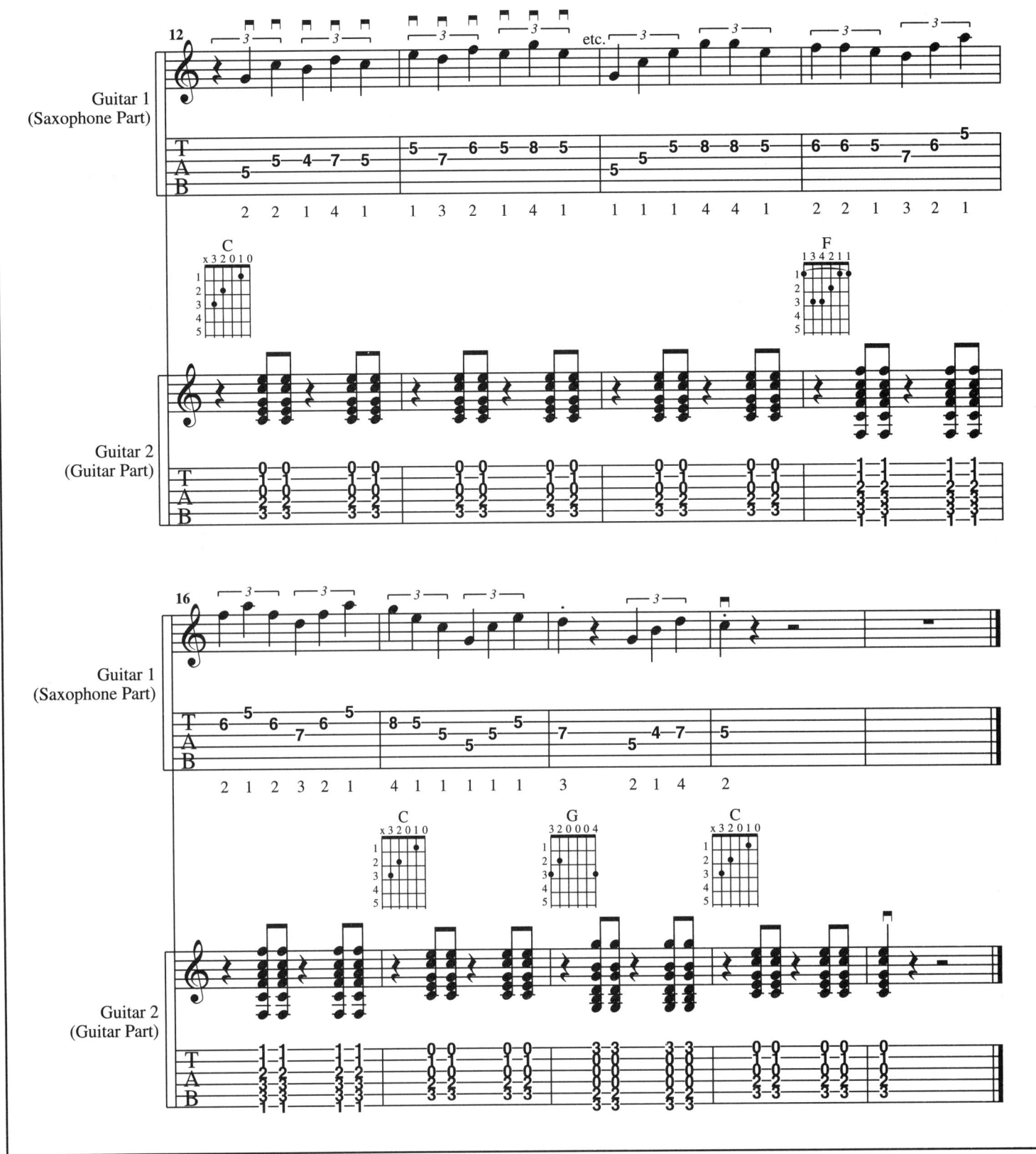

MENTO-CALYPSO

This final mento example (on the next page) is written in the style of "A Dash of the Sunshine" by Lord Tanamo. Lord Tanamo (Joseph Gordon), born in 1934 in Kingston, Jamaica, started out as a mento singer and rumba box player before going on to become one of the first lead singers of the legendary ska band The Skatalites. This is a unique tune because it contains mento, calypso, and jazz influences even though it was recorded in 1978, long after the golden age of mento had passed. It is a challenging piece to play due to the sophisticated strumming pattern and a dense, quickly moving chord progression. This song uses three-note chord voicings often found in ska and reggae styles.

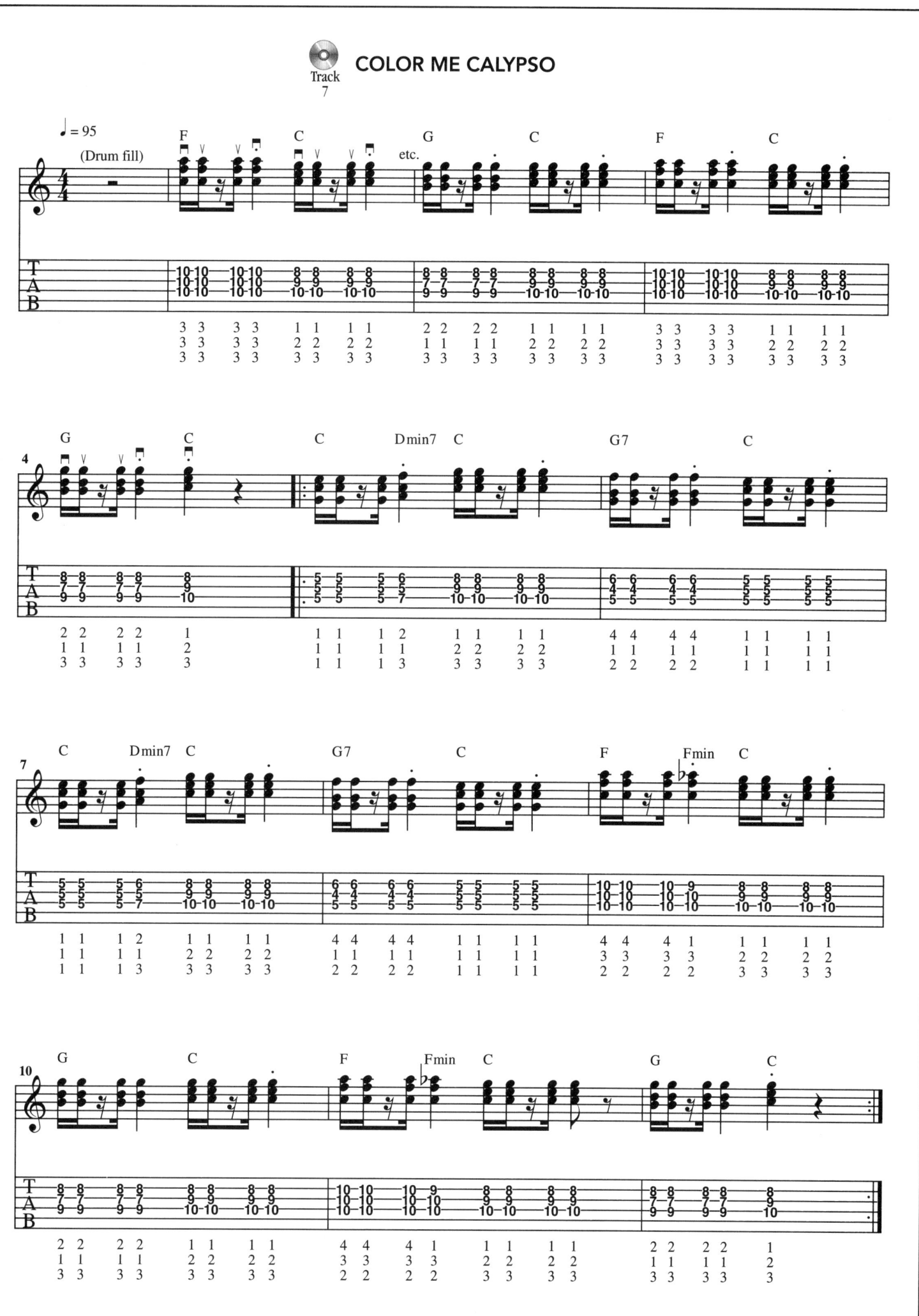

Chapter 2   SKA

THE BEGINNINGS OF SKA

As mento's golden age waned in Jamaica, American R&B hits and early rock 'n' roll recordings exploded in Jamaican dancehalls known as *sound systems*. As the mento sound was fading out of popularity, American R&B and rock 'n' roll influences were becoming firmly assimilated into the Jamaican musical mainstream. By the early 1960s, Jamaican music had taken all of these influences and morphed them into something new, a fast and upbeat musical style called ska. Duke Reid and Clement "Coxone" Dodd, owners of two competing sound systems, saw a huge opportunity for growth. Reid and Dodd created the Treasure Isle and Studio One record labels, respectively, in order to produce exclusive recordings for their sound systems. Before long, the pressing plant Caribbean Records was established, and the Jamaican recording industry took off.

Ska was a huge success because it was such a danceable music; it fit in perfectly with the wildly popular Jamaican sound systems. It also reflected the newfound joy and optimism gained from Jamaica's independence in 1962. By 1964, ska had swept through Jamaica, and soon it would spread to England as well.

Let's take a look at the song that started it all: "Oh Carolina." When The Folkes Brothers went to RJR studios in 1960 to record, Jamaican producer (and former employee of Coxone Dodd) Prince Buster (Cecil Bustamente Campbell) brought in an unlikely rhythm section: Rastafari *Nyabinghi* (see page 42) drummers from the Wareika Hills of Jamaica, led by Jamaican drummer Count Ossie (Oswald Williams). The resulting number one hit song was called "Oh Carolina," and it is widely considered to be the tune that paved the way for the formation of ska. When playing the following piece, which is in the style of "Oh Carolina," take notice of the brisk tempo. Also, notice how the rhythm emphasizes the *offbeats;* this is known as *syncopation* and is a key component of the ska styles to follow. (The offbeat is the second half of a beat, or the "&;" see measures 5–9.)

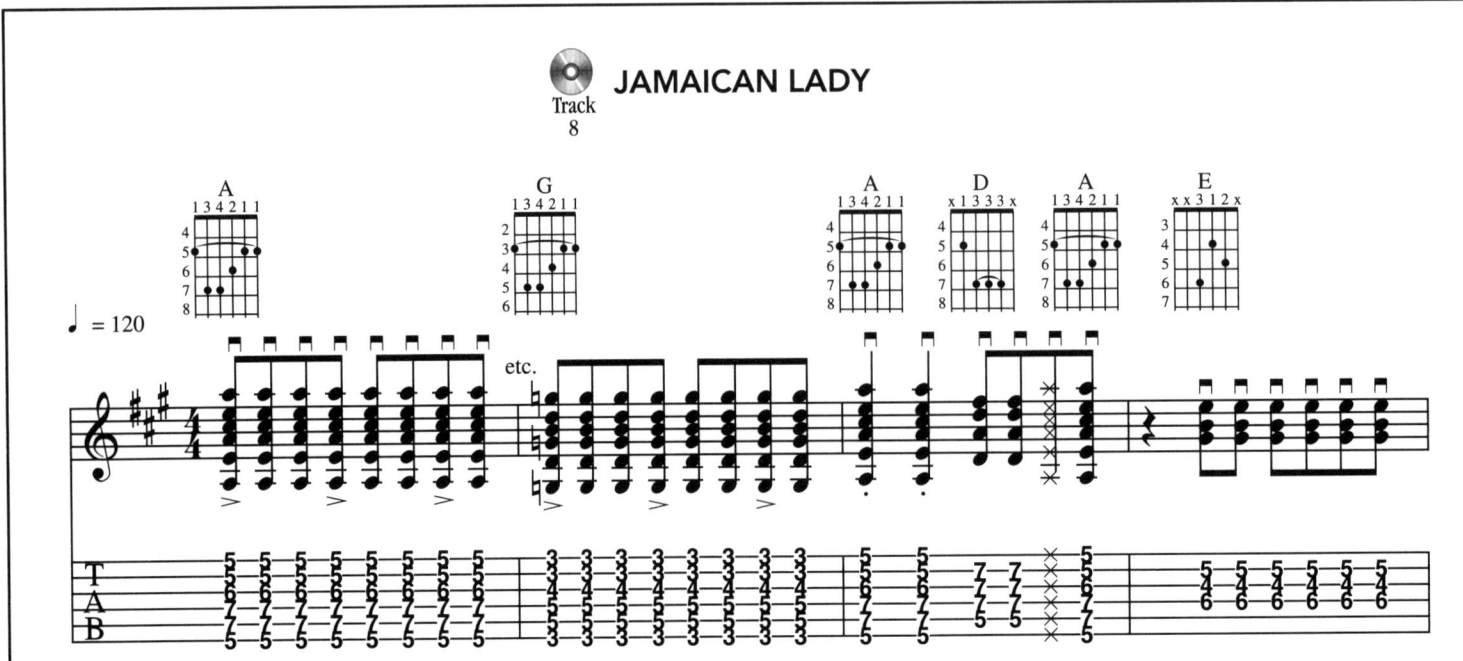

JAMAICAN LADY

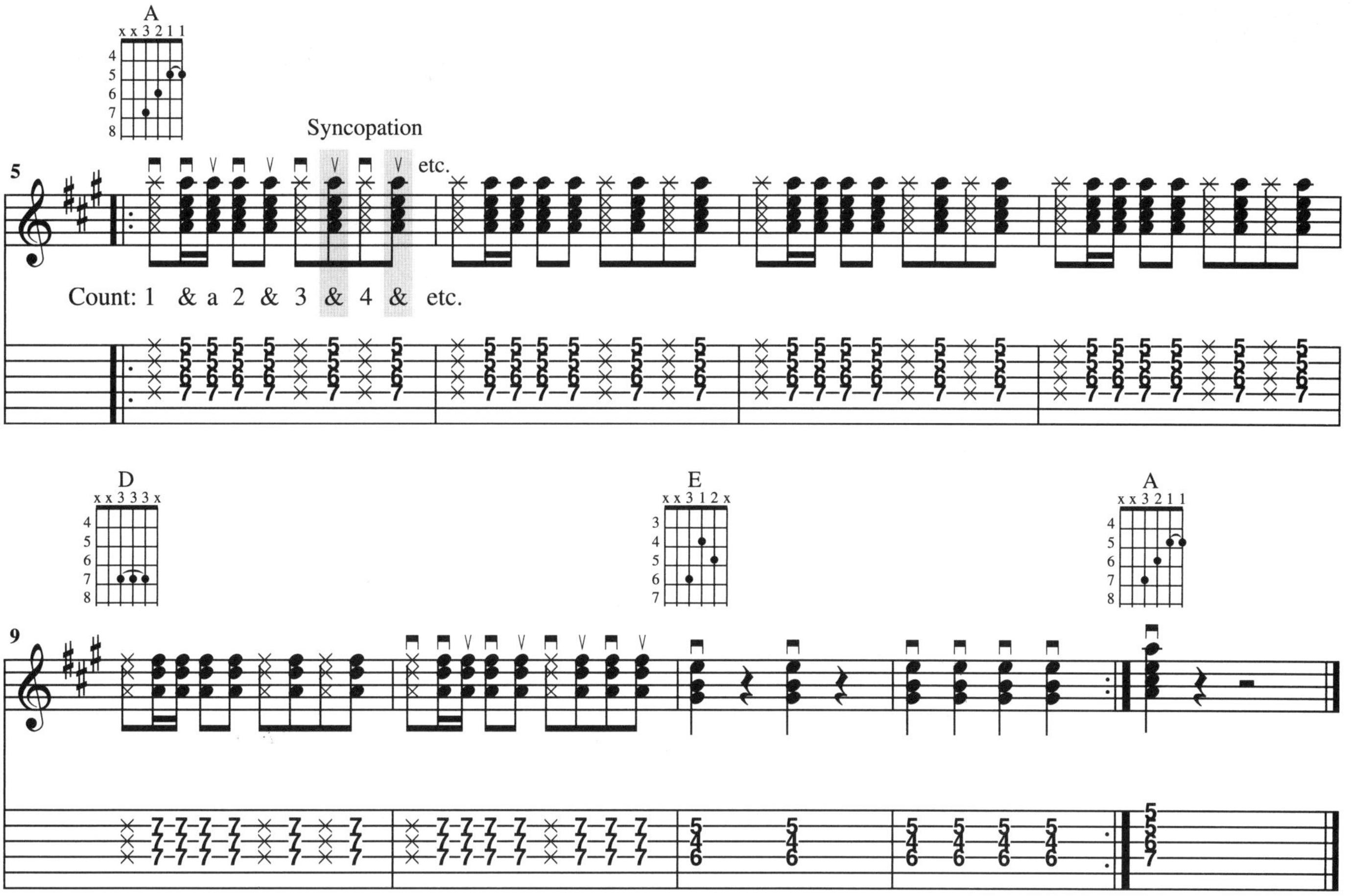

THE SKANK

The defining characteristic of ska guitar playing is a rhythm guitar technique called the *skank*. The skank was first used by the Jamaican guitarist Ernest Ranglin (see Chapter 6), who, while trying to imitate American R&B styles in the late 1950s, started strumming chords with sharp upstrokes on the offbeats of every measure. By the early 1960s, the skank had become a required technique for all ska guitarists (including Jerome "Jah Jerry" Haynes, a member of The Skatalites and a guitar student of Ernest Ranglin). Skanks are often played with three- or four-note chord voicings, and the upstrokes are usually preceded by muted downstrums played on the beats (1, 2, 3, 4, etc.). Ska music is sometimes played with a straight-eighth note feel and sometimes with a swing-eighth, or shuffle, feel. The following example illustrates a swing-eighth skank with a four-note voicing and muted downstrums.

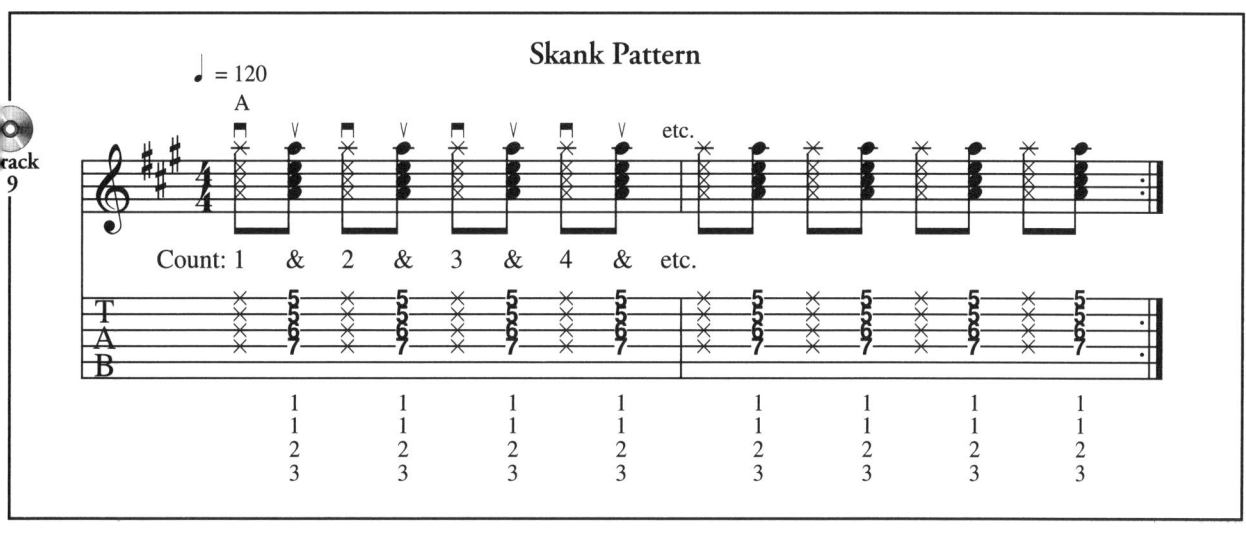

This following ska tune is in the style of "Forward March" by Derrick Morgan. "Forward March" holds an important place in Jamaican history not only because it was a hit on the charts, but also because it was the first emancipation song written in celebration of Jamaica's independence in 1962. In the early '60s, Derrick Morgan (who is still the only Jamaican artist to hold the top seven slots on the national pop-single charts simultaneously) was considered by many to be the "King of Ska." As the story goes, legendary Jamaican singer and producer Prince Buster recorded an instrumental break that was stolen from "Forward March," which set off an infamous, yet relatively shortlived, feud between the two. The arrangement below features the classic offbeat skank rhythm as well as some choice ska voicings.

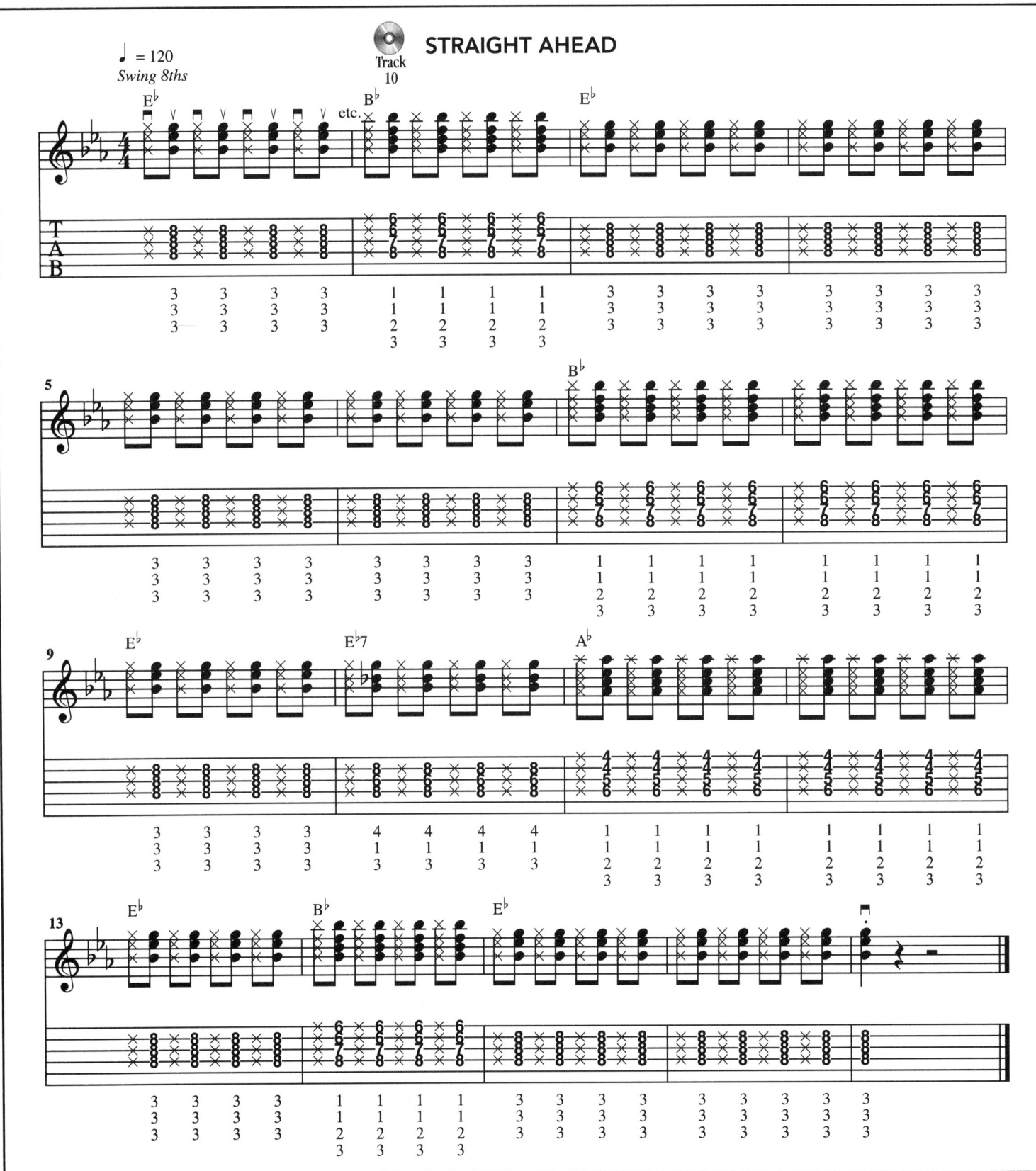

Below is a ska example arranged in the style of "I'll Never Grow Old" by The Maytals (who changed their name to Toots and The Maytals in 1972). This 1964 ska classic was produced by Coxone Dodd at Studio One. The recording featured the legendary backing band The Skatalites and a guest appearance by Ernest Ranglin on guitar. In the following example, you will be playing a straight-eighth skank, as well as some R&B-style dominant 9th chord voicings.

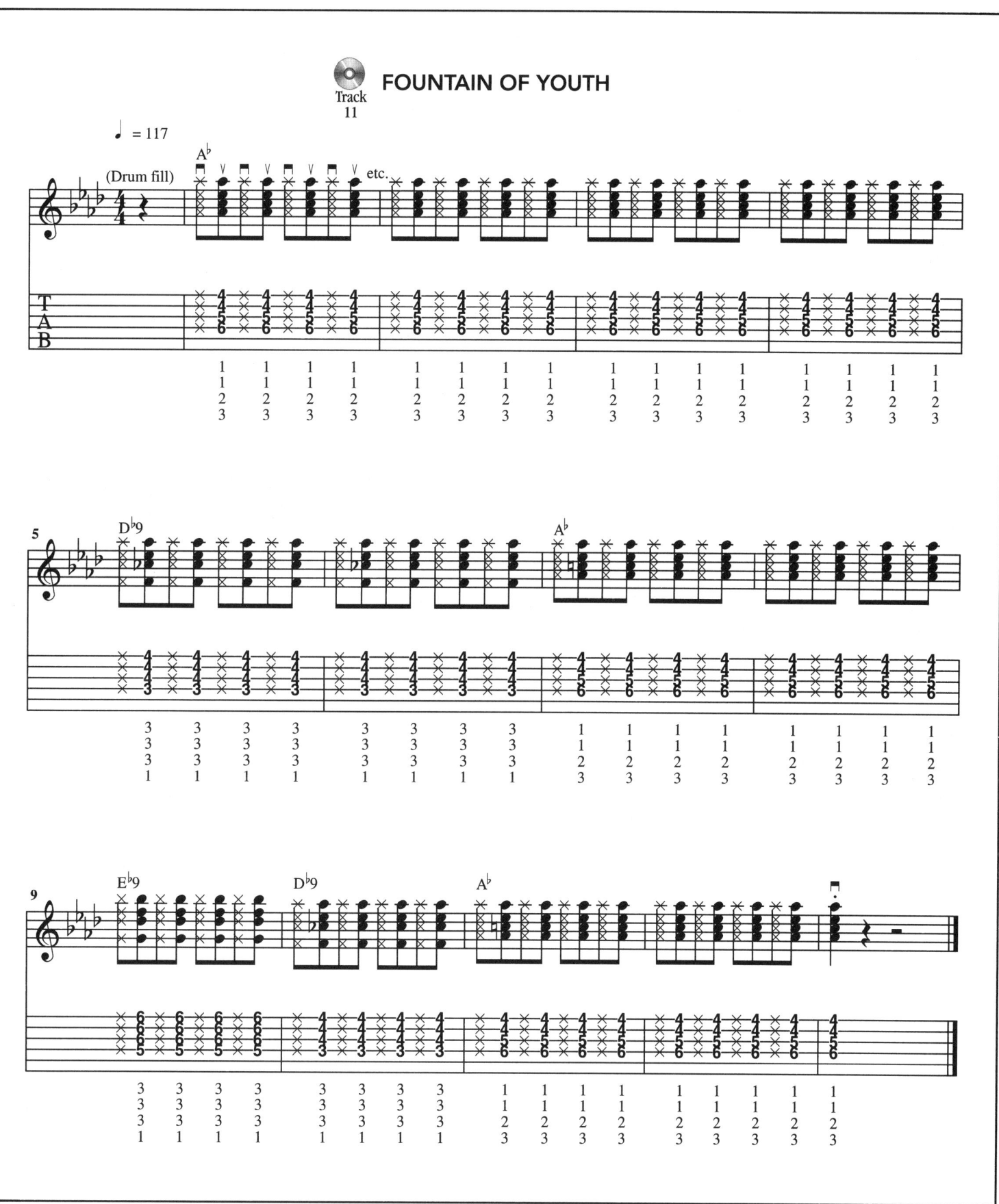

SKA HORN LINES

One of the most distinct characteristics of ska music is the inclusion of a horn section. These horn sections play short, catchy melodies during intros and interludes, then often switch to offbeat chord *stabs,* along with the rhythm section, during the verses and choruses of the song. (A stab is a sharp, rhythmic "hit," or attack.) In the example below, a horn line in the style of the intro to "Simmer Down" by The Wailers has been arranged for guitar. The rhythm guitar in this example features an offbeat skank rhythm, a quickly changing chord progression, and three-note ska voicings.

The original tune "Simmer Down" was the first single released by The Wailers, recorded at Studio One by Coxone Dodd in 1963 (with the Skatalites backing them up in the rhythm section). It's a significant song not only because it was a number one hit in Jamaica in 1964, but also because it marked the start of the recording career of Bob Marley, one of the most influential musicians in the history of music.

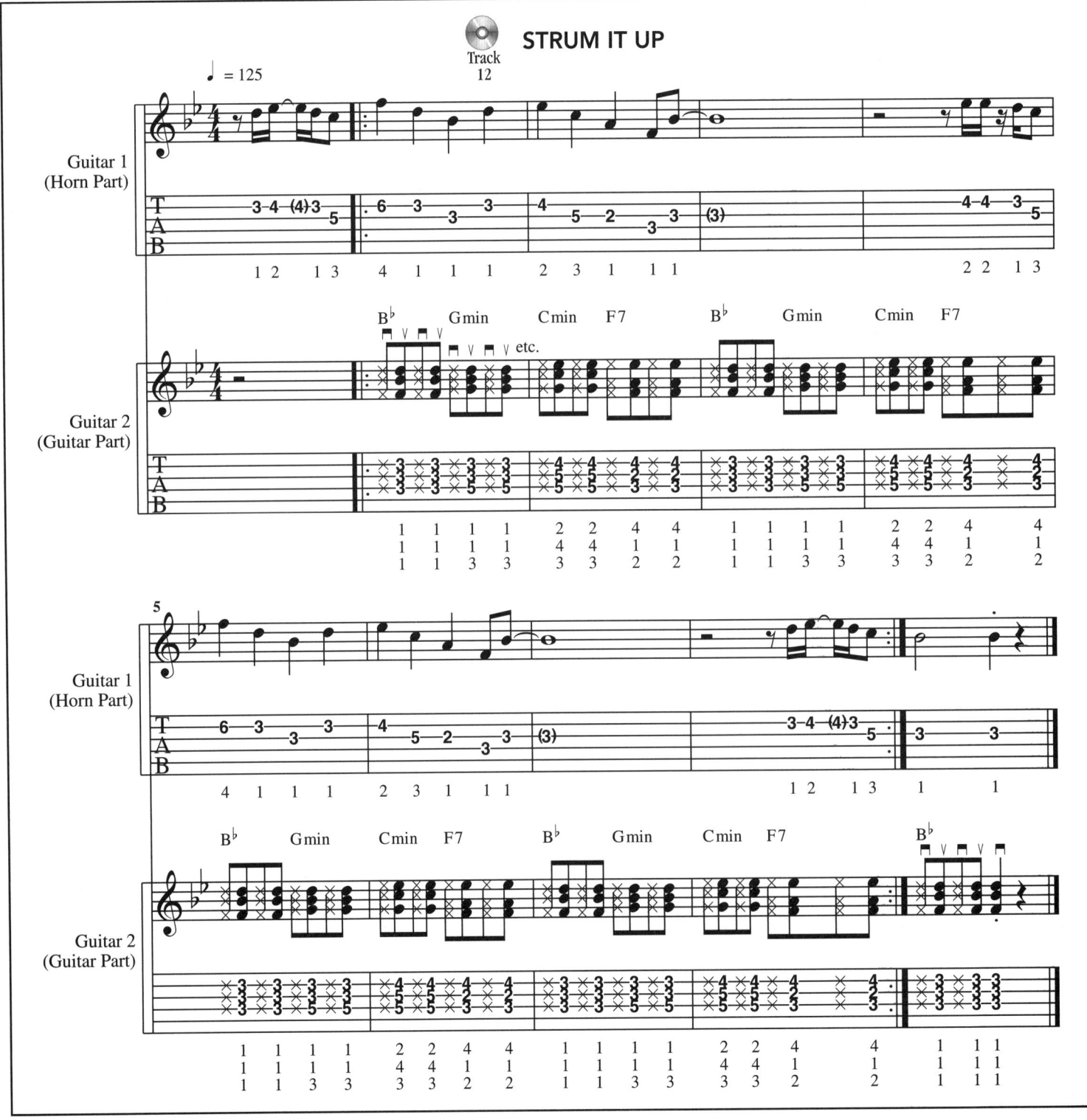

20 *Guitar Atlas: Volume 2*

With a career spanning more than five decades, Laurel Aitken, known as the "Godfather of Ska," was Jamaica's first international recording star. Born in Cuba in 1927, Aitken moved to Jamaica (his father's homeland) when he was 11. He was winning talent competitions by age 15, and before long, he was a popular nightclub performer known for his wide range of singing and songwriting styles, including jump blues, R&B, calypso, and mento. In 1960, Laurel emigrated to England where he established himself as one of the key artists and producers developing Jamaican ska in the U.K. One of his biggest hits, "Rudi Got Married," was released in 1980 during the *2-Tone ska movement* in England (named after the English record label 2-Tone Records). By the late 1970s, a major revival of ska had emerged in England, which is why this 2-Tone period is also known as ska's *second wave*. The following example is written in the style of Laurel Aitken's second-wave ska classic "Rudi Got Married." It features three-note ska chords (voiced exclusively on the top three strings) and a harmonized horn melody arranged for guitar.

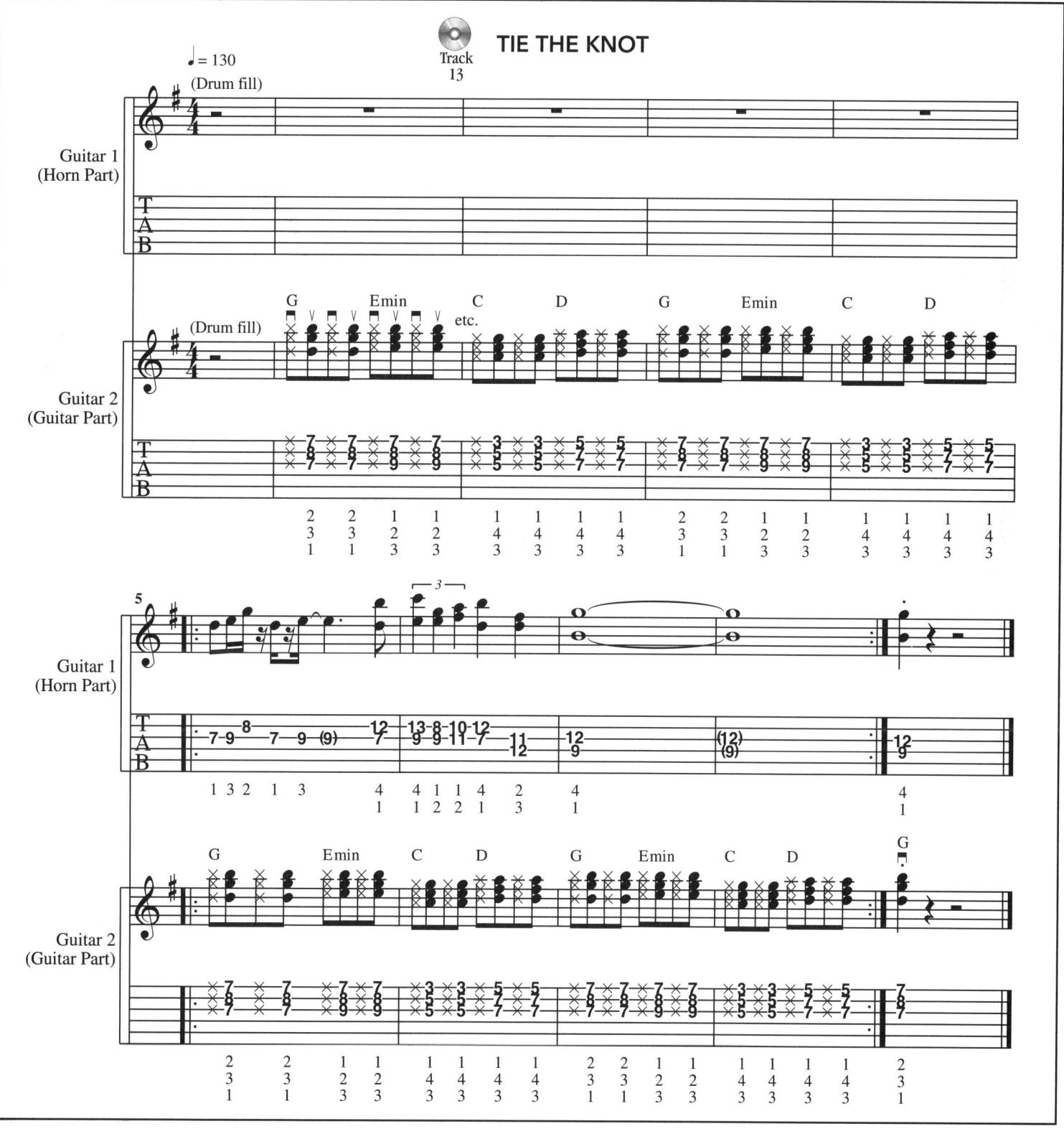

Guitar Atlas: Jamaica

THE SKATALITES

Arguably, no other band defined and influenced the sound of ska more than The Skatalites. Formed in 1964, the original Skatalite lineup consisted of nine of Jamaica's top jazz musicians, including Tommy McCook on tenor sax and flute, Don Drummond on trombone, Rolando Alphonso on tenor sax, Lester Sterling on alto sax, Johnny Moore on trumpet, Lloyd Knibb on drums, Lloyd Brevett on bass, Jah Jerry Hains on guitar, and Jackie Mittoo on Piano and Organ. In addition, they were often joined by guitarists Ernest Ranglin and Nearlin "Lynn" Taitt in the studio.

Under such producers as Coxone Dodd, Duke Reid, Prince Buster, Leslie Kong, and Randy Chin, The Skatalites gained significant fame as the supergroup that backed most of the top Jamaican artists of the mid-1960s. Unfortunately, their first run was shortlived. Their trombonist, Don Drummond, was jailed and convicted for the murder of his girlfriend, which led to the breakup of the band by August of 1965 (Don died in prison four years later). Almost 20 years after their breakup, The Skatalites reformed in 1983 and have been going strong ever since.

This final ska example is representative of the current incarnation of The Skatalites, written in the style of "Flowers for Albert" from the 1994 Grammy-nominated album *Hi-Bop Ska*. The challenging rhythm guitar part combines both three- and four-note ska voicings with quickly moving chord changes and a key change halfway through the tune (in measure 14, the key changes from A Major to B♭ Major). Happy skanking!

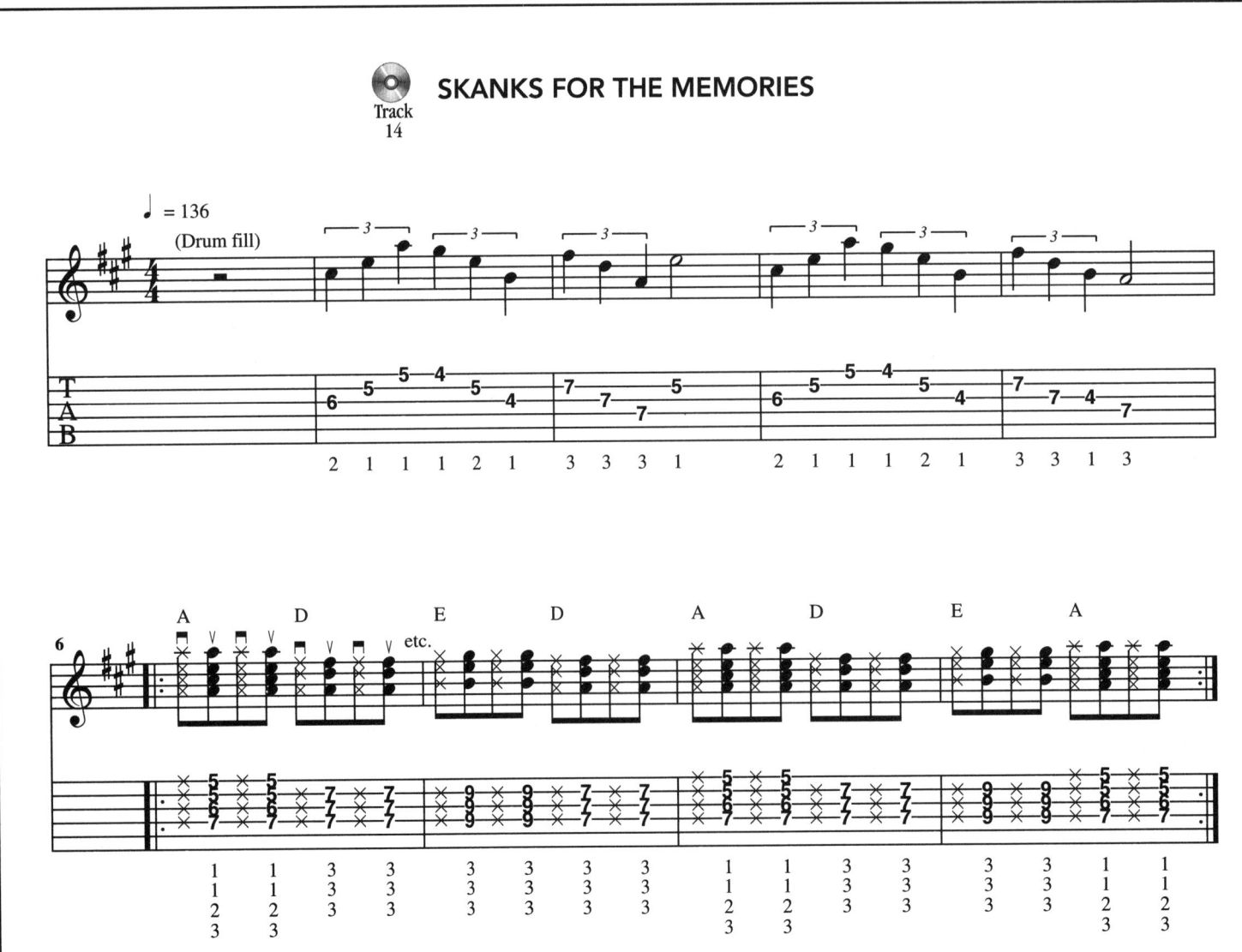

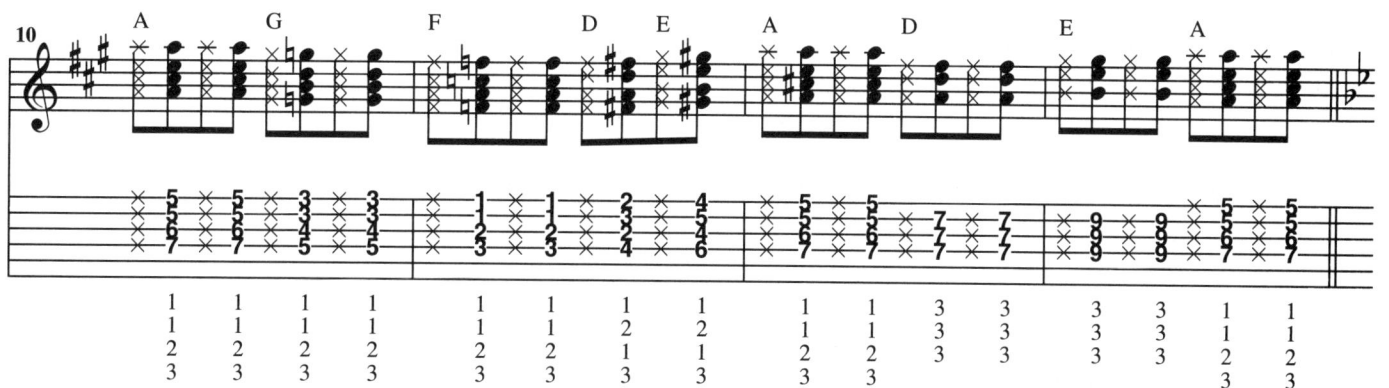
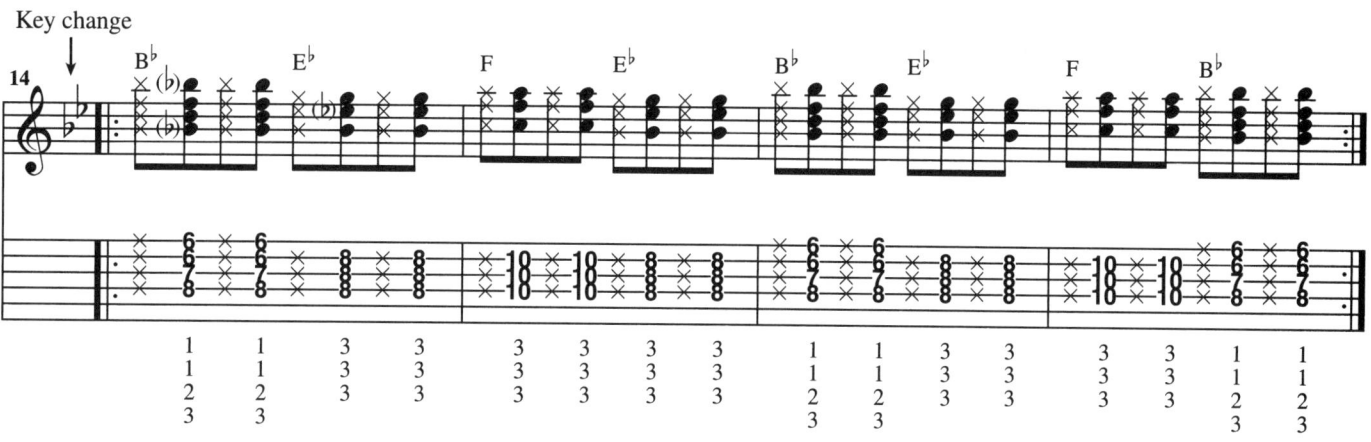
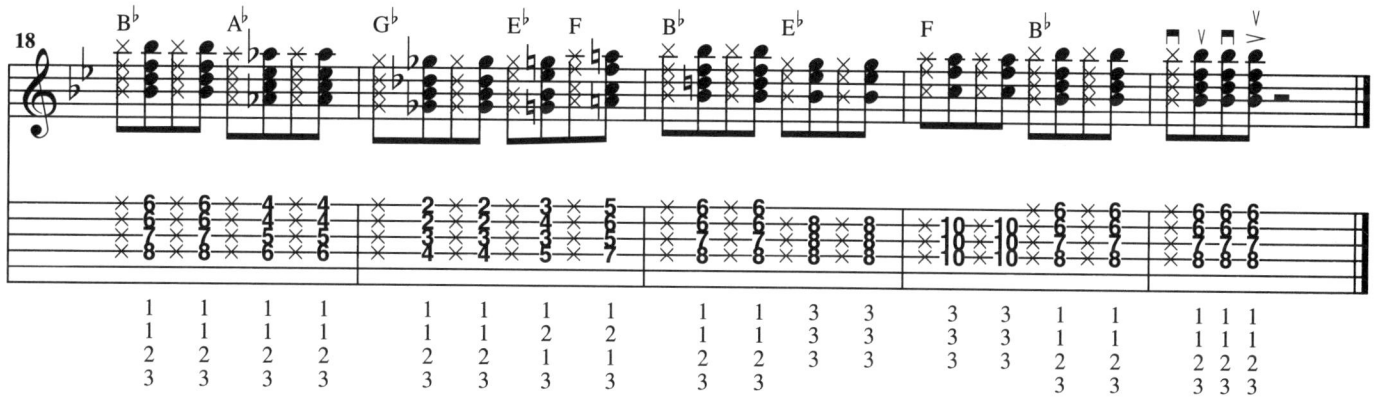

Guitar Atlas: Jamaica

Chapter 3 — ROCKSTEADY

HISTORY OF ROCKSTEADY

Just as ska was born from the optimistic climate in Jamaica after gaining independence, a new type of music, rocksteady, reflected a growing dissatisfaction with the serious problems that remained. The youth who had flocked to the cities looking for opportunity often found themselves stuck in ghettos with no work or money; this led to a life of crime and gangs for many young Jamaicans. These *rude boys,* as they were called, had a wide impact on Jamaica's social structure, as well as the music scene. Through their cool style and often delinquent behavior, the rude boys' dissatisfaction with the quick tempo of ska became evident.

Before long, ska had run its course. By 1966, ska was replaced by the shortlived, yet enormously influential, musical style known as rocksteady. Rocksteady was a fairly drastic departure from ska, with a slower beat, no horn section, a more prominent bass line, and intricate vocal harmonies. Even though this style only lasted about two years, rocksteady left a profound mark on Jamaican music.

Figuring prominently in the history of rocksteady is guitar legend Lynn Taitt. Born in Trinidad, Lynn Taitt moved to Jamaica in 1962 and hit the ground running as a highly sought after session player. Four years later, Lynn Taitt was backing nearly every artist making records in Kingston. By the late 1960s, he had been involved in well over 1,500 recordings, distinguishing him as an unsung hero of Jamaican music. Lynn Taitt emigrated to Canada in August of 1968. Perhaps it is no coincidence that his departure coincided with the end of the rocksteady era.

SLOW IT DOWN

Alton Ellis, the "Godfather of Rocksteady," first started recording in an R&B style for Coxone Dodd at Studio One in 1959. By the mid-1960s, however, after a few years on the ska scene, Alton Ellis found his true calling as the undisputed leader of the new rocksteady movement. Alton started recording with Duke Reid's Treasure Isle label in 1965. One year later, he released a string of hits including "Girl I've Got a Date," which, according to many experts (including Alton himself), was the first rocksteady song ever recorded.

The example on the next page, in the style of "Girl I've Got a Date," retains a hint of the momentum of ska due to the offbeat strums. However, the slower tempo creates a much more relaxed feel. Also, notice the melodic emphasis on the bass line, which is doubled by the guitar (Guitar 2). This doubling technique is used often and is one of rocksteady's distinguishing characteristics.

RUDE BOYFRIEND

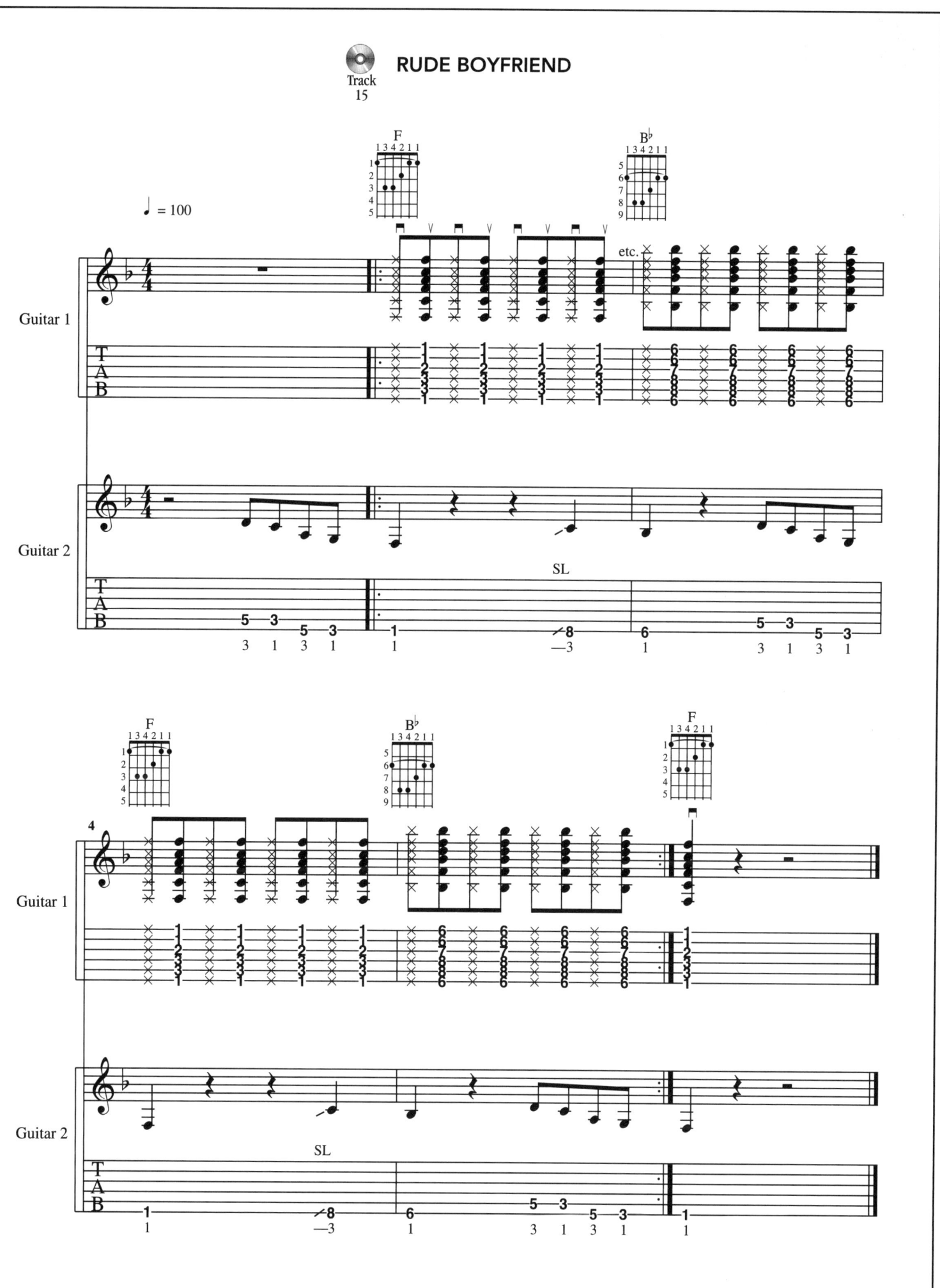

Below is an example in the style of "Get Ready Rock Steady" by Alton Ellis. By all accounts, this 1967 masterpiece coined the term "rocksteady." Produced by Duke Reid's Treasure Isle label, Alton was backed by Tommy McCook & The Supersonics (with Lynn Taitt on guitar). It's a great example because the original track perfectly captured the essence of Lynn Taitt's syncopated percussive guitar intros. In order to emulate Lynn Taitt's electric guitar sound, set your amp for a clean tone with a bit of reverb. Then, place a heavy palm mute on each note in Guitar 1 to get a staccato sound (this is accomplished by placing the heel of your right hand on the strings where they meet the bridge). Also, due to the relatively leisurely tempo of this rocksteady tune, the rhythm guitar part (Guitar 2) is played with sharp downstrums rather than ska-style upstrokes.

KEEP IT MUTED

This example is written in the style of the first rocksteady hit, "Take It Easy" by Hopeton Lewis, which was released in late 1966. This early rocksteady tune helped signal a clean break from ska not only by relaxing the tempo, but also by the lyrics, which tell the listener to literally "Take It Easy." The rhythm section for the original track was, no surprise, Lynn Taitt and his group The Jets (although it is said that Ernest Ranglin was on this session as well). As is often the case with Lynn Taitt-style riffs, the guitar begins with a palm-muted melodic intro that is doubled on the bass. Then, for the main body of the tune, offbeat chord strums are played, except for the few instances where chord changes are anticipated by slides (see measures 4 and 5, for example).

STEADY SIXTEENTHS

Jamaican singer, songwriter, and stage showman Roy Shirley (born Ainsworth Roy Rushton in 1944) was known both as King Roy Shirley and The High Priest. His 1967 hit song "Hold Them" is considered one of the formative tunes that solidified rocksteady as a new movement. In the style of "Hold Them," the example below features a more active Lynn Taitt-style of guitar playing. One benefit of rocksteady's slower tempo is that there is more space available for the development of guitar and bass melodies. In particular, notice how the addition of sixteenth-note embellishments sound surprisingly laid back when combined with the relaxed rocksteady beat.

By the late 1960s, the musical winds of change were starting to blow in Jamaica. Rocksteady was quickly morphing into reggae. A prime example of a rocksteady song that started to show clear reggae traits is "ABC Rocksteady," recorded by the Jamaican vocal trio The Gaylads. Produced by Sonia Pottinger, this song was one of the first with an authentic reggae beat (it featured a *one-drop* rhythm, covered on page 33). The following example is written in the style of the 1968 rocksteady classic "ABC Rocksteady," highlighting Lynn Taitt's percussive palm-muted sixteenth-note style. The sixteenth notes in Guitar 2 are to be played with a swing feel (*Swing 16ths*). Swing sixteenths are played like sixteenth-note triplets with the first two sixteenths tied.

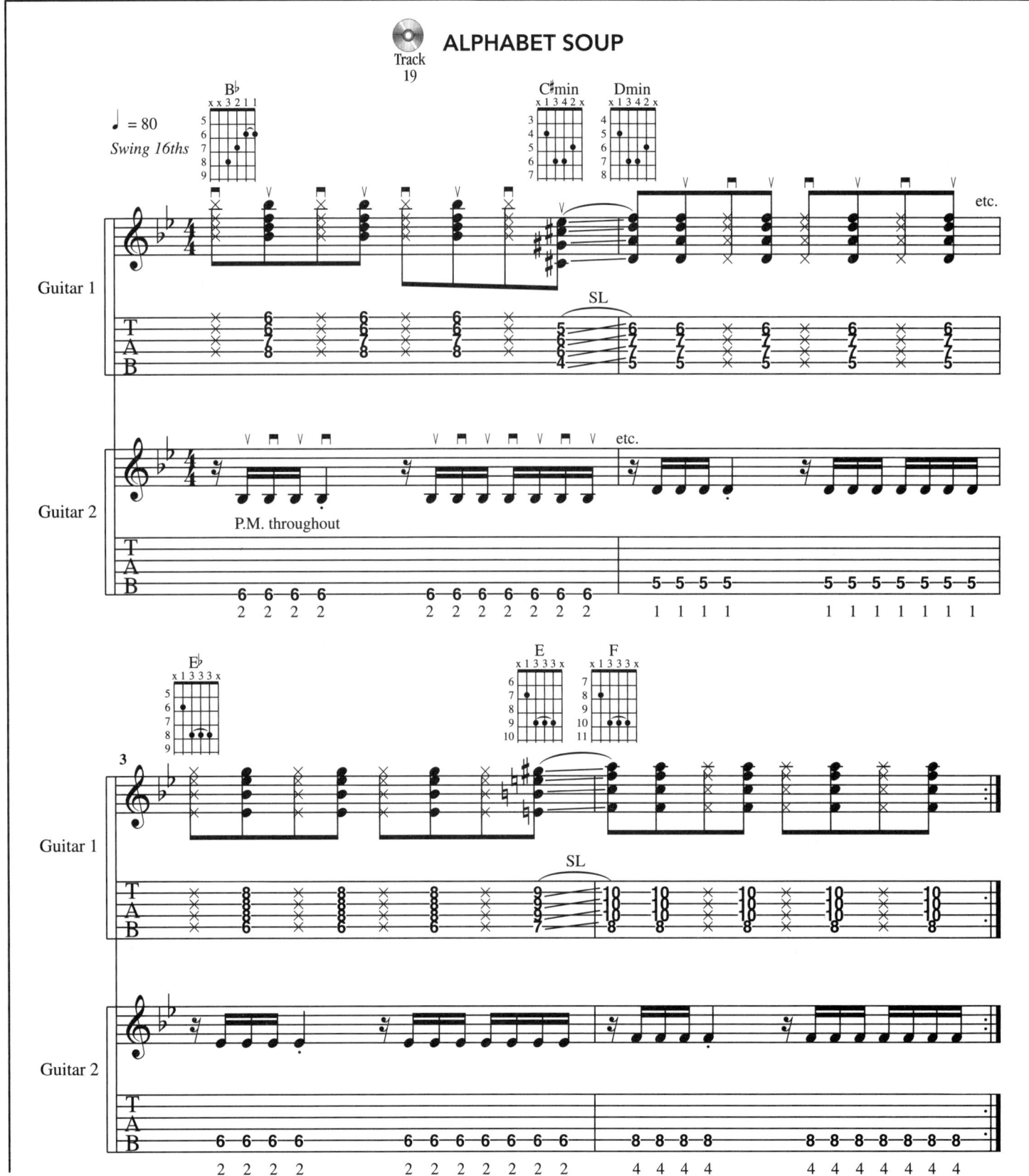

30 *Guitar Atlas: Volume 2*

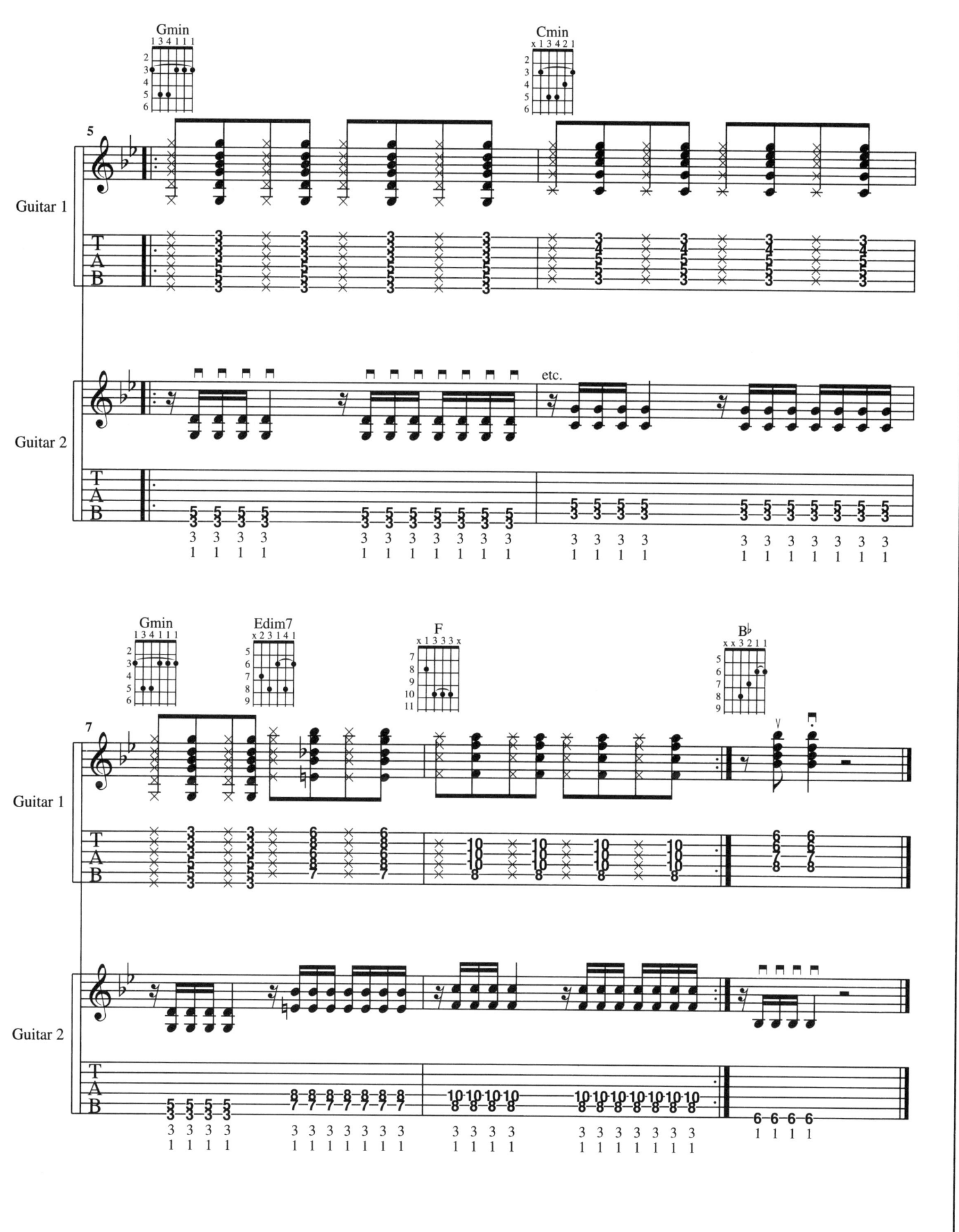

Chapter 4: REGGAE

EARLY REGGAE

At the end of the 1960s, with the influence of traditional African music, Caribbean music, American R&B, and, most importantly, ska and rocksteady, Jamaican music evolved yet again. The result was reggae, a form that defined an entire generation of Jamaican music. Starting in 1968, early reggae began working its way into Jamaican popular music alongside *dub* and *toasting*. Although reggae, dub, and toasting are all distinct Jamaican art forms, they are deeply connected. Essentially, dub is a style that involves the remixing of existing tunes, over which the deejay toasts. Toasting is a precursor to rapping, in which the deejay talks and rhymes in a half-sung, rhythmic way in an effort to motivate the audience to dance.

Starting in the 1960s, a key component of both the music and the music business in Jamaica was the concept of the *riddim*. On a practical level, the riddim is the groove created by the specific drum and bass riff of a given tune. However, the term "riddim" also refers to the background, or rhythm section, portion of the song used by deejays for toasting—or as the basis for an entirely new song (otherwise known as a *version*). Due to the nonexistent copyright laws in Jamaica at the time (Jamaican copyright laws weren't enacted until 1993), and the speed with which these versions could be created, it's easy to see why Jamaican music spread so quickly: one riddim might be used on hundreds of tunes! This chapter looks at the music of some of the most prominent reggae artists from the early '70s to the mid-'80s, including examples in the style of a few highly "versioned" riddims, like the one that follows.

The example below is written in the style of the 1971 hit single "Cherry Oh Baby" by singer-songwriter Eric Donaldson. This tune, which is considered a milestone in the development of the reggae genre, highlights some of the stylistic differences between reggae and its musical predecessors. In particular, notice the stark simplicity of the rhythm section. The unison starting and stopping of the guitar, bass, and drums creates a focused emphasis on the riddim. With this pared-down arrangement (no horns, background singers, or lead guitars), the original "Cherry Oh Baby" tune is one of the most heavily used riddims ever, having laid the foundation for over 100 tunes and remixes!

Throughout 1972 and 1973, Jamaican singer Jimmy Cliff was thrown into the spotlight as the star of the film *The Harder They Come*. Based on the story of a real-life Jamaican criminal from the late 1940s, the movie and the hit soundtrack brought reggae to a whole new level of international popularity.

The following example, based on Jimmy Cliff's title song on the soundtrack from *The Harder They Come,* illustrates a close interaction between the organ and the rhythm guitar that is common in reggae music. Guitar 1 is the organ part arranged for guitar, and Guitar 2 maintains a palm-muted sixteenth-note pulse throughout. Also present in this example is one of the most defining characteristics of reggae music, the *one-drop* rhythm. A one-drop rhythm is created when the drummer, playing in 4/4 time, simultaneously plays a snare drum stroke and a bass drum kick on the third beat of every measure. As you listen to Track 21 on your CD, shift your attention to the drums for an example of the one-drop rhythm in action.

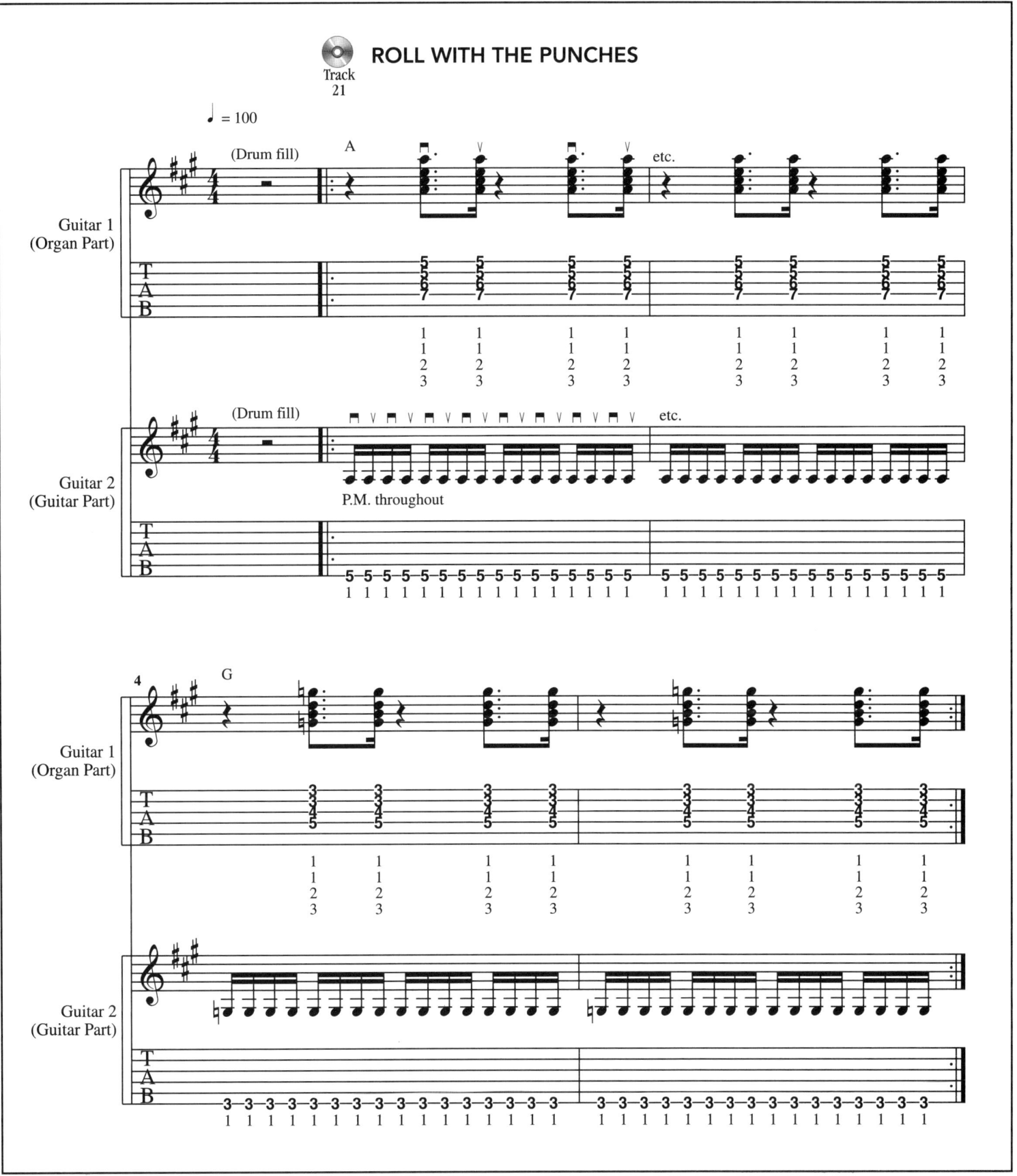

Guitar Atlas: Jamaica 33

Dennis Brown (known as the "Crown Prince of Reggae") was one of Jamaica's most beloved and prolific artists, recording over 75 albums during his career. In 1973, Dennis Brown's early reggae classic "Westbound Train" was number one on the Jamaican charts. Interestingly, the intro and interlude of the original "Westbound Train" featured a verbatim guitar riff from Al Green's classic tune "Love and Happiness." Produced by Winston "Niney" Holness, this tune featured the masterful guitar work of Earl "Chinna" Smith and Tony Chin from Soul Syndicate (Niney's house band). The example below is in the style of "Westbound Train." It begins with staccato offbeat strums played by the rhythm guitar, to which is added a sixteenth-note lead guitar riff.

THE RASTAFARI MOVEMENT AND ROOTS REGGAE

The Rastafari movement began with the philosophies of Jamaican black nationalist Marcus Garvey, who, in the 1920s, promoted the Universal Negro Improvement Association (UNIA). In 1927, Marcus Garvey, who had recently been deported from the United States back to Jamaica, spread the word that African redemption would come through the crowning of a new king of Ethiopia. In 1930, Ras Tafari Makonnen was crowned Haile Selassie, the new Emperor of Ethiopia, which was seen by many as fulfillment of Marcus Garvey's prophecy. This led to the belief that Haile Selassie was Jah (Jehovah, or God) reincarnate. Rastas believe that Jah lives within the human body in the form of the holy spirit; this is why they often refer to themselves as "I and I." However, the Rastafari movement is not considered an organized religion, but rather, a way of life.

In the 1950s, the Rastafari lived on the fringes of society. They were looked down upon in mainstream Jamaica due to their dreadlocks and beards (Rastas didn't comb or cut their hair because of their belief that the body must remain whole) and their ritualistic use of cannabis, or marijuana. As reggae became increasingly influenced by Rastafari culture and concerns, the term *roots reggae* was coined. The last half of the 1970s is generally considered the golden era of roots reggae. During this time, bands and artists like Bob Marley, Burning Spear, Horace Andy, Black Uhuru, and The Abyssinians popularized roots reggae and brought the Rasta belief system to the international stage. At its heart, roots reggae is a spiritual music primarily concerned with issues such as peace, poverty, government oppression, Afrocentric repatriation, and the worship of Jah through the Rastafari tradition. Largely through the influence of Bob Marley, the Rastafari movement has spread throughout much of the world. Today, there are estimated to be over one million Rasta living worldwide, however, only about five to ten percent of Jamaicans identify themselves as Rastafari.

THE "BUBBLE"

It is very common for roots reggae keyboard players to create what is called a "bubbling" effect by playing their chords with an alternating left-hand, right-hand, left-hand pattern. In the example on the next page, Guitar 2 is an arrangement of this "bubbling" keyboard style. Instead of playing an alternating left-hand, right-hand, left-hand pattern like a keyboard, a similar effect is created on the guitar with a bass-chord-bass pattern. Although this technique can be accomplished with a pick (as it is notated here), it can also be played fingerstyle, assigning the thumb to the bass notes, and the index, middle, and ring fingers to the top notes of the chords.

The example on the next page is in the style of the song "Slavery Days" from the groundbreaking 1975 album *Marcus Garvey* released by reggae legend Burning Spear. The guitar players on this album were Earl "Chinna" Smith and Tony Chin, who were supported by a top-shelf rhythm section that included Robbie Shakespeare on bass and Leroy "Horsemouth" Wallace on drums. Born Winston Rodney in 1948 in St. Ann, Jamaica, Burning Spear is a two-time Grammy Award winner (he has been nominated for a total of 12 Grammys) and is a devout Rastafari.

NEVER FORGET

Released as a single in 1971, The Abyssinians' reggae classic "Satta Massagana" is one of the first African-oriented reggae tunes and a frequently versioned riddim. It's a classic roots reggae song not just because of the spiritual overtones of the lyrics (which are partly sung in the Ethiopian Amharic language), but also because it provides another opportunity to examine the tight, rhythmic interaction between the guitar and keyboards. The following example is written in the style of "Satta Massagana." Guitar 1 plays downstrums on beats 2 and 4, while Guitar 2 is an arrangement of the offbeat keyboard line. Notice how the two parts interlock, with the strums of Guitar 1 alternating with the offbeat strums of Guitar 2. This interaction creates a syncopated, rhythmic bubbling effect similar to the example on the previous page.

REGGAE RHYTHM EMBELLISHMENT

One of the most distinctive vocalists to emerge from the Jamaican music scene is Horace Andy. Born Horace Hinds in Kingston, Jamaica in 1951, "Sleepy" Horace Andy is known for his high tenor voice and pronounced vibrato. The following example is in the style of "Child of the Ghetto," a tune recorded in the early 1970s at Studio One, but not released until the 1998 Horace Andy compilation *Mr. Bassie*. This example illustrates an effective technique for embellishing a basic roots reggae rhythm guitar part. The trick is for the rhythm guitar to add an eighth-note upstroke on the "&" of beats 2 and 4, frequently holding this chord over for the next beat. Then, every once in a while, this upstrum is held over the barline (see measures 4 and 5). When used sparingly, this can be an effective device, especially when contrasted with staccato sixteenth notes played by a second guitar.

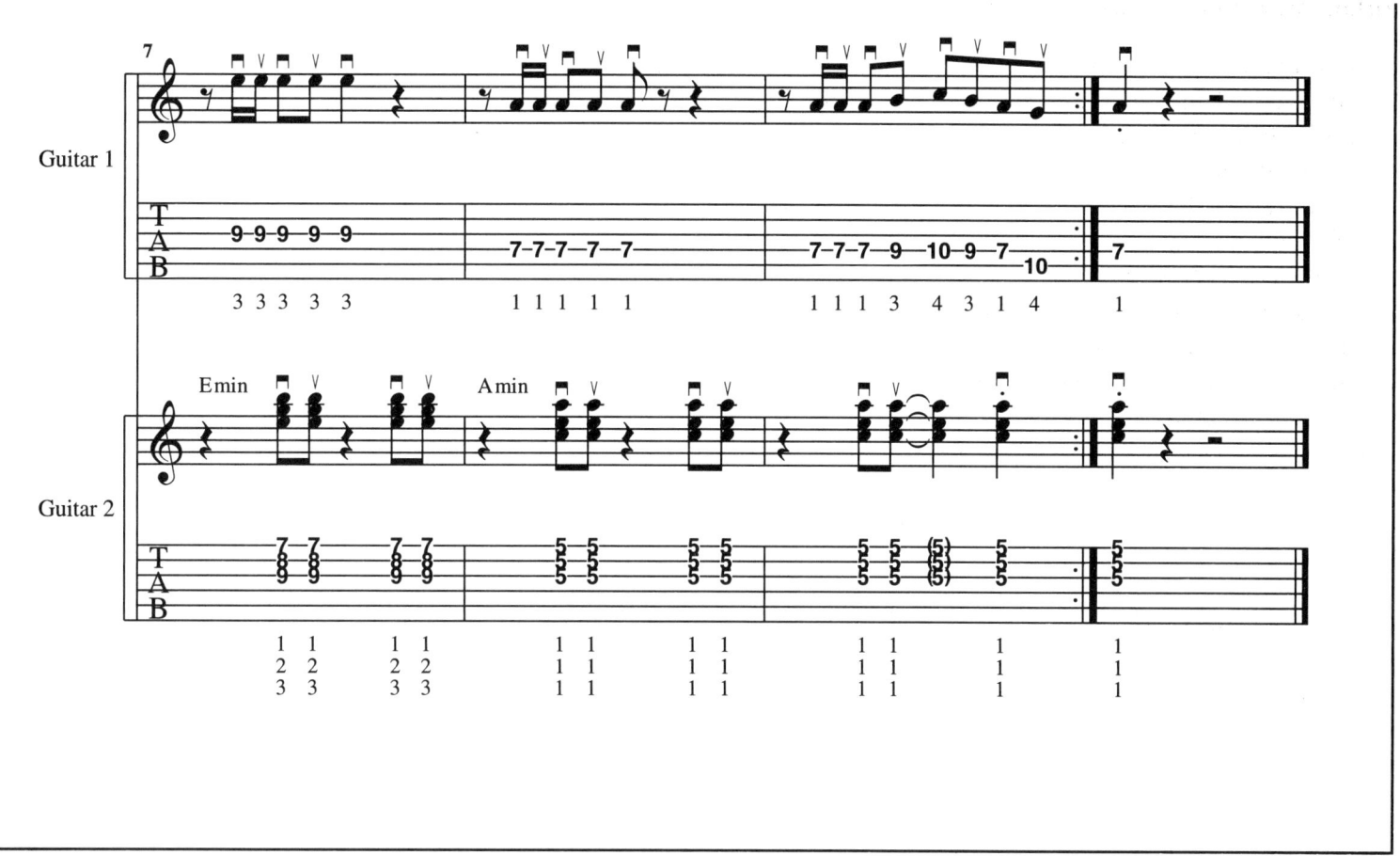

DUB-STYLE EFFECTS

Black Uhuru ("uhuru" is the Swahili word for freedom) is one of the most internationally successful Jamaican roots reggae bands. In 1985, they were the first artists to win a Grammy in the newly introduced reggae category for their hit song "What Is Life?" This song, like many Black Uhuru tunes, has a fairly progressive sound, with American pop-rock and Jamaican dub influences.

The example on the next page is in the style of Black Uhuru's song "What Is Life?" It features the use of *echo,* a remix trick common in Jamaican dub recordings involving a delay effect. On the accompanying CD, Guitar 1 is running through a *delay pedal* with the repeat set roughly to a quarter-note triplet pattern. (A delay pedal records the signal from the guitar and plays it back at various speeds and volumes.) Guitar 2 is going through a *chorus pedal,* giving it a shimmering pop-rock tone. (A chorus pedal takes the guitar signal and combines it with delayed copies of itself that have been altered in pitch). On the original recording, prolific reggae gurus Sly Dunbar (drums) and Robbie Shakespeare (bass) laid down their rhythm section magic, giving this recording what is known as a *rocker's beat.* Rocker's reggae drum beats usually contain a heavy kick-drum accent on beat 1, in addition to the usual one-drop accent on beat 3.

THE QUESTION

Chapter 5 — BOB MARLEY

JAMAICA

More than anyone, Robert "Bob" Nesta Marley, born in Saint Ann, Jamaica in 1945, was the cultural icon that made Jamaican music an international sensation. By the time of his death in 1981, Bob Marley had survived an assassination attempt, toured the world three times, fathered 12 children (two were adopted), composed hundreds of songs (many of which are considered archetypal masterpieces), received Jamaica's Order of Merit Award, received the United Nations Medal of Peace on behalf of five-hundred million Africans, brought international attention to the Rastafarian faith, and inspired millions of people with a deeply spiritual message of peace through music.

A testament to his world-wide popularity, the compilation album *Legend*, released three years after his death, went platinum 10 times over in the U.S. alone, becoming the best-selling reggae album in history. All in all, Bob Marley's accomplishments are truly amazing considering he only lived to be 36. In fact, his superstar status, gifted vocal ability, and brilliant songwriting make it easy to overlook the fact that he was also an excellent guitar player. But ultimately, through all of the fame and fortune, he remained a humble artist, spreading a positive message and a peaceful vision of humanity. This chapter examines a few of the Bob Marley masterpieces that helped reggae become a world-wide phenomenon.

Bob Marley (1945–1981).

IN THE STYLE OF "STIR IT UP"

This example is written in the style of "Stir It Up," composed by Bob Marley in 1967. The song was popularized by pop singer-songwriter Johnny Nash in 1972. Released a year later on The Wailers' *Catch a Fire* album, "Stir It Up" proved to be one of Bob Marley's biggest international hits. The example below features a classic reggae one-drop beat, with Guitar 1 laying down eighth-note strums on beats 2 and 4, and Guitar 2 doubling the bass line.

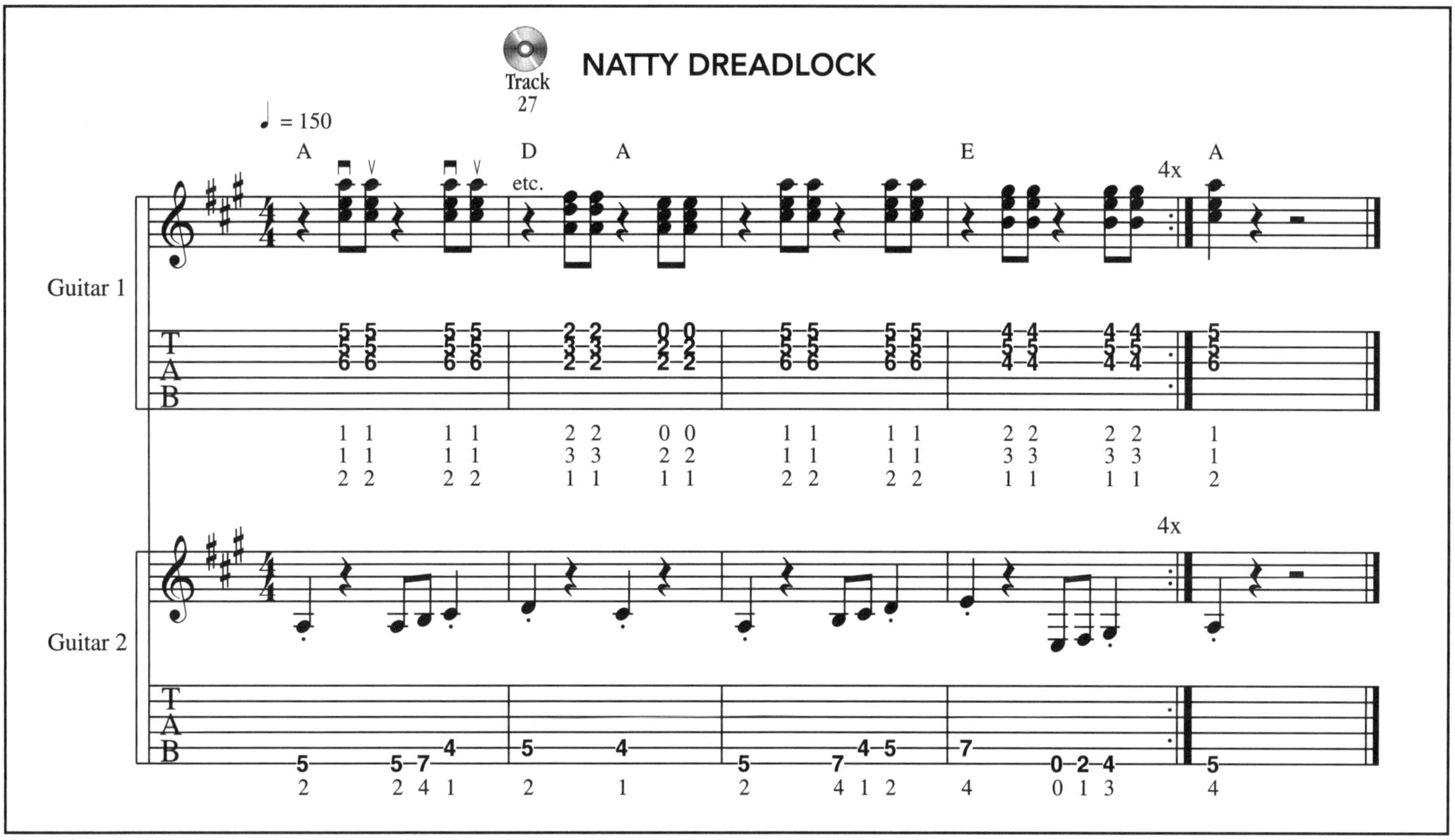

NATTY DREADLOCK (Track 27)

IN THE STYLE OF "RASTA MAN CHANT"

The next example is written in the style of "Rasta Man Chant" from the 1973 *Burnin'* album by The Wailers. The original recording of "Rasta Man Chant" was based on Nyabinghi drum ceremonies. Nyabinghi ceremonies are Rastafarian gatherings in which the celebrants praise Jah through chant, dance, and sacred drumming. The Nyabinghi rhythm emphasizes two eighth-note strums on beats 1 and 3, creating a heartbeat rhythm. Notice the similarity with the previous example, where the same strums are placed on beats 2 and 4. As in the previous example, Guitar 2 doubles the bass.

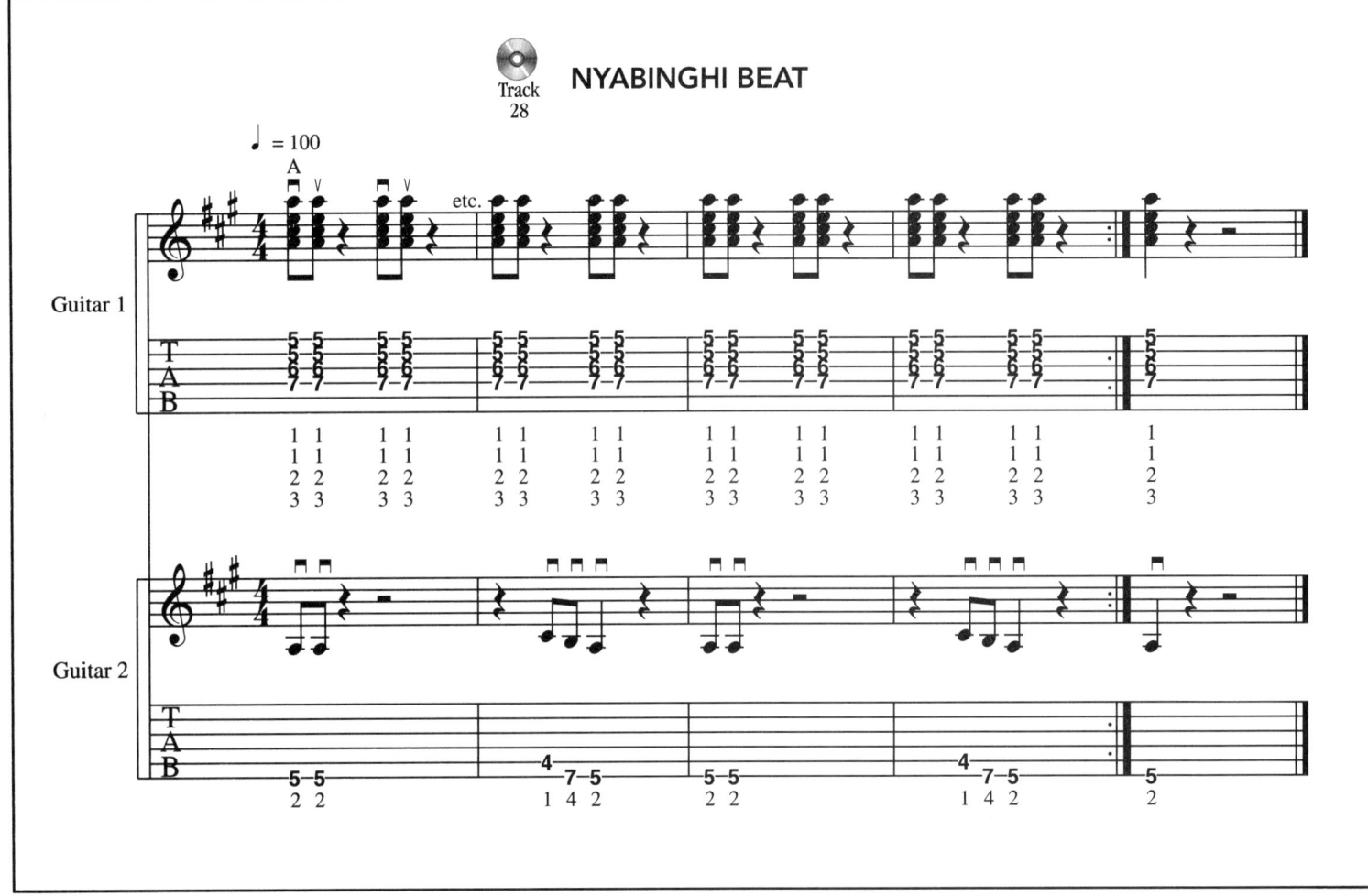

IN THE STYLE OF "I SHOT THE SHERIFF"

The Wailers' fourth major-label album, *Burnin',* is significant because it was the last album The Wailers released before co-founders Peter Tosh and Bunny Wailer left the group to pursue solo careers (at which point the band became known as Bob Marley and The Wailers). Plus, it featured "I Shot the Sheriff," a tune that became an international hit due largely to Eric Clapton's cover version. Clapton's "I Shot the Sheriff" was a number one hit on the American charts, which helped propel Bob Marley even further into international fame. The example on the next page is written in the style of "I Shot the Sheriff," and it features a longer song form and simple three-note chord voicings.

IN THE STYLE OF "EXODUS"

In late 1976, Bob Marley agreed to perform in Smile Jamaica, an outdoor concert organized by Michael Manley, the Prime Minister of Jamaica. Unfortunately, agreeing to appear in this concert proved dangerous, because two days before the show, Bob Marley, his wife, and manager were shot at Marley's home in a politically motivated assassination attempt. Thankfully, everyone survived, but after this incident, Bob and his family immediately relocated to London, where he recorded what many people consider his most groundbreaking album, *Exodus*. Released in 1977, at the height of the British punk movement, *Exodus* was a huge international success. In addition to being their first gold album, Exodus received widespread critical acclaim, so much so that in 1998, Time magazine voted it the best music album of the 20th century.

The following example is in the style of the title track of the *Exodus* album. It's a Bob Marley classic that features what is known as a *steppers,* or "four to the floor," rhythm. The defining characteristic of the steppers beat is that the drummer plays the kick drum on all four quarter notes of the measure, which gives a momentum and urgency to the beat. The guitar is playing a syncopated rhythm figure that accents every third eighth-note strum. Immediately after the accented strum, lift up your fretting finger slightly (still touching the string) to create a fret-hand mute. To get a tone similar to the original recording, pick your muted chords with quick and choppy strums. The effect is a washboard-like raking sound.

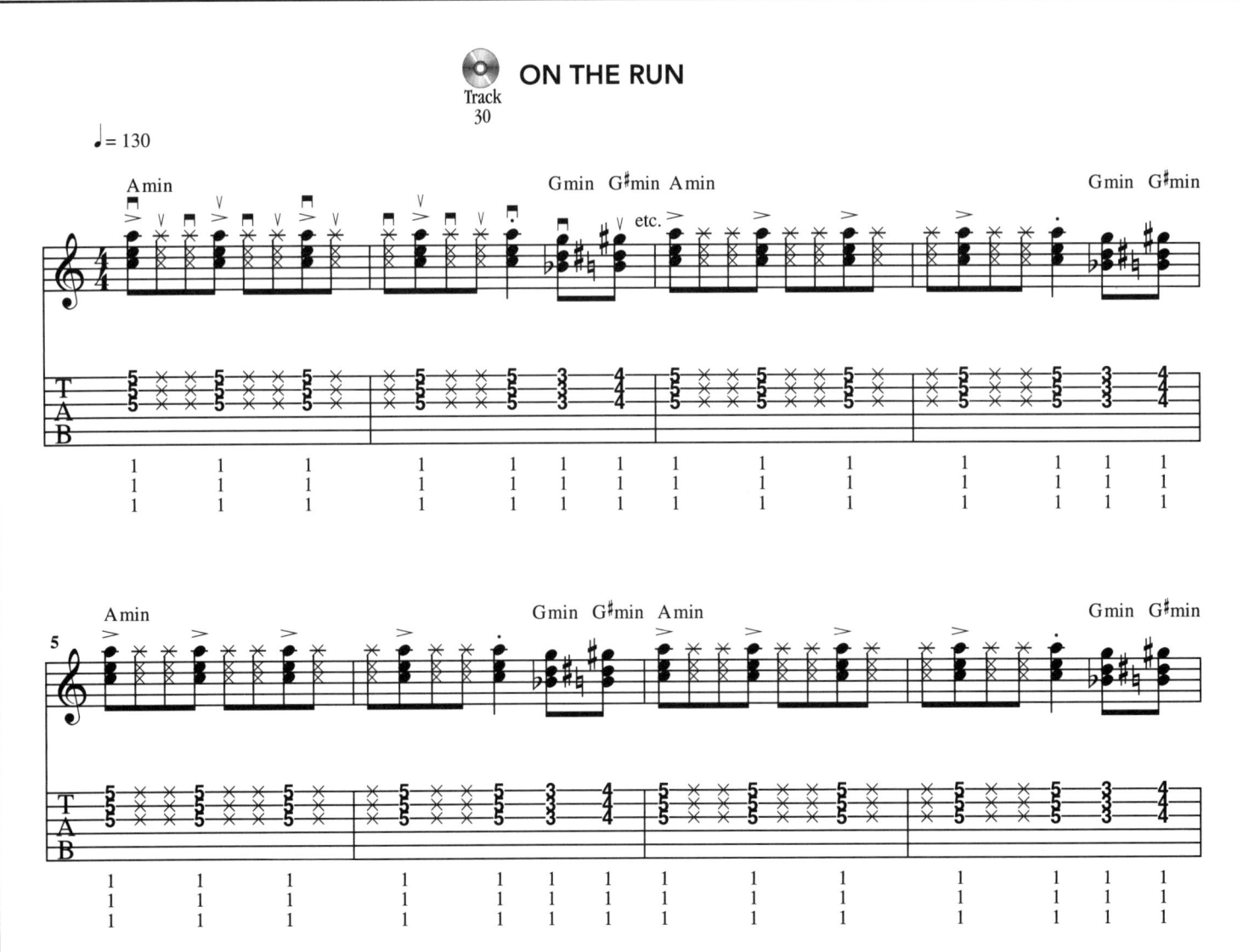

IN THE STYLE OF "REDEMPTION SONG"

Bob Marley was diagnosed with cancer in July of 1977, only a month after *Exodus* was released. Amazingly, even with the knowledge of his illness and deteriorating health, Bob Marley released three more studio albums: *Kaya* in 1978, *Survival* in 1979, and *Uprising* in 1980. *Uprising* was a particularly important work, in part because it was the last studio album Bob Marley ever recorded, and it also featured the tune that some believe was his greatest composition, the last track on the album, "Redemption Song."

The example on the next page, written in the style of "Redemption Song," features a single-note melodic introduction, and a folk-style strumming pattern on the acoustic guitar. The original "Redemption Song" is an excellent example of melodic and harmonic simplicity, serving as a backdrop for brilliant lyrical content that is both deeply personal and, at the same time, universally inclusive. "Redemption Song" is the last song he ever performed before his passing in 1981. It is fitting that the career of master musician, songwriter, and cultural icon Bob Marley would conclude gracefully with a simple folk song.

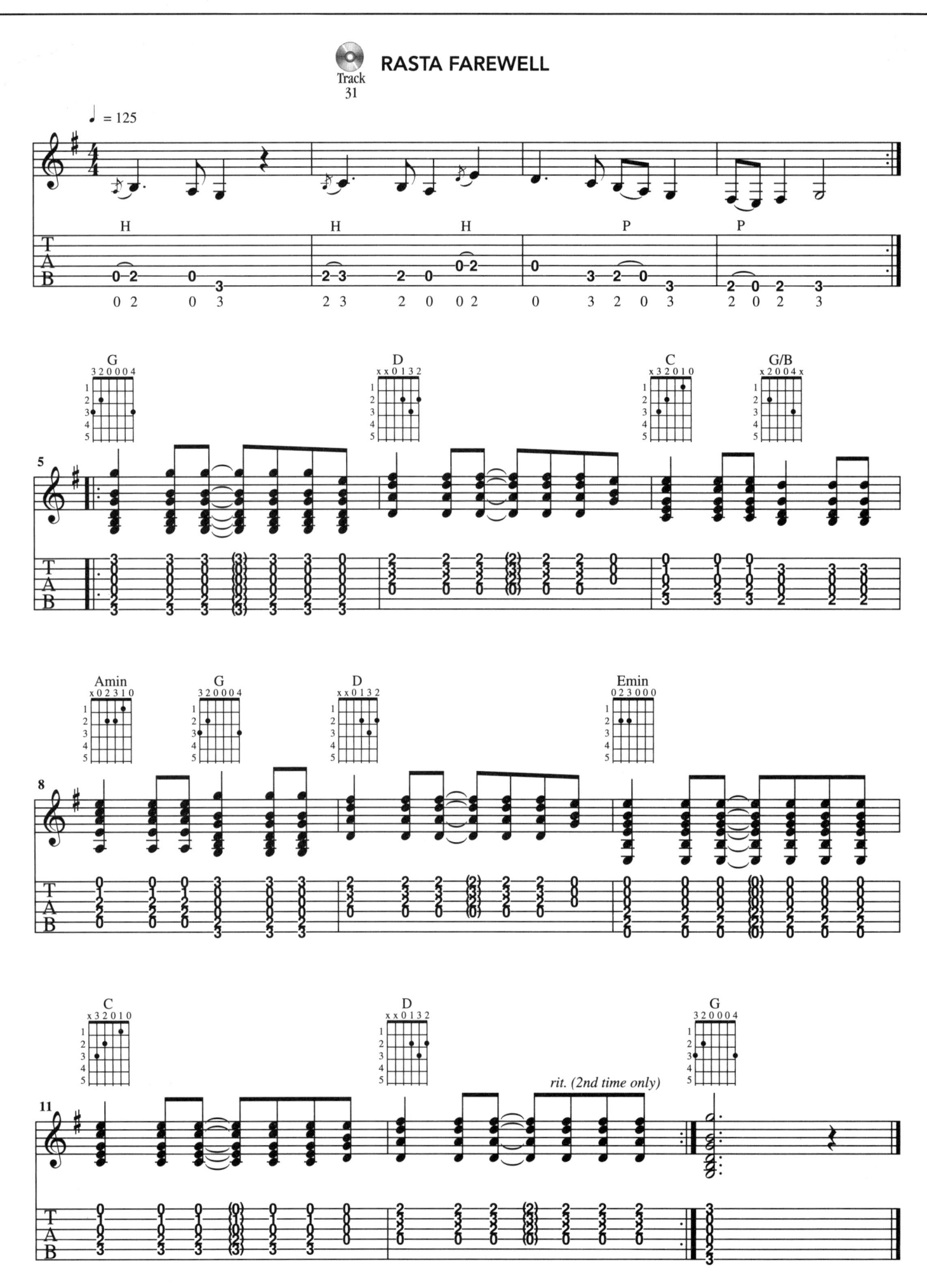

Chapter 6 — ERNEST RANGLIN

JAMAICA

Since this book focuses on the music of Jamaica from a guitar player's perspective, it's fitting to conclude by acknowledging one of Jamaica's truly legendary guitar players, Ernest Ranglin. Born in Manchester, Jamaica in 1932, this self-taught guitarist was well known in Jamaica as a rising star by the age of 16. In 1948, Ernest Ranglin joined his first group, the Val Bennett Orchestra, which played at local Jamaican hotels. His reputation grew quickly, and two years later, he was a member of one of Jamaica's best known big bands, the Eric Deans Orchestra, touring the Caribbean extensively and playing in the best hotels.

By the late 1950s and early '60s, Ernest was leading the way in developing the ska sound. His recordings for Island Records and Studio One are considered classics that influenced generations of musicians. In the '60s, he was in constant demand as a versatile guitarist and arranger. By the 1970s, Ernest had recorded with Millie Small (on her hit "My Boy Lollypop"), The Melodians, The Wailers, The Skatalites, Toots and The Maytals, and Jimmy Cliff just to name a few. Plus, Bob Marley had asked Ernest to be his live-in guitar teacher!

However, the true magic of Ernest Ranglin is that he has continued recording up to this day, pushing the boundaries of style by melding jazz, ska, reggae, and world music into a fusion all his own. To demonstrate this eclectic mix, our final example ("The Journey Begins" on the next page) features a layering of three independent guitar parts. This example is written in the style of a tune called "D'accord Dakar," the first track on the 1998 album *In Search of the Lost Riddim*, recorded in Senegal with the famous African singer Baaba Maal and his band.

The form of "The Journey Begins" is repeated five times. The first time through, only Guitar 3 is playing; the second time through, Guitars 2 and 3 are playing; and the third, fourth, and fifth times through, all three guitars are playing. On your CD, Track 32 features all three guitars. Track 33 consists of only Guitars 2 and 3, so you can take the part of Guitar 1. Track 34 consists of only Guitars 1 and 3, so you can take the part of Guitar 2. Track 35 consists of only Guitars 1 and 2, so you can take the part of Guitar 3. Have fun with this Ernest Ranglin-style arrangement!

Ernest Ranglin (b. 1932) was a major force in the creation of ska in the late 1950s. Perhaps the most innovative guitarist in Jamaica's history, Ranglin made his first guitar out of a sardine can and wires. Known for fusing Jamaican styles such as ska and reggae with jazz and world styles, Ranglin has performed and recorded with many artists including The Wailers, Jimmy Cliff, Prince Buster, The Skatalites, and jazz saxophonist Sonny Stitt.

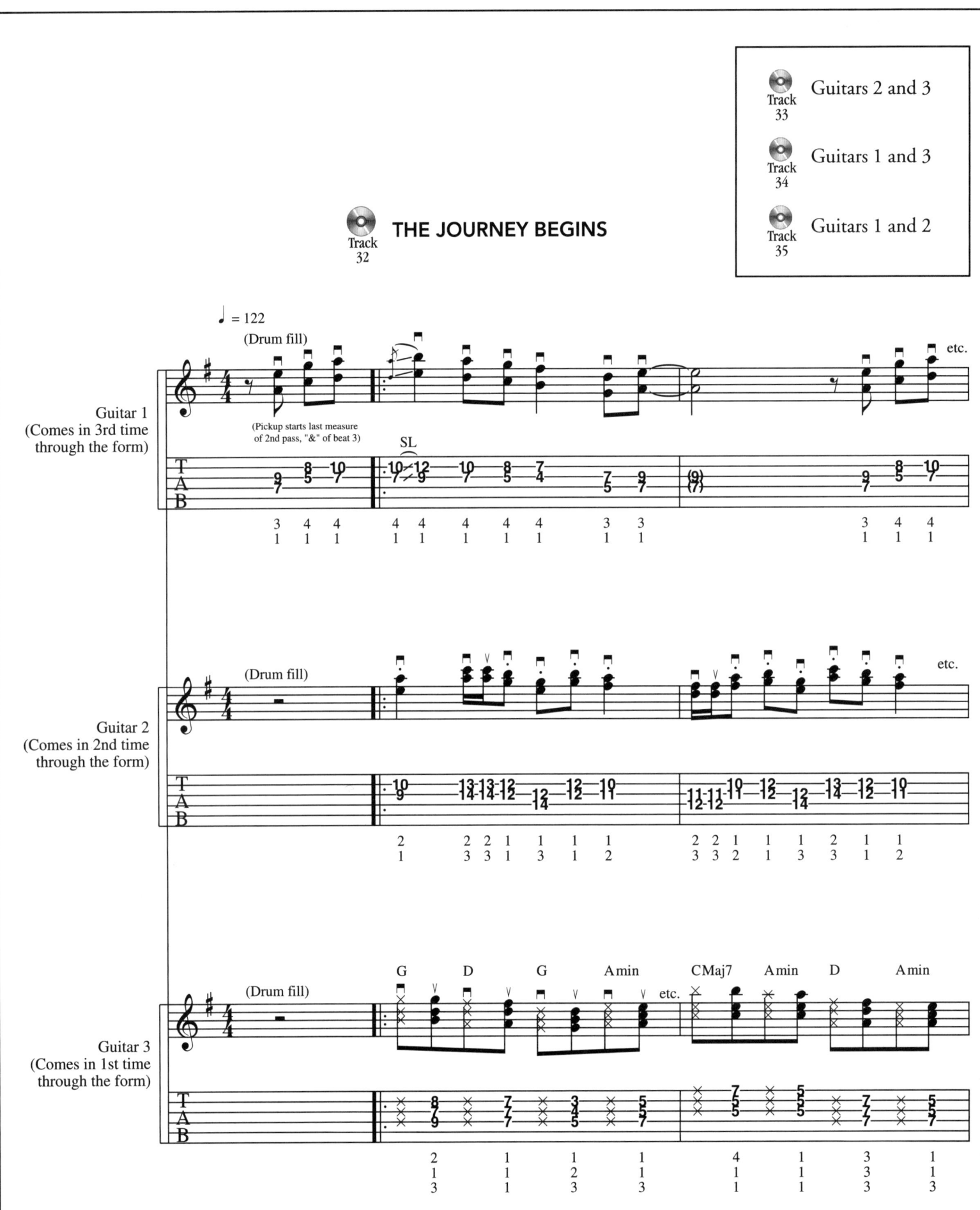

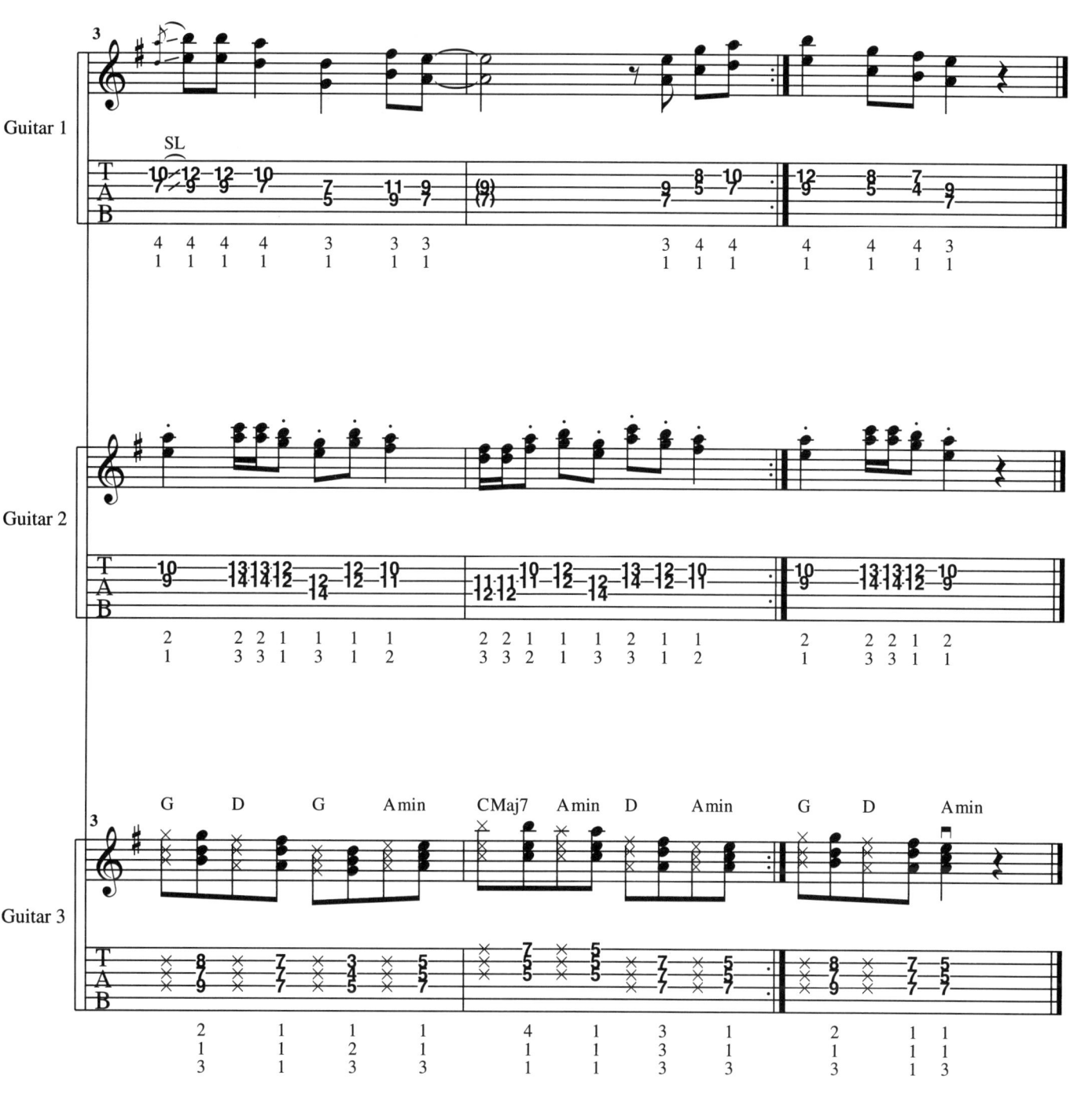

Final Word

I hope you have enjoyed this book, and it has given you a deeper appreciation for the rich tradition of Jamaican music. I encourage you to continue your own explorations by listening to and learning more about the artists covered here, also by applying the techniques and concepts that you've learned to your own playing. Jamaican music is here for all of us to enjoy. Peace.

Cuba

Jeff Peretz

*Guitar Styles
from Around the World*

*This book was acquired, edited and produced
by Workshop Arts, Inc., the publishing arm of
the National Guitar Workshop.*
Nathaniel Gunod, acquisitions, managing editor
Burgess Speed, editor
Matthew Liston, assistant editor
Timothy Phelps, interior design
Ante Gelo, music typesetter
Barbara Smolover, interior illustrations
CD recorded by Steve Rossiter at Axis Sound, NYC
Jeff Peretz (guitar), Tony de Vivo (percussion and bass)

Contents

ABOUT THE AUTHOR 53
  Author's Foreword 53

CHAPTER 1—History of Cuban Music 54
  The Golden Age 54
  African Influence 55
  European Influence 56
  The Migration of Cuban Music 56
  The Guitar and Tres in Cuban Music 58
  Rhythm Instruments 59
  Types of Cuban Groups 62

CHAPTER 2—Latin Rhythms 63
  Clave 63
  Cascara 65
  Tumbao 66

CHAPTER 3—Guajeo/Montuno 68
  Linking Guajeo with the Clave 69
  Triad Studies 71
    Agua con Gas 74
  Rhythmic Breaks 78

CHAPTER 4—Styles 80
  Son 80
    ¿Tu Tienes? 80
  Son Montuno/Guajira 83
    Hombre Calvo 83
  Changüí 86
    Cheena Morena 86
  Bolero 89
    Las Guajiras del Invernadero 89
  Nueva Trova 90
    La Proxima 90
  Danzón 92
    Una Mas 92
  Mambo 94
    Blue Brito 94
  Guaguancó 96
    Arroz con Pollo 96

FINAL WORD 98

  0
  Track
  1

A compact disc is included with this book. This disc can make learning with the book easier and more enjoyable. The symbol shown at the left appears next to every example that is on the CD. Use the CD to help ensure that you're capturing the feel of the examples, interpreting the rhythms correctly, and so on. The track number below the symbol corresponds directly to the example you want to hear. Track 1 will help you tune your guitar to this CD.

Have fun!

About the Author

Jeff Peretz was born in Newark, New Jersey. He studied music at Berklee College of Music and William Paterson University, with a focus on jazz performance. He is the author of *Zen and the Art of Guitar* (Alfred/National Guitar Workshop #21906) and *Guitar Atlas: Middle East* (Alfred/National Guitar Workshop #22711). He can be heard regularly with the Arabic/Jazz group Abu Gara, which he founded in 1999. Jeff has performed all over the United States, the Middle East, and Europe. While his main instrument is the guitar, he regularly performs on ud and dumbek as well. He has played ud with Grammy-nominated Latin group Yerba Buena. His jazz/hip-hop group, the Jeff Peretz Group, has shared the stage with the Fugees, Groove Collective, and Brooklyn Funk Essentials. He is the director of the electric guitar performance program at the Third Street Music School Settlement in New York City and is a faculty member at The New School and New York University. He also teaches at the National Guitar Workshop.

PHOTO BY NETA KATZ

Acknowledgements

This book is dedicated to my beautiful children Maya, Tristen, and Zohar. Everything I do is for you three. Thanks to Ben Lapidus and Julian Kleinerman for their patience with all of my questions. Extra special gratitude to Tony de Vivo for "killin' it" in the session and Steve Rossiter for pressing all the right buttons as usual.

AUTHOR'S FOREWORD

What is it about the music of Cuba that has caused such a great impact in the world music genre? This question can be answered in many different ways, but for me, a total rhythm junkie, the answer is quite simple: rhythm. Nowhere else in the Western world do African rhythms and European harmonies come together with such toe-tapping, hip-shaking intensity. This book is a compilation of exercises, historical facts, and general bits of wisdom I have picked up through many years of playing and listening to Cuban music. I hope to demonstrate that the guitar (along with its cousin the *tres*) plays an important role in the multi-layered rhythmic quilt of Cuban music.

To benefit from this book, you should be comfortable reading either standard music notation or TAB. Understanding the theory behind major scales and chords will help you make sense of the exercises. If you need a refresher, you can refer to *Theory for the Contemporary Guitarist* by Guy Capuzzo (Alfred/National Guitar Workshop #16755). Cuban guitar playing requires many of the same skills as jazz guitar, which you can learn more about in *Beginning Jazz Guitar* (Alfred/National Guitar Workshop #14120) or *The Total Jazz Guitarist* (Alfred/National Guitar Workshop #24417). The accompanying CD will help you interpret the rhythm and feel of each example. Before we delve into the power of Cuban rhythm, however, let's begin by exploring the cultural influences that have shaped Cuban music.

Chapter 1 — HISTORY OF CUBAN MUSIC

THE GOLDEN AGE

In 1940, after overthrowing the progressive government of Ramón Grau San Martin, Colonel Fulgencio Batista was elected to a four-year term as President of Cuba. In 1952, he overthrew the democratic government of Carlos Prío Socarrás to once again assume leadership. During his time in power, Batista courted investors and tourists from the United States. While this led to many mafia acquisitions of hotels, casinos, and mansions in and around Havana, it also led to an era of nightlife unlike any before. Despite the growing corruption of the Batista regime, music, dancing, and singing flourished in Havana in the 1950s. It was during this time that the music of Cuba became a major artistic force and established itself as a source of pride and identity for this island in the Caribbean. The 1950s are considered to be the golden era of Cuban music and nightlife.

The instability of the government didn't end with Batista. On December 31, 1958, Batista was ousted by Fidel Castro and his *barbudos* (bearded guerillas), including the revolutionary legend Ernesto "Che" Guevara. Despite the violence and fear that gripped the nation during these transitional times, the music and nightlife continued to attract people from all over the world. Legendary night spots like the Casino de la Playa and the Tropicana offered musical revues starring such celebrated performers as Celia Cruz (the "Godmother of Salsa"), Arsenio Rodríguez, Xiomara Alfaro, and the Valdés Brothers.

The excitement of the scene was not limited to the big night clubs and casinos. Small cafés such as El Paris and La Bombilla hosted local jam sessions known as *descargas* (which literally means "discharges"). These impromptu sessions attracted record companies from all over the world and are considered by many to be the precursor to the style of music that would later be known as *salsa* in New York. Some of these sessions were immortalized on classic recordings led by Israel "Cachao" López.

Aside from the night clubs, casinos, and café jams, radio was an important factor in the rise of Cuban music. It helped launch and sustain the careers of many titanic figures such as Arsenio Rodríguez, Isolina Carrillo, Orquesta Sensación, and Compay Segundo, who would later gain international stardom as the face of the Buena Vista Social Club.

AFRICAN INFLUENCE

Like most of the Caribbean and South America, Cuban culture is a mixture of indigenous, colonial (in this case, Spanish), and African influences. In Cuba, probably more so than anywhere else in the colonized world, the ties to traditional African religions and rituals remains strong even to this day. Nowhere is this more evident than in the music. When looking for the origins of Cuban music, we must start with the ritual music of the slaves who were brought to Cuba and the dances and song forms of the Spanish colonialists who brought them there.

There were three major *naciónes* (nations) of slaves brought to Cuba before slavery was abolished in 1887. There were the *Lucumi* (Yoruba) who came from western Nigeria, eastern Benin, and Ketu; the *Congo* (Bantu) who came from Burundi, Rwanda, and Namibia; and the *Calabaris* (Calabar) who were taken from Cameroon and the Lake Chad region. The people of each nación brought with them their own unique religions, rituals, and rhythms.

The different naciónes were often split up and spread out across the country in an effort to erase any connection to their origins. One of the ways that the slaves were able to maintain their identity was to gather to "beat the drum" when the plantation owners weren't looking or felt generous enough to allow it as a reward for hard work. As a result, many songs, dances, and rhythms found a home in the new world. Despite the efforts of many of the slave owners to rid the slaves of their African culture, the continued arrival of new slaves assured the connection to their origins was maintained. Rhythms, dances, and rituals were one way in which the slaves were able to do this.

Towards the end of slavery in Cuba, the various naciónes maintained their identities by sticking together in the cities and forming organizations known as *cabildos*. The cabildos were also a way for the government to keep tabs on the various former slaves. When slavery was eventually abolished in 1887, the cabildos were outlawed, and the different slave groups, who until then had been able to hold on to their identities, were assimilated into the greater society. The various cabildos were often forced to align themselves with the Catholic Church under the guidance of a patron saint.

From this point on, all that was left were the worship rituals, religious practices, and languages that defined the African identity in Cuban culture. These remaining cultural artifacts are preserved in the music.

Santería, or "The Way of the Saints," is a uniquely Afro-Cuban religion derived from the beliefs of the Yoruba people of Nigeria. Unable to openly worship the *orishas* of their native religion—orishas are spirits that manifest different aspects of the divine on Earth—they adopted Catholic saints as surrogates. By celebrating on the church-sanctioned saint's days, they were able to preserve many of their customs under the guise of Christianity. Santería's biggest influence on Cuban music was the importance of rhythm and dance. Many African religious ceremonies use sacred drumming as a means to communicate with the divine. The drummers play specific patterns for each orisha that combine to form complex, syncopated rhythms that are perfect for dancing. This is the root of the complex interplay of percussion instruments at the heart of Cuban music.

EUROPEAN INFLUENCE

If the African influence is responsible for the rhythmic content in Cuban music, the European (Spanish and, to a lesser extent, French) influence is responsible for the harmonic content and song forms. The music of Spain is itself a mixture of European, Arabic, Gypsy, Nordic, and Jewish influences, all of which made their way to Cuba.

With Catholicism being the main religion of the Spanish colonists, several Christian traditions survived the journey to the new world, such as the feast of the Epiphany and Corpus Christi. In Cuba, these became grand carnival celebrations, in which the cabildos were allowed to participate, in spite of the fact that they were still quite oppressed on every other level. It is during the parades of these festivals that the African influence and the Spanish influence came together in *comparsas* (groups of singers, dancers, and musicians that performed at carnivals).

Much like the carnival festivities of Brazil, each neighborhood and cabildo had its own comparsa. Each comparsa had its own unique flavor, evoking African deities with ritual masks, dances, and songs, while at the same time celebrating the harvest and seasonal changes that lead up to Lent. In modern times, each comparsa composes its own song and dance specifically for the procession. These processions are an expression of pride in one's neighborhood.

Cuba was also influenced by French culture, by way of New Orleans and especially Haiti (which was then known as Saint-Domingue). During the Haitian Revolution of the 1790s, many French colonists fled the country (sometimes bringing their slaves with them) and sought refuge in Cuba. The celebrations of the French slaves known as *tumba francesca* (or *tumba-francés*) were especially popular in the Oriente province. Much like the cabildos, tumba-francesca societies later became "freeman associations" when slavery was abolished. The tumba-francesca societies also participated in the Saint Day festivals performing a fast dance called the *cocoye*, which is based on a rhythm known as *cinquillo*. This rhythm later evolved into the *tumbao*, a rhythmic pattern that is the basis for the bass and conga in modern Afro-Cuban styles.

THE MIGRATION OF CUBAN MUSIC

It is important to realize that the music of Cuba and, for the most part, music in general during the Colonial era was primarily an accompaniment for dancing. The styles that exist today evolved from earlier versions that were based on European and African dances.

The *danzón*, which later evolved into the *mambo* and the *cha-cha-chá*, was based on the old English *contra dance*, which was adapted by the French and later transmitted to Cuba by way of Haiti. Over time, the *contradanza* (as it was known in Cuba) morphed into the less structured danzón in the Matanzas Province (see map on page 57).

While Havana is the capitol of Cuba, both politically and culturally, understanding the musical contributions of the rural regions of Cuba is essential. Most, if not all, of the classic styles of Afro-Cuban music were developed outside of Havana and brought there by the migration of those looking for a better life.

The *son* style grew out of several street song styles of Oriente (the eastern part of the country, encompassing provinces 11–15 on the map below) and is considered today to be the heart of Afro-Cuban music, more so than any other Cuban style. In Santiago de Cuba, the word "son" referred to all African styles of dance. The word later took on the meaning "festivity" in the western part of the island in and around Vueltabajo (a district in the Pinar del Río province). Since about 1920, the word "son" has encompassed not only the dances and the festive music but also the small bands that play it.

In 1909, a unique occurrence happened during President José Miguel Gómez's reign. Fearing that his army was conspiring against him, President Gómez ordered the company in Havana and the company in the Oriente to switch places. Several key son musicians including tres player Sergio Danger and guitarist Emiliano Difull were members of that Oriente company that was brought to Havana. According to legend, this was how the son made its way to Havana and, conversely, the guaguancó to Oriente.

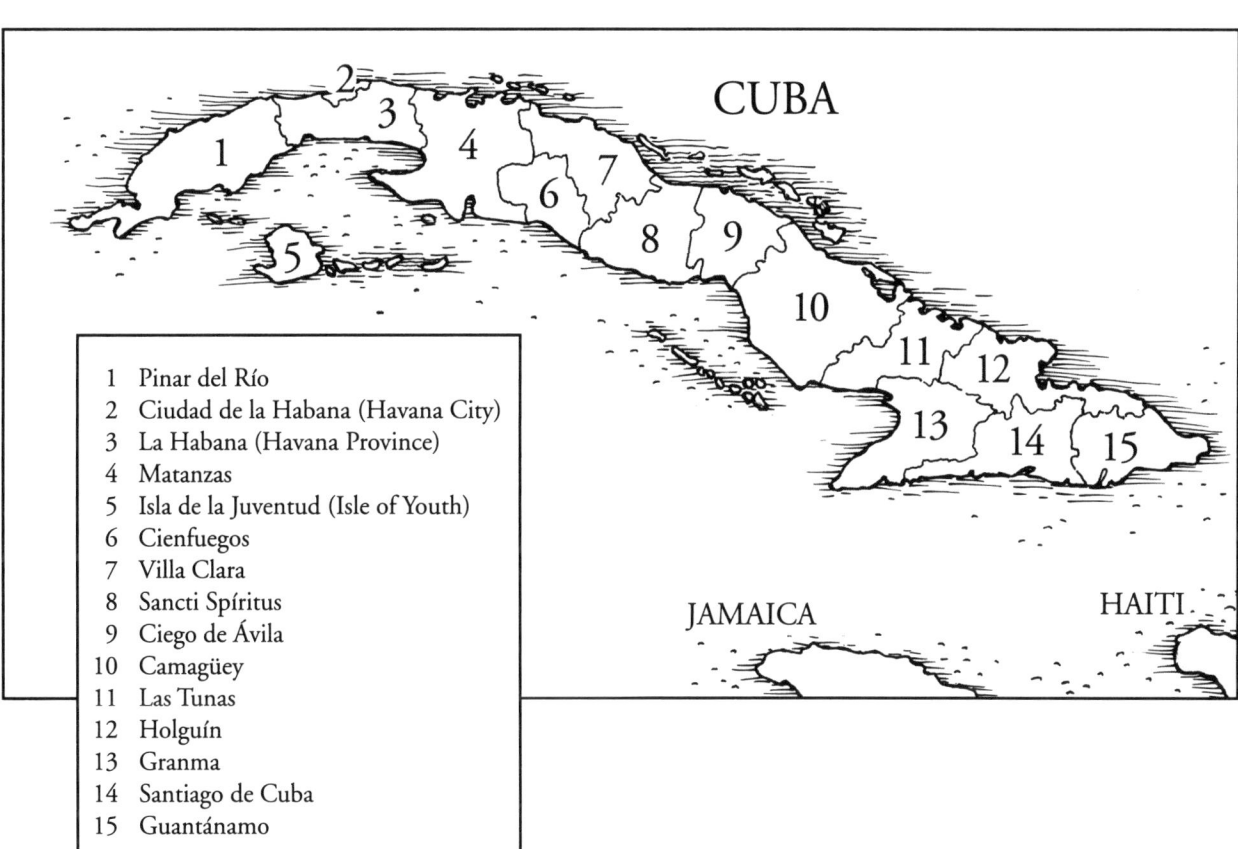

1. Pinar del Río
2. Ciudad de la Habana (Havana City)
3. La Habana (Havana Province)
4. Matanzas
5. Isla de la Juventud (Isle of Youth)
6. Cienfuegos
7. Villa Clara
8. Sancti Spíritus
9. Ciego de Ávila
10. Camagüey
11. Las Tunas
12. Holguín
13. Granma
14. Santiago de Cuba
15. Guantánamo

THE GUITAR AND TRES IN CUBAN MUSIC

The guitar and its relatives hold a special place in Cuban music. Cuba was colonized by the Spanish, and the guitar plays a huge role in the music of Spain, so it only makes sense that the guitar would make its way into the roots of Cuban music. The guitar probably made its way to Cuba sometime in the fifteenth century. There were many different variations of the guitar including the *bandurria, vihuela, requinto,* and *laúd (*or *lute)*. They were primarily used as accompaniment to singing. Eventually, the guitar-like instruments evolved into the Cuban *tres*, which is the essential stringed instrument in Cuban music.

The tres traditionally has a smaller body than a regular guitar, although many *treseros* (tres players) prefer to convert a regular acoustic guitar. The tres has three sets of double strings, or *courses*. It was originally tuned to a D Minor chord (D–F–A), but since the revolutionary influence of Arsenio Rodríguez, the predominant tuning is a C Major chord (G–C–E) with the G and E strings tuned in octaves and the C strings tuned in unison.

Arsenio Rodríguez, who many consider to be the father of modern tres playing, was born in Matanzas Province in 1911, the grandson of slaves from the Congo. Not only did he revolutionize the way that the tres was played and tuned, but he also was a legendary band leader and composer who single-handedly changed the direction of Cuban music. Although he went blind at the age of seven, he began his professional career at the age of eight playing *botija* (see page 59) and *marimbula* (see page 61), both precursors to the bass. He soon took up the tres and rose to fame in the 1920s and 1930s, combining the tribal rhythms of *rumba* with the Spanish harmonies and melodies which made up the bulk of the repertoire for the guitar. Some of his most memorable gigs were with conga player Chano Pozo in a small group that featured piano, tres, and percussion.

Arsenio was an important figure in bringing the son style to Havana in the 1920s. At a time when most other son bands were downplaying their African influence, Arsenio was doing the opposite and changing the way that Cuban music was approached from a rhythmic standpoint. As well as changing the rhythmic sound of the son and changing the way the instrument was tuned and played, he also changed the instrumentation that bands use. He expanded the lineup of the *septeto Habanero*, a group of seven musicians traditionally including strings, percussion, and a single trumpet. He added more trumpets, cowbell, and piano and opened up the form to include sections for improvised solos. By the late 1930s, he was bringing the *mambo* rhythm (based on a Congolese ritual pattern) into the mix, thus creating a whole new sound. The *conjunto* (big band) was the name given to the style that Arsenio had pioneered. This was the dawn of Cuban big band music.

Guitar (left); tres (right).

RHYTHM INSTRUMENTS

Bongos

Two small drums played between the knees. *Hembra* is the larger, "female" drum, and *macho* is the smaller, "male" drum. The bongos are usually responsible for accentuating and embellishing the rhythm.

Botija

A large clay jug originally used to carry water or olive oil. The player blows across the top of the jug to produce a bass note.

Cajón

A wooden box upon which the player sits. Typically found in rumba. Originally made by slaves out of wooden shipping crates.

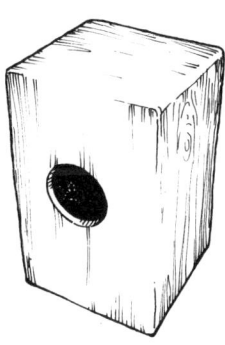

Claves

Two thick wooden sticks (one male, one female), which are struck together to create the clave rhythm. Possibly the most important rhythmic instrument in all of Cuban music.

Congas (Tumbadoras)

Barrel drums made from hardwood strips. Evolved from the *makuta* drums of Congo. Congas are grouped into three different sizes: *tumba* (large), *conga* (medium), and *quinto* (small).

Drumset

A set of drums consisting of kick (or bass) drum, snare drum, tom-toms, high-hat, and cymbals. Found in modern groups as well as Afro-Cuban jazz.

Güiro

A serrated calabash gourd that is scraped or hit with a stick or metal strip. Next to the clave, the güiro is one of the most important instruments in the rhythm section because it is responsible for keeping the pulse. It is typically the only instrument which keeps a steady downbeat.

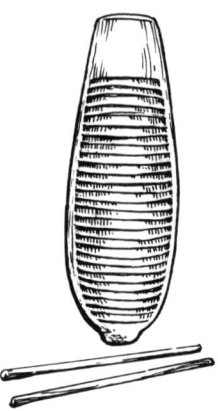

Maracas (Rumba Shakers)

Dried calabash or gourd shells filled with seeds, often played in pairs. It is believed that maracas came from ancient Morocco. Maracas are deceptively hard to play, in that the instrument relies on a delayed response. Once shaken, the seeds must travel inside the gourd to hit the other side. As a result, the player must anticipate the rhythm.

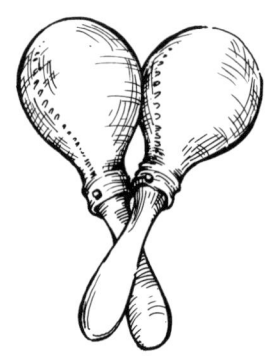

Marimbula
A wooden box fitted with metal prongs, like a larger version of the African *kalimba* or thumb piano. The player plucks the metal prongs to produce a percussive bass sound.

Shekeré
A large gourd covered in a mesh of beads or tiny shells. Brought to Cuba by the Yoruba, the instrument is shaken and hit with the palm of the hand for accents.

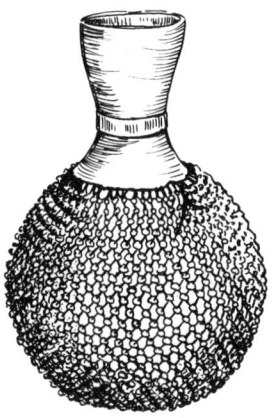

Timbales
Two mounted metal drums used for rhythmic embellishment and marking sections of a song. They are typically played with thin sticks striking both the shell and head of the drum.

TYPES OF CUBAN GROUPS

The Trio
As its name implies, a trio is a group of three singers who accompany themselves on guitar and small percussion instruments. The classic lineup consists of two singers playing guitar while the third played maracas. Sometimes, all three play guitars, and other times one plays tres or even clave. The trio is Cuba's version of the European *troubadour* or wandering minstrel tradition. It rose to prominence in the 1920s interpreting the bolero, guaracha, and son.

The Sexteto
The *sexteto* is the classic lineup of the son style, as Arsenio Rodríguez's "Sexteto Habanero," one of the first sextetos, demonstrated. The instrumentation consists of guitar, tres, bass, bongo, maracas, and clave. This type of collective came into existence in the 1920s.

The Septeto
As one would imagine, the *septeto*, which would go on to become the most important of Cuban bands, is a sexteto with the addition of a trumpet player. The most important of the septetos was Ignacio Piñeiro's Septeto Nacional, which started as a sexteto before adding a trumpet player in 1927.

The Conjunto
Further expanding of the traditional ensemble lineups continued into the 1940s when two or three trumpets as well as strings, vocalists, and a piano were added to the septeto. The final addition was the conga, first added to the conjunto by Arsenio Rodríguez. Today the conga is heard in almost all Cuban music.

The Combo
The combo is Cuba's version of a modern jazz group. There are no set lineups, but the traditional combination of trumpet, saxophone, bass, piano, and drumset is the template around which this type of group is based. There are versions that include electric guitar and tres as well. Again, like its American jazz counterpart, the combo is a reduction of a big band in order to fit into smaller venues and save costs when touring.

Chapter 2 LATIN RHYTHMS

CLAVE

The *clave* is not only the name of an instrument, but it is also the name of the rhythm it plays. The clave is the underlying rhythmic pulse of all Cuban music. It is a simple, yet deceptive two-measure rhythmic figure of African origin that provides a constant point of reference for each instrument. If you were to look at the complex rhythms of the various styles of Cuban music as a house, the clave would be the foundation upon which every instrument and part stands.

Not only is the clave the rhythmic point of reference for all of the other instruments, but each of the other instruments plays a highly syncopated part relative to the clave that all add up to create the quilt of Cuban music.

2/3 Clave

There are several different variations of the clave. The most common is the *2/3 clave.* The name simply refers to the fact that there are two attacks in the first measure and three in the second measure. In the chart below, the numbers refer to the downbeats, and the "&" symbols the upbeats.

1	&	2	&	3	&	4	&	1	&	2	&	3	&	4	&
		x		x				x			x			x	

3/2 Clave

The clave is also played in the reverse order; this is known as the *3/2 clave.* It is essential for each player to realize which clave is being played for each different style. When the wrong clave is played, the rhythm becomes *cruzado* or crossed.

1	&	2	&	3	&	4	&	1	&	2	&	3	&	4	&
x			x			x				x		x			

Guaguancó Clave

Certain rhythmic styles such as the *guaguancó* (which will be discussed at length in Chapter 4) have their own clave. It is also sometimes known as the *rumba clave*.

1	&	2	&	3	&	4	&	1	&	2	&	3	&	4	&
x			x				x			x		x			

Columbia Clave

In many Cuban rhythmic styles there are two separate rhythmic undercurrents happening simultaneously. One is in 4/4 and the other is based on groups of 3, 6, or 12. As a result, there are several claves where the rhythm in groups of three is dominant. The most common is the *columbia clave*.

1	2	3	4	5	6	1	2	3	4	5	6
x		x			x		x		x		

Combining Columbia and Guaguancó Claves

Notice how the columbia and guaguancó claves are approximately the same pattern, even though they are in different time signatures. These two undercurrents are present in many Afro-Cuban rhythms.

Columbia Clave	1	2	3	4	5	6	1	2	3	4	5	6
		x		x			x		x		x	
Guaguancó Clave	x			x				x		x		x		
	1	&	2	&	3	&	4	&	1	&	2	&	3	&	4	&

When seen in this light, it is easy to see how important a good relationship with the clave is. Rhythms are simply divisions of time. It's like evenly folding a piece of paper in half, quarters, thirds, or whatever number you want. The piece of paper is still the same size. Likewise, a beat or measure is always the same size. The ways in which to divide it are many. In Cuban music, there are two pieces of paper, one divided into quarters and one into thirds (both rhythms happening simultaneously); it's the clave that shows us how to line the pieces of paper up.

CASCARA

Cascara is a two-measure rhythmic pattern that interlocks with the clave. Sometimes, the actual claves (the instruments) will be absent, but the clave rhythm is still implied by the cascara. The word cascara literally means "rind" or "shell." It refers to the outside part of the drum where the rhythm is usually played. It's played either on the side of the conga or the side of the timbales with a wooden stick or sometimes on a woodblock.

Cascara for 2/3 Clave

Count	1	&	2	&	3	&	4	&	1	&	2	&	3	&	4	&
Cascara	x		x		x	x		x	x		x	x		x		x

Cascara with Clave

Notice how the cascara and the clave line up.

Count	1	&	2	&	3	&	4	&	1	&	2	&	3	&	4	&
Cascara	x		x		x	x		x	x		x	x		x		x
Clave			x		x				x			x			x	

The cascara for the 3/2 clave would simply be the opposite of the 2/3.

Guitar Atlas: Cuba

TUMBAO

A defining feature of Afro-Cuban music is its extensive use of *syncopation*. Rather than emphasize the downbeats, syncopated music emphasizes the upbeats or "ands" (&). We see this in the clave and the cascara and how they relate to each other. The avoidance of beat 1 by the bass is an essential part of the Cuban feel. Before there was bass in Cuban music, the lower register was played by the botija, a large clay jug that was used to transport olive oil from Spain. As you can imagine, the number of pitches that could be played were quite limited. This is the main reason why the harmonic/melodic content of an Afro-Cuban bass line is fairly simple, for the most part using only roots and 5ths. However, what these bass parts lack in melody, they make up for in rhythm.

The rhythmic pattern played by the bass is known as *tumbao*. Tumbao is a one- or two-bar figure that accents the "and" of beat 2 and beat 4. The *ponche* is the fourth beat of the measure on the "3 side" of the clave. This beat is extremely important because the bassline/harmony shifts on beat 4 as opposed to beat 1. The ponche is often tied to the first beat of the "2 side" of the clave, so once the rhythm is set in motion, in essence, all one hears is the "and" of 2 and beat 4.

Tumbao with Clave

Count	1	&	2	&	3	&	4	&	1	&	2	&	3	&	4	&
Clave			x		x				x				x		x	
Tumbao				x			x					x			x	

Ponche ↓ (above beat 4 of second measure)

Tumbao

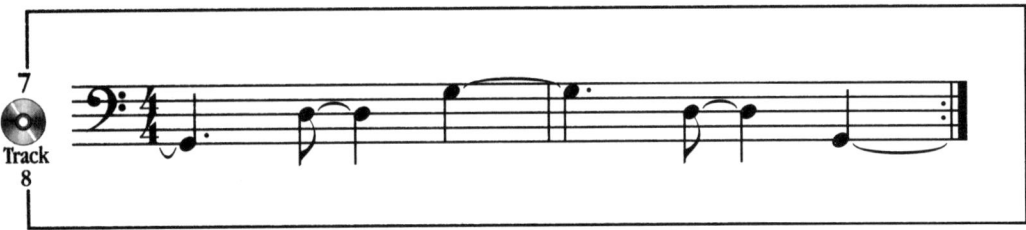

Tumbao Conga Pattern

The basic conga pattern is also a variation of the tumbao. The different conga strikes are notated P = Palm, T = Tip, S = Slap, O = Open High, and LO = Open Low.

Count	1	&	2	&	3	&	4	&	1	&	2	&	3	&	4	&
Palm	x				x				x							
Tip		x		x		x				x				x		
Slap			x								x					
Open High							O	O							O	O
Open Low												LO	LO			

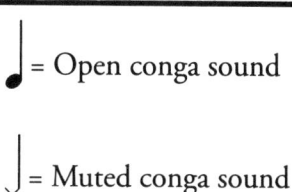

Complete 2/3 Pattern

The following example is the complete rhythmic accompaniment for the 2/3 clave and a summary of the different rhythmic patterns that we've explored so far.

Count	1	&	2	&	3	&	4	&	1	&	2	&	3	&	4	&
Clave			x		x				x		x				x	
Cascara	x		x		x	x		x	x		x	x		x		x
Bass Tumbao			x				x						x		x	
Conga Tumbao	P	T	S	T	P	T	O	O	P	T	S	LO	LO	T	O	O

Guitar Atlas: Cuba

Chapter 3: GUAJEO/MONTUNO

One of the key characteristics that sets Cuban music apart from many other types of music is the unique relationship between the fundamental elements of music: rhythm, melody, and harmony. In the music of Cuba, all three elements play an equal role in how the music sounds. Not only that, but each of the elements is highly developed.

The rhythms, as we learned in Chapter 2, are syncopated and quite challenging to master. As we will learn in this chapter, the harmonic content can be quite sophisticated, and the way in which the harmony is played—using arpeggios for a melodic effect—is also challenging.

The melodic manifestation of harmony in Cuban music, when played with the various syncopations, is known as *guajeo* or *montuno*. These two words have somewhat similar meanings, but in general, guajeo is played by a string instrument and montuno by the piano. Although they are often interchangeable, we will use the term guajeo in this book. The guajeo is the repeated melodic phrase or *vamp* that outlines the harmony.

Melodically and harmonically speaking, the music of Cuba is based on triads and 7th chords. Since 7th chords are in essence a combination of two triads, realizing how to play the triads in a melodic fashion over the complete fretboard is an essential skill to playing the guajeos that make up the bulk of the repertoire for the guitar and tres in Cuban music.

The following exercises and diagrams are designed to get you familiar with all of the triadic possibilities—both major and minor—as well as the dominant 7th chord possibilities across the entire fretboard.

CHORD THEORY REVIEW

A *chord* consists of three or more notes played simultaneously to create harmony. A *triad* is a three-note chord. All of the triads in this book are either major or minor. A major triad is constructed using the formula 1–3–5. The 1 or *root* is the note that gives the chord its name (for example, the root of a G Major chord is the note G). The next note is an interval of a major 3rd above the root. The final note is a perfect 5th above the root. For example, a G Major triad is spelled G–B–D.

Minor triads use the formula 1–♭3–5. They have a minor, or flatted, 3rd, which gives them their distinct sound. A G Minor triad is spelled G–B♭–D.

A *dominant 7th chord* has the formula 1–3–5–♭7. It is a major triad plus an extra note a minor 7th above the root. Dominant chords have a tense sound that wants to resolve back to the I chord. A G7 chord is spelled G–B–D–F.

Roman Numerals

When analyzing chord progressions, it is customary to assign each chord or triad a Roman numeral, indicating which scale degree of the key is the root of the chord. Upper-case numerals represent major chords, and lower-case numerals represent minor chords. For example, in the key of G Major, I stands for a G Major triad, ii is an A Minor triad, iii is a B Minor triad, and so forth. V7 indicates a dominant 7th chord built on the 5th scale degree (D7 in the key of G).

Roman Numerals
I or i 1
II or ii 2
III or iii 3
IV or iv 4
V or v 5
VI or vi 6
VII or vii 7

LINKING GUAJEO WITH THE CLAVE

The trick to executing the guajeos correctly is knowing how to link them with the correct clave and cascara. There are a few "telling beats" that indicate which clave is being used and serve as the connection point where the guajeo pattern rhythmically locks into the clave pattern. As with all other aspects of clave, linking the melodic pattern correctly to the rhythm is essential, otherwise the rhythm becomes cruzado (crossed). If this happens, the groove sounds awkward and is uncomfortable to dance to. Cuban musicians treat their relationship with the clave with great pride. A musician who is cruzado will soon be out of a job.

The following examples are meant to show you the rhythmic linking points to the various claves. Listen carefully until you can really hear the subtle differences of each.

The strongest two beats in either the 2/3 or 3/2 clave are beat 2 of the "2 side" and beat 4 of the "3 side."

Or, in other words, beat two of the first measure of the 2/3 or second measure of the 3/2 and beat four of the second measure of the 2/3 or the first measure of the 3/2.

Strong Beats of the 2/3 Clave

Count	1	&	2	&	3	&	4	&	1	&	2	&	3	&	4	&
Strong Beats			x												x	
2/3 Clave			x		x				x				x		x	

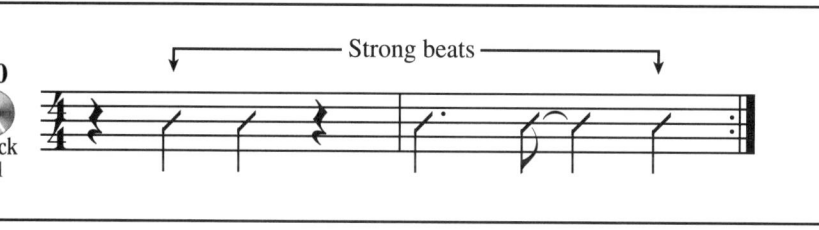

Strong Beats of the 3/2 Clave

Count	1	&	2	&	3	&	4	&	1	&	2	&	3	&	4	&
Strong Beats							x				x					
3/2 Clave	x			x			x				x		x			

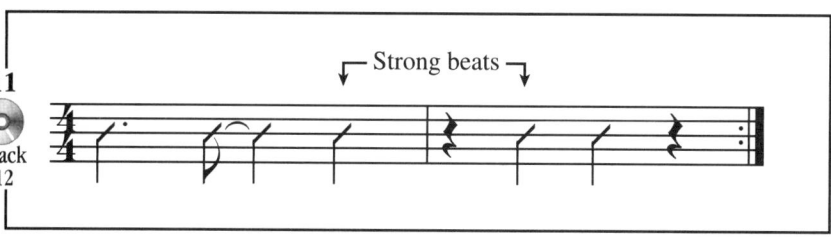

Son Montuno

The example below shows a typical guajeo that emphasizes the strong beats. Notice that the guajeo does not line up note-for-note with the clave, but rather dances around it to create a complex rhythmic pattern. Playing the accents on the strong beats will help you lock in with the clave.

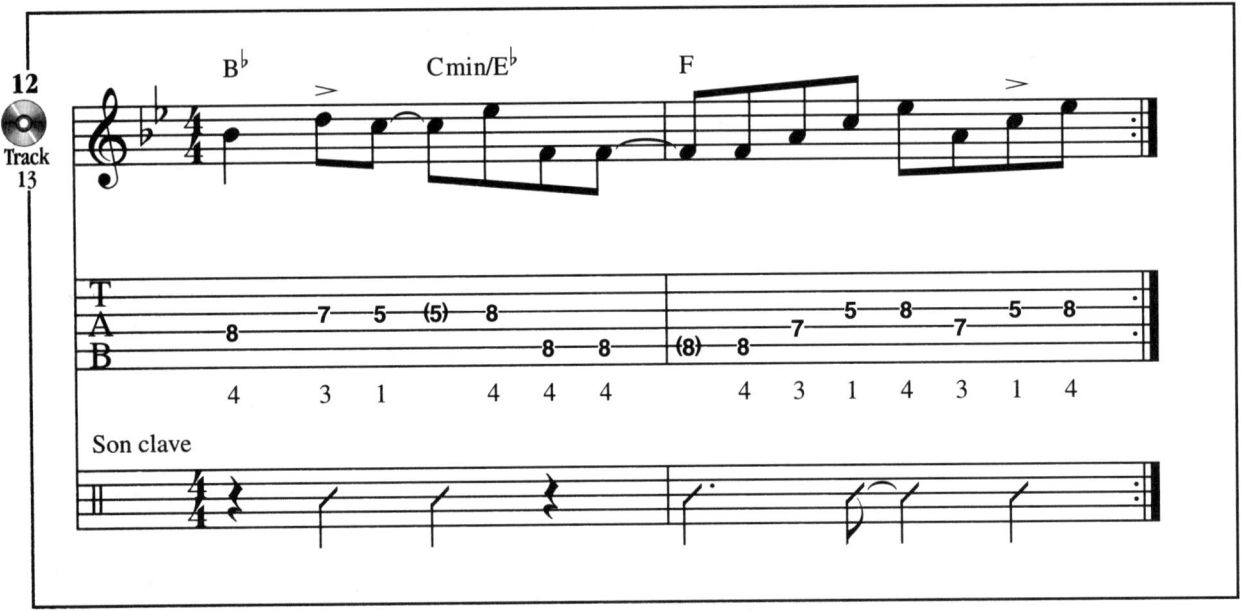

Against the Guaguancó Clave

Because the guaguancó clave is slightly different from the standard clave, it has slightly different strong beats. The accent on the "3 side" moves from beat 4 to the "and" of beat 4, as the following example illustrates.

TRIAD STUDIES

To gain the type of proficiency needed to express the complex rhythms discussed earlier, you must have a strong command of *triadic arpeggiation*, in other words, playing each note of the triad separately rather than strumming them all at the same time. The diagrams in this section show all of the possibilities on each group of three strings (EBG, BGD, GDA, and DAE). Limiting yourself to three strings at a time simulates the sound of the tres. Since most of the harmonic content of Cuban music is based on the I, IV, and V chords (either major or minor) of any given key, knowing how they relate is of chief importance. In the diagrams that follow, the I chord is always white, the IV chord black, and the V chord gray. The diagrams are in the key of G, but can be transposed to other keys by moving the shapes up or down the fretboard. The I–IV–V groups are shown separately, then together on one fretboard diagram.

◯ = Tones in the I chord
● = Tones in the IV chord
◐ = Tones in the V chord

Major I–IV–V (G, B, and E Strings)

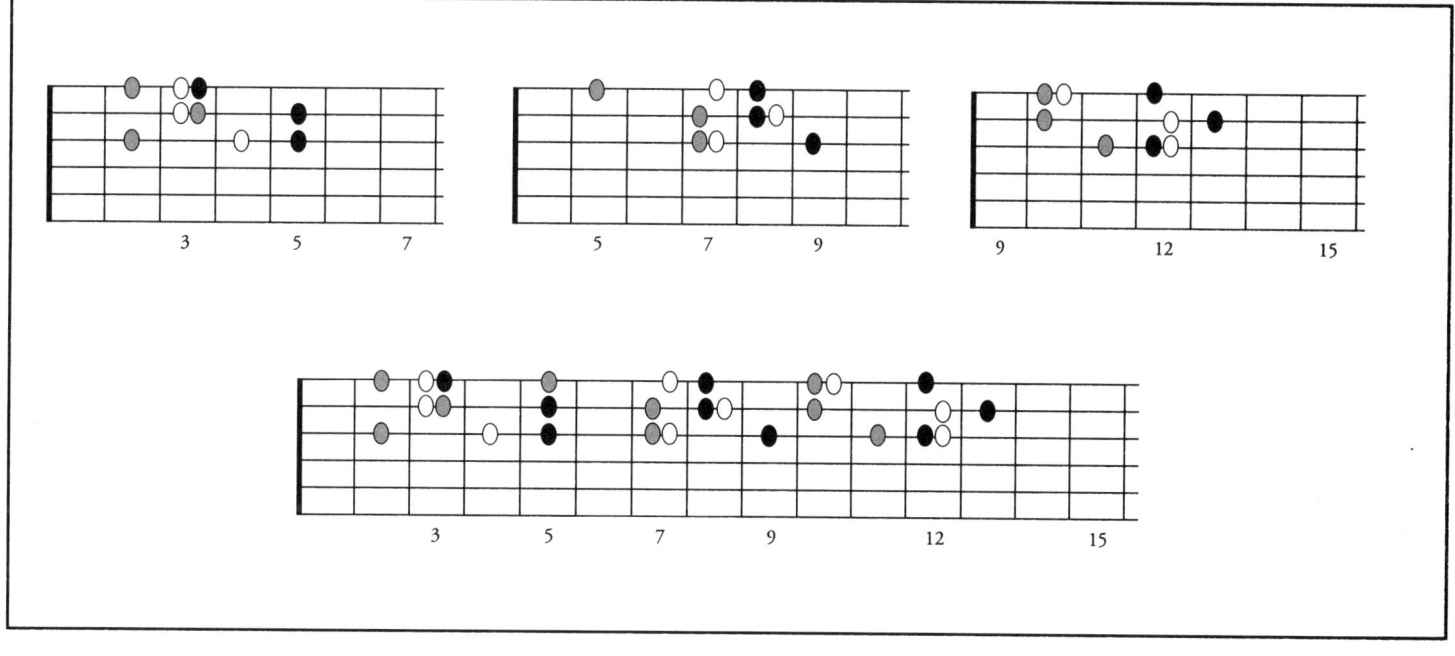

Major I–IV–V: Top Three Strings Against 2/3 Clave

Now that you have spent time some exploring major I–IV–V triads on the E, B, and G strings, you're ready to apply the same concept to the remaining three-string sets.

Major I–IV–V (D, G, and B Strings)

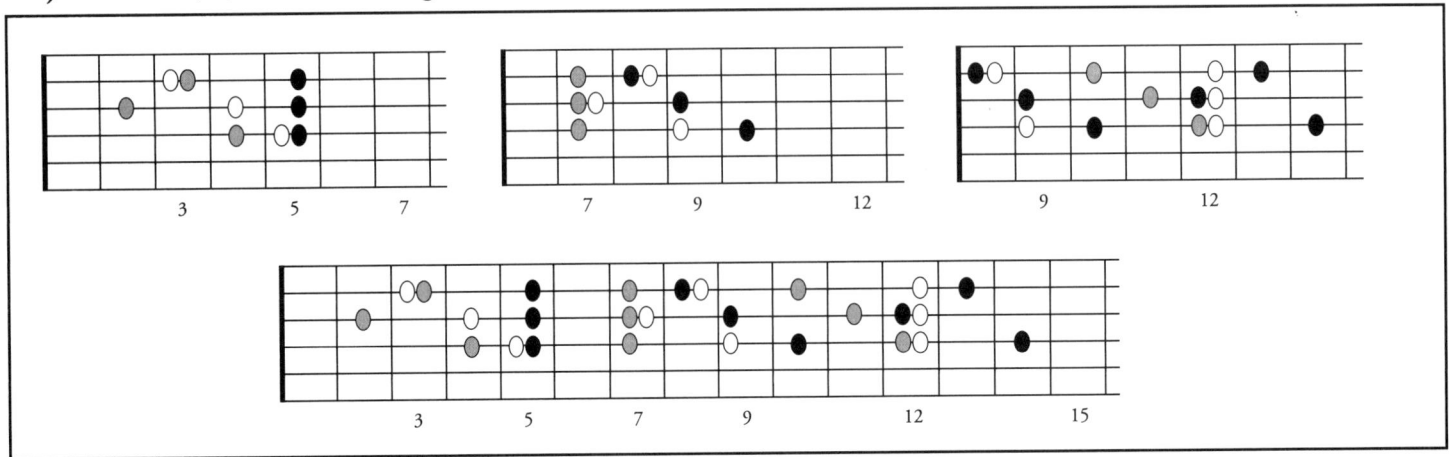

Major I–IV–V (A, D, and G Strings)

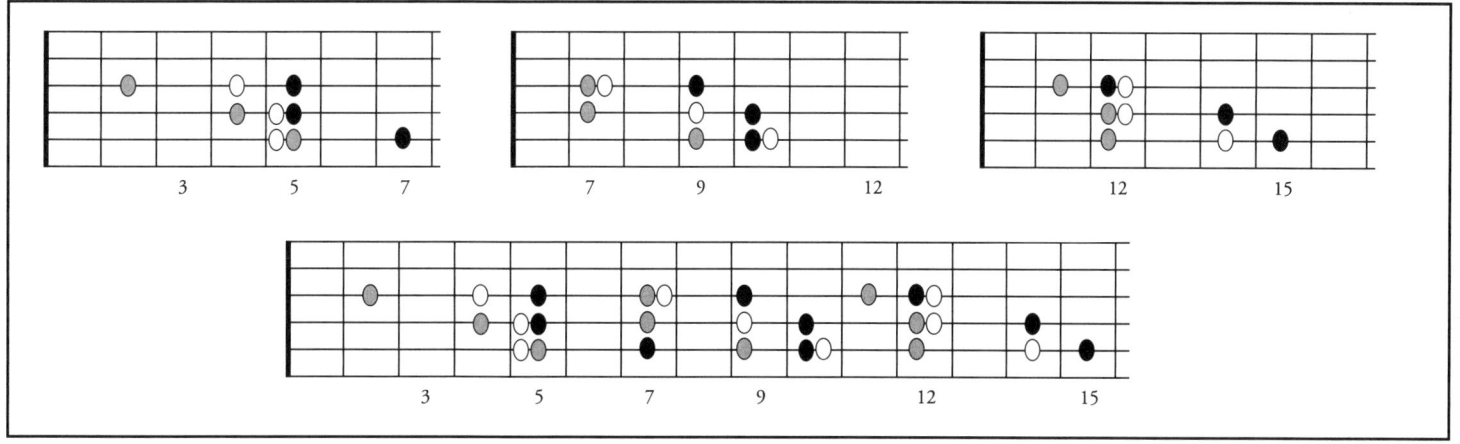

Major I–IV–V (E, A, and D Strings)

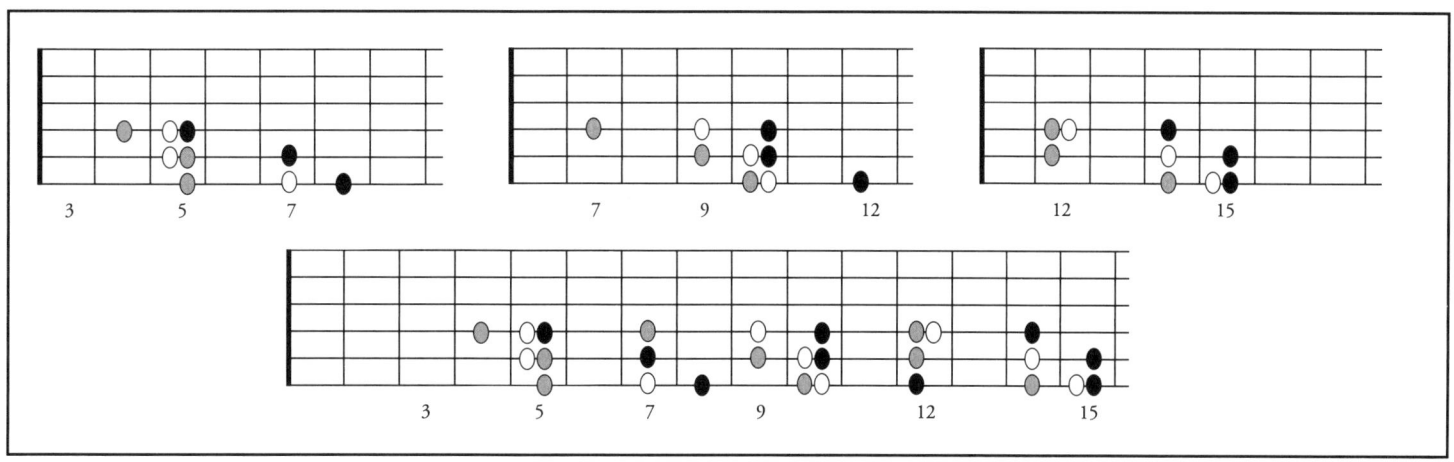

Just as important as the major I–IV–V progression is its minor counterpart, i–iv–V7. Both major and minor I–IV–V progressions are found in all of the various styles of Cuban music. These diagrams are in the key of G Minor, but can be transposed to any key. You may notice there are more gray dots; that is because the V7 arpeggio consists of four notes instead of three. Also, certain notes have been doubled so you can play them wherever they best fit the music.

Minor i–iv–V7 (G, B, and E Strings)

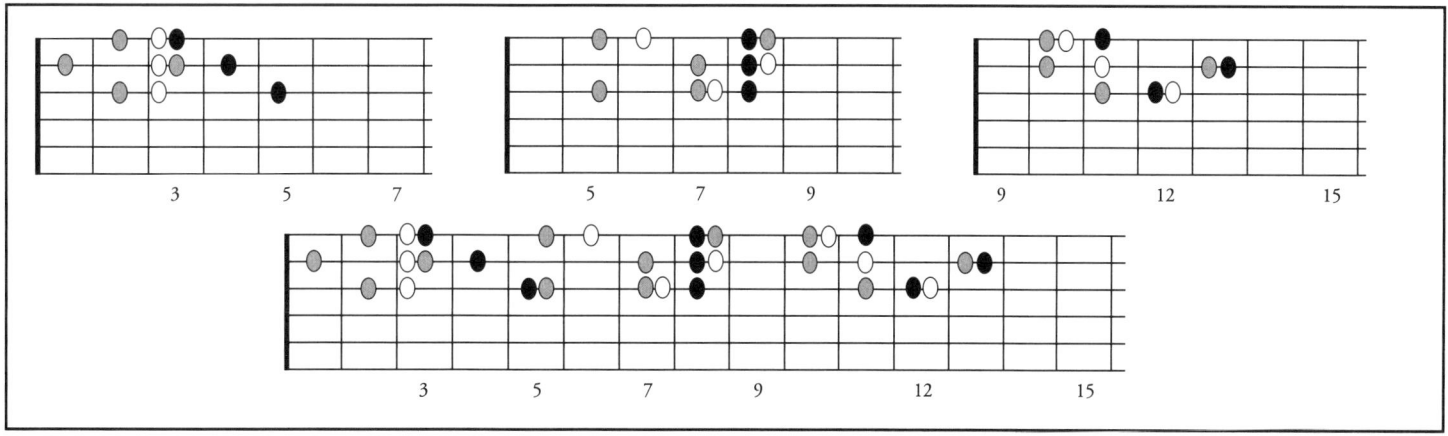

The following exercise is a i–iv–V7 progression in G Minor based on the 2/3 clave. It uses only the top three strings: E, B, and G. As already mentioned, Cuban music is highly syncopated. Often, with syncopation there also comes a *staccato* feel (notes played in a short, detached way); listen to "Agua con Gas" on the CD for a demonstration of this.

AGUA CON GAS

Track 16

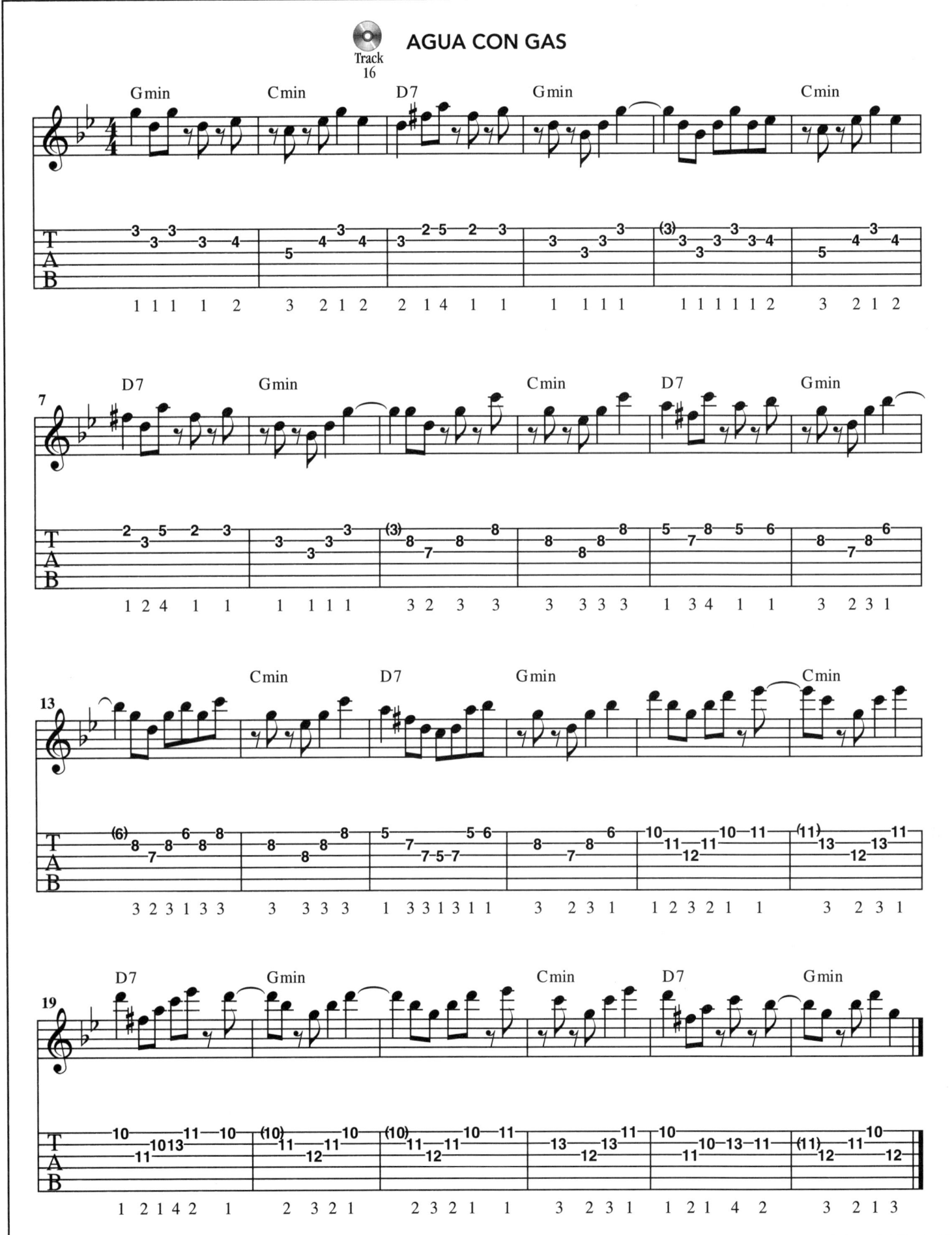

Now that you've spent some time on the minor i–iv–V7 progression on the E, B, and G strings, let's apply the same concept to the remaining three-string sets.

Minor i–iv–V7 (D, G, and B Strings)

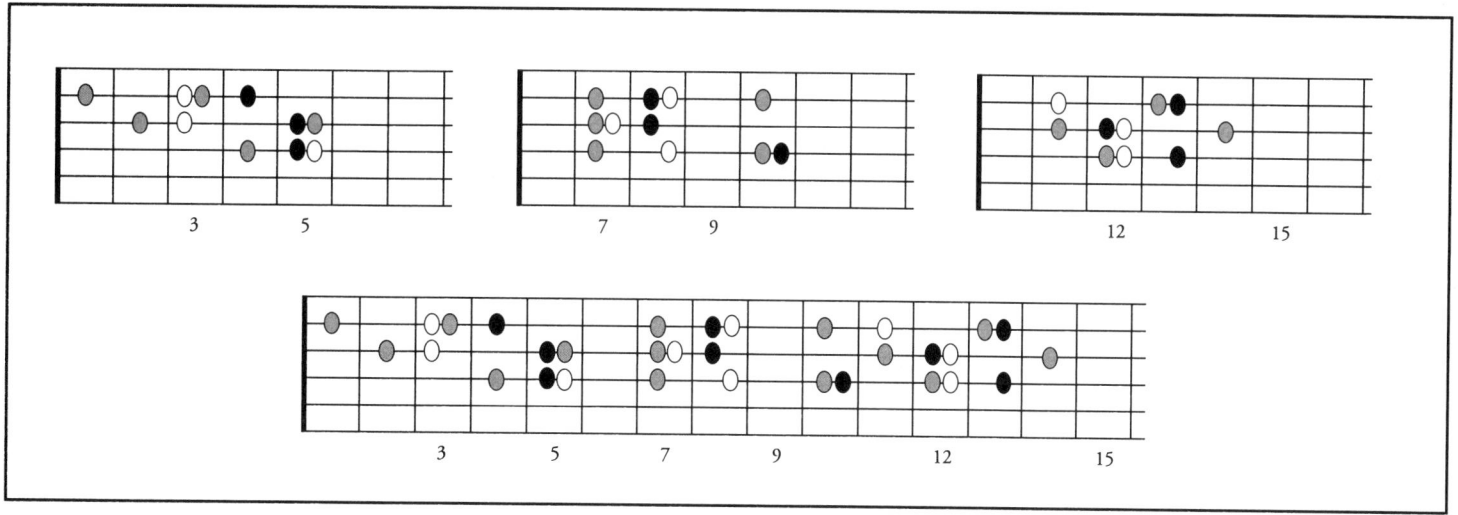

Minor i–iv–V7 (A, D, and G Strings)

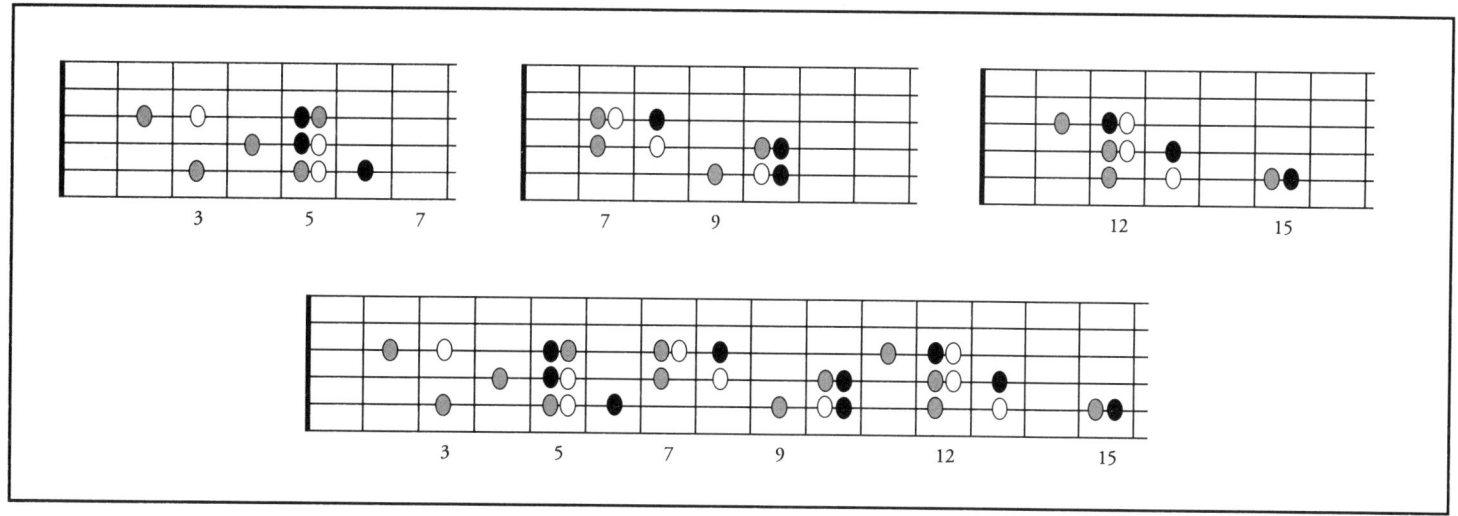

Minor i–iv–V7 (E, A, and D Strings)

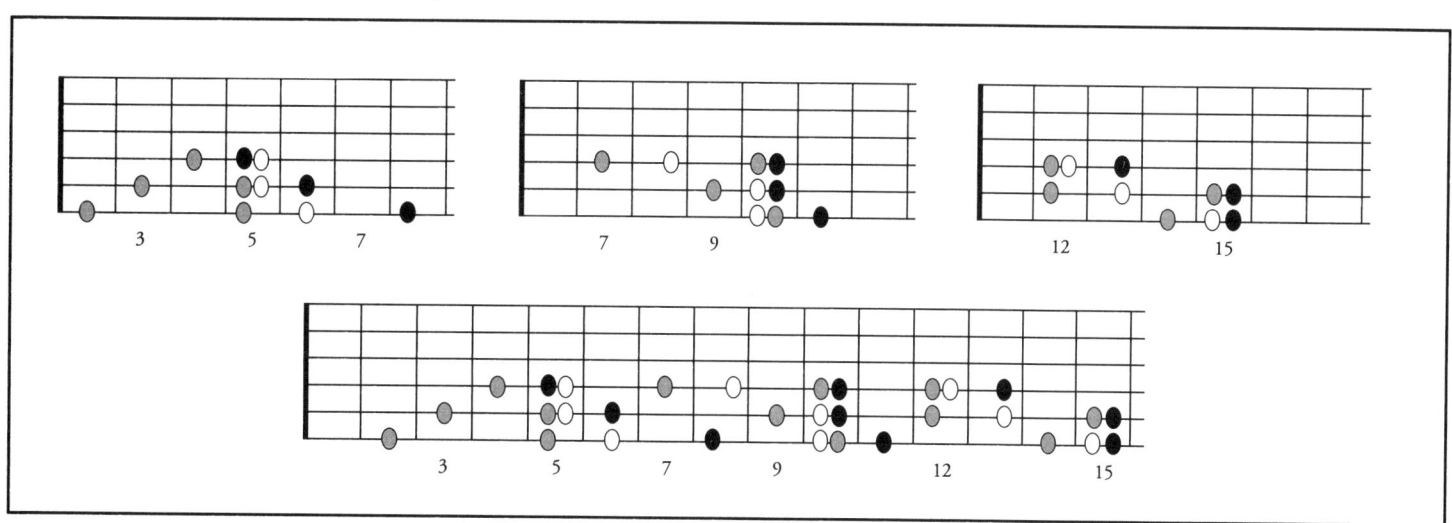

While I–IV–V progressions are a good place to start when learning to play guajeos, there are many other chord progressions you will come across when playing Afro-Cuban music. The following examples demonstrate a few of the more common progressions.

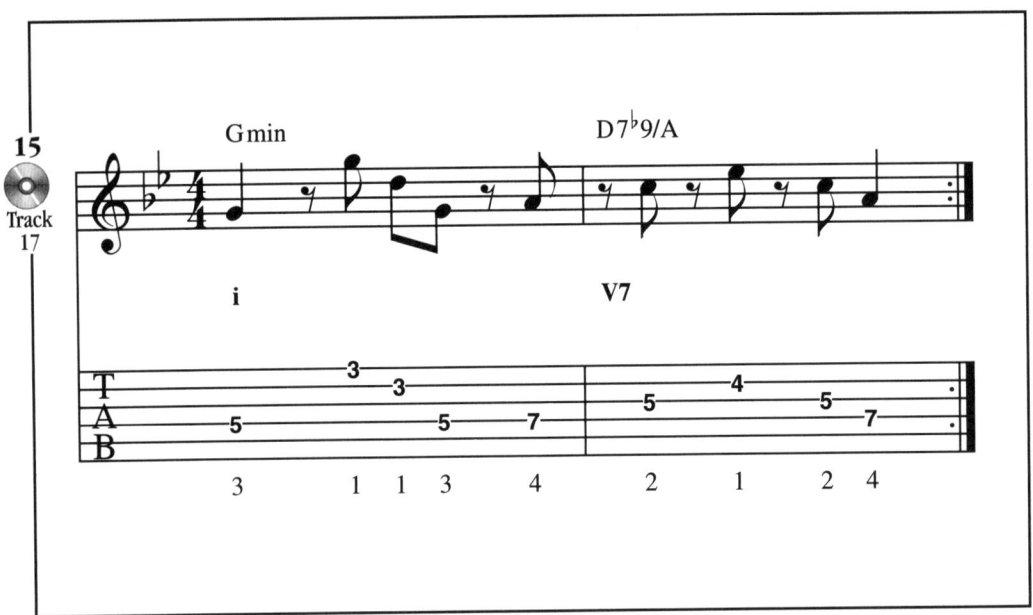

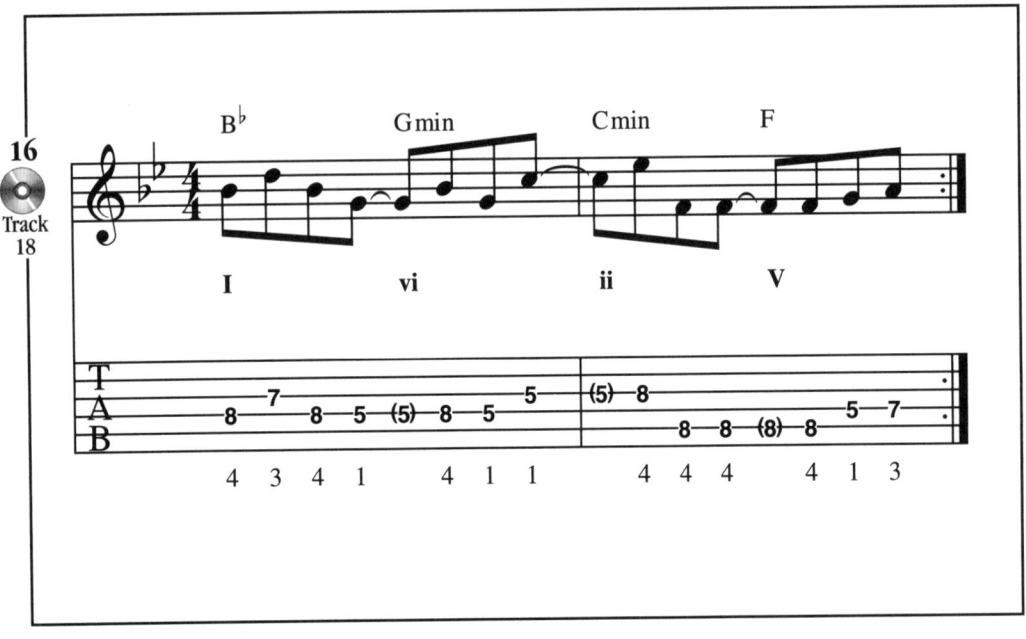

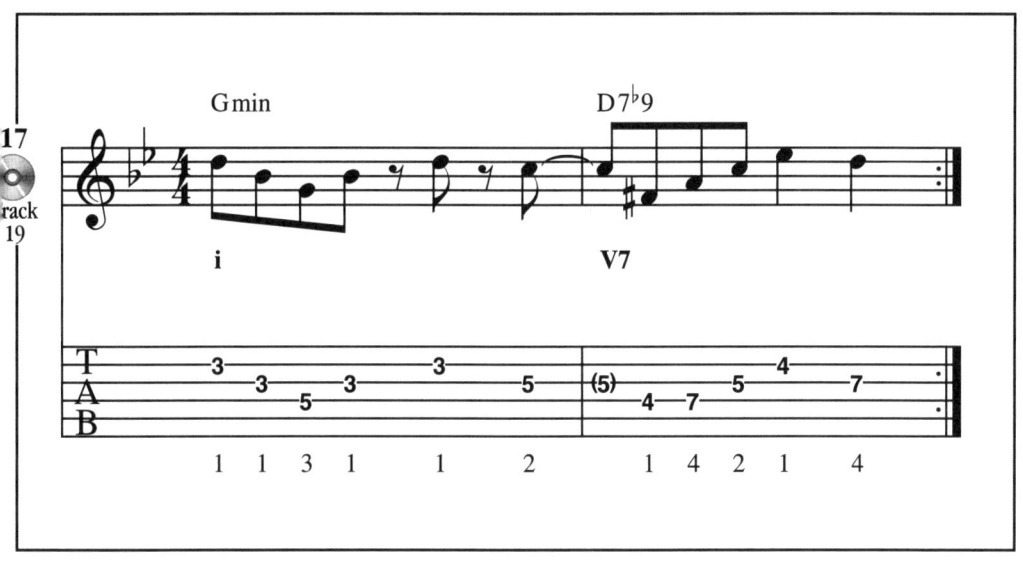

Fingerstyle Notation Key

p = thumb
i = index
m = middle
a = ring

The following example is easiest to play using the fingerstyle technique.

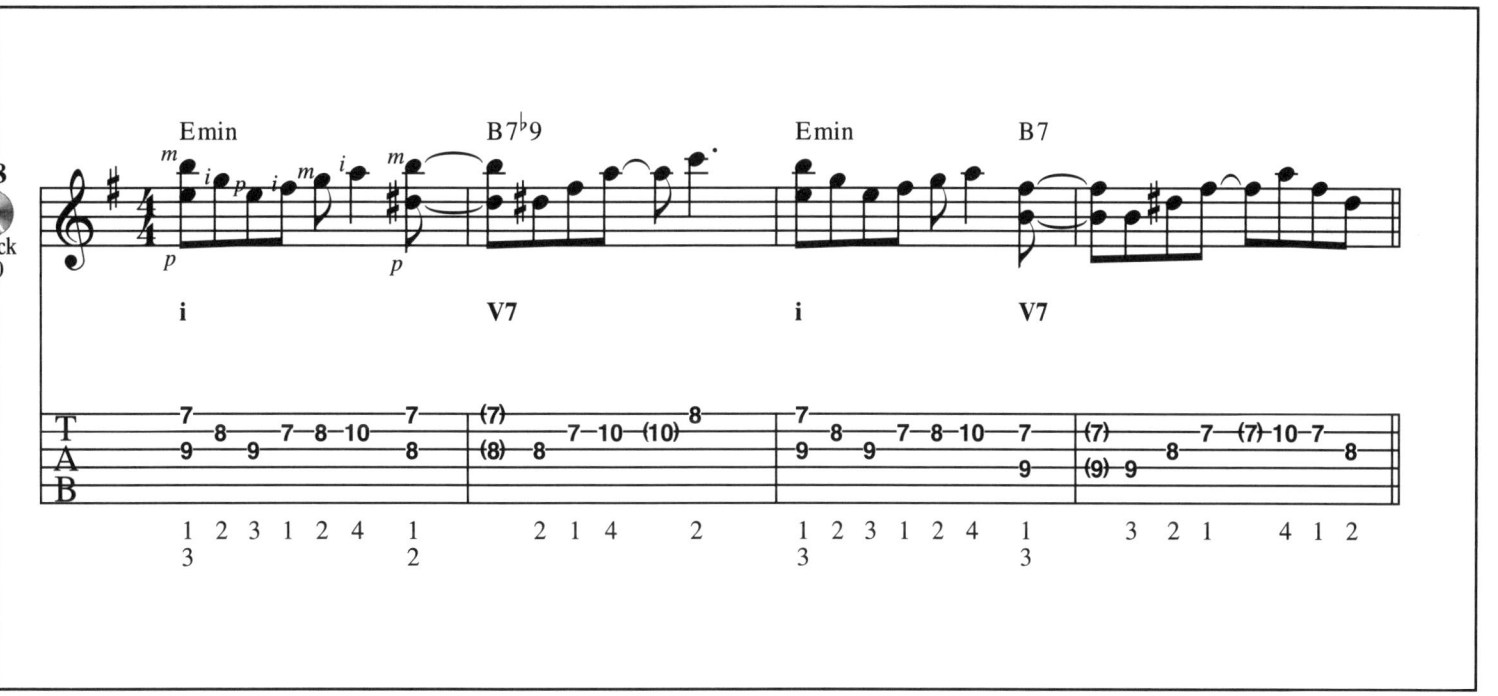

Guitar Atlas: Cuba 77

RHYTHMIC BREAKS

We have learned in this chapter that the melodic and harmonic element of Cuban music is quite unique. That being said, the main appeal of Afro-Cuban music for most people is its incredible rhythms. In some styles, such as the descarga (jam session), the entire song can be based on one continuous two-chord progression. One way to create distinct sections in a tune where the chord progression is the same throughout is to insert little breaks between sections. There exists a common set of rhythmic/melodic figures that are used to mark sections, or to separate an instrumental solo from the *coro* (part of the tune where everyone sings the main theme) and the coro from the montuno section.

The next few examples show some of the more common breaks.

Following is a descending arpeggio ending on the ponche in the 3 side of a 2/3 clave.

Count	1	&	2	&	3	&	4	&	1	&	2	&	3	&	4	&
Clave			x		x				x			x			x	
Break	x								x	x	x	x	x	x		

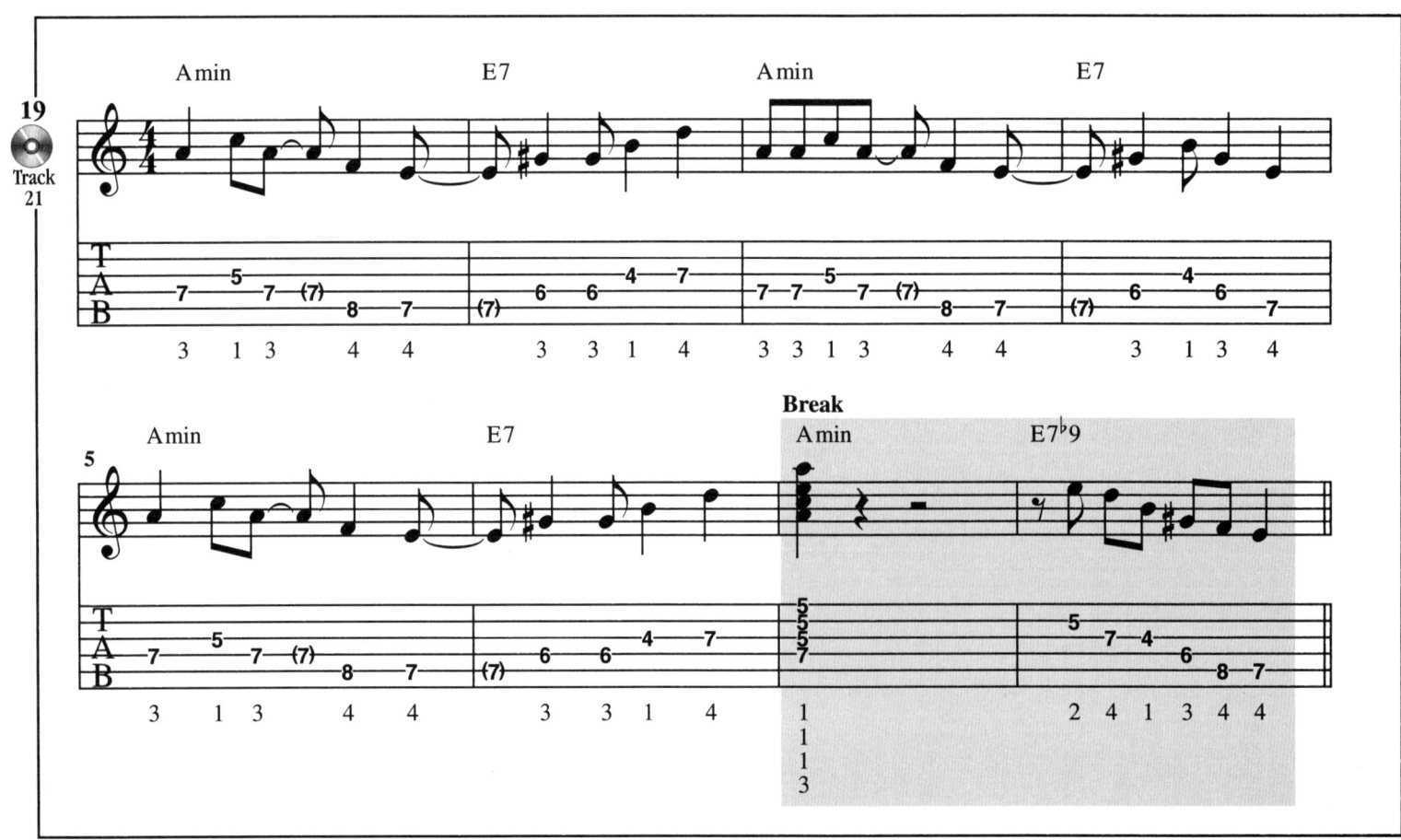

Next is an ascending arpeggio based on the 3/2 clave.

Count	1	&	2	&	3	&	4	&	1	&	2	&	3	&	4	&
Clave	x				x			x			x		x			
Break	x	x		x		x	x				x	x	x	x		

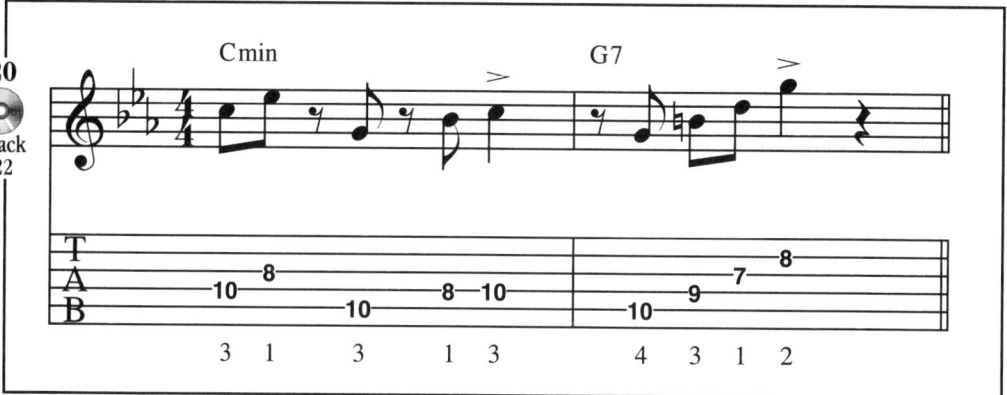

Finally, here is a rhythmic break that utilizes eighth notes and eighth-note triplets based on the 2/3 clave. Eighth-note triplets are one third of a beat in duration and are counted "1-trip-let, 2-trip-let, 3-trip-let, 4-trip-let."

Count	1	trip	let	2	trip	let	3	trip	let	4	trip	let	1	trip	let	2	&	3	&	4	&
Clave				x			x						x				x				x
Break	x		x	x		x	x	x	x	x	x	x	x		x	x				x	x

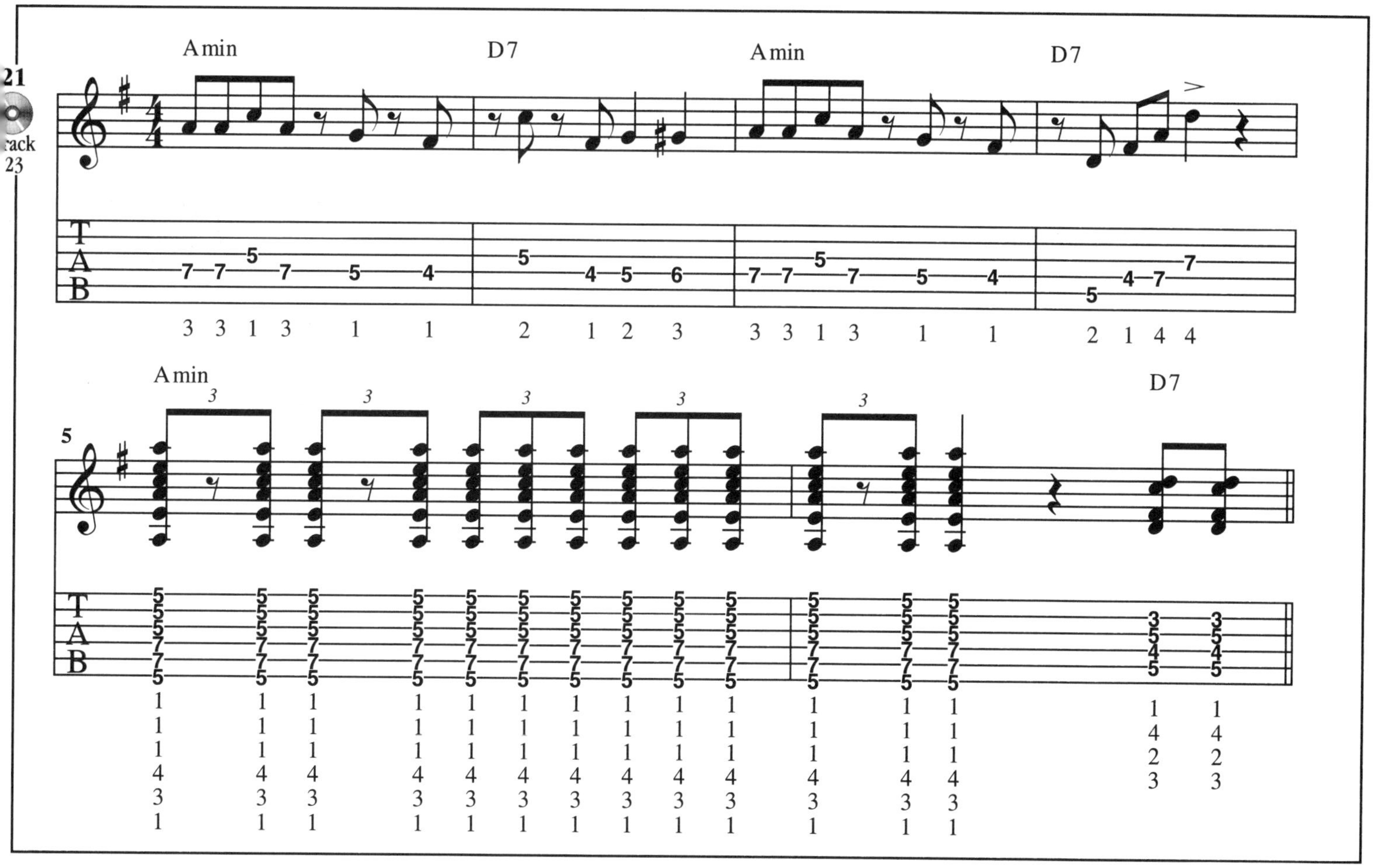

Guitar Atlas: Cuba

Chapter 4 STYLES

SON

The son emerged in Cuba around 1900 as an urban, popular dance-music style. It derived some features from Spanish music, including its harmonies and the use of the guitar and tres. To these, it added characteristics of the rumba. Features derived from the rumba include the clave rhythm and a two-part formal structure. This structure consists of a songlike first section followed by a longer second section featuring call-and-response vocals and instrumental improvisations over a repeated chordal pattern. By the 1940s, the son had become the most popular dance music in Cuba, Puerto Rico, and much of urban Africa; Puerto Ricans who moved to New York City brought the son with them. In the early twentieth century, son was a loose term which encompassed most of the rural music, much like the rural blues of the United States. By the 1920s, however, the standard configuration of son musicians was a septeto comprised of trumpet, guitar, tres, bass (or marímbula), bongos, maraca, and claves.

The son is characterized by the highly syncopated nature of its groove. None of the musicians accent the first beat of the measure.

The son begins with the statement of the theme followed by a break and then the montuno, which opens up the song for soloing. Usually the sections are punctuated by *mambos*, unison breaks played by the rhythm section. In the following tune, most of the guitar part can be played by forming chords with the left hand. For example, the entire intro can be played by keeping your left hand in the form of the Gmin chord shown to the right.

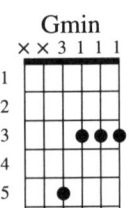

¿TU TIENES?

Track 24

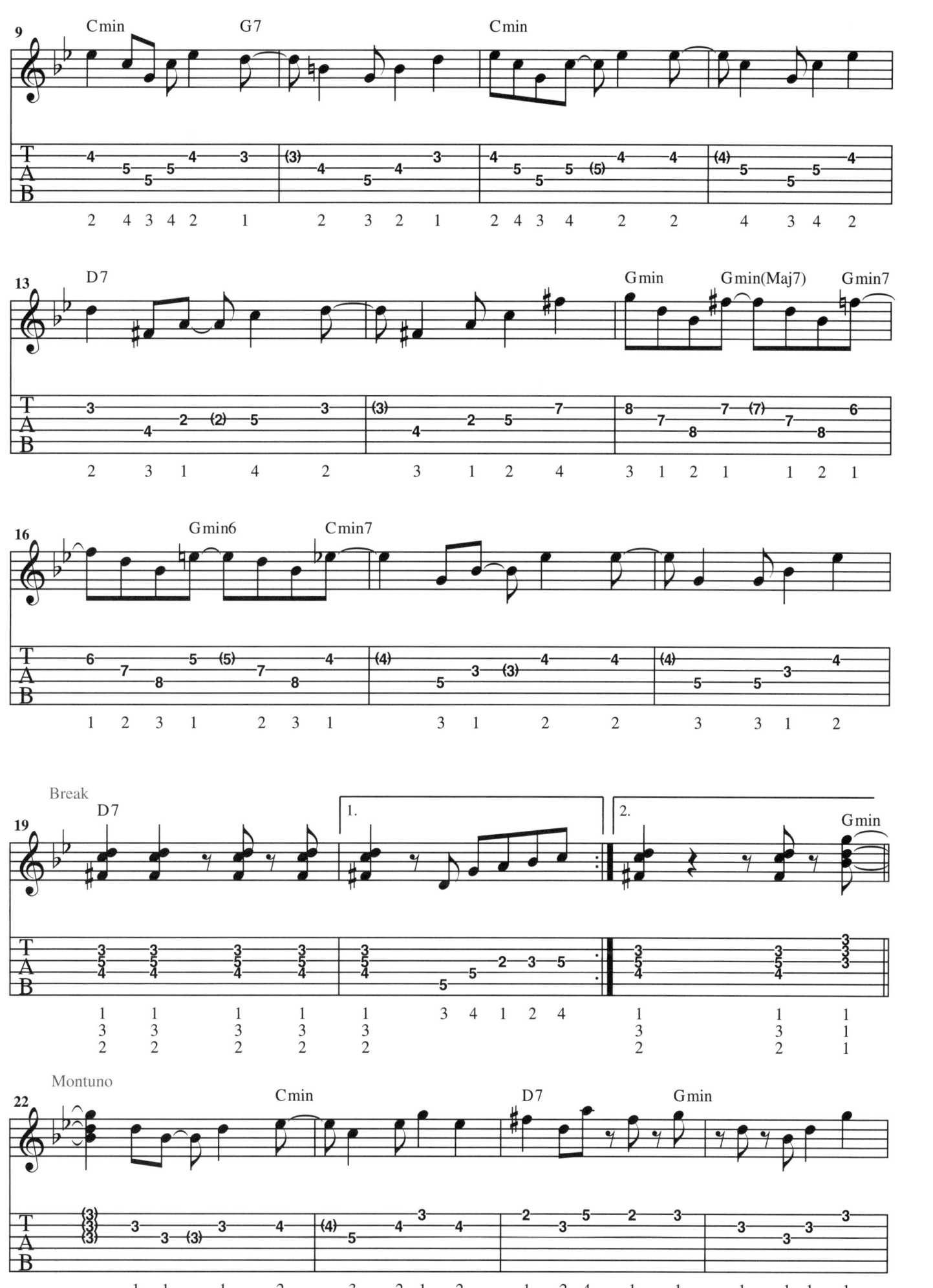

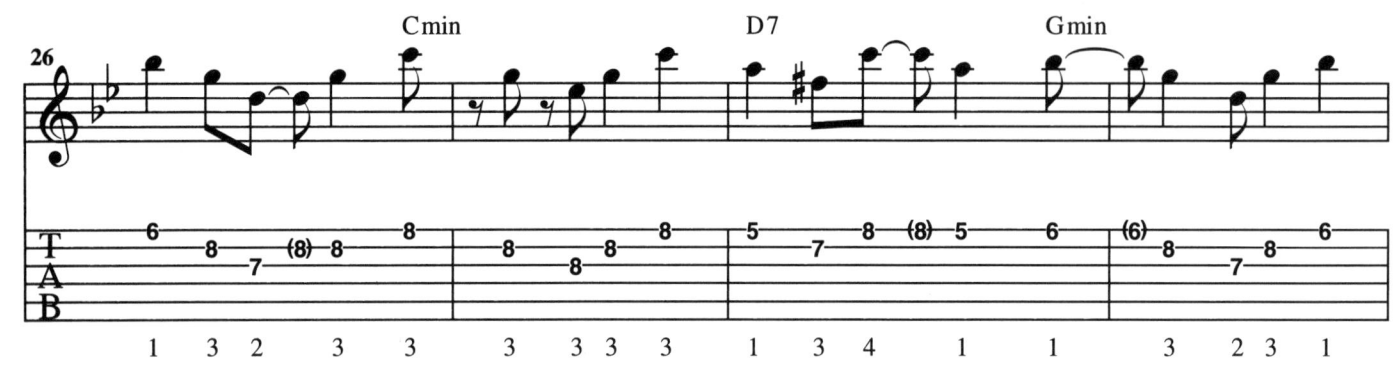
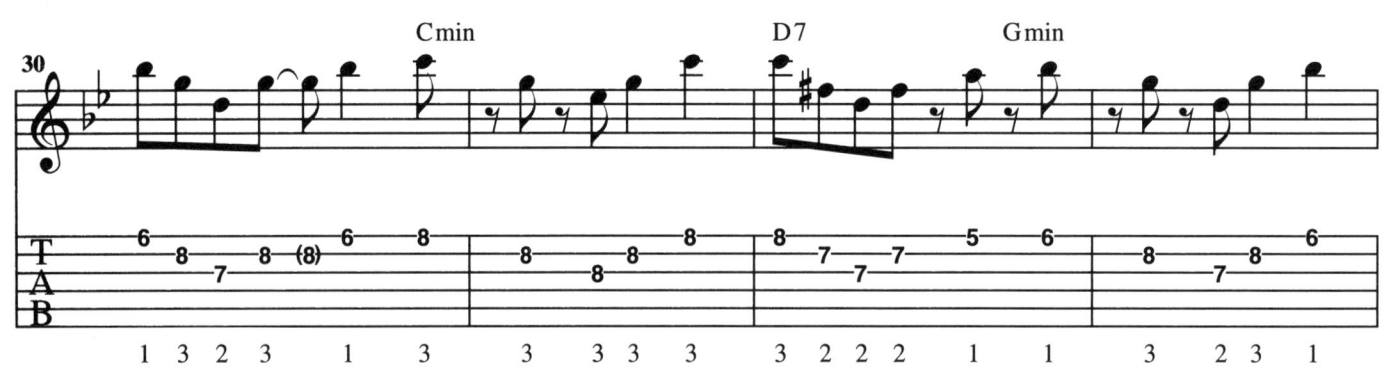
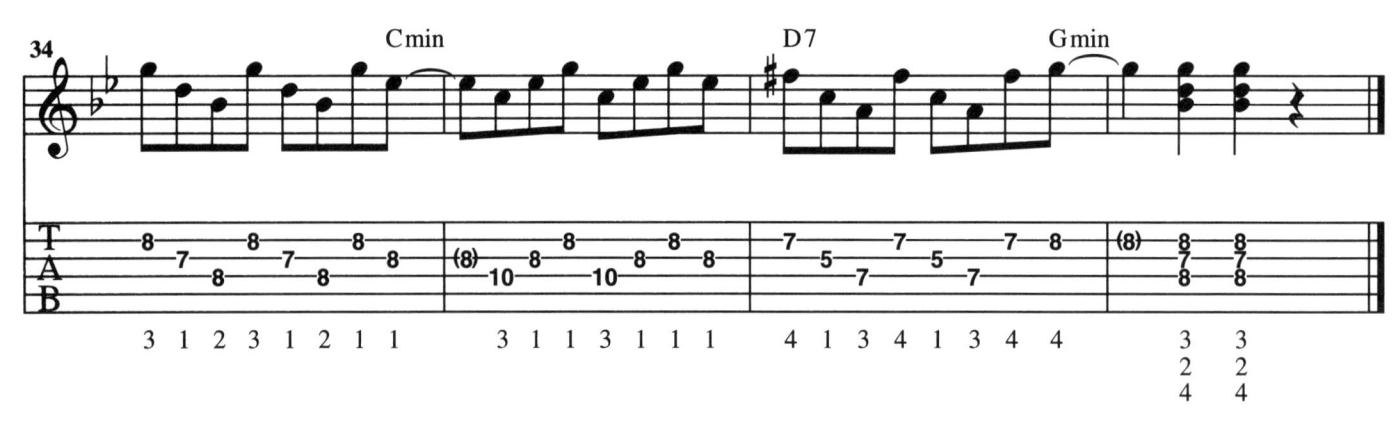

SON MONTUNO/GUAJIRA

Son montuno is a slower son influenced by the *guajira* (a style of rural song with Spanish origins that utilizes guitars and bongos). Usually, a simple I–IV–V chord progression is the vehicle for improvisation.

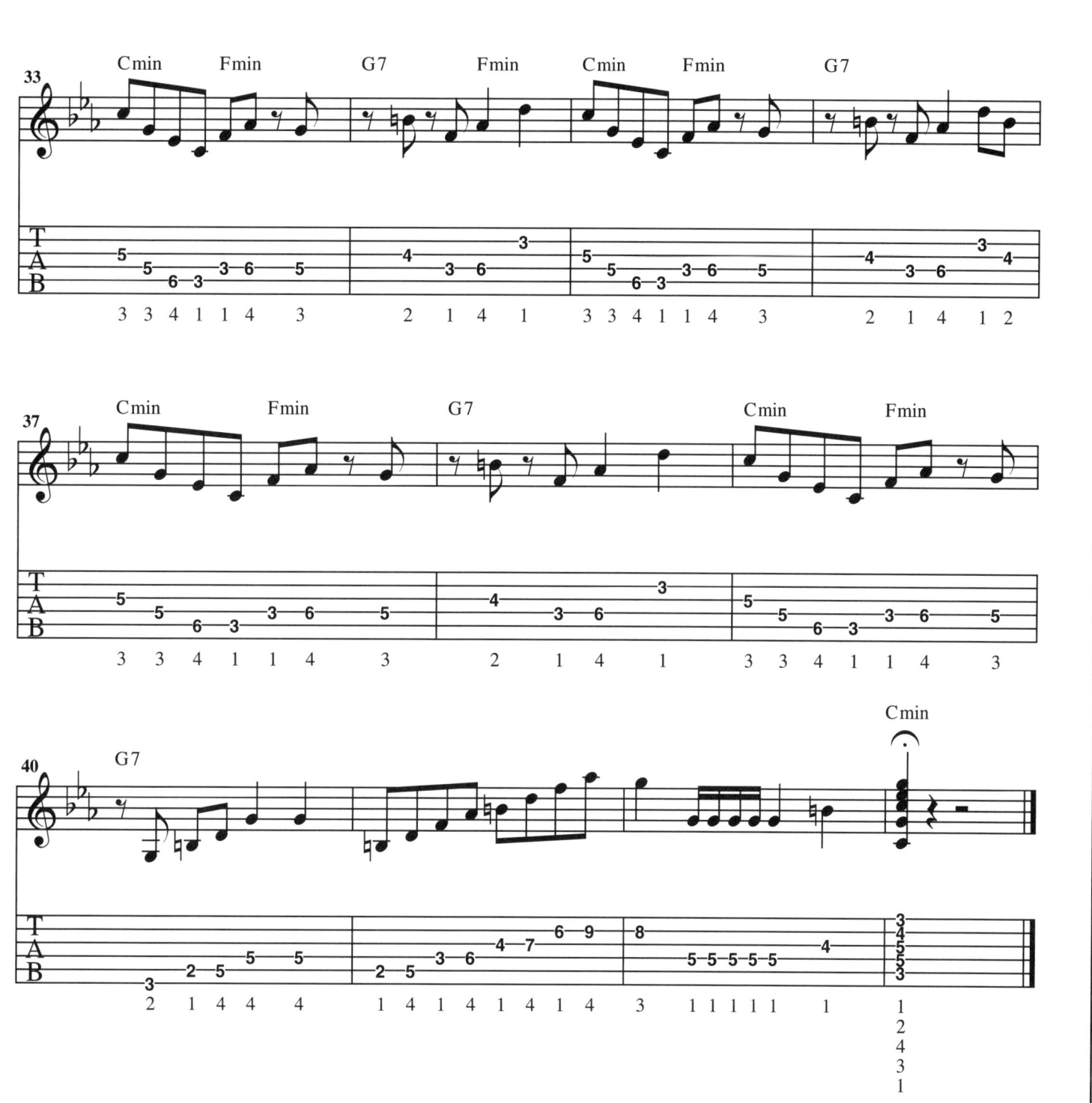

Guitar Atlas: Cuba 85

CHANGÜÍ

Changüí originated in the mid-nineteenth century in the rural areas around Guantánamo. The changüí is a highly syncopated style that is believed to have been a major influence on the son.

CHEENA MORENA

BOLERO

Bolero is a slow, romantic song style that is rooted in old Spanish dances. It arrived in Oriente around 1810. One of the first true Cuban boleros was "Tristeza," written in 1885 by Pepe Sánchez. The guitar is a prevalent instrument in bolero, usually used to accompany the singer. A semi-percussive strumming style known as *rayado* is utilized by bolero guitarists.

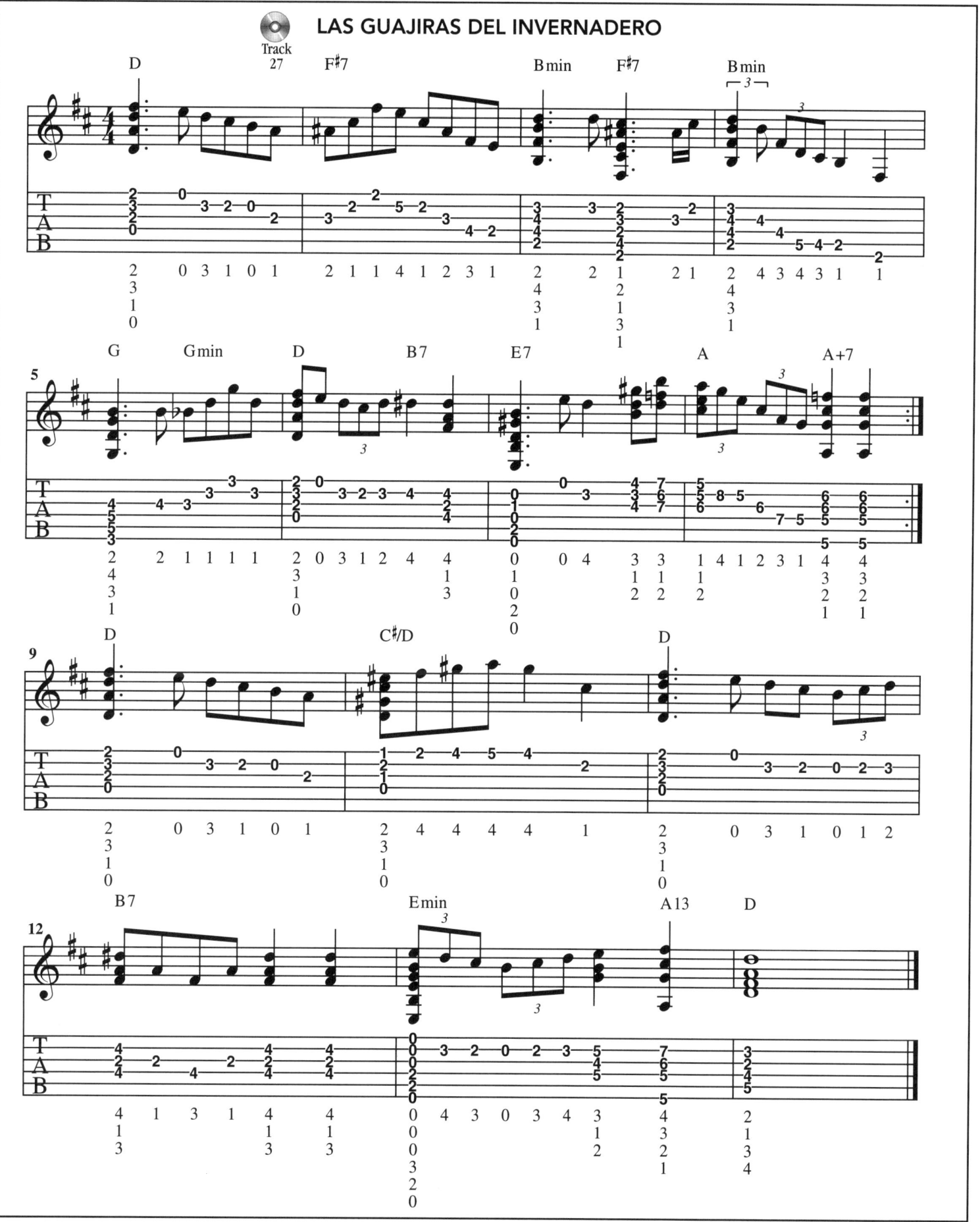

NUEVA TROVA

The term *trova* originally referred to a singer/guitar player from Oriente. The musical style of *nueva trova* emerged in the 1960s and can be considered Cuba's political folk music, as the lyrics often contain satirical evaluations of the government as well as social commentary. The style is defined by its flowing $\frac{6}{8}$ rhythm. This song uses the fingerstyle technique.

Guitar Atlas: Cuba 91

DANZÓN

Danzón is derived from early nineteenth century French contradanzas and European ballroom dances and was originally written to accompany similar dances for the upper classes of Cuba. Its strong rhythmic undercurrent lead to the evolution of the cha-cha-chá and the mambo.

MAMBO

The *mambo* came to prominence in the early 1950s. Pérez Prado is almost single-handedly responsible for putting the style on the map. The mambo is first and foremost a dance music, created as a backdrop for ballroom dancing events. It is normally performed by a big band, and notable singers include Benny Moré, Celia Cruz, and Daniel Santos. The following example can be played either fingerstyle or with the pick.

GUAGUANCÓ

The guaguancó is a type of rumba characterized by the highly syncopated rhythms based on the guaguancó clave. This style is also very connected to the spiritual and religious Santería dances found in the countryside.

ARROZ CON POLLO

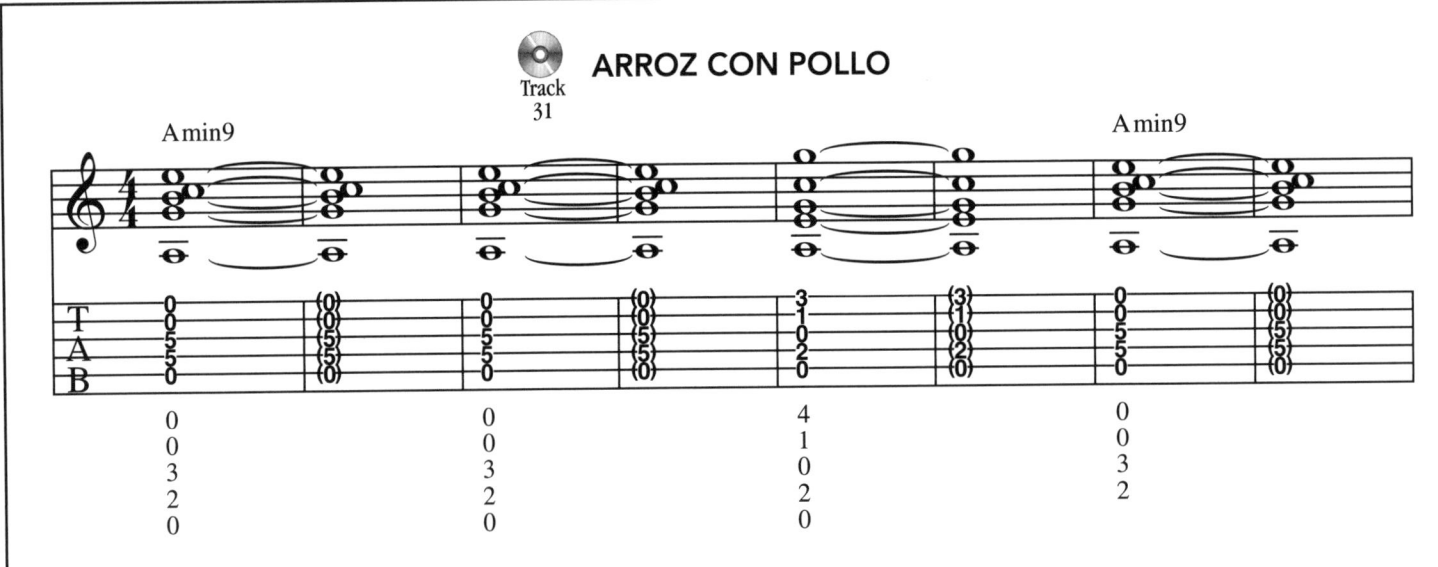

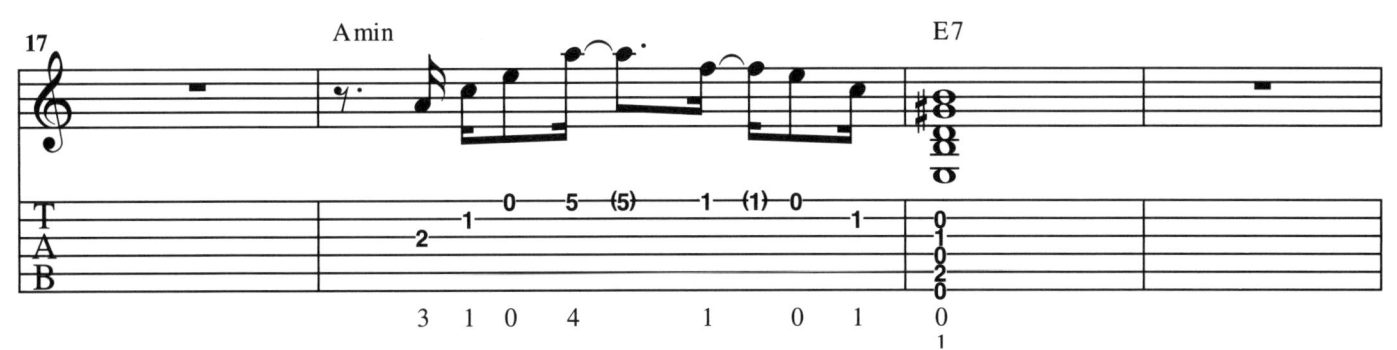
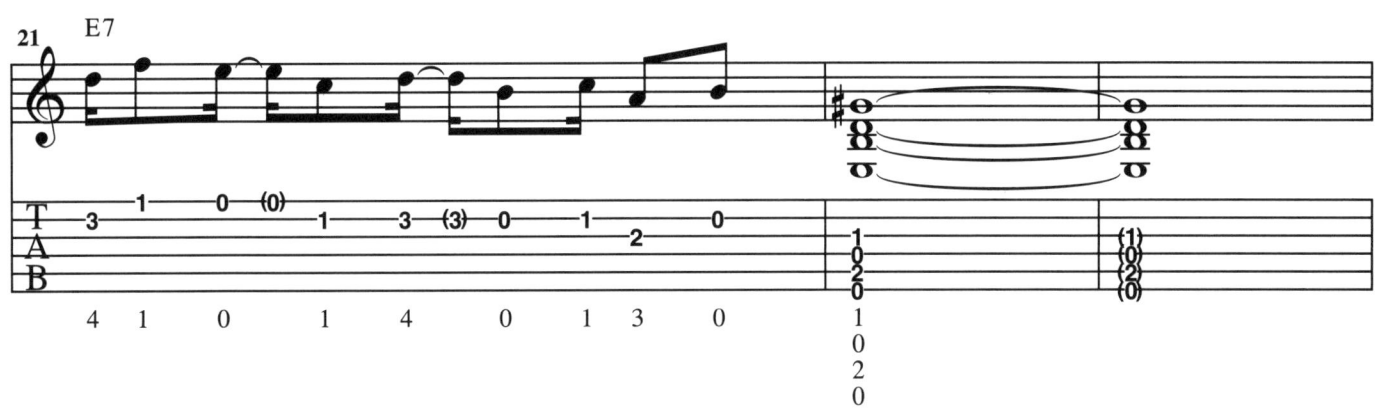
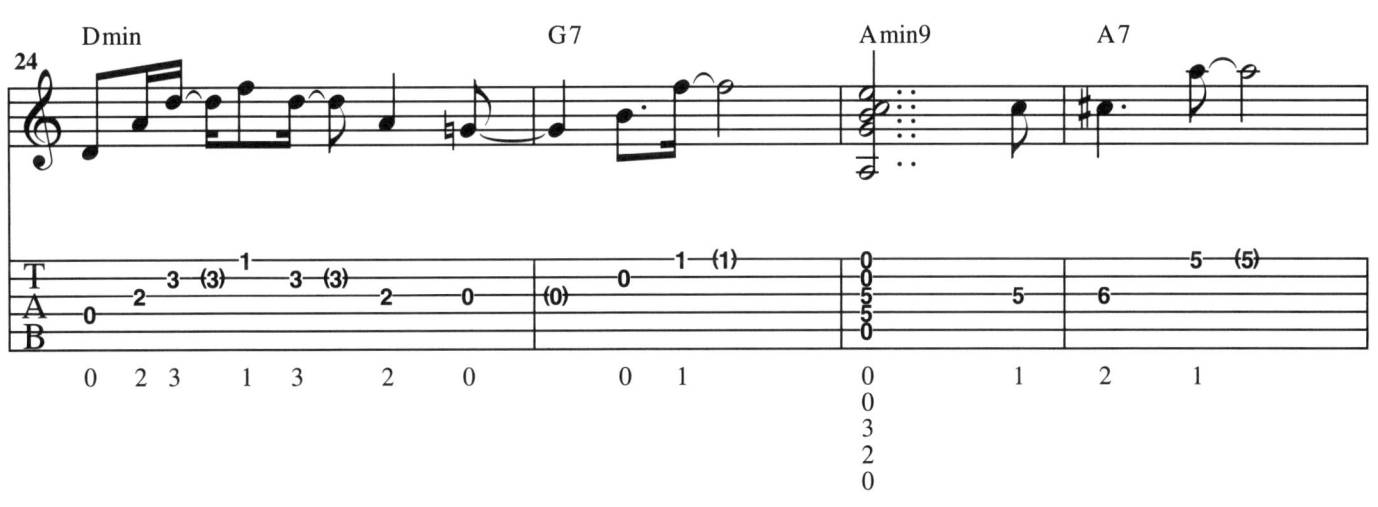

Guitar Atlas: Cuba 97

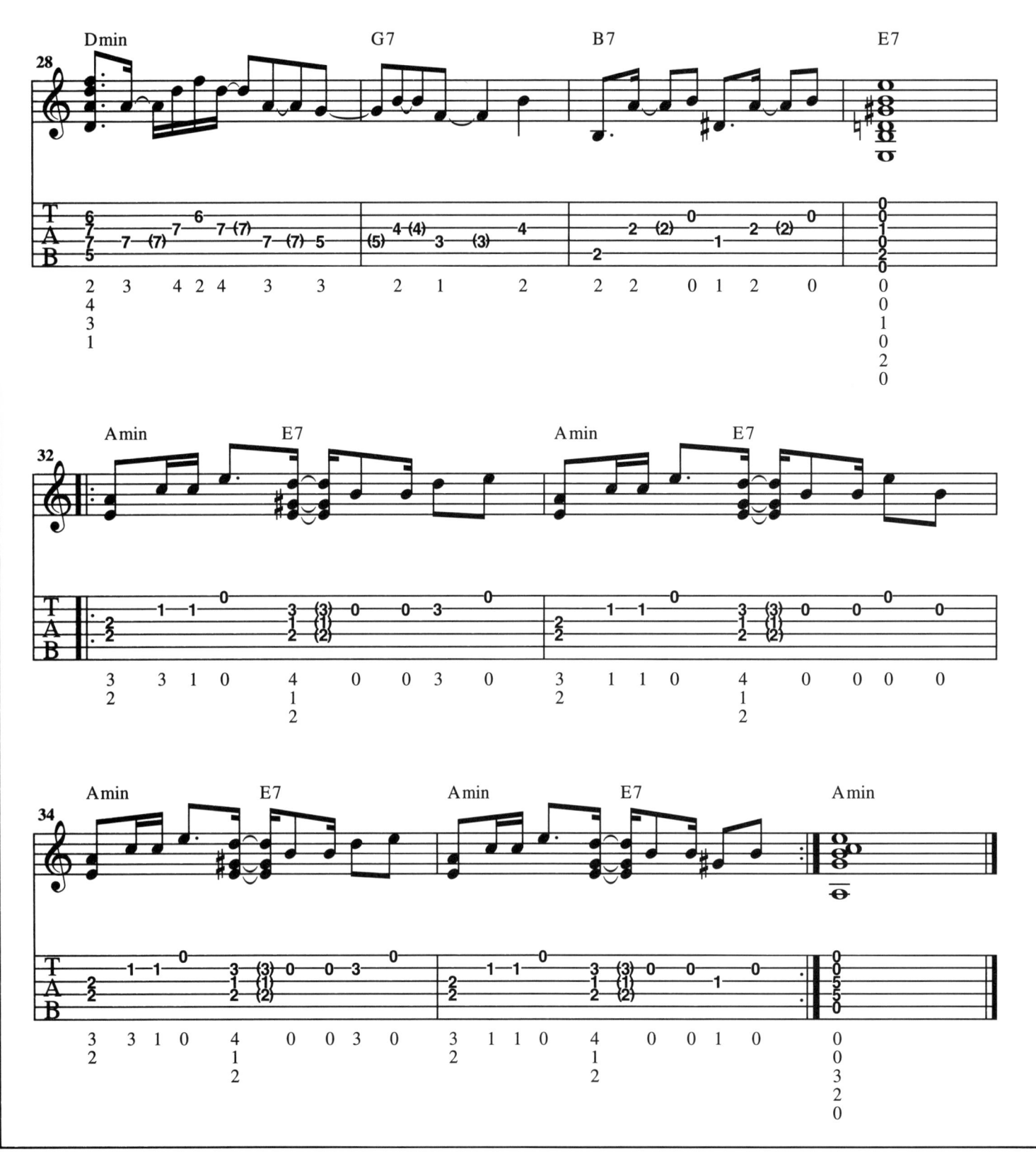

Final Word

This concludes *Guitar Atlas: Cuba*. The next step is to listen to as much Cuban music as you can, both recorded and live (if possible). Cuban music is all about rhythm and feel, qualities that are best developed through listening and practice. Good luck!

Celtic

David Ernst

*Guitar Styles
from Around the World*

*This book was acquired, edited, and produced
by Workshop Arts, Inc., the publishing arm of
the National Guitar Workshop.*
Nathaniel Gunod, managing and acquisitions editor
Timothy Phelps, interior design
Ante Gelo, music typesetter
CD recorded at Aesthetic Leverage Music, San Francisco, CA

Contents

ABOUT THE AUTHOR 101
   Acknowledgements..................................101

INTRODUCTION 102

CHAPTER 1—Getting Started 103
   The Guitar in Celtic Music 103
   Ornamentation 104
   Harmony and Arrangement 106
   Tuning 108
   Melodic Development...............................109
   The Songs and the Recordings 113

CHAPTER 2—Jigs 114
   Blarney Pilgrim 114

CHAPTER 3—Reels 118
   Conlon's 2 118
   The Morning Dew 120

CHAPTER 4—Slow Airs and Laments 122
   My Fair Young Love (A Lady to her Husband
      who was Killed at the Battle of Culloden) 122
   Harmonics 124
   My Fair Young Love (A Lady to her Husband
      who was Killed at the Battle of Culloden)
      (Harmonics)..126
   Highland Boat Song 128

CHAPTER 5—Hornpipes & Strathspeys 130
   Hornpipes 130
      The Scent of the Bog 130
   Strathspeys 132
      The Flax in Bloom 132

CHAPTER 6—O'Carolan Tunes 134
   George Brabazon, 2nd Air (Standard Tuning) 135
   George Brabazon, 2nd Air (DADGAD)..............136
   Shi Beg Shi Mhor (Standard Tuning)....................138
   Shi Beg Shi Mhor (DADGAD) 140

CHAPTER 7—Arrange It Yourself! 142
   Fairy Jig (Standard Tuning) 142
   Fairy Jig (DADGAD)..............................144

RECOMMENDED DISCOGRAPHY 145
   Solo Artists 145
   Duos and Ensembles 145
   Compilations 145

FINAL WORD 146

Track 1

A compact disc is included with this book. This disc can make learning with the book easier and more enjoyable. The symbol shown at the left appears next to every example that is on the CD. Use the CD to help ensure that you're capturing the feel of the examples, interpreting the rhythms correctly, and so on. The track number below the symbol corresponds directly to the example you want to hear. Track 1 will help you tune your guitar to this CD.

Have fun!

About the Author

David Ernst started playing guitar in 1977. After playing rock for several years as a teenager in Palo Alto, CA, David was lucky enough to see Michael Hedges play many times at a local cafe. About that same time, he met Tuck Andress and heard Pierre Bensusan, Ralph Towner, Egberto Gismonti, Keith Jarrett, Miles Davis, Dmitri Shostakovich, George Benson and Pat Metheny, to name a few. These experiences inspired him to pursue music with greater discipline. Over the years, he has explored Celtic music, jazz, flamenco and Balkan styles. His journeys took him throughout the U.S., Europe and Asia where he studied, played, taught and lived. David studied at the University of California in San Diego, Leningrad State University in what is now St. Petersburg, Russia, Berklee College of Music in Boston and the Arnon Jazz School in Thailand, as well as with some ridiculously talented private teachers. He's now the Director of the Music Theory Program at the Expression Center for New Media in Emeryville, California. In addition to this, David runs the guitar classes at Bronstein Music School in South San Francisco, teaches for the National Guitar Workshop, has a large number of private students and writes and arranges for a variety of local and international projects.

PHOTO • COURTESY OF DAVID ERNST

ACKNOWLEDGEMENTS

I'd like to express my thanks to those who have helped me with this project: Leigh Ann Hussey for her informed opinions and guidance; Tracy Farbstein for source materials and photos; Brian Hill for recording, text advice and photos; my students with whom I experiment; and most of all, my dear wife Nong, for her love, patience, support and artwork.

Introduction

Welcome to the Celtic edition of the National Guitar Workshop's/Alfred's Guitar Atlas series! This book is for you if you're an intermediate guitarist with a fairly developed fingerstyle technique, facility with hammer-ons, pull-offs and harmonics, an understanding of guitar tablature and at least the rhythmic aspects of standard notation. A basic knowledge of music theory and chords will help you understand the explanations in this book and will make it easier to create your own arrangements. However, if all you want to do is learn the tunes in this book, you don't have to be any kind of theory geek at all. If you're interested in theory, check out *Theory for the Contemporary Guitarist*, by Guy Capuzzo (NGW/Alfred #16755).

Celtic traditional music has been around for a long time. Its graceful, lively and earthy feel appeals to almost everyone. Sometimes it makes you laugh, sometimes it makes you cry and sometimes it makes you kick your feet about like a crazy person without moving your arms. We've all heard the music and we've all seen the word "Celtic" tossed around. But, who were the Celts? There's no flawless answer to that question, but there are a few basic things on which most people agree.

The term Celtic comes from the word Keltoi, which the Ancient Greeks used to refer to a number of barbarian tribes that dominated a large part of Central Europe during the first millennium BC. Interestingly, none of these tribes ever referred to themselves as Celtic; that's what Greeks and historians called them. In any case, these various tribes were constantly absorbing and integrating the characteristics and philosophies of those they conquered. All this flux makes them pretty hard to describe concretely.

The Celts eventually spread to Ireland and Scotland bringing their language and culture with them. Christianity gradually squeezed much of the "Celticness" out of the British Isles, but the language and certain elements of the culture remained. The Celtic dialects that survived in the British Isles became the most tangible link between various groups of people being persecuted by the English government in the mid 19th century. This connection led to the emergence of a new political and cultural force.

For the first time, groups emerged that actually called themselves Celtic. Their similarity to the historical Celts didn't extend far beyond certain elements of language. However, because Celtic language groups only survive in the British Isles and Western France, this has become known as the Celtic world. Some people in Ireland and Scotland embrace the term and feel a deep connection to their Celtic roots. Some of them, however, feel that they're just Irish or Scottish and want nothing to do with romantic notions of a Celtic heritage.

Whatever the case may be, "Celtic" is definitely a word that gets used a lot in the music world. It's usually used to refer to the traditional music of Ireland and Scotland. But, strictly speaking, this definition should include some of the music from Wales, Brittany (northwest France), Galicia (northwest Spain) and even parts of Canada. For the purposes of this book, however, we're going to focus on Irish and Scottish tunes since this is usually what people mean when they talk about Celtic music. So whether or not Irish/Scottish music is really Celtic or just Irish/Scottish, we're going to refer to all of it as Celtic.

Chapter 1 GETTING STARTED

THE GUITAR IN CELTIC MUSIC

Celtic guitar is certainly an intriguing topic. This is partly due to the beautiful traditional music which is often called "Celtic," and partly due to the fact that there is really no long-standing Celtic guitar tradition. The guitar was used only rarely in Irish and Scottish traditional music until the folk boom of the 1960s and 1970s, when British guitarists such as Davy Graham, John Renbourn, Bert Jansch and Martin Carthy began to arrange traditional Celtic melodies for fingerstyle guitar.

This doesn't mean that the guitar was completely absent from Celtic styles before that. The lute appeared in the 16th century and the English guitar, which is more like a *cittern* (a large mandolin) than a modern guitar, appeared in the 18th century. The Spanish guitar appeared in Scotland in the 18th century, but was not used to play traditional Celtic music. The instrument matching the modern idea of the guitar was used only during the last 100 years or so, and then only rarely and mostly for rhythmic and harmonic accompaniment, which didn't quite fit the bill of "traditional."

Celtic music is fundamentally *melodic* (single-note lines) rather than *harmonic* (two or more different notes happening at the same time). That means that this music is primarily played without chords. Certain instruments, such as *uileann pipes*, use drones, but they're still considered more melodic than harmonic. The widespread use of bass lines and chord progressions in modern Celtic music is a relatively new development, and therefore the "rules" of tradition do not apply in this regard.

Despite this relative freedom from tradition, it's crucial that we respect the primary importance of the melody. The grace, flow and color of the melody should be maintained (as much as possible) when adding harmony to a traditional piece. Therefore, it's a good idea to make sure that your arrangements are playable enough to preserve the beauty and phrasing of the melodic line. In other words, if you're working too hard to play all the harmonies and bass-lines, the phrasing of the melody will probably suffer. This can affect the spirit of the song.

Certain aspects of traditional Celtic music, particularly some of the very fast rhythms and ornaments are almost impossible to play on fingerstyle guitar. Often, the rhythms and phrasing have to be altered in order to be playable at all. Because of this, some purists consider fingerstyle guitar an inappropriate vehicle for this music. So here's a good general rule: *Don't let purists tell you what to play!* After all, if all we did was keep things the same, we'd still be banging on rocks! Celtic music has almost constantly been in flux, and while there are elements of continuity, many details of the forms have changed significantly over the years. So, don't be afraid to experiment and explore. After all, that's just what the architects of this music have been doing for thousands of years!

Have fun!

ORNAMENTATION

One of the most important and definitive aspects of Celtic music is the *ornamentation* (decoration) of the melody. Ornamentation varies significantly according to personal taste, regional style and the physical nature of the instrument being played. Therefore, it's a bit difficult to define a concrete set of rules for how it works. For example, on a guitar your options for ornamentation will be affected by which fretting-hand finger is playing the primary melody note, or whether the note is on an open string. Some composers and arrangers don't include written ornamentation so that the players can embellish the music as they see fit. This book will include some written ornamentation to match the performances on the CD, but feel free to ornament these pieces any way you like.

There are several common types of ornamentation that we will cover in this book as they are quite manageable and useful for guitar arrangements. All of these can be accomplished using standard guitar techniques such as hammer-ons, pull-offs and slides. They include *high grace notes, low grace notes, rolls, trills, slurs* and *slides*. Depending on the instrument and the culture, these approaches have been given different names. But to make things simple, we'll keep the terminology as guitar oriented as possible.

High Grace Notes

One of the most effective ornaments on the guitar is the *high grace note* (grace note from above). This is done with a quick pull-off from a note above the target note (usually within three frets). Grace notes can be played before the rhythmic placement of the note they ornament, or they can be included in the rhythmic value of that note (in the latter case, they're called *appoggiaturas*.) Grace notes are represented by tiny eighth notes that don't contribute any time value to the measure (tiny sixteenth notes are used for *double grace notes*.)

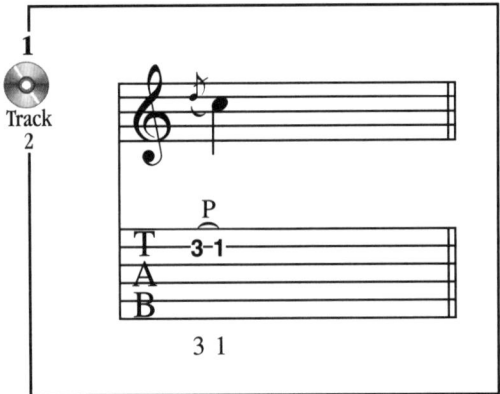

Low Grace Notes

The flip-side of the high grace note is, of course, the *low grace note* (grace note from below). This is done with a quick hammer-on from a note below the target note (usually within three frets). It can also be done with a quick *slide* (see page 105), usually from one fret below.

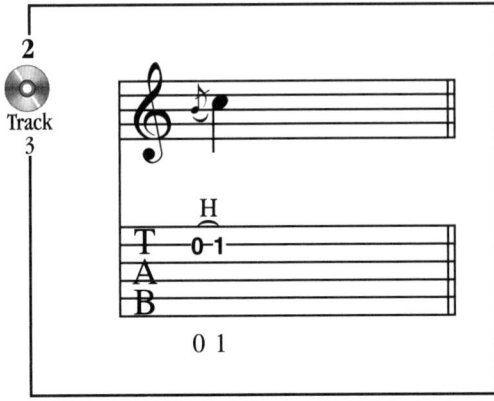

Trills

A trill is a very quick alternation between two notes. Trills are written as a single note value with ∿ written above the note. A trill lasts for the duration of the note.

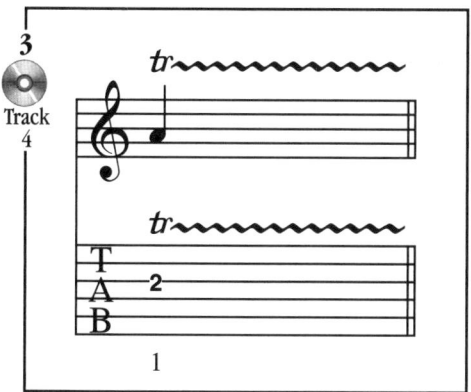

is played like:

Long Rolls

One of the more elaborate ornaments is the *long roll*, which can be difficult to perform accurately in certain positions on the guitar, especially at fast tempos. It involves converting a dotted quarter note into three eighth notes with high and low grace notes between them (see "Conlon's 2," page 118).

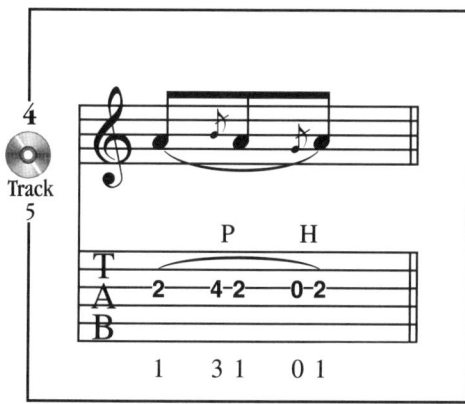

Slurs

While they're not really ornaments, *slurs* play a very important role in the phrasing of Celtic music. Slurs refer to two or more consecutive notes that follow a single pluck of the string. Slurs are notated with a curved line ⌢. Ascending slurs are accomplished with a hammer-on. Descending slurs are accomplished with a pull-off.

Slides

Slides are similar to hammer-ons and pull-offs, but sound a bit more slippery and allow your fretting hand to *shift* (change) positions. In a slide, a finger moves along a string to create a gliding sound. Because many fiddle melodies sound best played on the top two strings, position shifting is often unavoidable. Slides can be a big help in these situations. When the second note in a slide is not plucked, a slur is used.

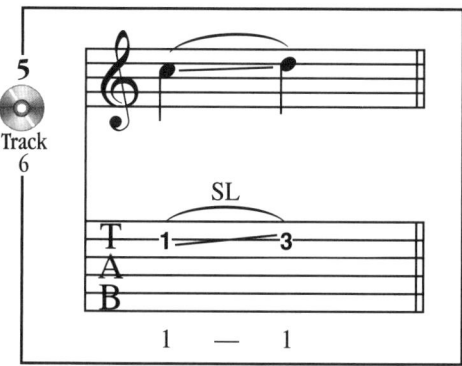

HARMONY AND ARRANGEMENT

Traditional Celtic music is fundamentally melodic rather than harmonic in nature. Contemporary Celtic fingerstyle guitar, however, commonly uses a lot of chords and harmonies to fatten up the melodies. Depending on the complexity of the melody, arrangements can vary from pure melody to melody with bass lines to lush and complex chord-melodies.

Due to the fast and intricate nature of dance tunes such as *jigs* (page 114) and *reels* (page 118), players will often embellish the melody with a simple bass line (see "Blarney Pilgrim," page 114). In the case of a slow *air* (page 122), one might choose to use very colorful chords and harmonizations to create a richer soundscape (see "Shi Beg Shi Mhor," page 138). The more ornate the melody is, the more sparse the harmony should be.

Often, a simpler arrangement is best. If you start playing chords in your arrangement, it sets up the expectation that more will follow. This can get pretty sticky because sometimes complex melodic sections make it almost impossible to work in a nice chord. If you try too hard to maintain the regularity of chords, the phrasing of the melody can suffer. Generally it makes better sense to focus on finding the right bass notes, and then work in supporting harmony when it's possible and tasteful.

Right-Hand Fingerings
p = Thumb
i = Index
m = Middle
a = Ring

Whether simple or complex, the rhythmic phrasing of the accompaniment should always support the melody. Sometimes this involves placing accompaniment directly on the beat in the style of the old *ceili bands* (bands that play for Irish dancing). This approach provides a steady pulse or groove that carries the melody along. If overdone, this can get boring. Here's an excerpt from an old Irish fiddle tune called "The Leg of a Duck."

Another approach involves accenting more freely to match the phrasing of the melody or merely to maintain interest and excitement. If overdone, this can be distracting.

* Unless otherwise indicated, examples and pieces are in standard tuning.

One good way to keep the rhythm of the accompaniment from being too boring or too complex is to occasionally vary the regularity of the bass notes, which involves establishing a steady rhythmic pulse and then either dropping bass notes or adding extras whenever you think the feel is getting stale.

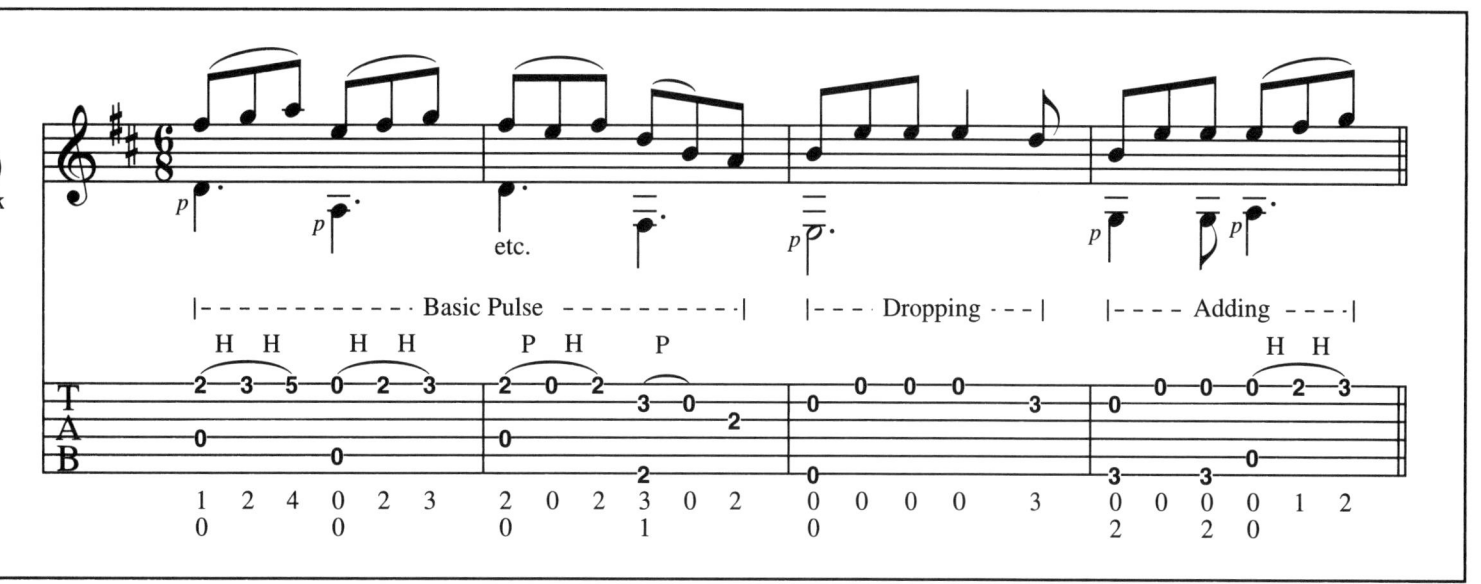

You'll notice that many of the tunes that follow appear to have two parts, and often, but not always, are eight bars each. These parts are commonly referred to as the "A" section and the "B" section. A standard way to play these tunes is AABB (play the "A" section twice, then the "B" section twice), but it's really up to you. This means that you should feel free to make any structural arrangement you like. You could do ABAB, AABA, etc.

You can embellish and harmonize these melodic sections differently each time they come around. For example, you can start with the melody alone and gradually add more elements of harmony. One mark of a sophisticated traditional musician is the ability to keep a simple two-part melody interesting for a long time with seemingly endless variation.

As you play the tunes in this book, it's highly recommended that you take a very open approach to the arrangements and the harmonies. As you become familiar with the melodic lines, experiment with different bass notes and try to throw in (or remove!) some chords. You might also try playing sections of these tunes completely without bass lines or harmony as is done with the beginning sections of "George Brabazon" (DADGAD version, page 136) and "Blarney Pilgrim" (page 114).

Your enjoyment of Celtic fingerstyle guitar will increase dramatically as you learn to arrange and embellish these melodies in your own way. When you've finished working through this book, consider purchasing a book of fiddle tunes written without accompaniment and start working them out. It's easier than you might think and it is tremendously fun and rewarding. Let everything you learn in this book be a step towards doing it yourself!

TUNING

All the tunes in this book are in DADGAD and/or standard tuning. This will allow you to develop some flexibility in these tunings. DADGAD was chosen because it is very resonant and works equally well for all the common modes used in Celtic music. It's also very commonly used in this style so it's quite easy to develop a deep technique, vocabulary and repertoire. Standard tuning was chosen to allow you to add some Celtic lines and feel to your standard vocabulary. To develop your skills in these tunings, you should try to avoid playing your arrangements the same way all the time. As you find yourself becoming familiar with this music, take some risks and see what you come up with.

Here is DADGAD tuning. You can check your tuning against the CD.

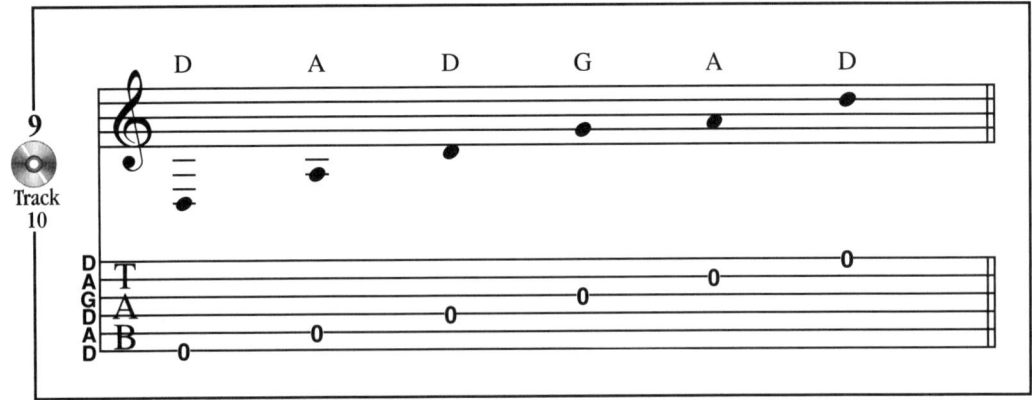

Here's a simple way to get your guitar into DADGAD tuning without using an electronic tuner:

Step 1. Play the 12th fret harmonic on the 6th string and tune it down one whole step so that it matches the 4th string open (D).

Step 2. Play the 2nd string open and tune it down one whole step so that it matches the 12th fret harmonic on the 5th string (A).

Step 3. Play the 1st string open and tune it down one whole step so that it matches the 12th fret harmonic on the 4th string (D).

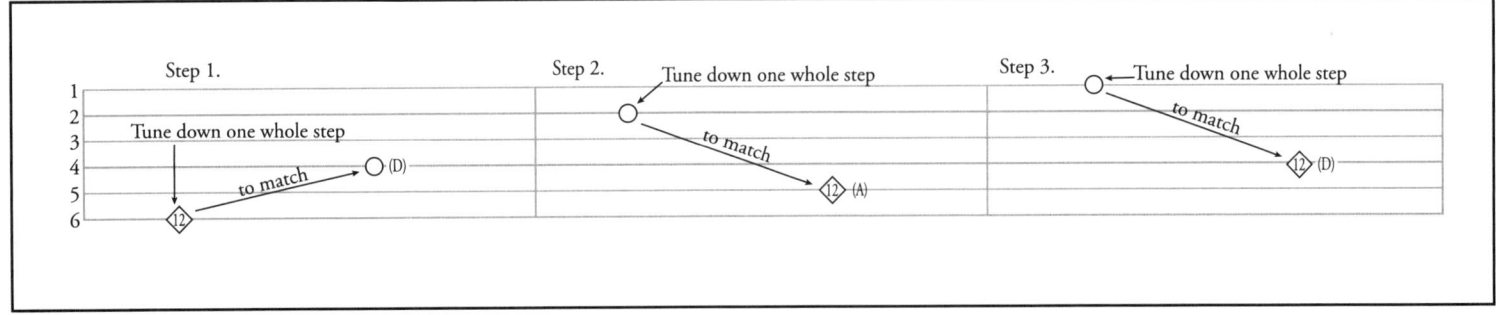

Tuning your guitar down will change the intonation a little bit, so you may have to do some tweaking before it sounds in tune throughout the fretboard.

MELODIC DEVELOPMENT

To help you learn to make your own arrangements, let's take some basic, unadorned melodies and develop them through a series of common steps. The first thing we'll do is develop the melody alone so that it sounds sweet, colorful and personal to you. Then we'll create a nice bass line that supports the melody. After that we can add whole or partial chords to fill out the harmony. Here's a summary of those steps:

Step 1. Choose an un-ornamented melody.

Step 2. Add ornamentation and phrasing as you see fit.

Step 3. Create a bass line.

Step 4. Add chords and/or harmonies if possible.

As a general rule, try to maintain the feel of the melody as it is in Step 2 when adding material in Steps 3 and 4. We'll start by running this process through the first few bars of "Planxty Eleanor Plunkett" (in standard tuning) by Turlough O'Carolan.

Step 1. Un-Ornamented Melody—You'll notice that when you play the melody as it's written here, it's pretty straight and dry. There are no hammer-ons or pull-offs, grace notes or trills. It's actually pretty boring.

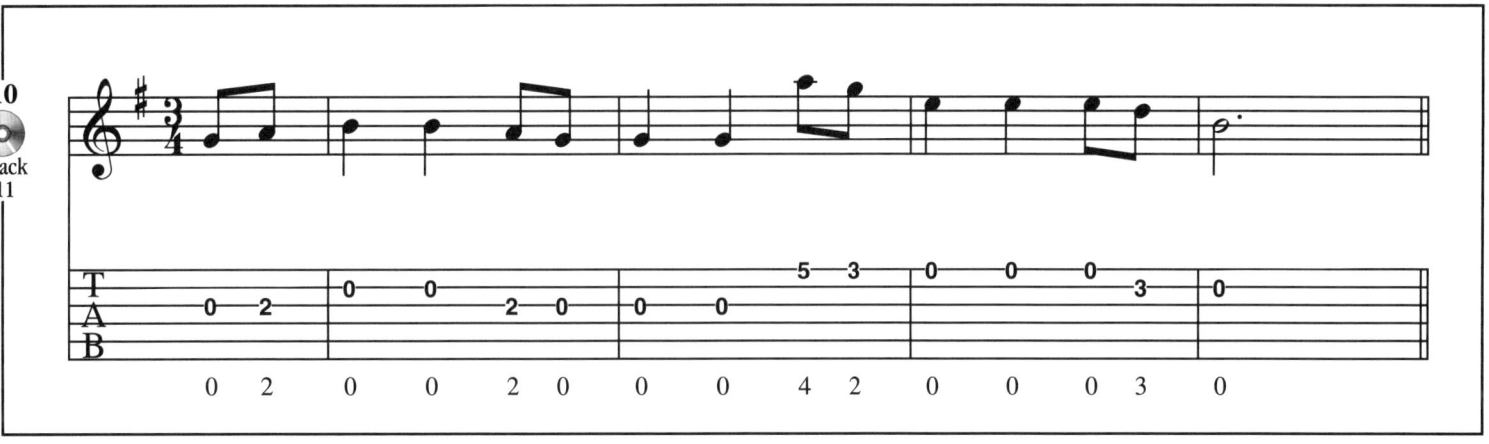

Step 2. Ornamented and Re-Phrased Melody—Here we've added some slurs and grace notes to liven things up. In addition, we've changed the rhythmic phrasing a little bit to give it a looser feel.

Step 3. With Bass Line—Notice that the phrasing in the second full bar changed a bit to accommodate the bass fingering (we're using slides now). These bass notes are all from the same key as the song and were chosen because they create a nice sense of direction for the melody. There are many other possible bass lines for this example, some of which would create a different sense of direction. At this point, you're truly adding material to the piece, making you the co-composer. The rhythm for this bass line is very simple and typical for a delicate air in 3/4 time. The first bass note is on beat one, and the second is on beat three.

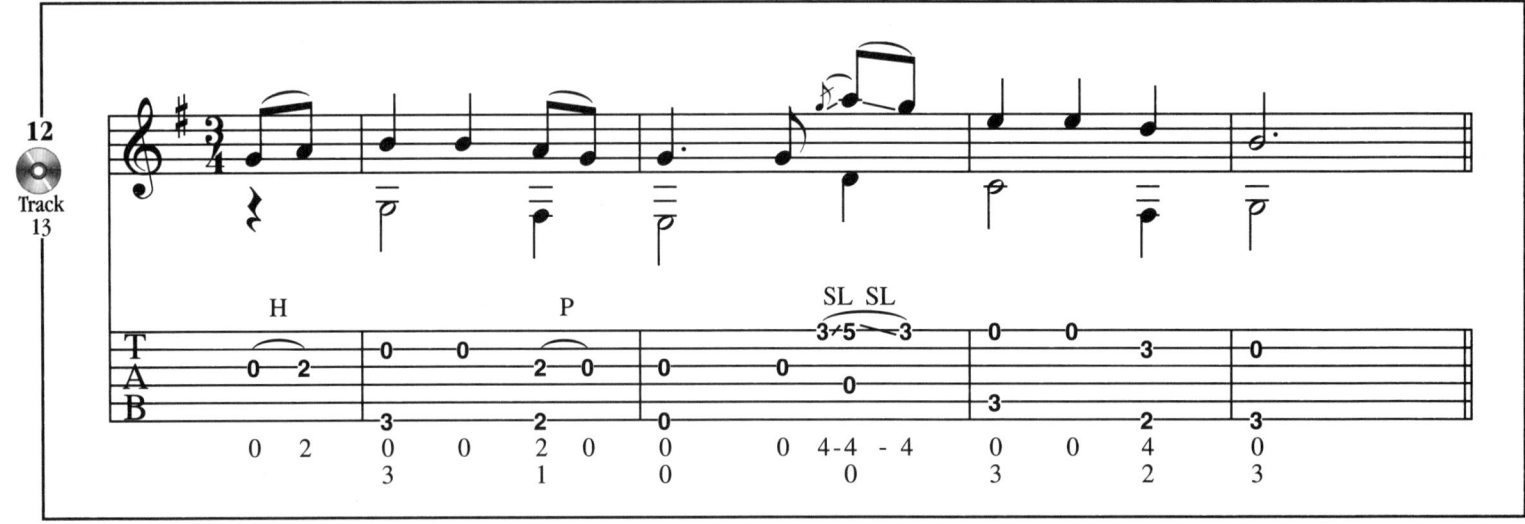

Step 4. Full Harmony—For this final step, we're simply expanding the bass notes into full and partial chords. It's important to choose your chord voicings wisely so the melody is still easy enough to play beautifully. You should also pay attention to how the *voices* (each note in a chord is a "voice") in each chord lead to the voices in the next chord. As with the previous example, the chords here are located on the first and third beats.

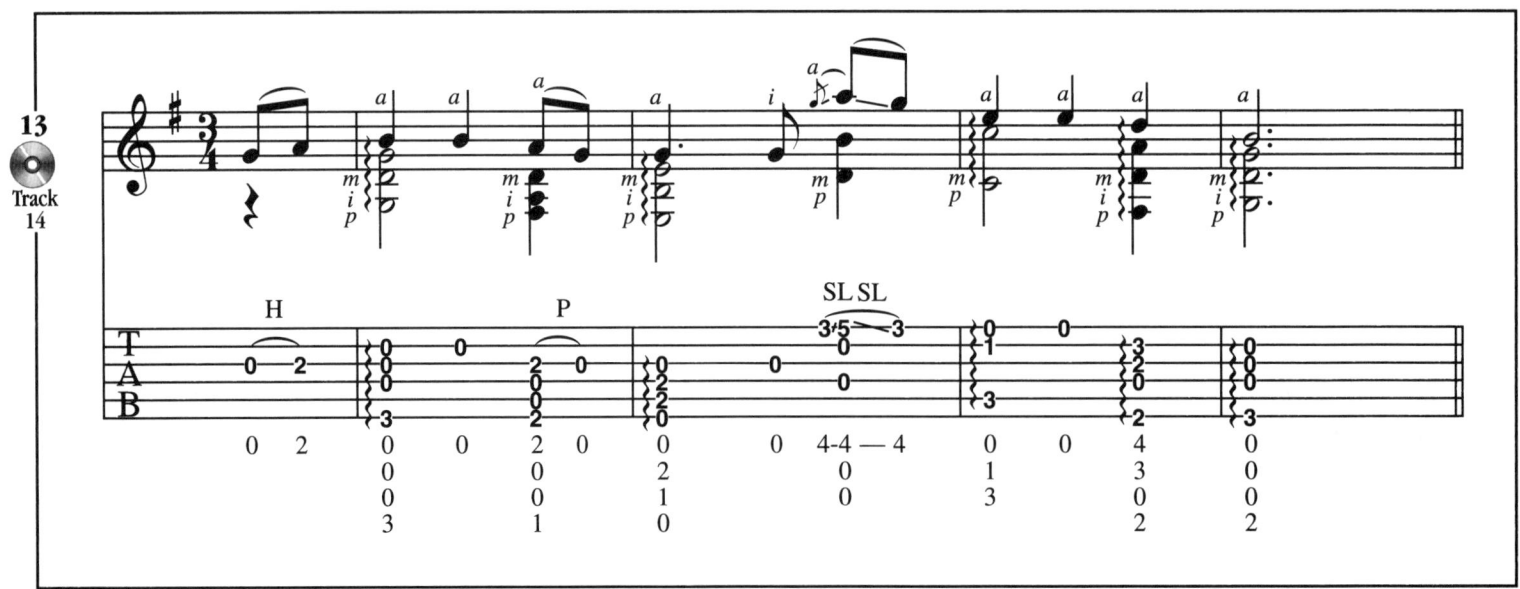

Now that you've gone through all four steps, go back and play the version at Step 1 again. You should hear quite a dramatic difference.

Let's try this again in DADGAD. This excerpt is from a traditional Irish reel called "O'Connell's Trip to Parliament." We've combined Steps 3 and 4 into one step, since it's quite easy to distinguish the bass line from the harmony.

Step 1. Un-Ornamented Melody—When played this way, it's pretty dry and boring.

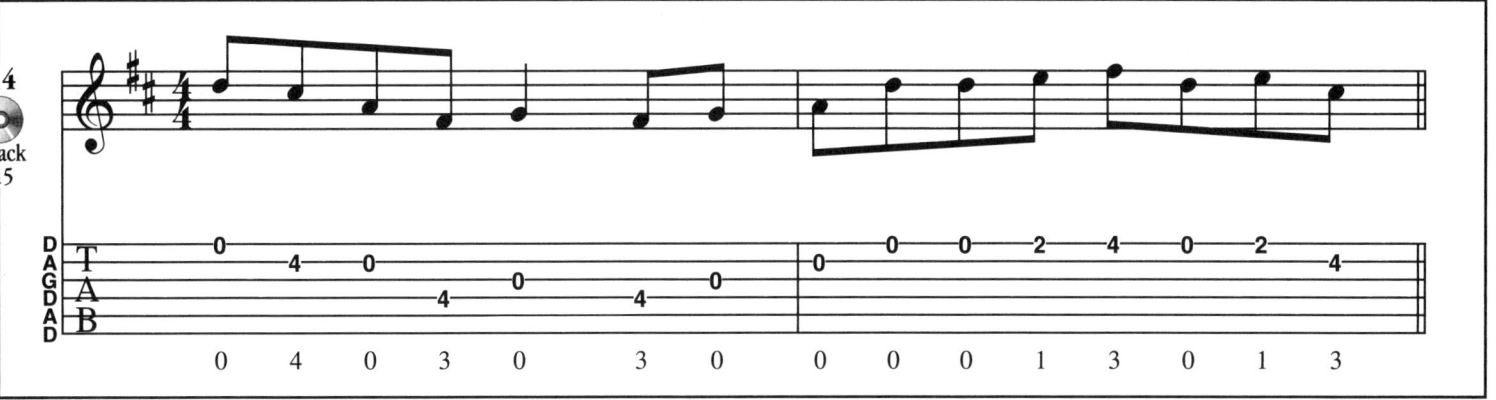

Step 2. Ornamented Melody—Slurs and grace notes have been added to give some color to the melody. Although the written rhythm is unchanged, this should be played with a fair amount of swing.

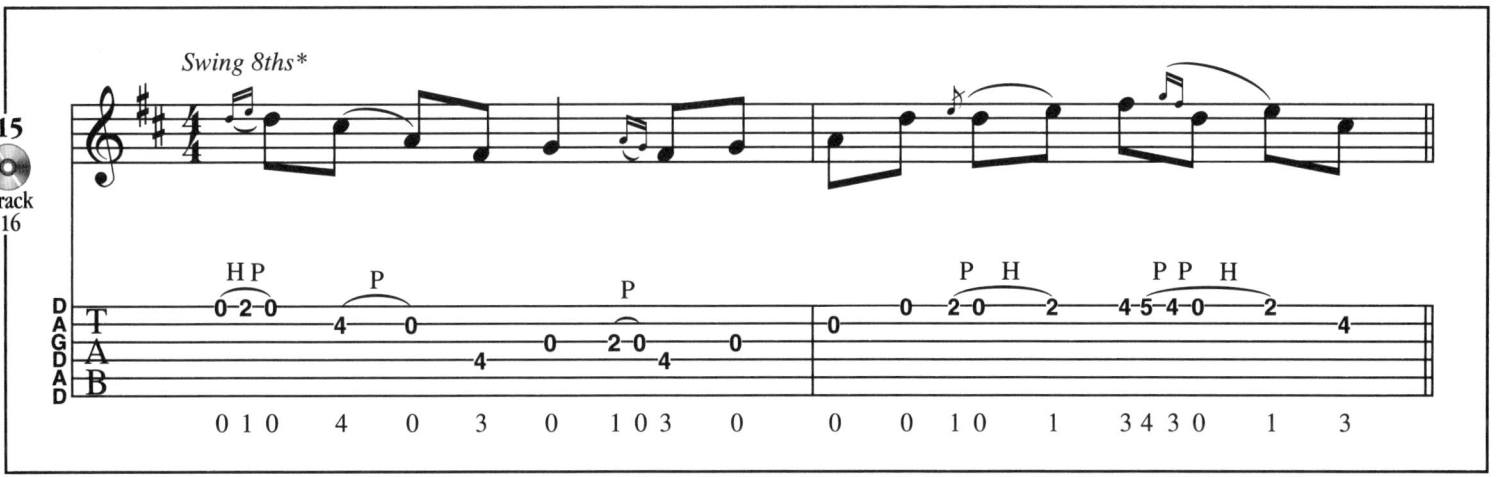

Steps 3 and 4. With Bass Line and Harmony—A fairly simple bass line and harmony were chosen to allow the melody to be played clearly and allow the open strings to resonate relatively freely.

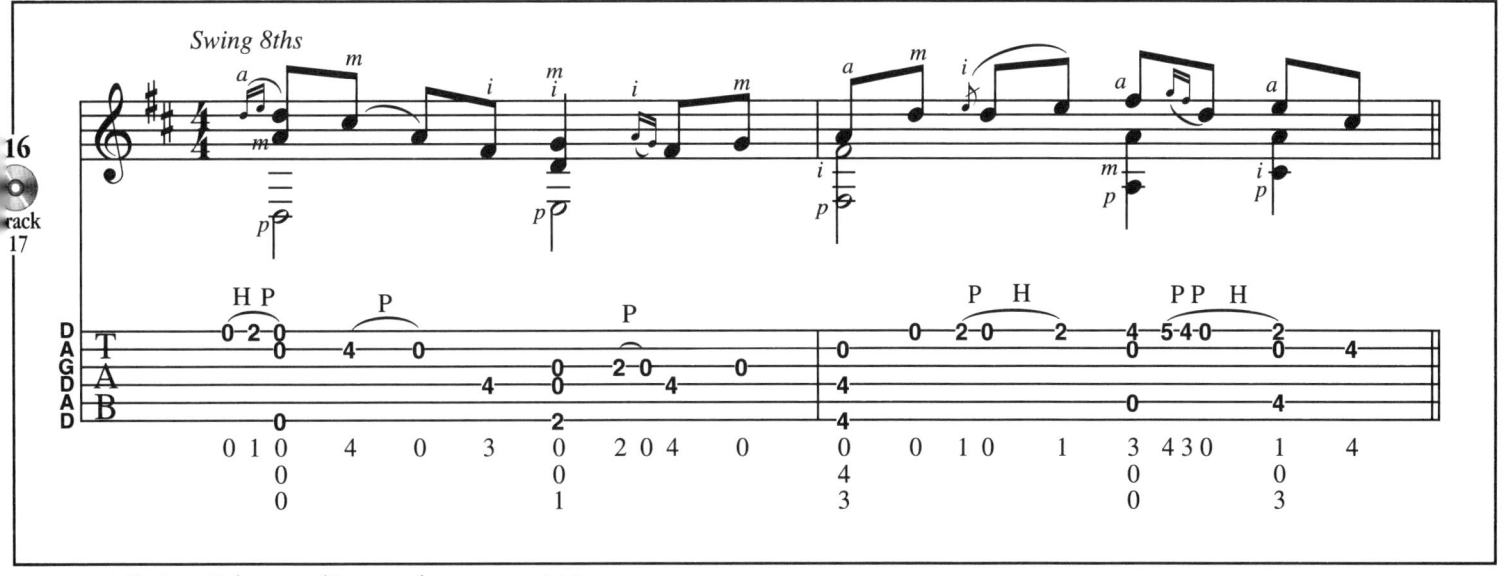

* Swing 8ths are discussed on page 113.

Guitar Atlas: Celtic   111

Harp Effect

One really great thing about DADGAD is how well it works for *harp effect*. The goal of the harp effect is to divide the melody between the strings so that several notes ring simultaneously. This usually involves spreading the melody out over more strings than would normally be required. As a result, it can be harder to play additional harmony and/or bass notes. This isn't really a problem, though, because with all those notes ringing together, the melody itself creates a very lush harmony. This example shows "O'Connell's Trip to Parliament" played with maximum harp effect.

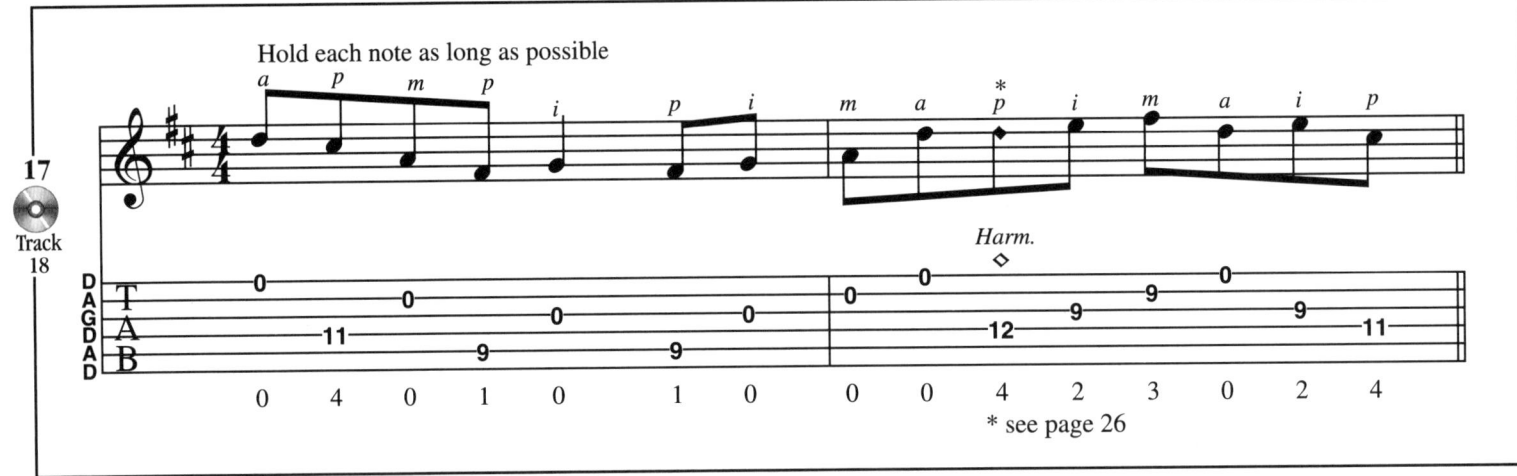

If you want to add bass notes to this, the easiest thing to do is to hit the tonic (D) at some regular interval to fill up the low end without creating a lot of harmonic chaos.

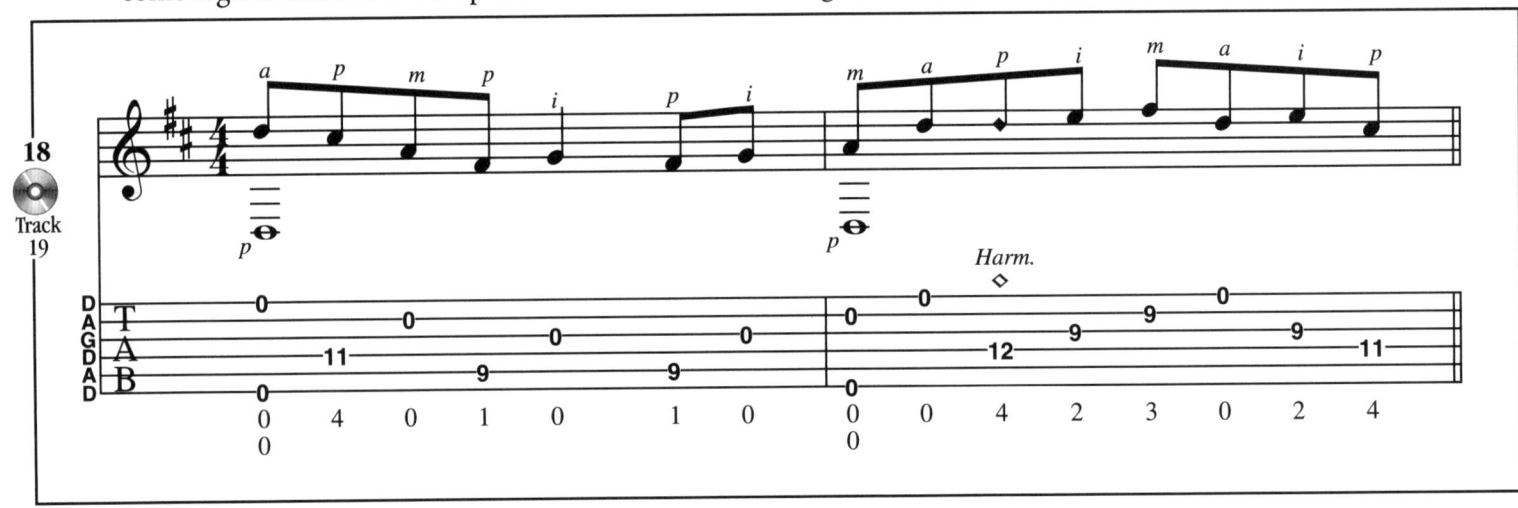

If you're interested in combining harp effect with more interesting bass movement, you'll need to sacrifice a bit of resonance. If you focus on shorter harp lines with less emphasis on duration, it'll free your fingers up to play more bass notes. Also, note that this allows you to play more on the lower frets, which is the more common range for bass lines.

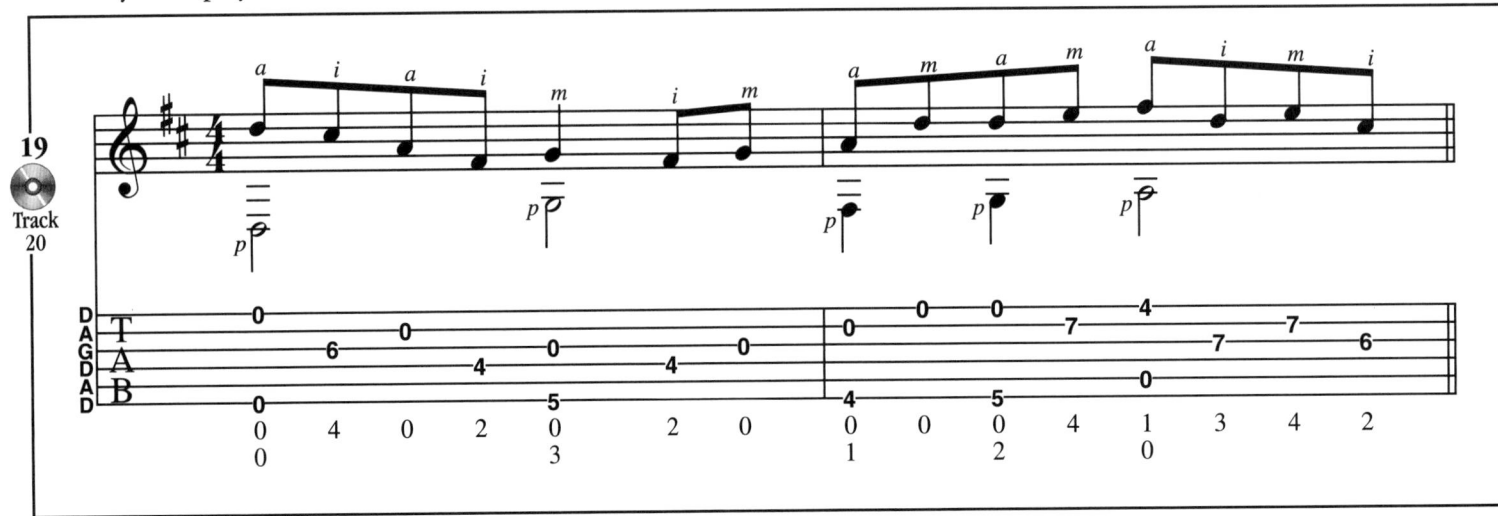

THE SONGS AND THE RECORDINGS

Now we're about ready to get into the music. The following arrangements cover a common range of Celtic styles. You'll find a jig, some reels, a hornpipe, a strathspey, a slow air, a lament, and some O'Carolan tunes. The specifics of each kind of tune will be discussed at the beginning of each section. The main things that separate different varieties of Celtic music are rhythm and tempo. In addition to this, however, categories vary according to the amount of *swing* or the type of techniques used. Swing refers to how the eighth notes are played. As in jazz or blues, we often play eighth notes unevenly in Celtic music: long-short, long-short. This is called *swinging the eighths*. Even within a particular category, like jigs for example, many details will be different from region to region, and from country to country.

The arrangements presented in this book offer a variety of technical challenges. When learning any new tune, try to think of it as a collection of lessons. Approach each new technique, each new challenge, as an independent thing. Also, the more you focus on the difficult sections, the more quickly you'll learn the tune.

The point of this book is to introduce you to this music, give you some ideas and make you a better player. If you dive in deep and really master something new, you'll be ready to apply it to a new song. If, however, you gloss over new material, merely trying to get through it, every new song will be like starting over again entirely. Focus on depth and quality while taking a very gentle but realistic stance toward how you sound at any point; don't be too hard on yourself, just be as honest and objective as you can. As you get better at doing this, the process of learning new songs will get easier and easier to do.

All the songs in this book are included on the CD. The various sections of each song are indexed separately so you can learn them as independent parts to mix and match as you like. It's important to remember that the way a piece is performed is up to you. How you vary the density and color of the arrangements is how you make these songs your own. So please use these sections as ingredients and bake your own cake.

When you're learning a new tune, listen to it as often as possible. This will make the process go much faster. Because many of these tunes are written with straight eighth notes, there's really no other way to learn the amount of swing except by listening. The same is true for all elements of feel: there's only so much you can communicate with written music. So listen carefully, then read and play, then listen again, etc.

Fretting-hand fingerings are provided throughout the arrangements (underneath the tablature). These are suggestions, not rules. If you decide to do something else, make sure that it is in the service of the music. Very few picking-hand fingerings are provided because the range of possibilities is too extensive and too personal. However, it is almost universal to pick all bass notes with the thumb.

Chapter 2 JIGS

When most folks refer to jigs, they're actually talking about *double jigs*. These are considered normal because most jigs are of this type. Double jigs are in 6/8 time with primary accents on the first and fourth eighth notes. *Slip jigs* are in 9/8 and some *single jigs* are in 12/8. The name comes from the 16th century word "jigg," which referred generally to fiddle music. Most jigs were composed by fiddlers and pipers from the 18th and 19th centuries.

The "Blarney Pilgrim" jig is extremely popular and fun to play. This DADGAD arrangement is written in F Major (capoed at the 3rd fret*), which sounds very sweet and provides a nice contrast to so many songs in D Major and G Major. It starts with a section of unaccompanied melody played in harp style. Make sure that your fingerings allow the notes to ring out as much as possible. Harp style creates a lovely effect and should be practiced very slowly and carefully until you get the hang of it. There are some stretches in this section, so warm up before you try them and stop if you feel any pain in your hands, wrists or arms. In the last sections of this arrangement, the melody is played an octave lower. You don't need to play these parts at the end. You can place them anywhere you like within the flow of the piece in order to create contrast and maintain interest. As is generally the rule, the various parts of a traditional Celtic tune can be played and repeated in any order you like. If you can learn to combine these parts freely and creatively, it'll feel like your own tune in no time!

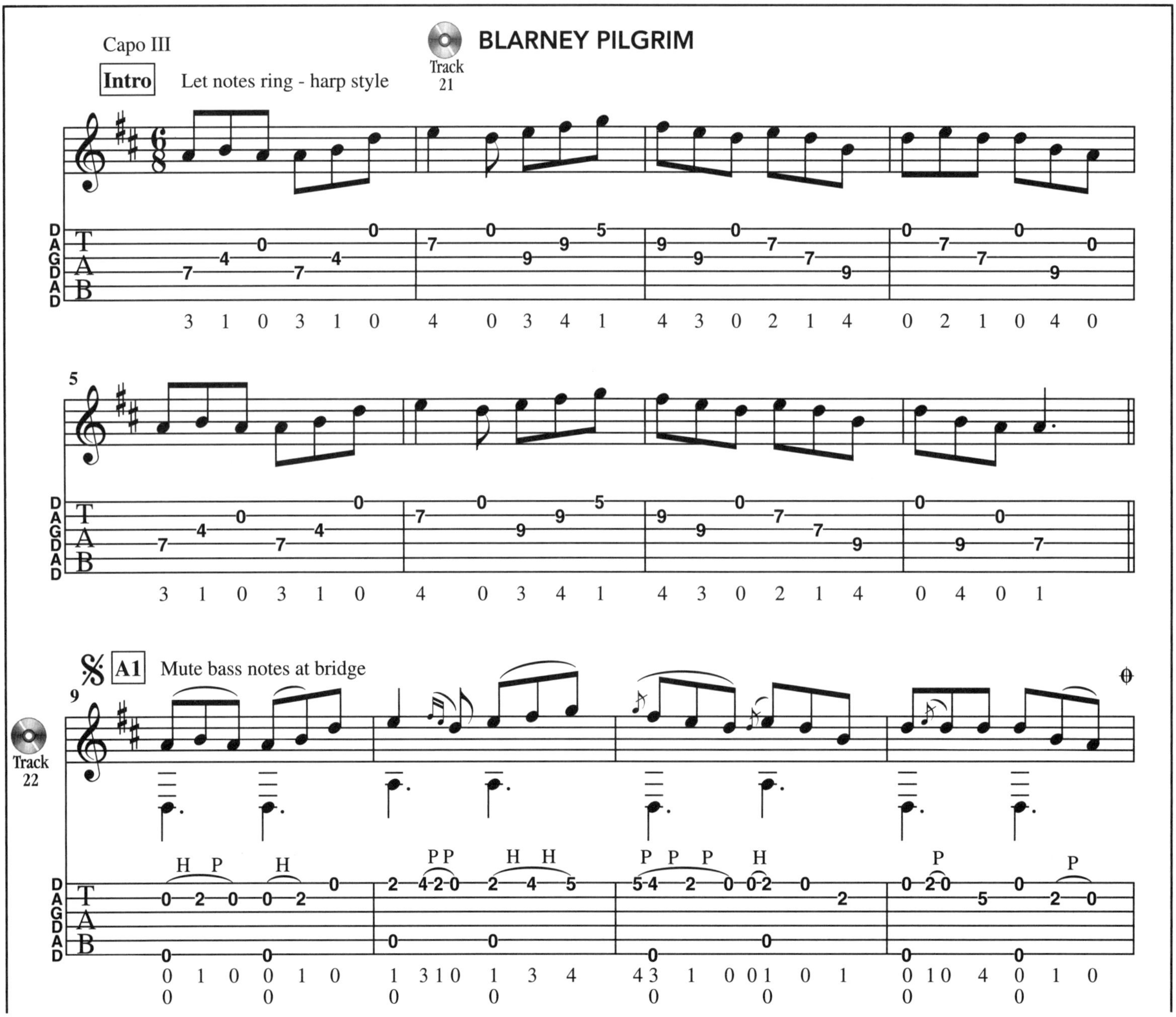

BLARNEY PILGRIM

Track 21

Capo III

Intro — Let notes ring - harp style

Track 22

A1 — Mute bass notes at bridge

* In this and many other guitar books, music intended to be played with a capo is written at the fretted pitch, not the sounding pitch. In other words, with the capo at the 3rd fret, we still write the open 1st string as a D (DADGAD tuning), even though it sounds an F. This is for ease of reading.

Chapter 3 — REELS

Derived from the 16th century word "reill" which meant "circular," reels appear to be of Scottish origin. This name reflected the fact that country dancers often moved in a circle. In the old days (18th century) in Scotland, the word "reel" referred to all manner of country dancing, including what are now called jigs, reels and strathspeys. "Reel" eventually came to refer to fast tempo, flowing dance music in 4/4 time, although reels are occasionally played at slow and moderate tempos. Accents normally fall on the first and third beats (where a quarter note equals a beat.)

"Conlon's 2" is a lovely Scottish reel. There are some unusual and playful movements in it. The use of the ♯4 (G♯) in the "B" section gives this tune a bit of a jazzy feel (Dixieland, not bebop). Notice, also, that the melodic phrase at the beginning of the "B" section is only three beats long and starts on the "&" of beat 4. This creates a striking rhythmic effect. This tune also employs some *frails* (FR), which are hard strikes by the middle fingernail of the picking hand. This is accomplished by tucking the picking hand middle finger into the pad of the thumb and launching an aggressive inward strike against the string ("into" the guitar). This creates a very percussive effect. If you find that you can't do this right away, don't sweat it. Just play it any way you can.

FR	=	Frail
T	=	Tap

CONLON'S 2
Track 29

Swing 8ths

*T = Tap this note with the left hand. Not plucked.

Guitar Atlas: Celtic

"The Morning Dew" is a popular Irish reel in E *Dorian*, which is the mode built from the 2nd degree of the D Major scale (the notes of D Major starting from E). This arrangement has a very simple and repetitive accompaniment designed to focus attention on the melody in a more traditional way. The bass notes should be muted with the palm of your picking hand to simulate the sound of the traditional Celtic frame drum known as the *Bodhran* (pronounced "bow-ran"). It takes some practice to play cleanly and powerfully with your hand in this position, but it's worth the effort. Among other things, it enhances the illusion of more than one instrument playing.

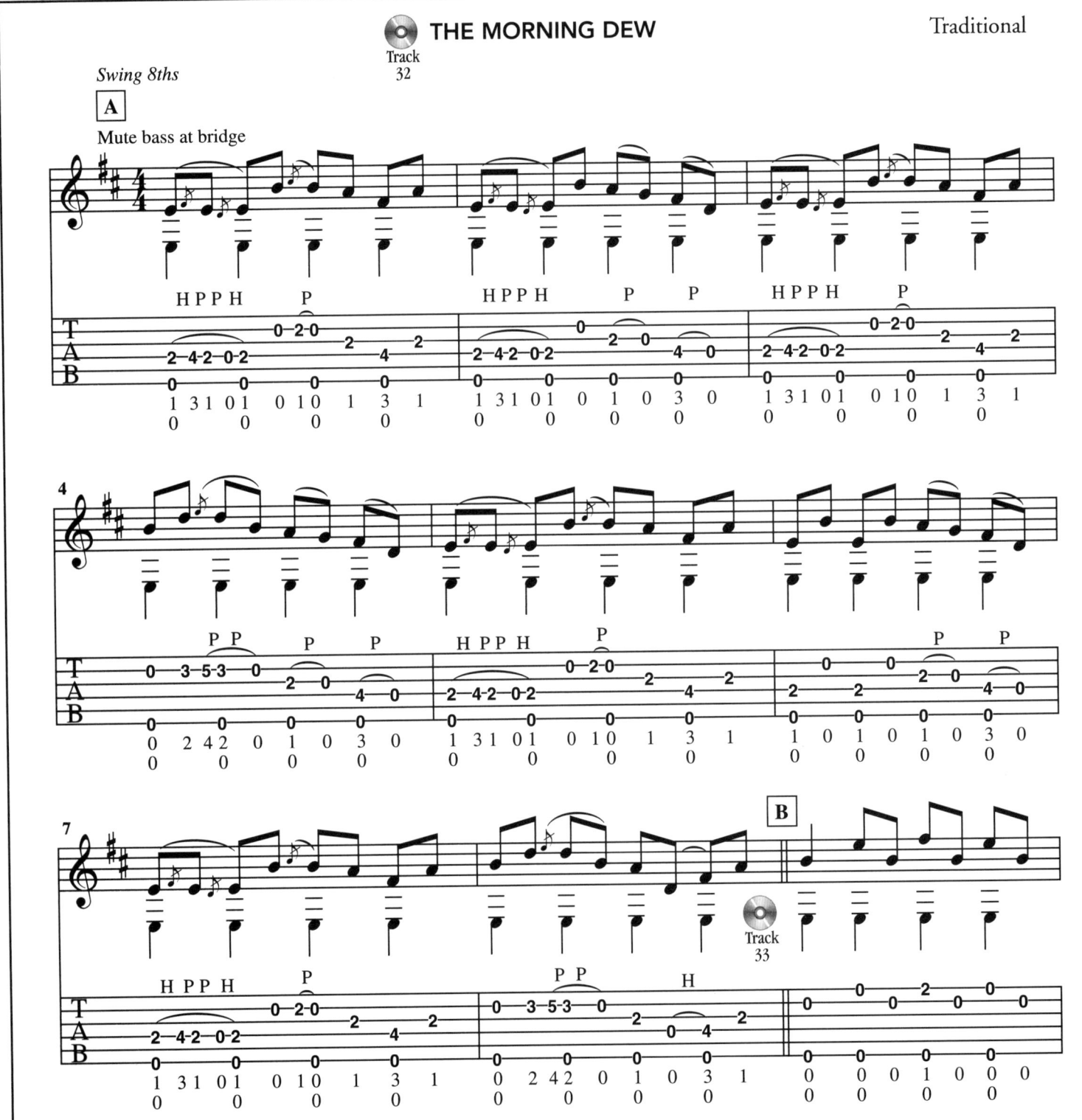

Chapter 4 — SLOW AIRS AND LAMENTS

Air simply means "melody" or "tune." Slow airs are derived from old-style Gaelic singing. They are played slowly with a free rhythmic feel, meaning that the tempo can speed up or slow down as the player likes. *Laments* are musical expressions of sorrow. Like slow airs, they should be played slowly, freely and expressively.

"My Fair Young Love (A Lady to her Husband who was Killed at the Battle of Culloden)" is a lovely and simple Scottish lament that is interesting for a couple of reasons. First, it has 19 measures per section. This is unusual and adds to the peculiar sense of sadness and longing given by the melody. Secondly, there's very little rest in the melody until the end of each section. If phrased well, this lack of rest can create a very melancholy effect. There are two versions of this tune here. Since they're both in standard tuning, you should try combining them into more complex arrangements. You can mix and match whole sections, or borrow short phrases from each other (or anything in between). Both of these versions should be played extremely expressively in terms of both *dynamics* (loudness and softness) and tempo (rubato). The rhythm of the eighth notes can be interpreted quite loosely.

This first arrangement is very simple, allowing emphasis on the flow of the melody. It is written entirely without grace notes. This is not to suggest that you shouldn't ornament this piece. You should, but you should do it entirely as you see fit. The rhythmic phrasing on the recording is very loose. Take this as an indication that you have a lot of freedom to interpret. Chord symbols have been included as suggestions for additional harmony, should you choose to add some. This is easy to do with this piece because of the slow tempo and the simplicity of the arrangement.

MY FAIR YOUNG LOVE (A LADY TO HER HUSBAND WHO WAS KILLED AT THE BATTLE OF CULLODEN)

Track 35

122 *Guitar Atlas: Volume 2*

HARMONICS

This section is intended to prepare you for the second version of "My Fair Young Love." In this very challenging arrangement, the bulk of the melody is played with *harmonics*, which create a lovely bell-like tone. Before we get started, let's take a brief look at harmonics and how they work.

A harmonic is created when you place your fretting-hand finger very lightly on the string at a specific location and then pluck the string with your other hand. These points, called *nodes*, are found where the string is divided into two, three or four. The string is divided into two directly at the 12th fret; three at the 7th fret; and four at the 5th fret. These locations create the following pitches:

Harmonic Location	Harmonic Pitch
12th fret	One octave above the open string
7th fret	One octave above the 7th fret
5th fret	Two octaves above the open string

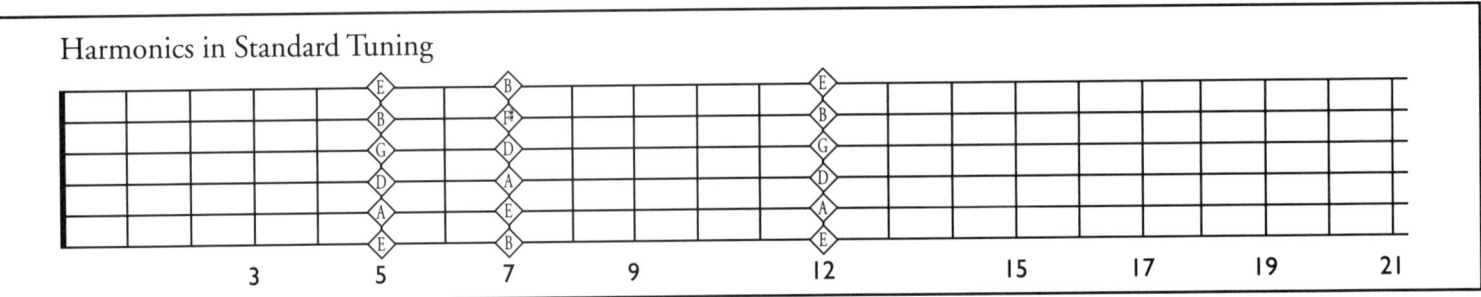

NOTE: To play a harmonic, the finger must lightly touch the string *directly above* the fretwire. This is in contrast to normal playing, wherein we press the string down into the fretwire, placing our finger just behind it.

Harmonics are indicated with diamond-shaped notes, and with diamond-shaped symbols and "*Harm.*" above the TAB.

*Born in 1965 in Paisley, Scotland, **Tony McManus** is considered by some to be the world's greatest Celtic guitarist. His astonishing technique and unmatched ability to capture the complex phrasing of traditional Celtic music truly set him apart in the world of fingerstyle guitarists.*

8va = *Ottava*. Sounds an octave higher than written.

Let's look at the scale created from the lowest to the highest of the common harmonics in standard tuning.

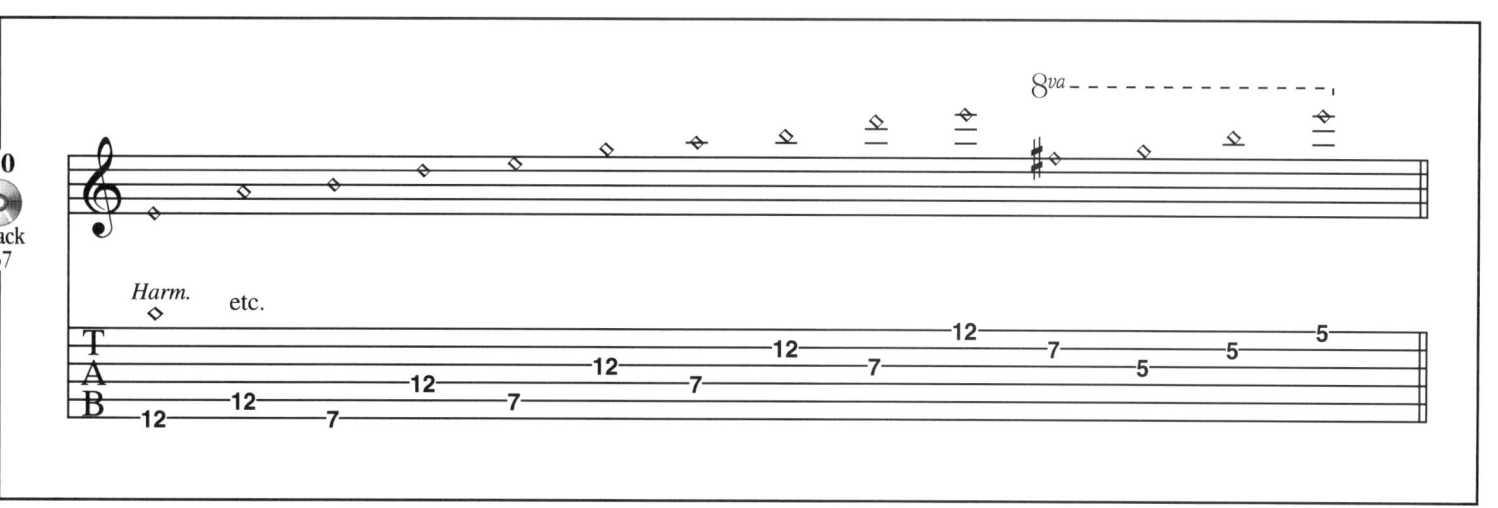

This collection of notes is a substantial subset (six out of seven notes) of several common scales. These include G Major and D Major as well as their respective relative minor scales; E Minor and B Minor. That means that in these keys, harmonics can be used to play many of the melody notes, adding a fresh and unusual quality to the song.

Guitar Atlas: Celtic

MY FAIR YOUNG LOVE
(A LADY TO HER HUSBAND WHO WAS KILLED AT THE BATTLE OF CULLODEN)

Track 38

Harmonics

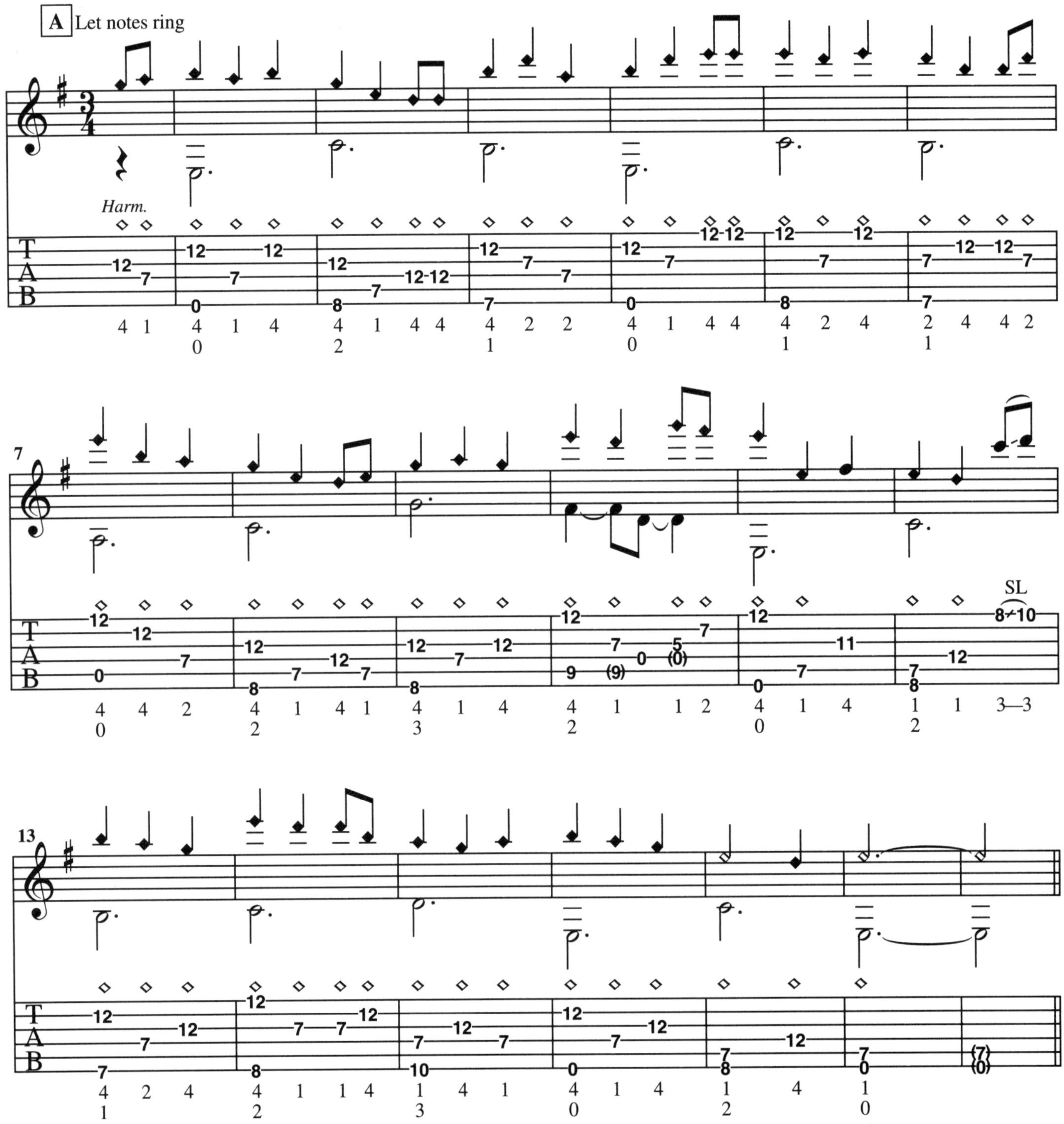

Guitar Atlas: Celtic 127

"Highland Boat Song" is a slow Scottish air in E Minor. It is capoed at the 7th fret, which gives it a very bell-like quality. This arrangement makes use of some colorful chords and a bit of subtle *dissonance* (clashing). The non-standard resolutions contribute to the feeling of melancholy. There are probably a million different ways to arrange a simple melody like this. If you hear a different harmony than the one presented here, feel free to change it in any way you like. As always, intelligent fretboard fingerings will allow you to sustain the chords in a musical way.

Chapter 5 — HORNPIPES & STRATHSPEYS

HORNPIPES

The *hornpipe* originated in England and was named after a 16th century reed instrument. It was originally in 3/2 time, but changed to common time (4/4) in the middle of the 18th century. Hornpipes are like reels, but are generally slower with a more pronounced accent on the 1st and 3rd quarter notes. They have a light, bouncy rhythm and are played with a very strong swing feel.

We're going to look at an Irish hornpipe called "The Scent of the Bog." One could fairly assume that this isn't a love song, unless the composer's lover smelled of mud and rotting wood. Still, it's a beautiful song. This arrangement isn't particularly easy, but it's quite fun to play once you get it. Make sure that the bass notes don't interrupt the flow of the melody. Start out slowly and pay close attention to the left-hand fingerings, or you'll end up moving your hand unnecessarily and the song will end up sounding lumpy. Remember, this is a hornpipe, so swing it!

THE SCENT OF THE BOG

Swing 8ths
Capo V
Track 42

130 *Guitar Atlas: Volume 2*

STRATHSPEYS

Strathspeys are uniquely Scottish and were brought to prominence by 18th-century fiddlers, although they're mentioned as far back as 1653. They are in 4/4 time and are similar to reels, but are played with a much slower, less-flowing rhythm. They make use of a rhythmic device known as the *Scots Snap*, which is written like this:

but is actually performed more like this:

"The Flax in Bloom" is sometimes written as a reel and sometimes as a strathspey. This arrangement represents a combination of the two. The phrasing of the "A" section is meant to be more strathspey-like, making use of scots snaps and a less flowing rhythm. The "B" section becomes a bit more reel-like, more sweet and flowing, while maintaining the stately pace and playfulness of the "A" section.

132 *Guitar Atlas: Volume 2*

Chapter 6 O'CAROLAN TUNES

Turlough O'Carolan was a Harper who lived from 1670 to 1738. He started playing harp at the age of 18 when smallpox left him blind. He was apparently not a very good player due to the fact that he started so late, which led him to focus his efforts on composition. Though his music shows some Irish folk and traditional harp influence, he was far more interested in Italian Baroque composers such as Antonio Vivaldi (1678–1741), Arcangelo Corelli (1653–1713) and Francesco Geminiani (1687–1762).

The written versions of his music that survive today are in the form of single-line melodies. Although he almost certainly accompanied himself with harmonies and bass lines, detailed information about his approach is hard to find. There is one book (only one known original copy exists, although modern editions of his melodies are available) of his music, which suggests that he accompanied himself with single-line bass with few complex harmonies.

The first tune presented in this chapter is "George Brabazon, 2nd Air." This is a beautiful piece, with a delicate, flowing melody. The second piece is "Shi Beg Shi Mhor," which is one of O'Carolan's most famous pieces. There are two different arrangements of each song included here, to give you a sense of how you might approach a single piece with different tunings.

This first version of "George Brabazon, 2nd Air" is in standard tuning. It's easy to play and very simple harmonically. There are no chords in this arrangement so as not to distract from the beautiful melody. Adding more harmony is easy to do in this case, since all the open strings are in the key, so give it a try if you feel the urge.

El McMeen *started playing guitar as a student at Harvard University in the 1960s. His arrangements of Celtic tunes are characterized by unusually lyrical sensitivity, clear technique and a very warm and sweet feel.*

134 *Guitar Atlas: Volume 2*

This arrangement of "George Brabazon, 2nd Air" is in DADGAD tuning and begins with an unaccompanied "A" section. You can start the arrangement with this section and then occasionally reintroduce it to give your performance a simple, sweet feeling. Focus on a flowing harp-like quality, since that is the instrument on which this piece was composed. These tunes respond well to a smooth and gentle touch.

"Shi Beg Shi Mhor" was based on a local legend about a war between two fairy armies. Many folks believe it to be O'Carolan's first composition. Among the numerous versions you might hear, there are many that stray far from the original melody. The fact that you can still identify the tune is testament to its strong personality and originality. This first arrangement is in standard tuning and uses fairly simple and common chord forms.

This version of "Shi Beg Shi Mhor" is in DADGAD and is a bit more harmonically complex, although it never strays from the key. You should practice this one very slowly to make sure that your fingerings allow the melodic line to emerge clearly from within the chords. Some of these chords require that you pluck with all five fingers of your picking hand. This usually means that your little finger (pinky) will be playing the melody note. This may seem difficult at first, but you'll get it if you stay with it.

Chapter 7 — ARRANGE IT YOURSELF!

The following are two versions of the "Fairy Jig," which is in D Mixolydian (G Major started from the 5th scale degree). The first is in standard tuning, the second is in DADGAD. All that is written here is the melody. Your job is to put in bass lines and harmony however you see fit. Try writing ideas in pencil directly onto the staff. The scales are supplied to give you a pool of notes to draw from. Have fun!

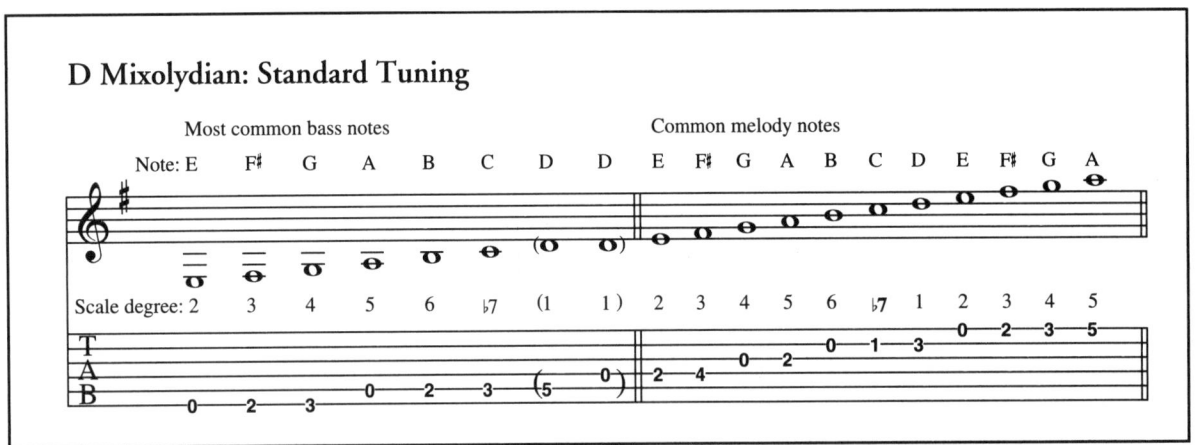

FAIRY JIG
(Standard Tuning)
Track 55

142 *Guitar Atlas: Volume 2*

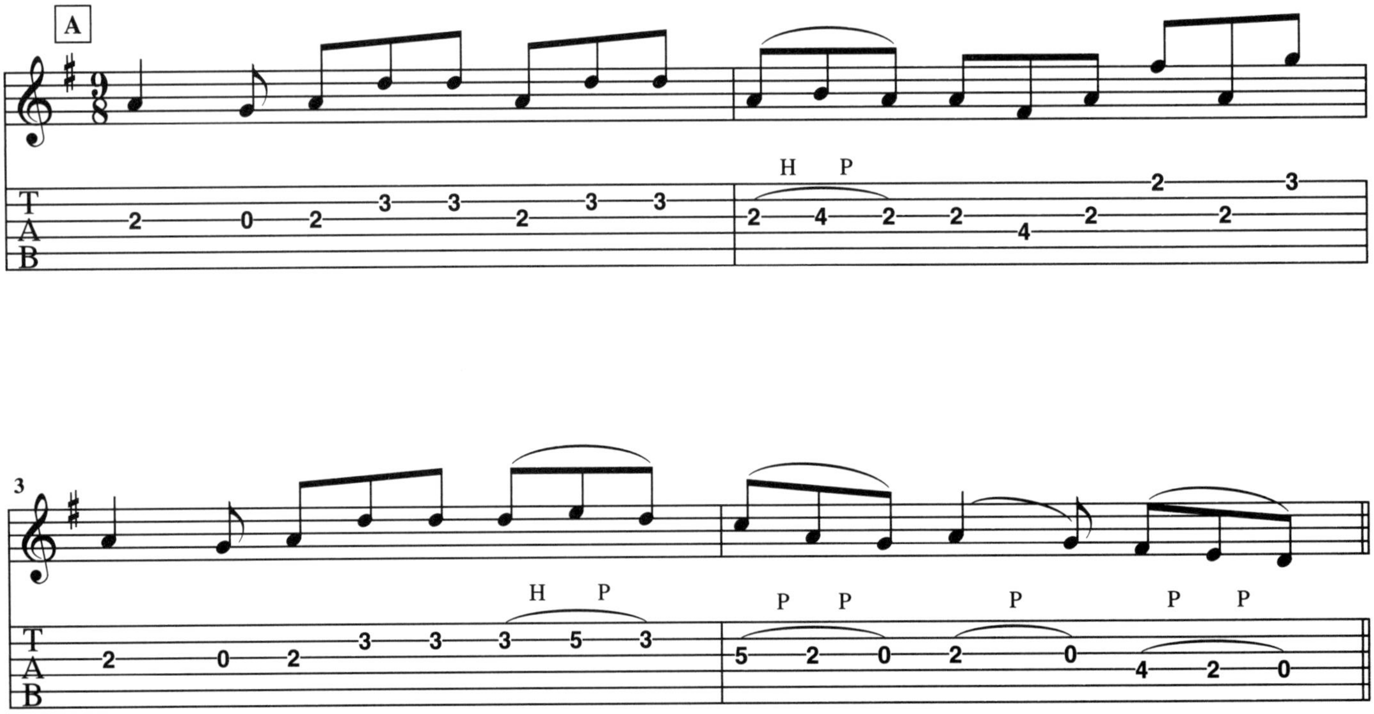

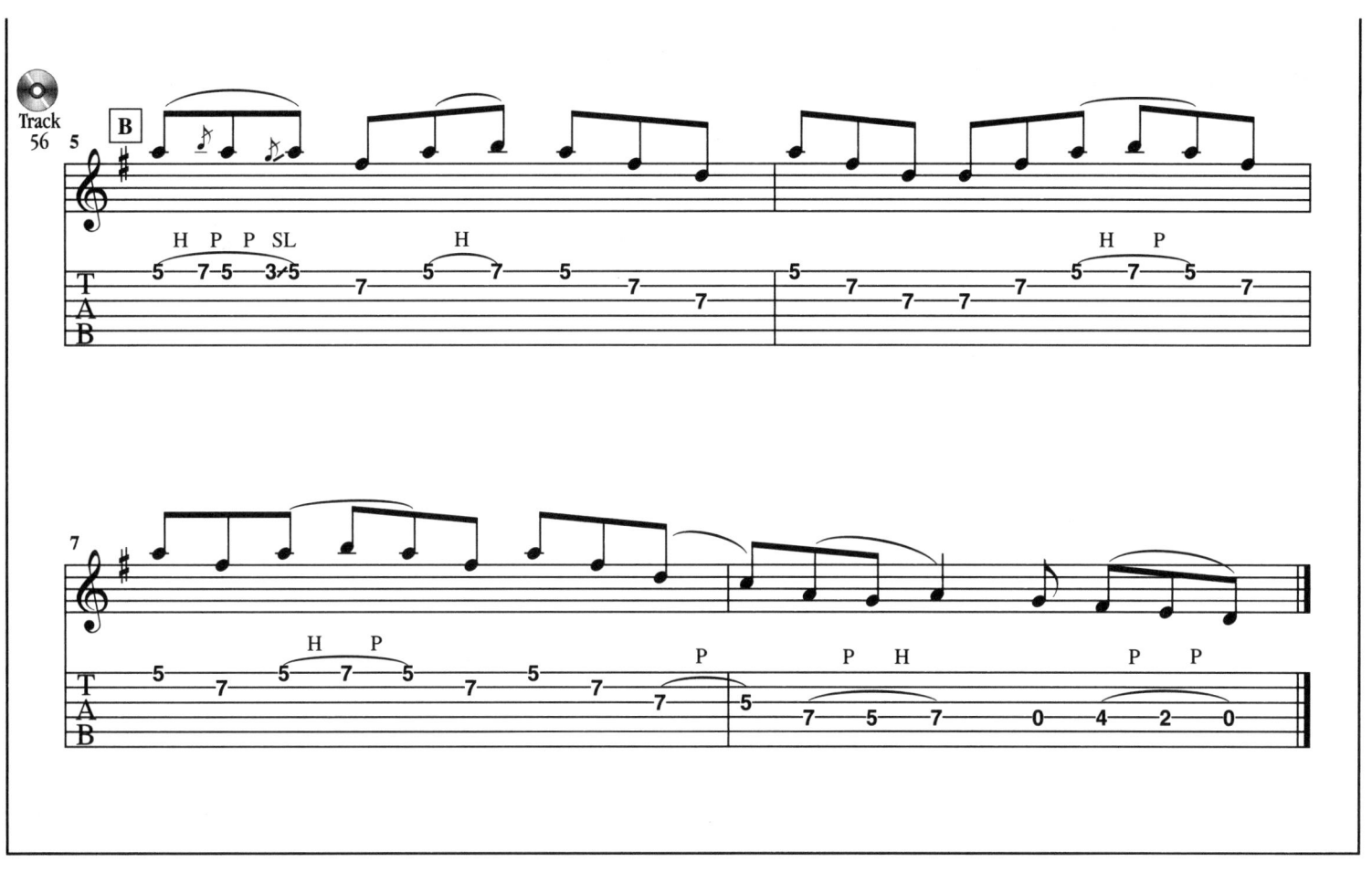

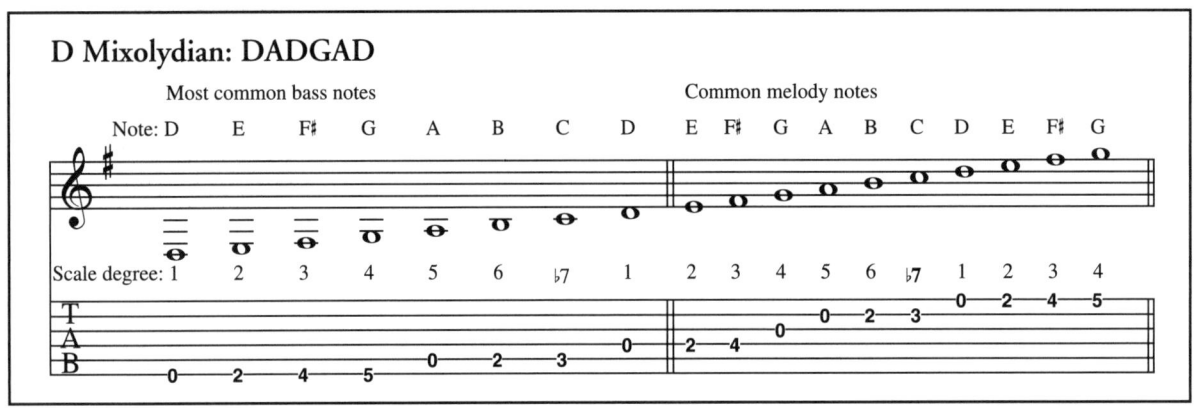

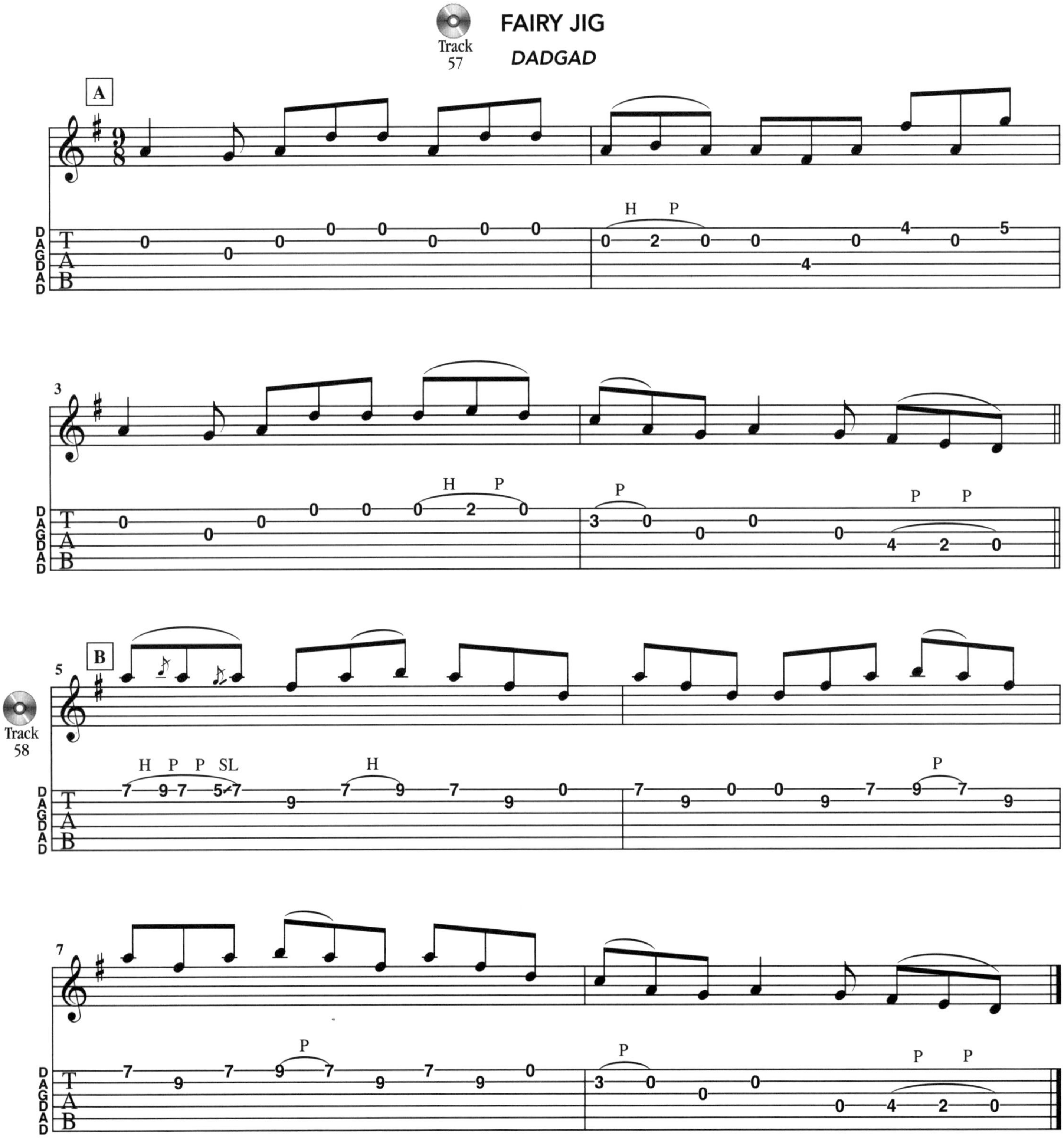

Recommended Discography

Here is a list of some great recordings. This is in no way a complete list. Not even close! Go find a good record store and used record store and take some chances on things you've never heard of. Some of the best players and bands aren't well known at all in different parts of the world. Read about your favorite players and find out who they listened to. Then go buy those records. It creates a magnificent chain reaction. The Internet is also a great resource for these kinds of searches.

SOLO ARTISTS

Pierre Bensusan: Intuite (Dadgad)
Pierre Bensusan: Pierre Bensusan 2 (Dadgad)
Pierre Bensusan: Pres de Paris (Dadgad)
Paul Brady: Welcome Here Kind Stranger (Mulligan LUNCD024)
Martin Carthy: The Collection (Green Linnet GLCD1136)
Pat Kirtley: Irish Guitar (MainString Records PKCD9701)
Tony McManus: Ceol More (Greentrax Recordings/Compass Records)
Tony McManus: Pourquoi Quebec (Greentrax)
Tony McManus: Tony McManus (Greentrax)
El McMeen: Acoustic Guitar Treasures (Piney Ridge 106)
El McMeen: Irish Guitar Encores (Shanachie 97017)
John Renbourn: Traveller's Prayer (Shanachie 78018)
Martin Simpson: Leaves of Life (Shanachie 97008)
Martin Simpson: When I Was On Horseback (Shanachie 97016)

DUOS AND ENSEMBLES

Alasdair Fraser and Tony McManus: Return to Kintail (Culburnie CUL113D)
Altan: Island Angel (Green Linnet GLCD1137)
The Baltimore Consort: On the Banks of Helicon (Dorian Dor-90139)
The Bothy Band: The Best of the Bothy Band (Mulligan LUNCD041/GLCD3001)
The Chieftains: Celtic Wedding (RCA 6358-2-RC)
Martin Hayes: Under the Moon (Green Linnet GLCD 1155)
Donal Lunny: Coolfin (Metro Blue)
Sharon Shannon: Sharon Shannon (Solid ROCD8)
Davey Spillane: A Place Among the Stones (Columbia 4769304)
Tommy Peoples and Paul Brady: The High Part of the Road (Mulligan SHCD29003)

COMPILATIONS

Lament (Real World/Carol 2325-2)
Music of Ireland (Shanachie 97004)
The Music of O'Carolan (Shanachie 95009)
The Rough Guide to Scottish Folk (World/Rough Guides RGNET 1038 CD)

Final Word

Congratulations! At this point, you've either skipped to the end of book, or you've actually finished it. Assuming the latter, you're ready to tackle most of the fingerstyle Celtic guitar music out there. The techniques and vocabulary you've developed will help you in a variety of styles, but these things need to be maintained. Your practice needs to involve a combination of learning the new and remembering the old. If you can keep this balance, your musical world will continue to expand.

Like jazz musicians, Celtic players are partly gauged by the number of tunes that they know. In addition to this, they're judged by their ability to keep the tunes fresh through improvisational rephrasing, ornamentation and creative arranging. So treat these tunes as living things; let them move and grow. Learn to combine different melodic sections of similar tunes to create medleys that can keep people dancing or crying for a long time. Even if you're not trying to make people dance or cry, imagine that you are. Infuse your arrangements with the great joy and sadness that inspired these songs throughout the ages.

As with any tradition, one of the most important things to do is to listen and listen and listen and then listen some more. Get it into your soul; etch it onto your brain. If you can do that, your fingers will find the music.

It is also a big help to involve yourself in some sort of musical community. Make friends with other players and enthusiasts with similar interests. This can dramatically increase the amount of cool stuff to which you are exposed. Go to shows and try to meet the players. Try to get a lesson here and there from those you respect. The music is definitely out there....

Go out and find it!

Flamenco

Dennis Koster

*Guitar Styles
from Around the World*

This book was acquired, edited, and produced
by Workshop Arts, Inc., the publishing arm of
the National Guitar Workshop.
Nathaniel Gunod, acquisitions and managing editor
Michael Rodman, editor
Timothy Phelps, interior design
Matt Cramer, music typesetter
Dennis Koster, interior illustrations
CD recorded at Gizmo Enterprises, Inc. New York, NY
and mastered at Bar None Studio, Northford, CT

Contents

ABOUT THE AUTHOR 149

PRONUNCIATION GUIDE 149

INTRODUCTION 150

THE GUITAR IN FLAMENCO 151

CHAPTER 1—Flamenco Forms and Rasgueado 152
    Rasgueado 152
    Lesson 1—Rasgueado with *i* 152
        Compás 153
        Soleares 153
        The Compás of Soleares 153
        Alegrías 154
    Lesson 2—Five-Stroke Rasgueado 154
    Lesson 3—The Golpe and *a-m* Stroke 158
        Golpe 158
        The *a-m* Stroke 158
    Lesson 4—Llamada 159
    Lesson 5—Extended Compás Sequences 160
        Compás por Alegrías 160
        The Remate 162
    Lesson 6—Bulerias 164
        Hemeola and Flamenco Compás 164
        Playing Bulerias 165
    Lesson 7—Other Flamenco Rhythms 167
        La Farruca 167
        Tangos 167
        Fandangos 168
        Siguiriyas 169

CHAPTER 2—Flamenco Technique and the Falseta 170
    Lesson 8—The Thumb in Flamenco 170
        Por Soleares 171
        Por Alegrías 172
    Lesson 9—Arpeggio Falsetas 172
        Escobillas por Alegrías 172
        Por Soleares 173
        Por Bulerías 174
    Lesson 10—Alzapúa 174
        Alzapúa por Soleares 175
        Alzapúa por Bulerías 175
    Lesson 11—Flamenco Tremolo 176
        Por Alegrías 176
        Por Soleares 177
    Lesson 12—Toque Libre: Granadinas and Tarantas 178
        Granadinas 178
        Tarantas 179

CHAPTER 3—Concert Solos 180
    Final Words 180
        Solo por Soleares 181
        Solo por Alegrías 185
        Solo por Bulerías 190

Track 1

A compact disc is included with this book. This disc can make learning with the book easier and more enjoyable. The symbol shown at the left appears next to every example that is on the CD. Use the CD to help ensure that you're capturing the feel of the examples, interpreting the rhythms correctly, and so on. The track number below the symbol corresponds directly to the example you want to hear. Track 1 will help you tune your guitar to this CD.

About the Author

PHOTO COURTESY OF DENNIS KOSTER

Dennis Koster's New York debut was hailed in the New York Times as "a considerable success … a brilliant, aptly fantastic performance." One of New York's most sought after teachers for over 25 years, Dennis has guest lectured and performed at the Peabody Conservatory, the Juilliard School, the American String Teachers Association, and the New York Bach Gesellscaft. A brilliant classical guitarist and flamenco player in equal measure, Mr. Koster studied with Juan D. Grecos, Mario Escudero and the legendary Sabicas, who called him "an excellent interpreter of my compositions." He has toured extensively in the U.S. and Japan, and has been broadcast throughout Spain. A frequent artist at the National Guitar Workshop, Dennis teaches in New York City and is the author of the three-volume method, *The Keys to Flamenco Guitar*. His classical and flamenco CDs are on the Music Masters label of the Musical Heritage Society.

Pronunciation Guide

Aire	= EYE-ray
Alegrias	= ah-leh-GREE-ahs
Alzapua	= ahl-thah-POO-ah
Apoyando	= a-poh-YAHN-doh
Baile	= BUY-ee
Bulerias	= boo-leh-REE-ahs
Cante	= KAHN-tay
Escobillas	= es-coh-BEE-yahs
Falseta	= fahl-SET-ah
Fandangos	= fahn-DAHN-gohs
Farrucus	= fah-ROO-kah
Golpe	= GOL-pay
Golpeador	= gohl-pee-AH-dohr
Granadinas	= grahn-ah-DEEN-ahs
Huelva	= WELL-vah
Jondo	= HON-doh
Llamada	= ya-MAH-dah
Madre	= MAH-dray
Picado	= pee-CAH-doh
Rasgueado	= rahs-gay-AH-doh
Remata	= ray-MAH-tah
Siguiriyas	= sih-geh-REE-ahs
Soleares	= sol-aye-ARE-es
Soledad	= sol-aye-dahd
Tangos	= tahn-GOHS
Tarantas	= tah-RAHN-tas
Toque	= TOKE
Verdiales	= vair-dee-AH-less

Introduction

In the minds of many guitarists, flamenco is "the king of guitar styles," combining the most appealing aspects of all guitar playing: Its spectacular, driving rhythms rival the most exciting popular styles; it shares improvisational freedom and great harmonic sophistication with jazz; it equals the musical depth and complete right-hand technique of classical guitar; and today's flamenco players perform with a level of virtuosity that leaves even heavy metal players breathless.

What was once an art limited to the narrow confines of ethnic boundaries—the Gypsies of southern Spain—today, flamenco is played all over the world by guitarists whose enthusiasm appears limitless. Many are first drawn to flamenco by exposure to superficial "pop-flamenco" styles; many begin playing flamenco by "faking it" in an attempt to "sound Spanish." But, oh-so-often, these same guitarists, once they've heard the real thing, forget all that is fake and devote themselves to learning authentic flamenco.

From classical to rock, guitarists of other styles often express frustration about solving the mysteries of flamenco: "How can that technique *possibly* be done?" or, "I could *never* learn that complex rhythm," and so on. It's my goal to answer all of your questions about flamenco and have you experience the thrill of playing true flamenco guitar.

This introduction to flamenco is designed for guitarists who have some classical training or are adept at fingerstyle playing. This book also assumes that you read standard music notation and/or tablature and that you have a good understanding of the fundamentals of harmony and rhythm.

In this book, we'll explore the complex strumming techniques of flamenco as well as flamenco percussion effects, thumb technique, arpeggios, tremolos, *picado* (flamenco scales), and performance style.

Not only is flamenco guitar technique complex, the art of flamenco itself is complex, encompassing literally dozens of songs and dances from nearly every region of Spain. In this book you will sample many different flamenco forms, but in an effort to provide some depth into the study, the lion's share of the forms will be from the "first family of flamenco rhythms"—the *soleares* family, which includes *soleares, alegrías*, and *bulerías*. All the techniques explained will be applied to these three rhythms, building your flamenco vocabulary and leading to three concert-level solos at the conclusion of the book. These solos incorporate all the techniques, rhythms, and melodic variations explained in these pages. Along the way, many other flamenco forms will be introduced in short examples.

The Guitar Atlas series welcomes you to Spain and the thrilling world of flamenco guitar.

The Guitar in Flamenco

Flamenco is the art of the Andalusian Gypsies—their song (*cante*), dance (*baile*), and guitar playing (*toque*). Although its origins go back hundreds of years to the time of Ferdinand and Isabelle, flamenco as we know it emerged in southern Spain during the mid-19th century.

In its early history, the guitar in flamenco was a humble accompaniment to the song and dance, which were considered far greater arts, if the guitar was considered an art at all! By the turn of the century, guitarists such as Maestro Patiño began to give a more expressive voice to the guitar, but it was not until the 1930s that flamenco guitar achieved recognition as the expressive equal of the song and dance. Ramón Montoya revolutionized flamenco guitar. A friend of classical master Miguel Llobet, Montoya not only brought classical guitar technique to flamenco—all the arpeggios, scales, tremolos, and so on—but the *language* of classical music as well. Montoya was the first to perform solo flamenco guitar concerts. His Paris concerts during the Spanish Civil War caused a sensation. His style was further developed by followers Niño Ricardo and concert artists Sabicas and Mario Escudero, who performed solo flamenco guitar in the great concert halls of the world.

In the 1970s, another revolution took place in flamenco. Paco de Lucía, who, in his early 20s, was already considered one of history's greatest guitarists, created a new modern style of flamenco incorporating the harmonic language of progressive jazz and a sophisticated Latin-influenced approach to traditional rhythms. Paco's revolution inspired an entire new generation of flamenco artists in Spain, where there are now more high-caliber flamenco artists than at any other time in history, largely due to the enormous influence of Paco de Lucía.

Flamenco can be played on any nylon-string guitar as long as it is equipped with some type of a *golpeador* (tap-plate or top-guard, similar to the pickguard on a steel-string acoustic guitar), to protect the guitar from stylistic rhythmic tapping. Traditional flamenco guitars are cypress bodied, have low action and a more percussive and brilliant sound than classical guitars.

Flamenco players are very casual about their sitting positions. Most sit cross legged, many use footstools, and some sit in the traditional Gypsy position with both feet on the floor and the lower bout of the guitar resting on the right thigh.

Flamenco left-hand technique is identical to that of classical guitar; right-hand position is only modified as needed to perform specific flamenco techniques. Fingernails are used to play flamenco just as they are in classical guitar.

The very best way to learn flamenco is to accompany flamenco dancers, and later, flamenco singers. If there are no flamenco artists near you, listen to all the flamenco recordings you possibly can—not just modern flamenco, but also historical recordings of the past masters and especially the cante.

Traditional Gypsy position.

Chapter 1: FLAMENCO FORMS AND RASGUEADO

RASGUEADO

Flamenco strumming technique is called *rasgueado*. A remarkable variety of rasgueado techniques are applied to flamenco rhythms—and the resulting sound can be electrifying. To most guitarists, expertly played rasgueado sounds like almost impossible virtuosity, but the technique can be broken down into basic movements, which can be learned through patient practice.

Rasgueado strokes are played by extensor muscles (the muscles that extend the fingers). Outside of flamenco, these muscles are rarely used in guitar playing. Their strength and agility must be developed carefully over time. It takes about one year of intelligent practice to master basic rasgueado techniques.

One of the biggest mistakes a flamenco student can make is to equate excessive force with the fire they hear in great rasgueado playing. Flamenco masters play rasgueado effortlessly. The fire comes from their expression.

Never strain or use excessive force when playing rasgueado technique. Great rasgueado is played by relaxed hands using free unrestrained motions learned through patient practice—*not* by brute force!

Right-Hand Fingers
Thumb............p
Index i
Middle ....m
Ring ....a
Little (pinky)....e

LESSON 1—RASGUEADO WITH i

In flamenco playing, the rhythm is often marked by downstrokes and upstrokes of the index finger (i), which uses a free, swinging motion from the large knuckle joint (the joint that connects the finger to the hand). This technique is performed from a steady and comfortable hand position in which the thumb (p) rests on the 6th string to balance and support the hand. When i alone plays rasgueado strokes, the little (e), ring (a), and middle (m) fingers remain passively extended and are never curled into the palm.

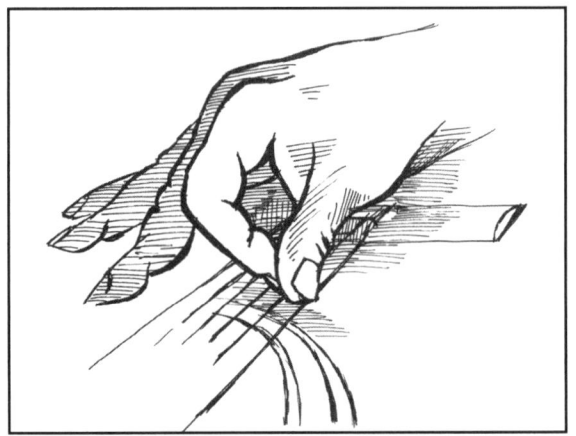

Starting position: i is folded in toward the palm; e, a, and m are extended passively.

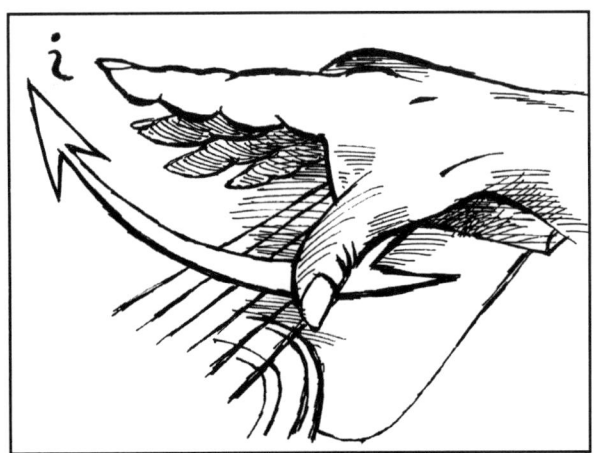

1. Downstroke: i extends fully with a free, swinging motion.

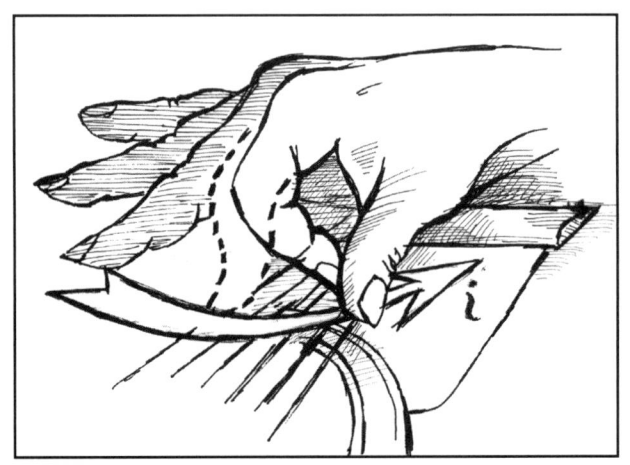

2. Upstroke: i returns to its starting position, brushing (not hooking) the strings.

COMPÁS

Compás, which means "rhythm," may be the most important word used in flamenco. Its meaning subtly changes depending on the context in which it is used. Compás can describe rhythm in general, or it can be used to describe the specific rhythmic structure of a flamenco form. For example, in this lesson, we will be learning the compás of soleares. Compás can also be used to describe the individual phrase of a flamenco form. Example 2 on page 154, for instance, is one compás of soleares, whereas example 3 includes two compáses.

SOLEARES

The Gypsies call *soleares* "*La Madre de Cante*" ("The Mother of Song"), as it is generally considered the oldest form of flamenco. Soleares derives its name from the Spanish word *soledad*, which means either "loneliness" or "solitude." A slow and serious song, soleares is an example of flamenco's *cante jondo* or deep song. Its lyrics are among the most moving and profound in Spanish poetry.

In the exotic key of E Phrygian (the scale you hear when playing all natural notes from E to E), typical chords in soleares are shown below. Notice that the E chord in the last bar is major. This is typical, even though the other chords are clearly Phrygian (a minor mode).

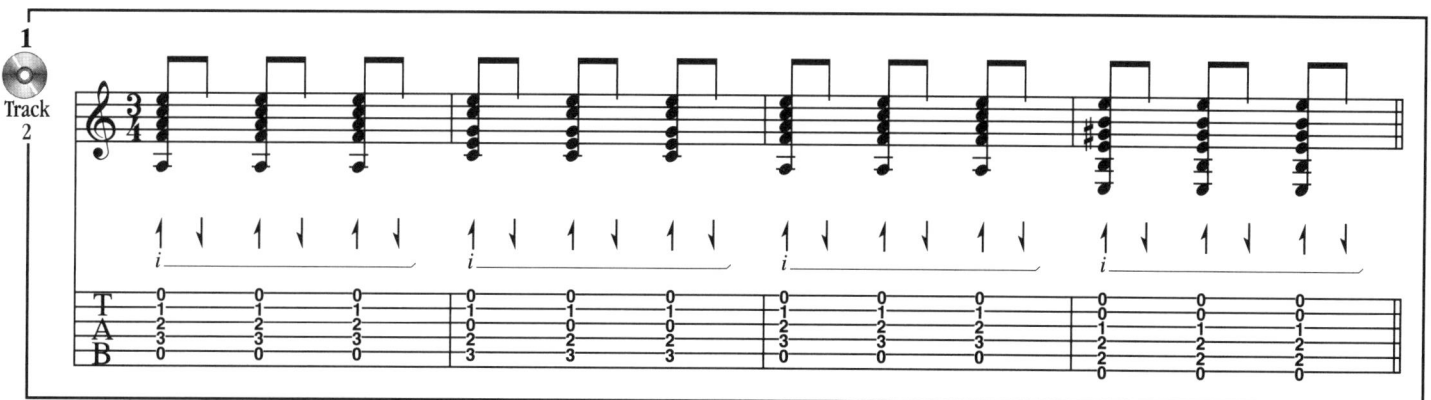

Note:
In flamenco music notation, it is customary to show all of the notes in a rasgueado chord only once per beam. Further occurrences of the chord under that beam are indicated with a noteless stem.

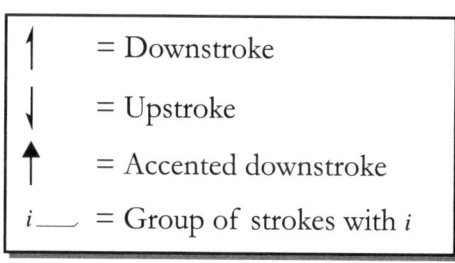

THE COMPÁS OF SOLEARES

Soleares and the dances that derive from it, *alegrías* and *bulerías*, share a very distinctive rhythmic structure. Often written in 3/4 time for easier reading, soleares is actually performed in 12-beat phrases with a very specific series of accents:

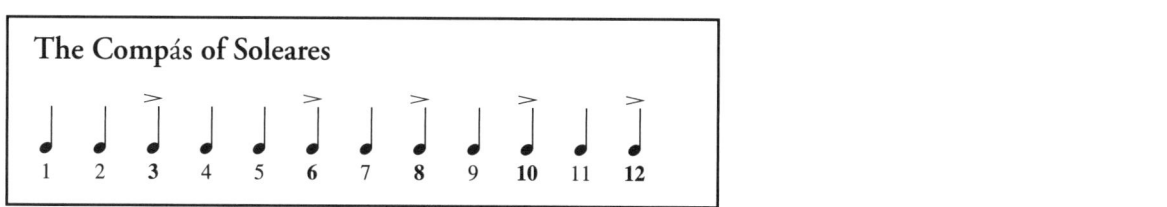

> = Accent

See Lesson 5 on page 160 for a more in-depth study of this rhythmic structure.

Adding accents on beats 3, 6, 8, 10, and 12 transforms an exercise of steady eighth notes into true flamenco. Play accented downstrokes with slightly more force than the unaccented beats.

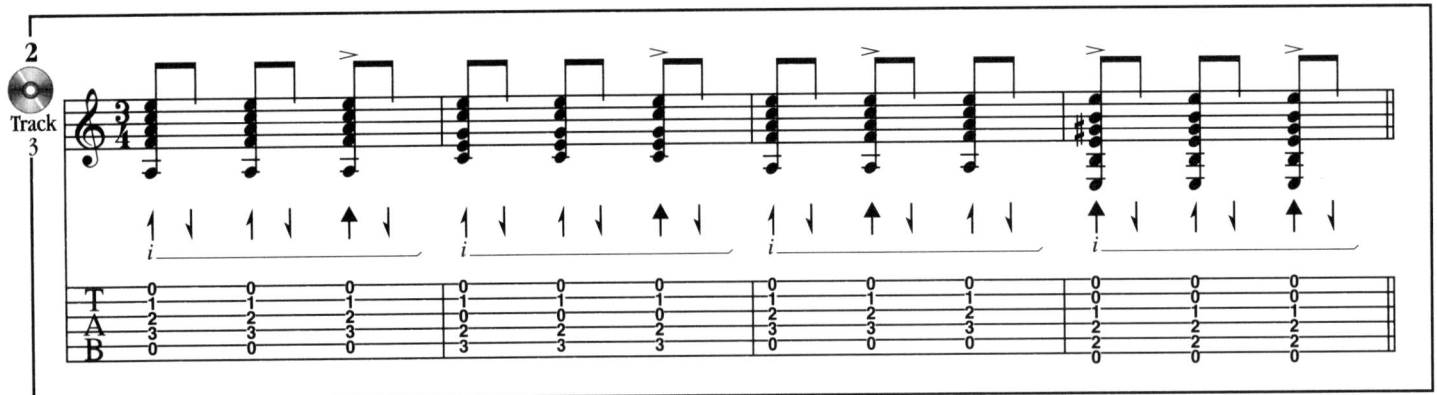

ALEGRÍAS

Next we turn to one of flamenco's most joyous expressions—*alegrías*, which is Spanish for "happiness." The emotional opposite of soleares, alegrías shares the same rhythmic structure but is played at a quicker tempo and in a major key. The alegrías in example 3 is in A Major. Note that flamenco guitarists use two fingers to play the first-position A Major chord; the tip section of the 1st finger covers the notes on both the 3rd and 4th strings (see the diagram on the right).

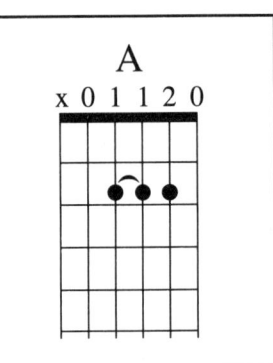

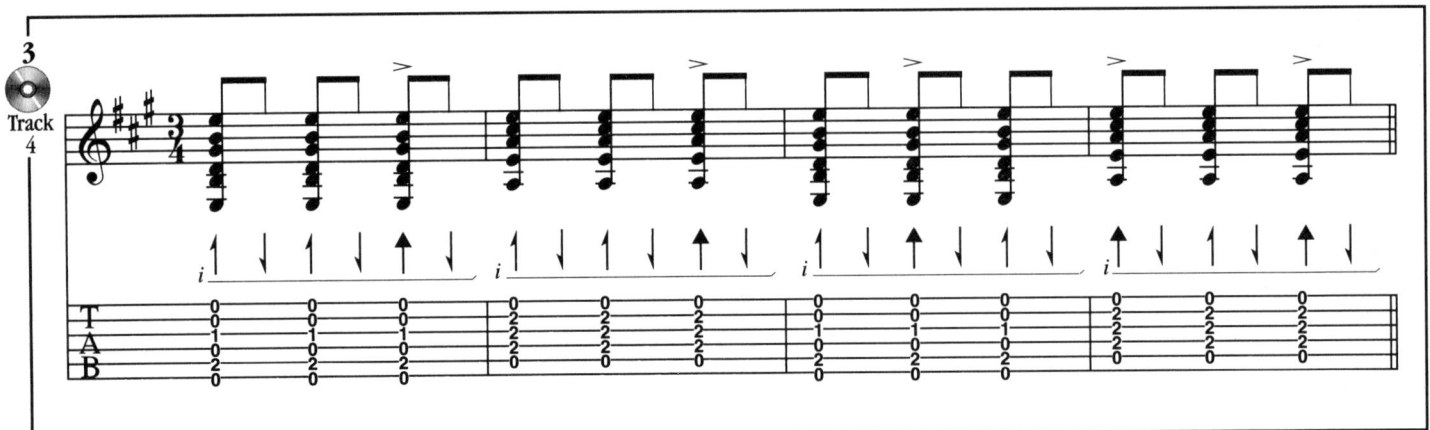

LESSON 2—FIVE-STROKE RASGUEADO

When rasgueado technique incorporates all the fingers of the right hand, it blossoms into a full language of remarkable guitar sounds and seemingly limitless rhythmic articulations. The most commonly used rasgueado, known as the Ramon Montoya rasgueado, is the five-stroke rasgueado. Four downstrokes are followed by an *i* upstroke. This rasgueado pattern is excellent for preparing the hand for other flamenco techniques.

Your ultimate goal in learning the five-stroke rasgueado is to achieve complete independence of the fingers, resulting in evenly spaced rasgueado strokes, each heard individually. The hand is held in a steady and comfortable position, the thumb resting on the 6th string for balance and support. In the starting position, the fingers are folded in toward the palm in a loose fist. The fingers are held close to the strings with the fingertips just behind the 6th string (even though the thumb is resting there). Each finger, beginning with the *e*, then *a*, *m*, and *i*, is fully extended in a series of completely independent downstrokes. Each finger completes its stroke *before* the next finger moves. The five-stroke pattern is completed by an upstroke with *i*, which brushes (rather than hooks) the strings.

The Five-Stroke Rasgueado Pattern
e down
a down
m down
i down
i up

Starting position

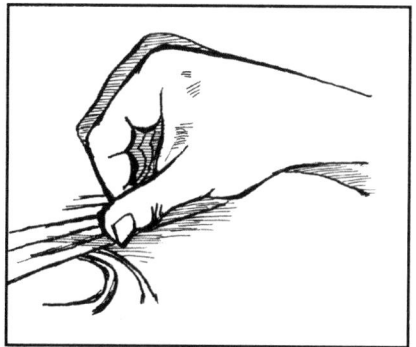

1. Downstroke with *e*

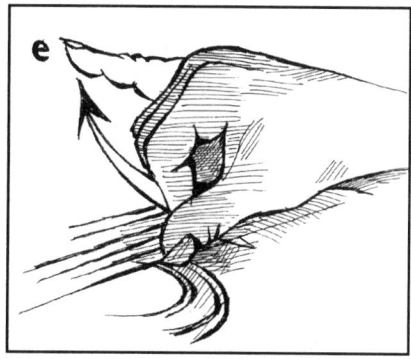

2. Downstroke with *a*

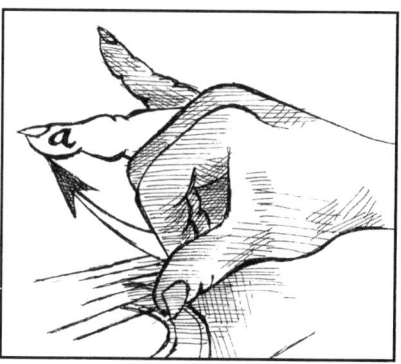

3. Downstroke with *m*

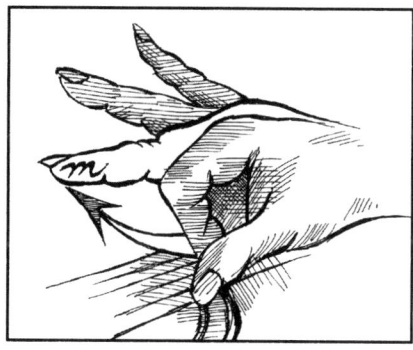

4. Downstroke with *i*

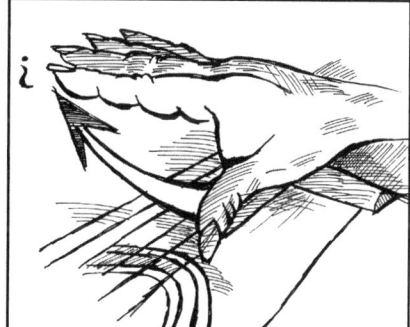

5. Upstroke with *i*

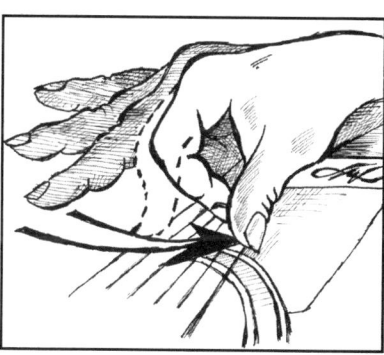

Remember that in beginning to learn five-stroke rasgueados, you will be training new muscles. Be sure to keep your hand supple and relaxed during your initial attempts at this technique. Never force or strain (it can't be mentioned often enough). As you practice five-stroke rasgueados, your finger independence and extension will develop—but this only takes place over time.

Next, we will introduce five-stroke rasgueados into the compáses of soleares and alegrías. Here, the five-stroke pattern will be used to articulate even, quintuplet rhythms (one beat divided into five equal parts). This technique will be indicated in the notation as follows:

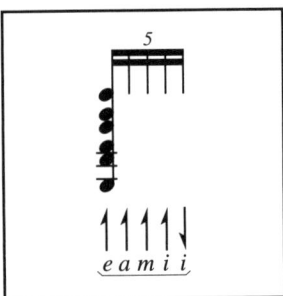

In example 4, a five-stroke rasgueado precedes each accented beat. Notice how the accents now stand out in stark contrast to the more fluid rasgueados.

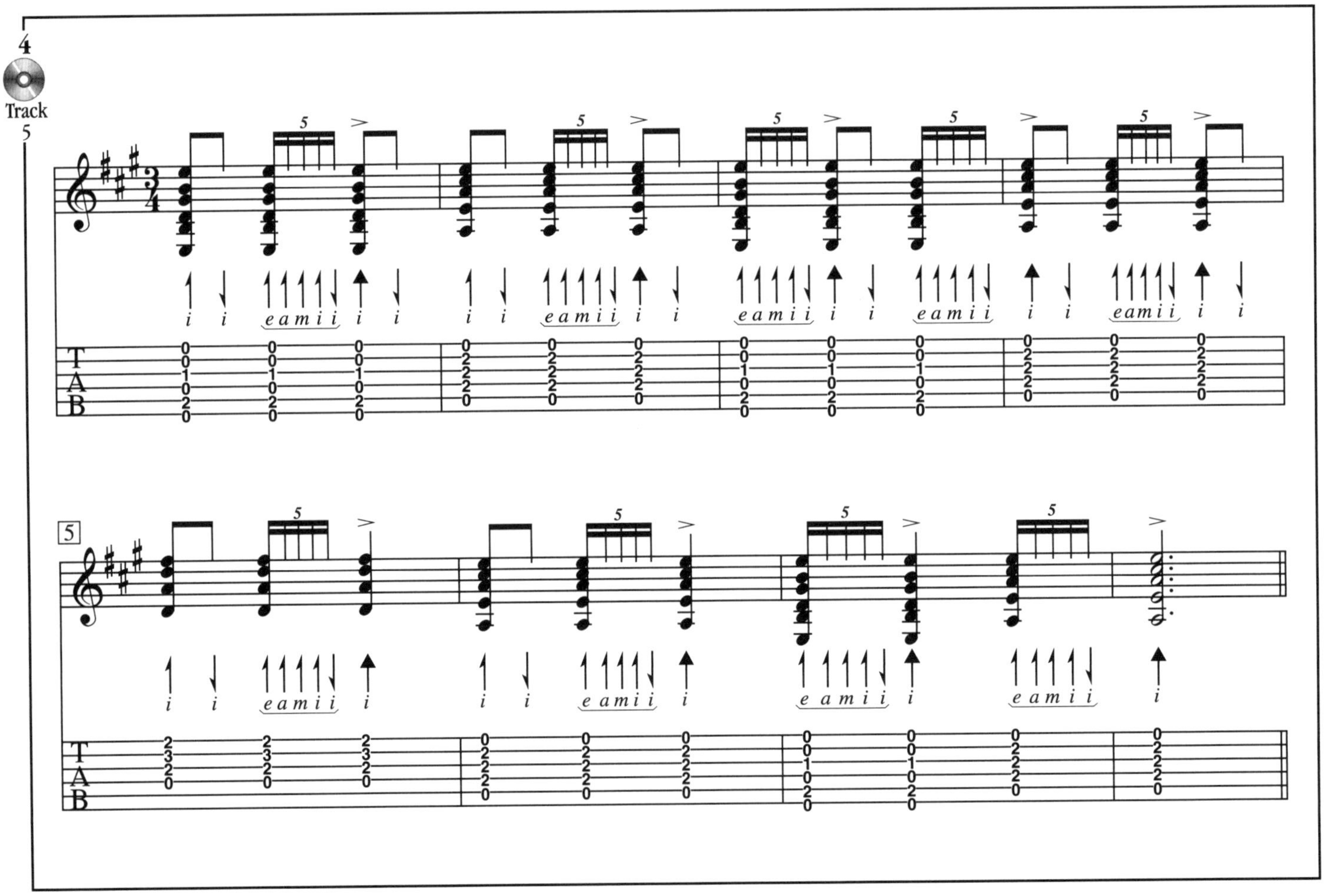

156   *Guitar Atlas: Volume 2*

Flamenco dancers often lead into each accent with a volley of machine-gun-like *taconeo* (heelwork). The effect is very dramatic, like a giant wave cresting and then breaking. Guitarists create a similar effect by leading into accents with multiple rasgueados. The desired effect is achieved when there are no perceptible pauses between the rasgueados or the accented beats.

Here, continuous rasgueados lead into every accented beat of the soleares compás. When mastered, this rasgueado pattern reveals the true *aire* (spirit) of soleares. Note that the second compás of this example has the added spice of chord alterations, which are typical of the style.

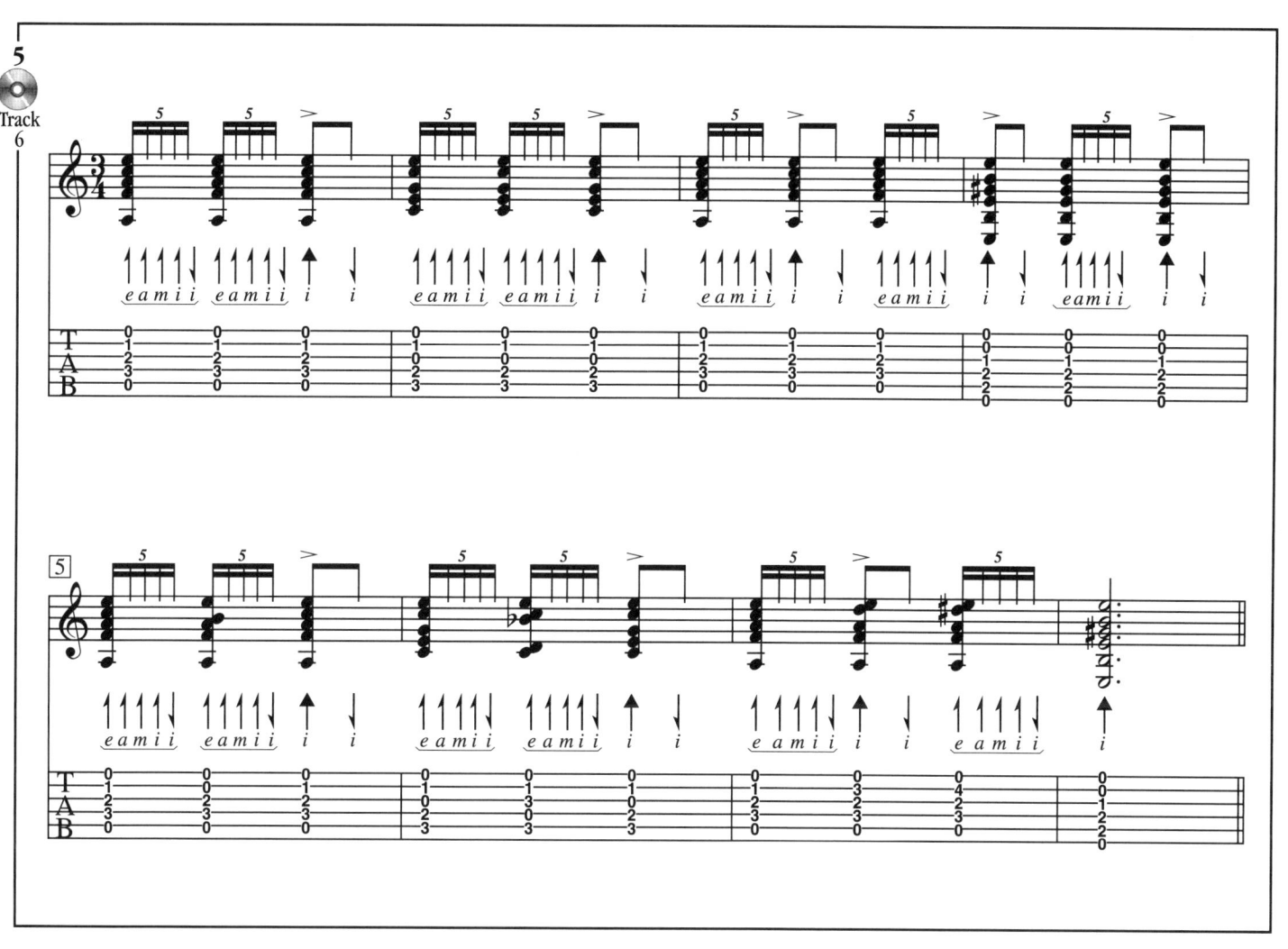

LESSON 3—THE GOLPE AND *a-m* STROKE

This lesson explores two particularly strong rhythmic expressions of flamenco guitar: the *golpe*, a percussive tap on the face of the guitar, and the *a-m* stroke in which two fingers are used as one.

GOLPE

The golpe is used to mark time during silences or to mark accents. It is used alone or adds greater emphasis to accented notes and chords. Golpes are played with the *a* finger in a motion that is almost identical to a *rest stroke* (the technique in which the striking finger lands on the adjacent lower string), except that the fingernail (not the pad of the finger) contacts the face of the guitar about one-half inch from the 1st string. Golpes are played with very little force. The face of the guitar is very responsive and produces a clear golpe sound with the lightest touch. Overly loud golpes can sound very ugly—or worse, break your fingernail!

| ♩ with x = Golpe alone in standard music notation |
| x = Golpe in tablature or in standard notation when combined with other notes or chords |

Important Note: Never play golpes on a guitar that does not have a golpeador (tap-plate or top-guard). Golpes will leave permanent scars on the face of an unprotected guitar.

Here is a very simple use of golpes combined with four-note chords to achieve a striking (pardon the pun) rhythmic effect.

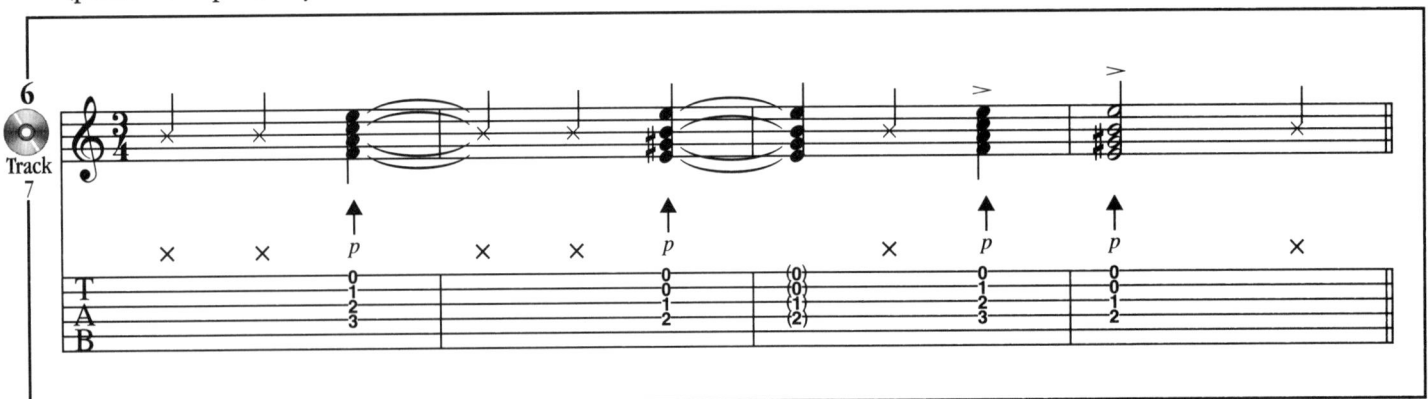

It is important to note that golpes, like much else in flamenco, are often added on the spur of the moment. It is unlikely that a flamenco guitarist would play the same piece twice and apply this technique exactly the same way both times.

THE *a-m* STROKE

The *a-m*, stroke is the loudest rasgueado stroke, using two fingers as if they were one, large finger. This stroke can be performed in two distinct manners.
1) With the hand held steady and the thumb resting on the 6th string, *m* and *a* are folded into the hand while *e* and *i* remain passively extended. Then, *m* and *a* are fully extended, striking the accented chord. This stroke is used for five-note chords.
2) An even stronger accent can be achieved by adding forearm rotation to the stroke. The entire hand moves, and the thumb does *not* rest on the 6th string. As *m* and *a* are folded into the hand, the wrist rotates so that you see into your palm. Then, as *m* and *a* are extended, the hand and arm turn so that by the time the stroke is completed, you see the back of your hand. This is a very loose, whip-like motion in which the hand is almost completely passive. *The looser the hand, the stronger the stroke.* Any rigidity in the hand or arm will weaken the sound.

The use of *a-m* strokes is essential to the accompaniment of the most important of all flamenco dance steps—the *llamada*.

LESSON 4—LLAMADA

In flamenco, it is the dancer who controls the length, speed, structure, and intensity of the dance. In almost every other form of dance, people dance to the music, but in flamenco it is the job of the guitarist—even if you're Paco de Lucía himself—to follow the dancer. An important aspect of the relationship between the flamenco dancer and guitarist is the dance step known as *llamada* (the call). In soleares, alegrías, and bulerías, large sections of the dance are brought to a close by the llamada, often marked with a strong, stamped 1–2–3, and always ending on the 10th beat of the final compás.

Just as the llamada is a specific step, there is specific music used to accompany it. Following are examples of llamadas por soleares* and alegrías. Both use strong *a-m,* strokes to match the strength of the dancer's heelwork. The golpe on the 4th beat of each example is very typical in llamada accompaniment.

Llamada por Soleares

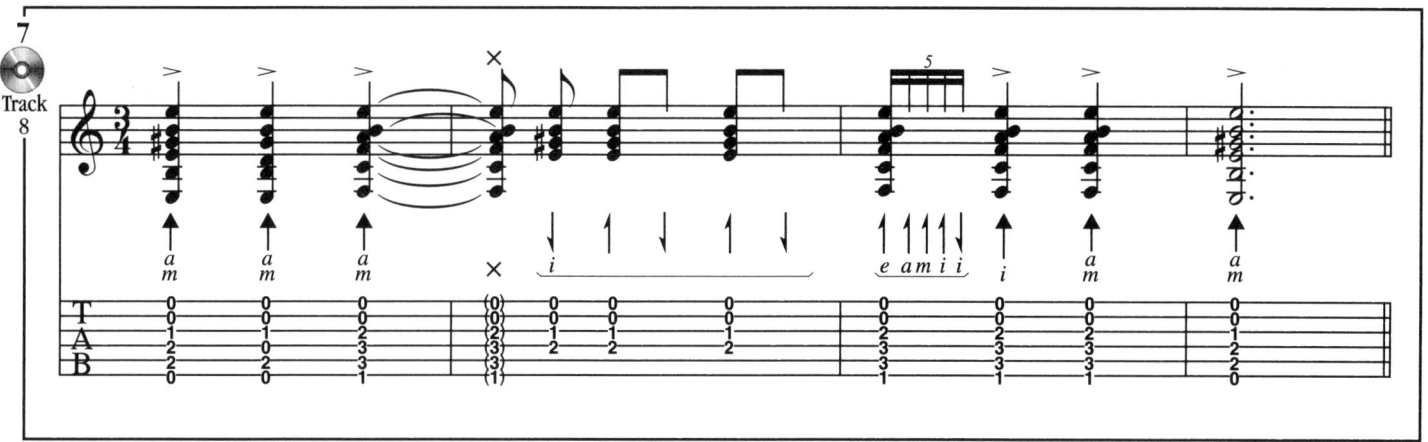

Llamada por Alegrías

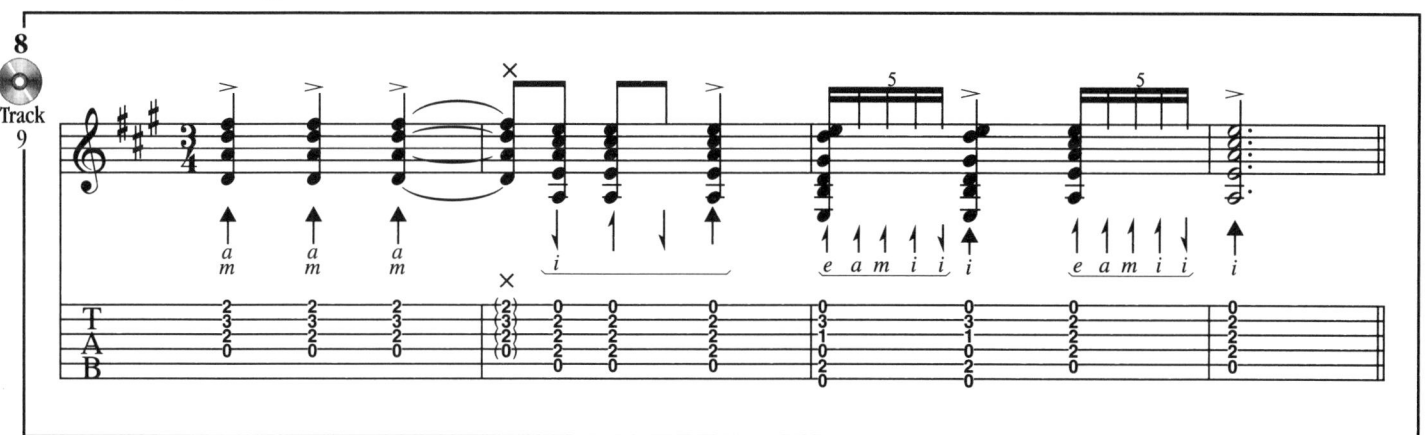

* "por Soleares" means "in the rhythm of Soleares."

Guitar Atlas: Flamenco

LESSON 5—EXTENDED COMPÁS SEQUENCES

In the following examples, the chord progressions, techniques and musical structures introduced so far are combined and expanded into longer compás sequences. These are typical patterns used to accompany the flamenco dance.

COMPÁS Por ALEGRÍAS

The repeated slur from F# to E on the 1st string of the A Major chord is a very typical ornament in alegrías, and certainly underscores the joyous aire of the dance. Another traditional touch in this example is the tasty use of chromaticism (non-chord tones) on the E7 chord of the fourth compás (fourth system), and the sliding D and A chords of the fifth compás.

160   *Guitar Atlas: Volume 2*

½CI = Half barre (three strings) at the 1st fret
CII = Barre at the 2nd fret

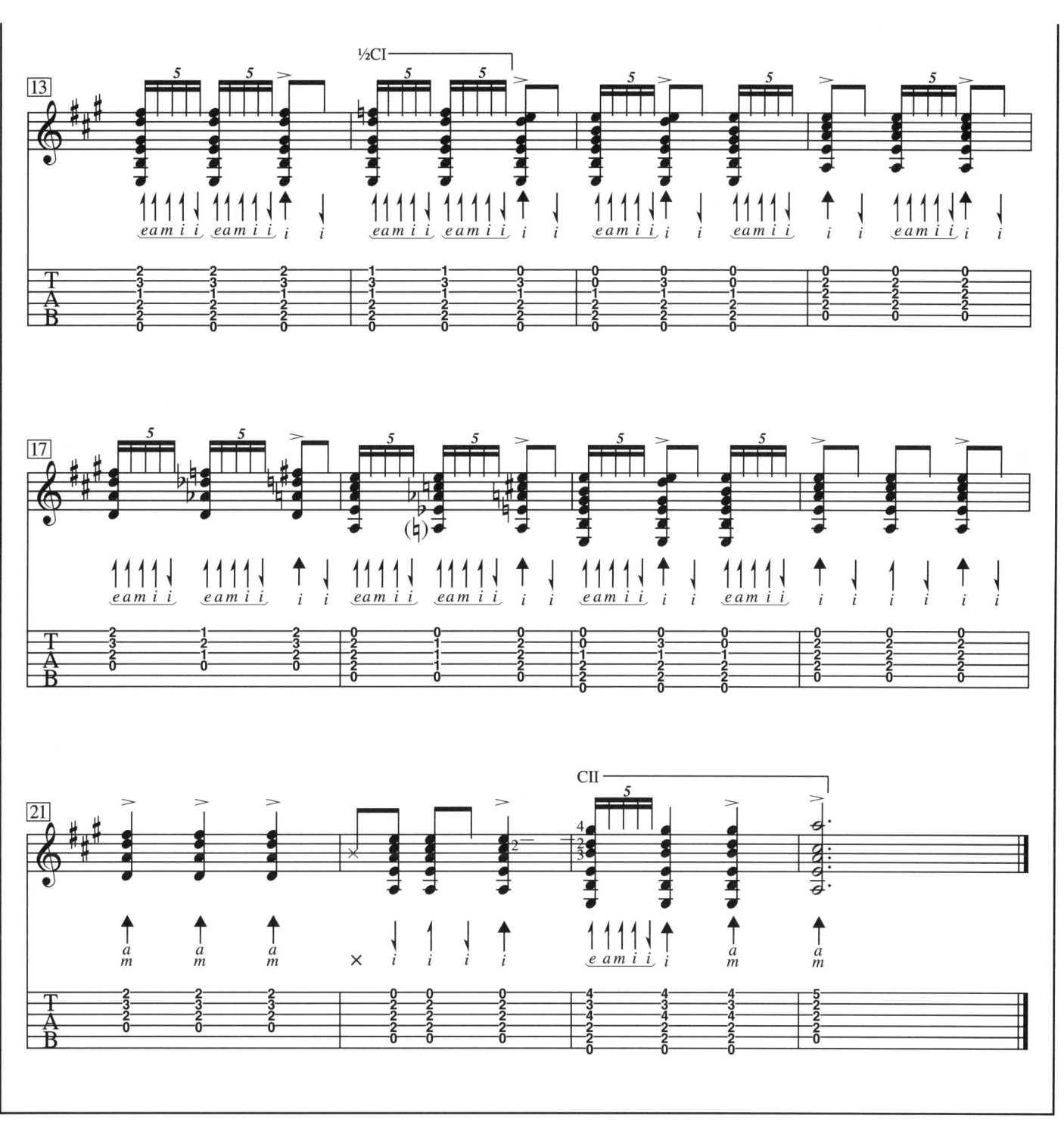

Guitar Atlas: Flamenco

THE REMATE

As in example 9, the use of slurred ornaments adds authenticity and character to the compás sequence in example 10. You'll notice that three of the compáses in this example end with arpeggio figures instead of rasgueado on the 10th, 11th and 12th beats. This typical manner of ending a compás is called the *remate*, which literally means "re-kill," a rather gruesome term borrowed from bullfighting. Each flamenco form has its own distinctive remate that is its signature.

Note that both soleares and alegrías always end on the 10th beat of the final compás.

LESSON 6 —BULERÍAS

Bulerías is the most firey and exciting of flamenco dances. It is also the fastest version of the 12-beat compás derived from soleares. To reflect the faster tempo bulerías is written as a compás of 12 eighth notes rather than 12 quarter notes.

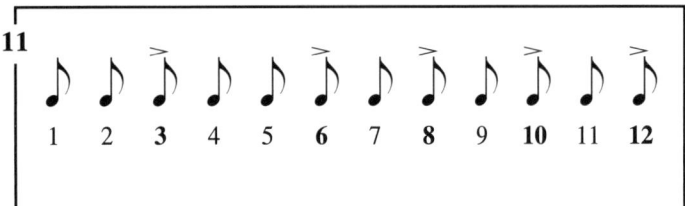

When seen in beamed eighth notes (example 12, below), readers with classical training will agree that the origin of this accent pattern (used for soleares, alegrías and bulerías) becomes more apparent.

HEMEOLA AND FLAMENCO COMPÁS

Examples of Spanish music dating back hundreds of years demonstrate alternating measures of two and then three accents. When expressed in eighth notes, both $\frac{3}{4}$ and $\frac{6}{8}$ will have six eighth notes per measure; the difference between the two meters is the placement of their accents:

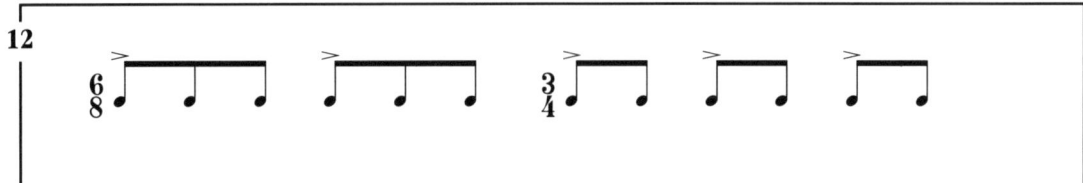

Alternating measures of $\frac{6}{8}$ and $\frac{3}{4}$ time is called a *hemeola* rhythm. Examples of this rhythm are heard in the opening bars of Rodrigo's *Concierto de Aranjuez*, in Gaspar Sanz's *Canarios*, and Leonard Bernstein's "America" from *West Side Story*.

The hemeola rhythm in soleares, alegrías and bulerías is not quite so obvious because the 12-beat phrase begins after the downbeat, and ends on a downbeat.

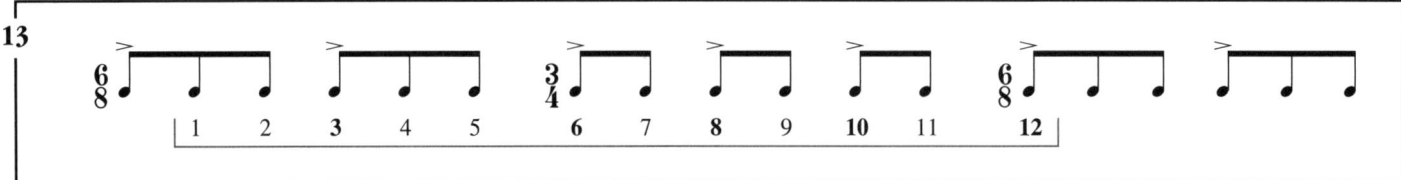

Unfortunately bulerías is very confusing to learn when written "correctly" in alternating bars of $\frac{6}{8}$ and $\frac{3}{4}$ time. To express bulerías rhythm as clearly as possible, we will portray each 12-beat compás as one bar of 12 eighth notes. We will not, however, use a $\frac{12}{8}$ time signature, since that does not accurately represent what is happening in the bulerías, either. There will be no time signature at all. Each eighth-note beat will be beamed individually, and the counting of each compás (with accents in bold) will be written below the TAB staff.

PLAYING BULERÍAS

In the Phrygian mode (such as from A to A with an F Major key signature—A–B♭–C–D–E–F–G–A), the most important chord change is ♭II–I: two major chords, one half step apart. The bulerías in example 16 is played in A Phrygian. The II chord is B♭ Major, played in a "flamenco version" that includes the open 1st string.

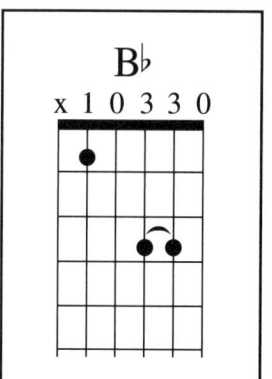

Since bulerías is played at a much faster tempo than either soleares or alegrías, the compás is expressed in much simpler beat divisions than are generally used in the slower dances. The compás of example 14, for example, simply uses golpes to mark the unaccented beats, and chords on beats 3, 6, 8, 10, and 12 are played with *i* upstrokes.

Bulerías can be easily learned if you conceive of the compás as two phrases of six beats.

14 **The First Compáse of Example 16**

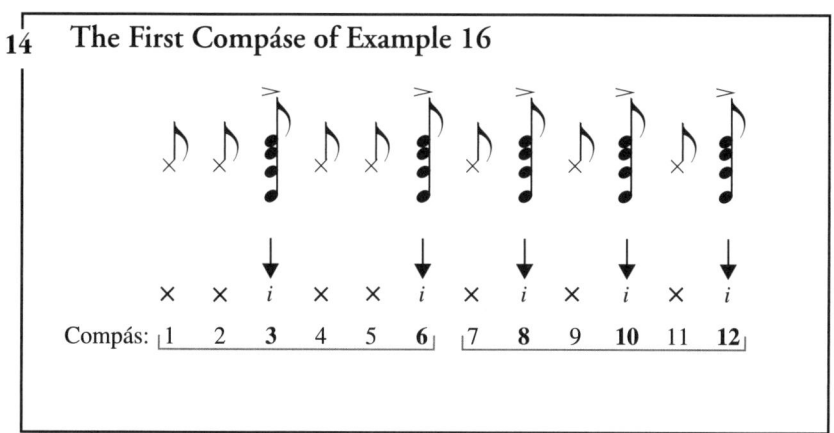

The compás below (example 15) is identical to the one above (example 14) except that the second half (beats 7–12) is elaborated upon with the use of two five-stroke rasgueados. Because of the quick tempo, one rasgueado is most often used to express two beats in bulerías. Be sure that the final upstroke of each rasgueado receives a full beat.

15 **The Second Compáse of Example 16**

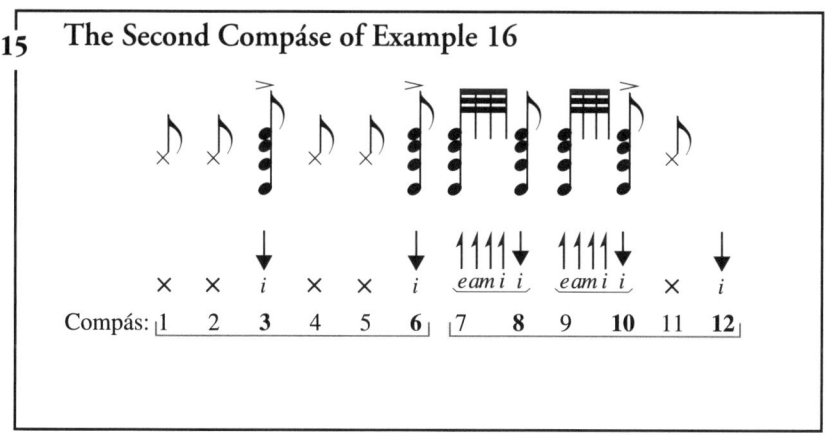

It is also important to note that a buleriás is often phrased from beat 12. Look ahead to the *Solo por Bulerías* on page 190. The fifth, sixth, and seventh compáses begin on beat 12, which is why the second and third systems have *open* measures at the end (no bar lines).

Guitar Atlas: Flamenco 165

Example 16 demonstrates seven different ways to play bulerías compás. These variations are very much like a vocabulary. Master each of them individually, and then begin to interchange them freely. In this way, you will become fluent in the language of bulerías.

Bulerías, like soleares and alegrías, always ends on the 10th beat of the final compás.

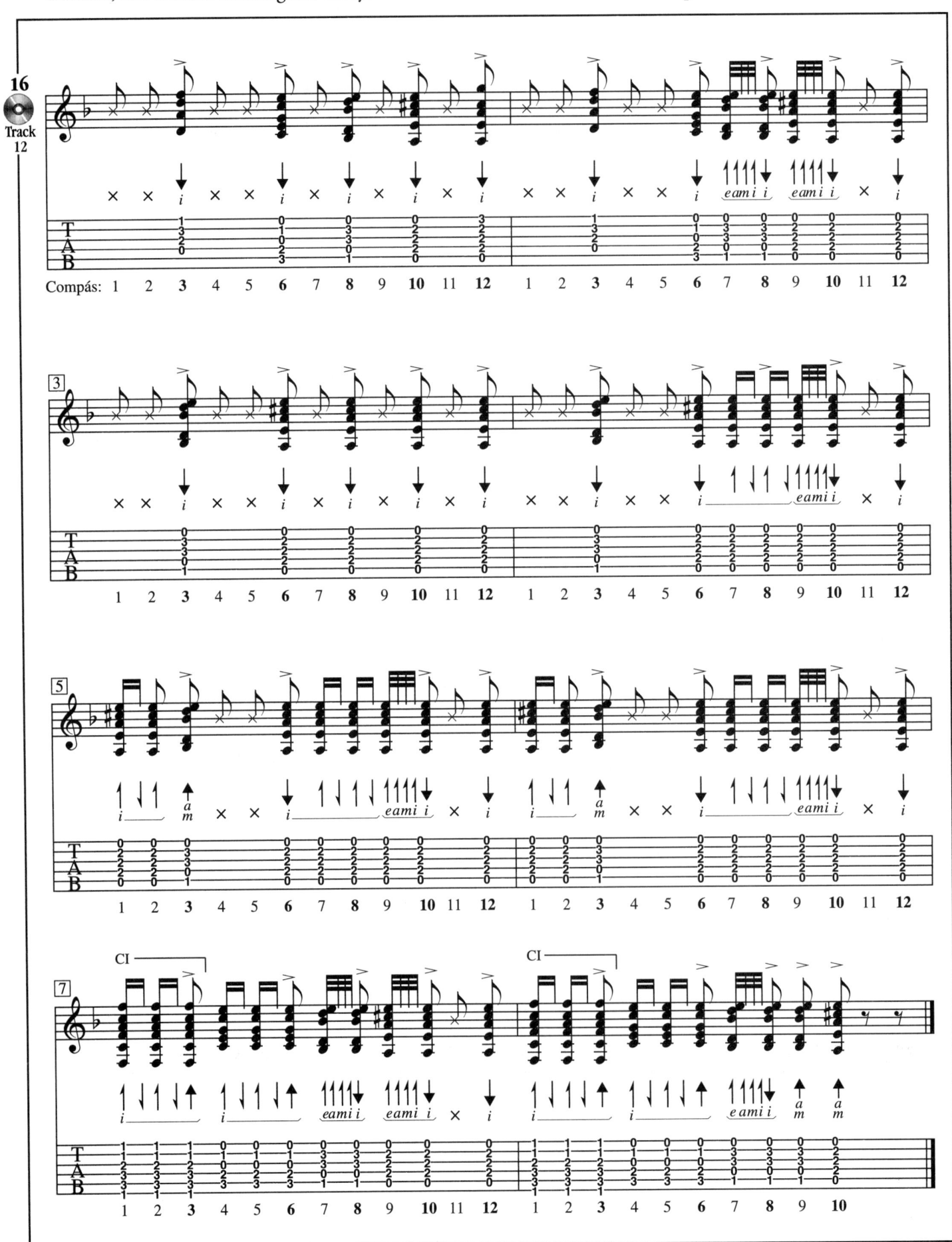

LESSON 7—OTHER FLAMENCO RHYTHMS

Soleares, alegrías, and bulerías represent one family of flamenco rhythms. Several others exist, and we'll sample some of these forms in this lesson.

LA FARRUCA

La Farruca, a folk dance from northern Spain, is in 4/4 time and the key of A Minor. Although neither Gypsy nor Andalusian in origin, flamenco artists have embraced and performed La Farruca for more than a century.

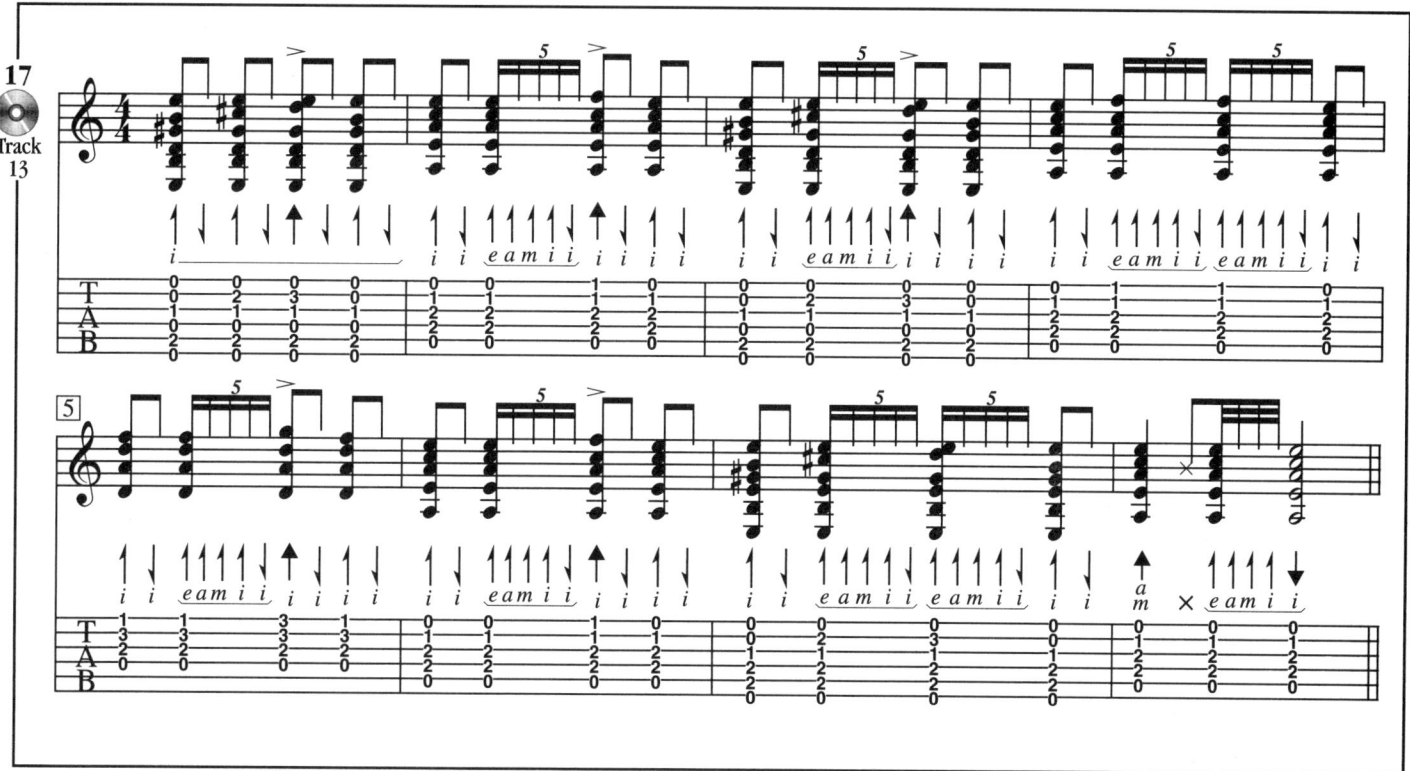

TANGOS

Tangos, by contrast, is pure Gypsy flamenco in 4/4 time and the Phrygian mode. Even this short sampling of tangos demonstrates a depth of expression La Farruca could never hope to approach. The eighth notes in this tango have a swing (uneven, long–short) feel.

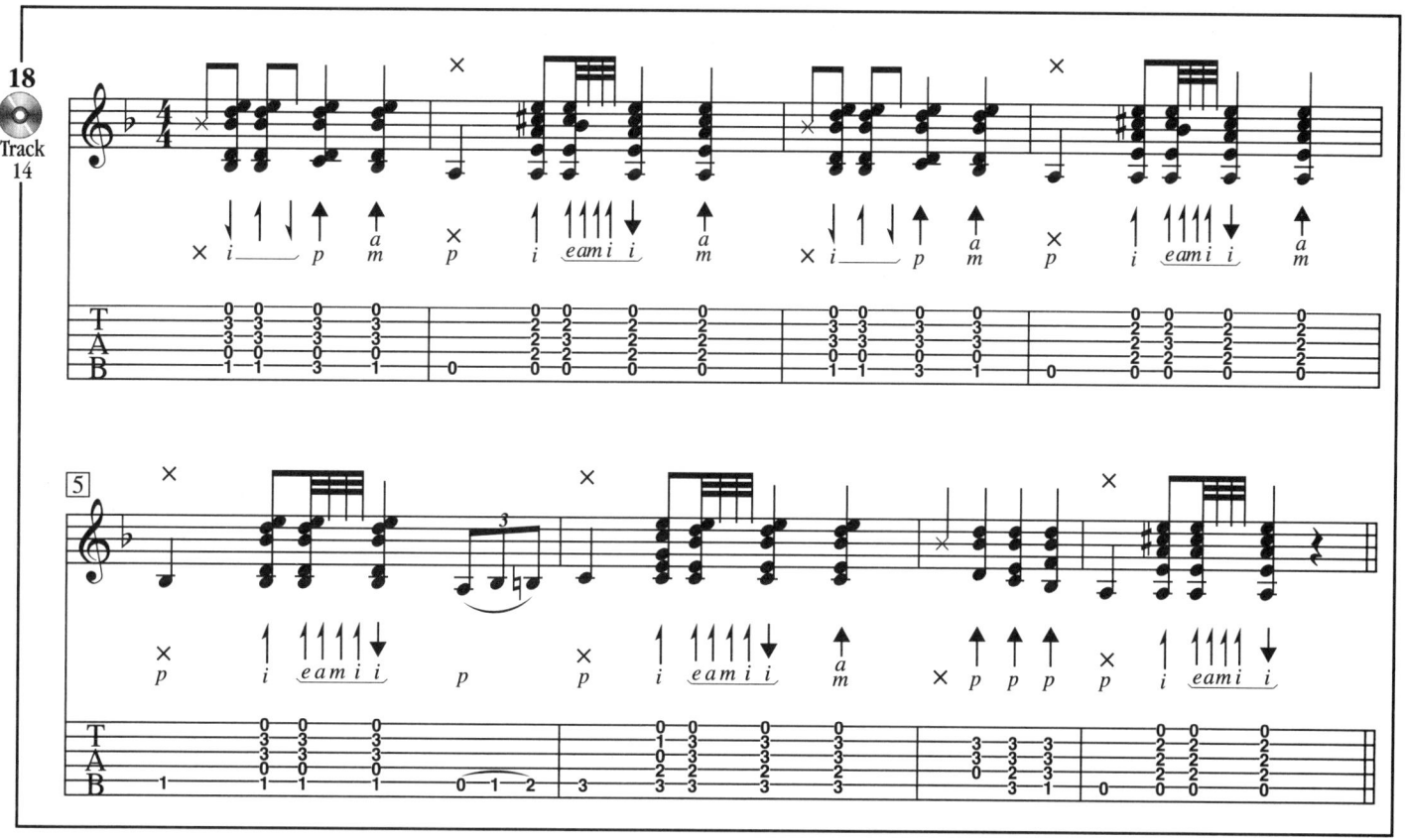

Guitar Atlas: Flamenco

FANDANGOS

Fandangos are songs and dances that date back hundreds of years to the Moorish domination of Spain. Every region of Spain—nearly every city—has its own particular version of fandangos. Some forms of fandangos are strictly vocal and never danced (see lesson 12, page 178). When danced, fandangos are very much like flamenco waltzes—in $\frac{3}{4}$ time, and almost always with a golpe on the first beat of each $\frac{3}{4}$ bar.

Verdiales

A lively dance from Malaga, *verdiales* is one of the most familiar and frequently imitated Spanish rhythms.

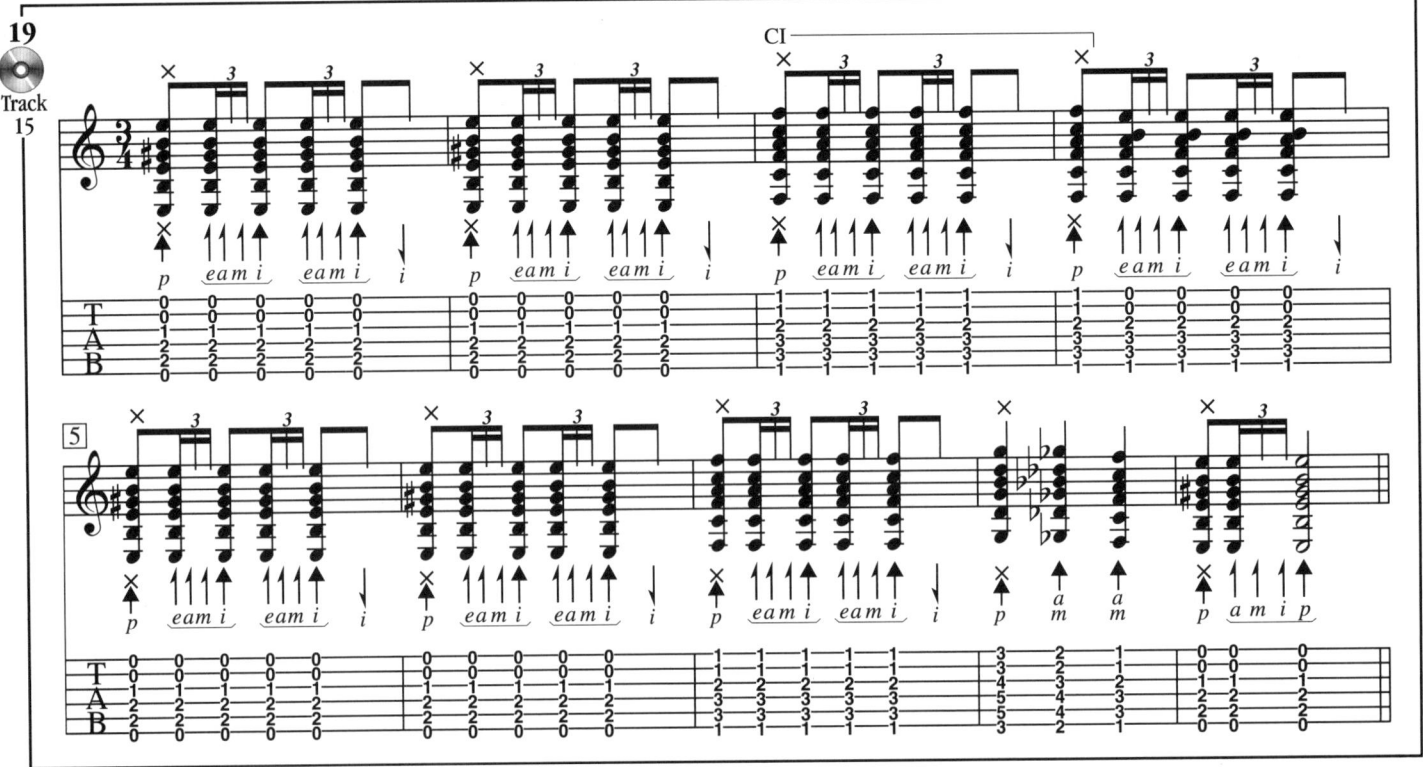

Fandangos de Huelva

Fandangos de Huelva is the most popular form of fandangos among flamenco artists. It is a more sophisticated and syncopated version of fandangos compás. Notice the use of indefinite ties to show that the chord continues to ring through the golpe.

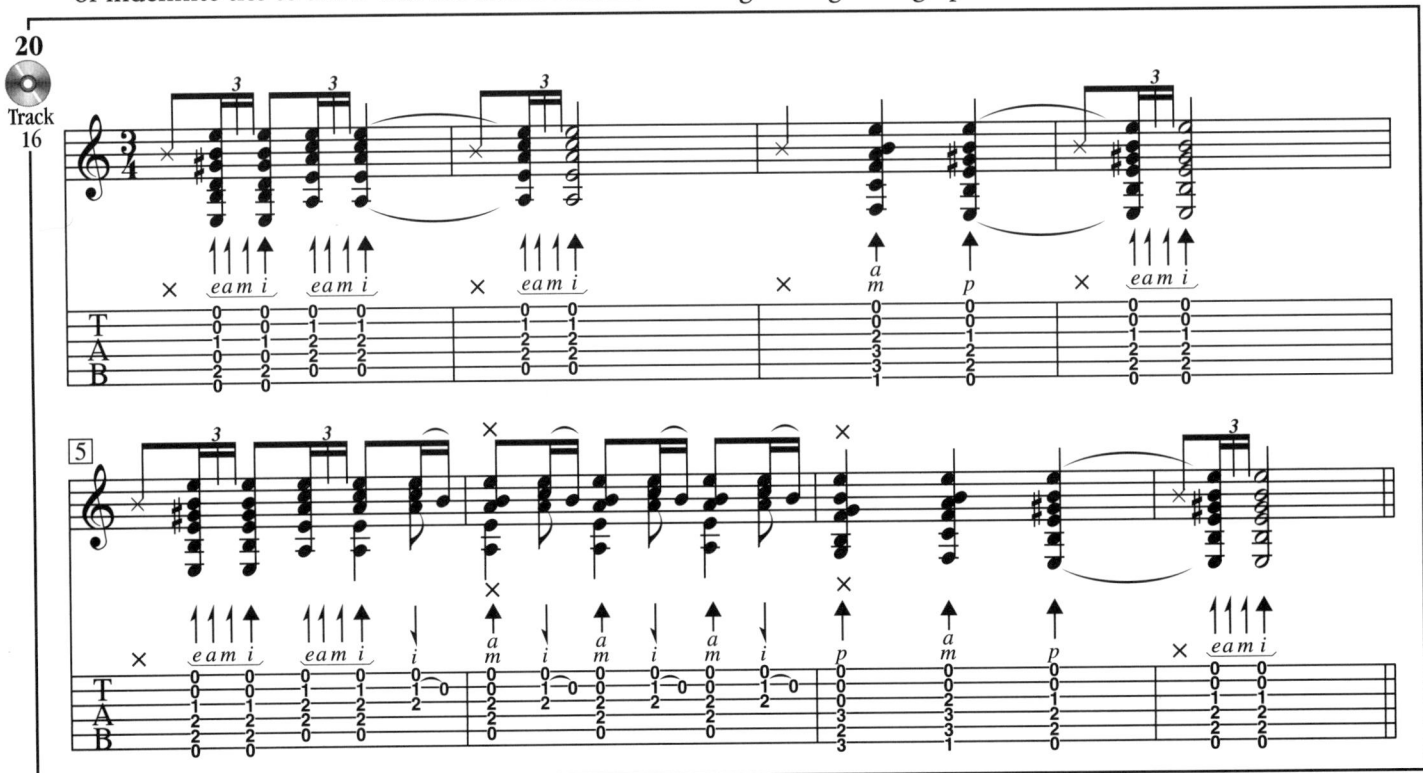

SIGUIRIYAS

One of flamenco's most profound and tragic expressions, the lyrics of *cante por siguiriyas* often question the very meaning of life. Siguiriyas has a very particular aire—a slow drag, which is never rushed and never used as virtuoso display.

The compás of siguiriyas is another variant of the hemeola rhythm. In siguiriyas, the compás begins on the second beat of the $\frac{3}{4}$ bar and is counted as five unequal beats.

Chapter 2

FLAMENCO TECHNIQUE AND THE FALSETA

So far, we've only expressed flamenco compás through the use of rasgueado. In a sense, this mirrors flamenco history—the earliest role of the flamenco guitarist was to strum chords in dance accompaniment. But as the art of flamenco guitar developed, the musicians began to assert themselves by incorporating melodies into their chordal accompaniments. The melodies are called *falsetas*.

The earliest falsetas were undoubtedly simple melodies played with the thumb, but in the hands of the great flamenco guitarists of the 20th century, the art grew to encompass the full range of guitar technique. All manner of scales, arpeggios and tremolos were used to realize the full harmonic potential of the guitar fingerboard.

In this chapter, we'll explore the flamenco approach to these techniques and demonstrate how they are used to express both the rhythm and the emotional content of various flamenco forms.

LESSON 8—THE THUMB IN FLAMENCO

In the early history of flamenco, tiny small-voiced guitars were most often played in outdoor settings. To have their falsetas heard under these conditions, early flamenco guitarists developed the thumb technique of *apoyando* (rest stroke). While in most respects, the right-hand techniques of both classical and flamenco guitar are identical, a subtle but profound difference between the two is the use of apoyando thumb technique. Most classical guitarists rarely play rest strokes with the thumb, whereas in flamenco almost all thumb strokes are played apoyando. The flamenco hand position favors apoyando thumb work, a more arched wrist and more emphasis on hand and arm weight in the playing than is generally used in modern classical guitar technique.

The following examples explore various uses of apoyando thumb strokes, especially in combination with *i* free strokes. In these falsetas, allow the thumb to fall effortlessly yet weightily from string to string. Use gravity rather than force to play these falsetas.

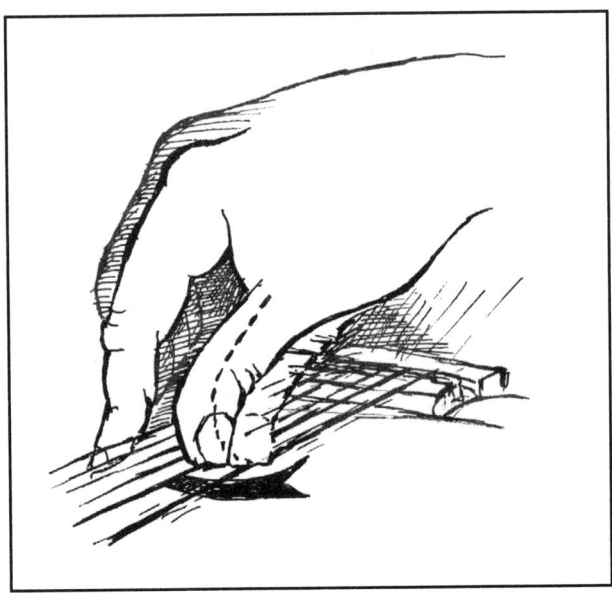

Rest stroke with p.

POR SOLEARES

This falseta is very similar to the rasgueado compás in example 5, but expressed with *p–i* technique. The arpeggios on the first beat of each bar are played by gliding *p* from string to string until the high note of the chord, which is played free stroke with *i*. This technique produces a stronger arpeggio than is possible with *p–i–m–a* free strokes. The second compás of this example seems a repeat of the first until it is interrupted in beats 6 through 9 by a bass melody in ♩. ♩ rhythm. Bring out this melody with very strong apoyando thumb strokes.

Ramon Montoya was one of the earliest flamenco virtuosos. He was born on November 2, 1880. Though born in Madrid, faraway from Andalucia, he developed the ability to play flamenco so well that by the time he was 14, he was employed in a Madrid cafe to accompany cantaores *(singers)*. His virtuosity grew as fast as his fame. He began recording in about 1910. He was active as a performer until about 10 years before his death in 1949.

Guitar Atlas: Flamenco

POR ALEGRÍAS

Here, a simple bass melody in a triplet rhythm is played with thumb rest strokes. The open 1st string is a *pedal tone* (a sustained or continually repeated note) played with *i* free strokes. Interspersed within this pattern are flowing melodies played with as many slurs as possible. This is another very important aspect of flamenco guitar style that will be explored in many upcoming examples.

LESSON 9—ARPEGGIO FALSETAS

Ramón Montoya was most likely the first flamenco guitarist to play *p–i–m–a* arpeggios. His recordings document seemingly limitless arpeggio patterns on chord progressions covering the entire fingerboard. The importance of thumb apoyando carries over into arpeggio falsetas, the vast majority of which have arpeggio patterns accompanying apoyando bass melodies, as in example 24.

ESCOBILLAS POR ALEGRÍAS

Escobillas is a very important section of the dance alegrías in which the dancer displays spectacular heelwork. Escobillas means "brushes," describing a particular dance step. Example 24 is the most traditional accompaniment to escobillas. The melody is played entirely with apoyando thumb strokes.

172 *Guitar Atlas: Volume 2*

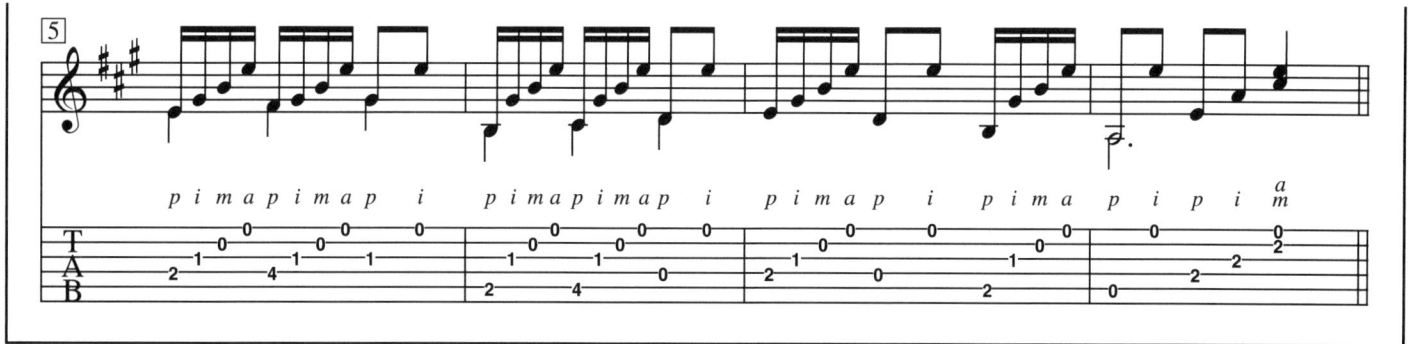

POR SOLEARES

This example demonstrates two different versions of the most traditional of all soleares falsetas. In the first and second measures of both compáses, the 1st and 3rd fingers remain in place throughout the entire measure; the melody is played by the 2nd and 4th fingers. In the second compás, *ligato* (slurred) melodies are added to the traditional falseta. Be careful not to rush these slurs.

Some of flamenco's most virtuosic passages can leave an audience breathless but actually are not all that difficult to play. This is illustrated in beats 7, 8, and 9 of the second compás (found in the 3rd bar of example 25's second system). This spectacular lick combines a right-hand arpeggio with flowing left-hand slurs, one of flamenco's most popular and dazzling techniques. Place all fingers on beat 7, and hold them in position as long as possible throughout the measure.

Guitar Atlas: Flamenco

POR BULERÍAS

Here is the slur/arpeggio technique applied to bulerías.

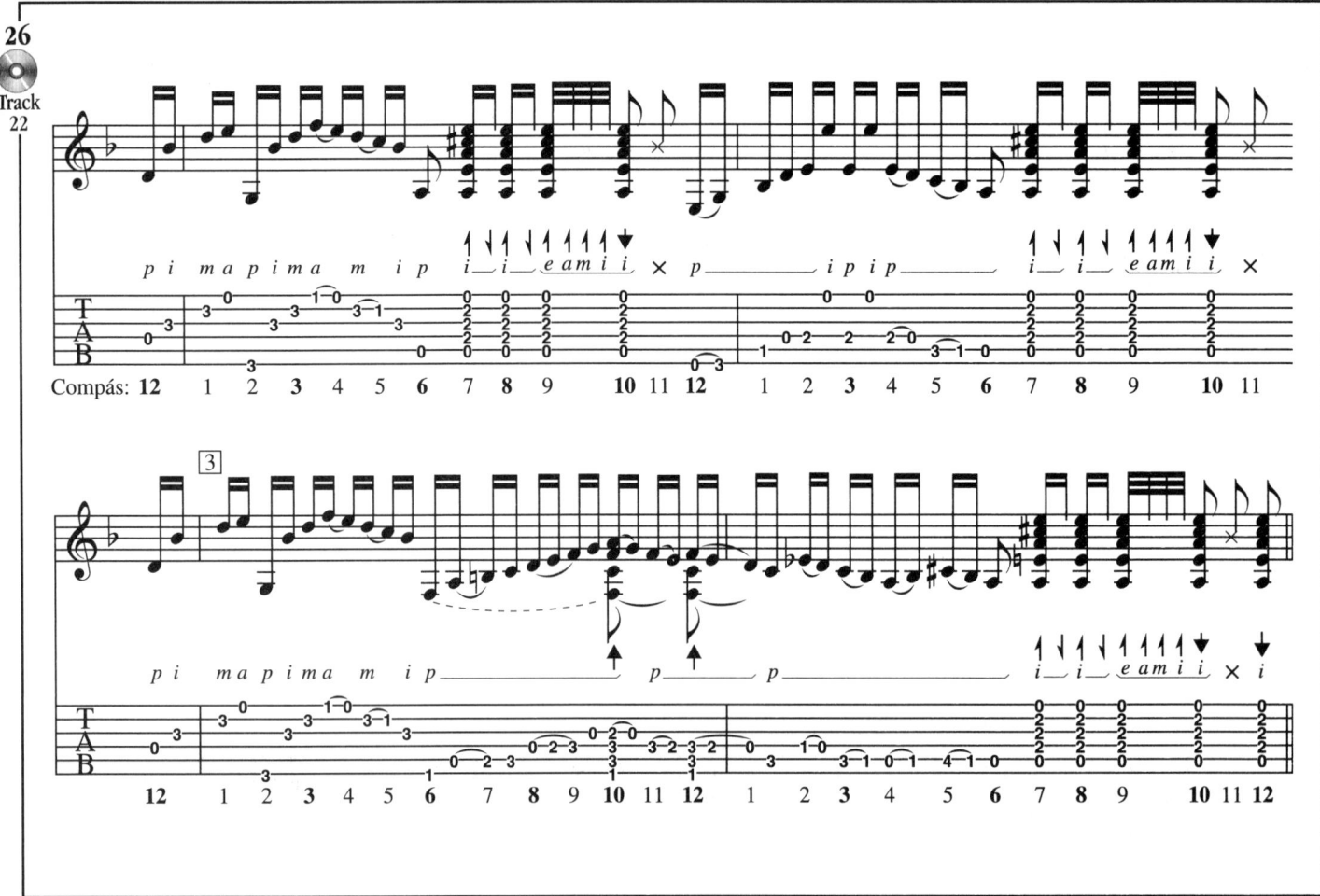

LESSON 10—ALZAPÚA

Alzapúa, a Gypsy word meaning "to raise the thumb," is another electrifying flamenco technique. Alzapúa combines a single-line bass melody with an accompaniment of downstrokes and upstrokes on chords, *all performed by the thumb*! The back of the thumbnail is used to execute the upstrokes.

Alzapúa is used in a variety of contexts and can articulate many complex rhythms, but the following three movements are the essence of alzapúa technique:

1) **Single note** — The melody note is always played apoyando. If the single note is played on the 6th string, the thumb comes to rest on the 5th.

2) **Downstroke** — The downstroke begins without the thumb lifting away from the 5th string. The downstroke is an arc-like movement in which thumb just misses the 1st string. The stroke is propelled more by forearm rotation than by thumb movement.

3) **Upstroke** — The back of the thumbnail hooks the strings in reverse of the same arc as the downstroke. Once again, forearm rotation turns the hand and thumb.

ALZAPÚA POR SOLEARES

This is the most traditional of all soleares alzapúa falsetas.

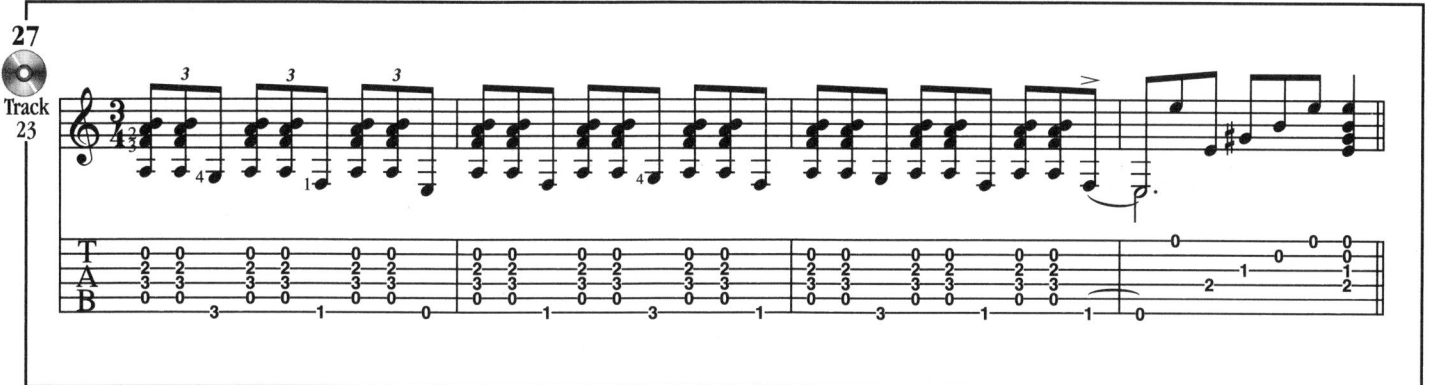

ALZAPÚA POR BULERÍAS

Here, the bass melody is elaborated with slurred figures between the down/up alzapúa strokes.

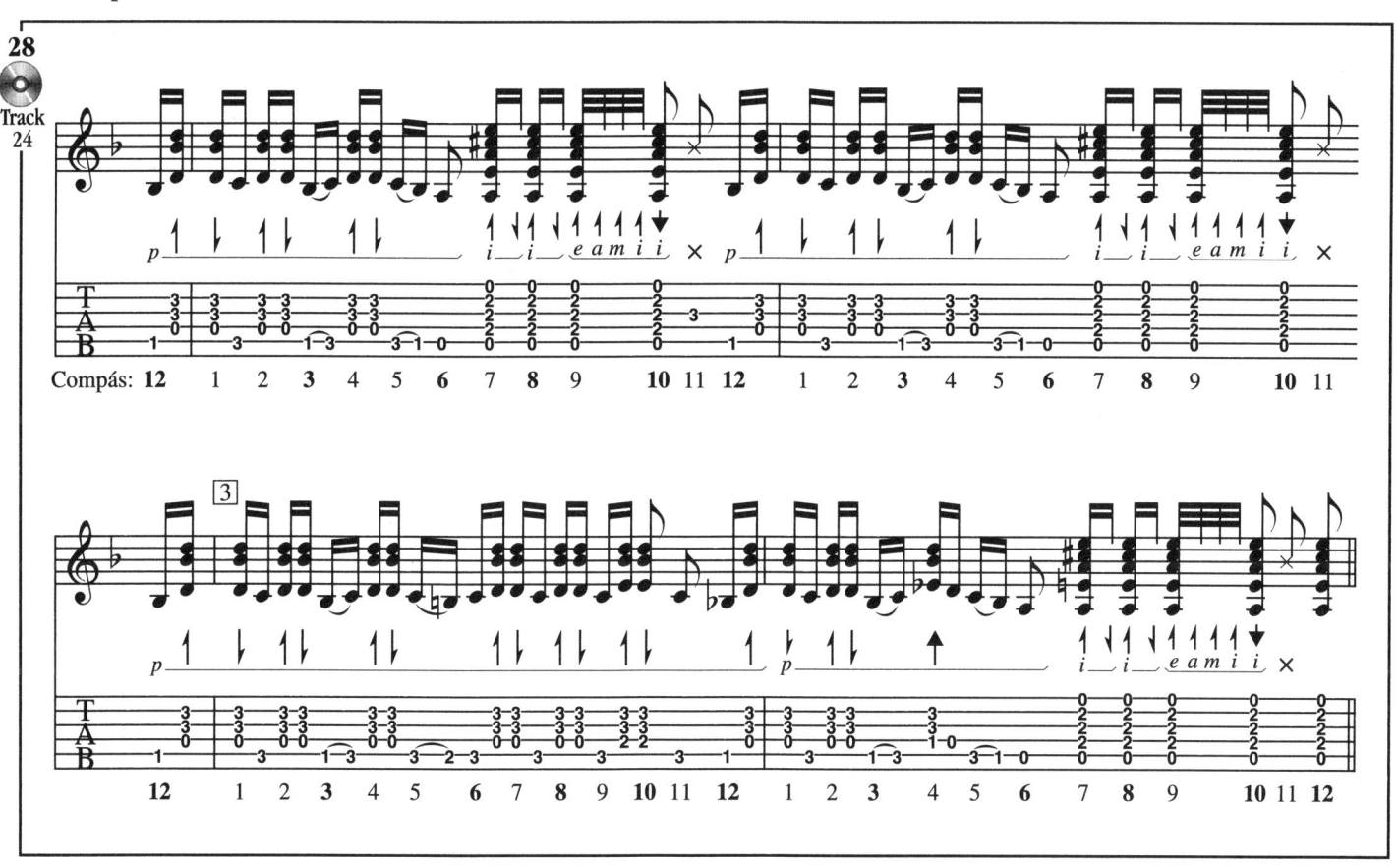

LESSON 11—FLAMENCO TREMOLO

Flamenco *tremolo* (in guitar music, this refers to rapidly repeated notes) completes the expressive range of flamenco guitar. Tremolo answers the rhythmic fire of rasgueado with the guitar's most singing melodic expression.

Using a technique borrowed from classical guitar, Ramón Montoya altered classical tremolo to create a new technique, which many listeners find even more beautiful then its classical counterpart. Classical guitar tremolo divides each beat into four equal parts: a bass note played with *p*, and three repeated melody notes played *a–m–i*. Flamenco tremolo adds an additional melody note, turning each beat into an even quintuplet fingered *p–i–a–m–i*.

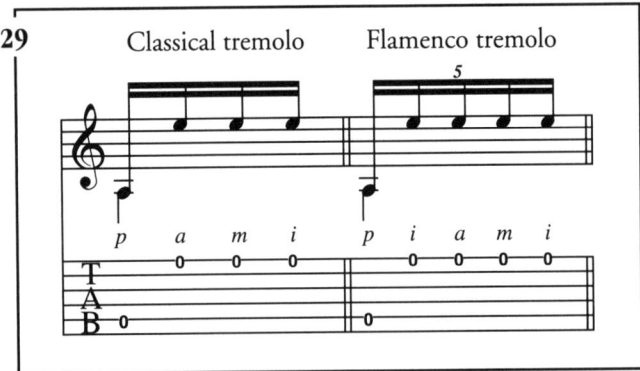

The flamenco tremolo has two distinct advantages over the classical: It can be played at a slower tempo without sounding mechanical; and its uneven beat division "fools the ear," creating its essential illusion of an unbroken melodic line.

One cannot rush mastery of tremolo. The secret to a great tremolo is not speed but *evenness*. If you are in a hurry to learn tremolo, practice very slowly. Focus your attention on dividing each beat into five exactly equal parts. Once a perfectly even quintuplet is achieved, tremolo can easily be brought up to the desired tempo.

POR ALEGRÍAS
This is a tremolo version of escobillas por alegrías.

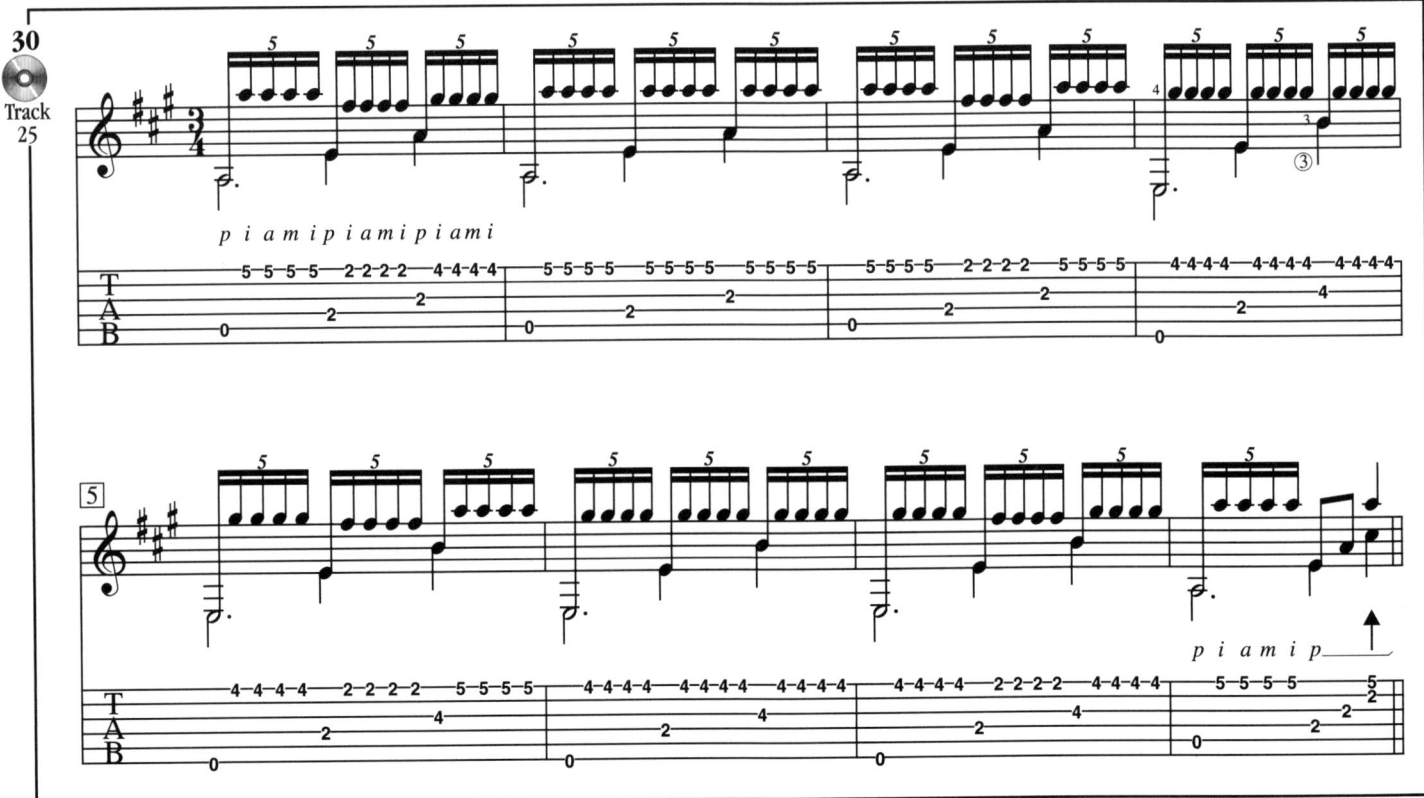

176   *Guitar Atlas: Volume 2*

POR SOLEARES

This falsetta demonstrates how effectively tremolo can be used to express counterpoint between the bass and melody lines.

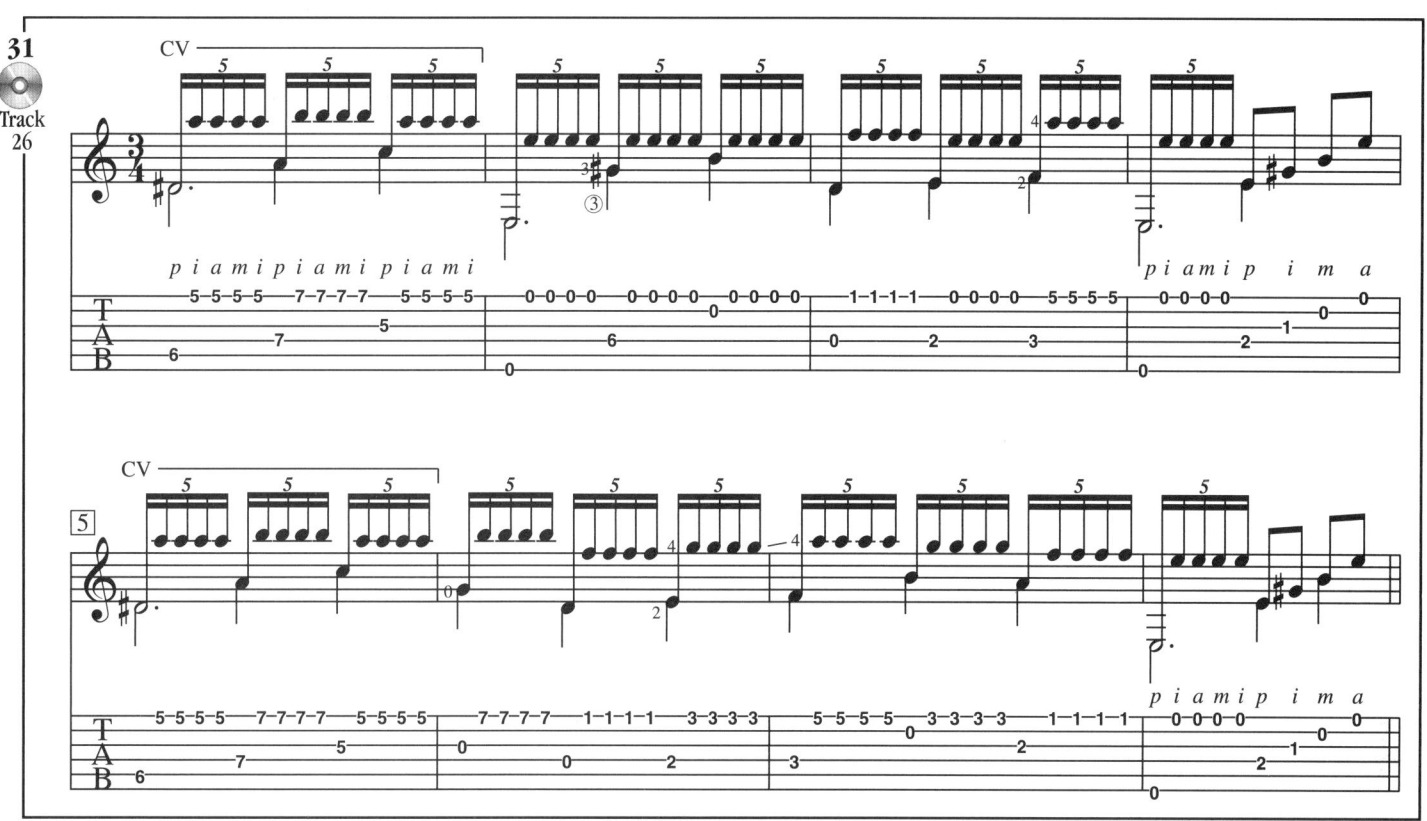

The author (far right) with Sabicas (center) and Mario Escudero (far left). If you look closely at the top of this photo, you may be able to detect where Escudero and Sabicas signed it. The photo was taken in New York City, in 1981.

Mario Escudero's *(b. 1928) compositional innovations ushered the art of flamenco into a new era. As a child, he studied classical guitar with Tarraga-disciple Daniel Fortea, and flamenco with the great Ramon Montoya. At age 14 he began touring the world as a guitarist for Spain's finest flamenco dance companies. Throughout the 1950s and '60s he enjoyed great international recognition as both a recording artist and a solo recitalist. The bold and sophisticated harmonies of his solo guitar works had a tremendous impact on Paco de Lucia, who called Mario Escudero "the Father of Modern Flamenco."*

Sabicas (Augustine Castellon) *(1912–1990) was unquestionably flamenco's greatest concert artist. His phrasing, tone, and effortless virtuosity were such that he could as easily be compared to history's great violinists and pianists as to other flamenco guitarists. A self-taught genius, Sabicas was famous throughout Spain by the time he was nine years old and was the first solo flamenco guitarist to tour the world. His concerts and the dozens of albums he recorded inspired guitarists from all over the world to learn flamenco, transforming it into an international art.*

Guitar Atlas: Flamenco

LESSON 12—TOQUE LIBRE: GRANADINAS AND TARANTAS

In Lesson 7 on page 168, we mentioned that certain forms of fandangos are strictly vocal; they are never danced and have no rhythmic constraints. Singers improvise freely on each line of the verse in what is called *cante libre* (free song). When these forms are performed as guitar solos they are called *toque libre*. These are very free instrumental fantasies in which the entire expressive range of the guitar can be fully explored and exploited.

In this lesson, we will sample two extraordinary forms of the toque libre: *granadinas* and *tarantas*.

GRANADINAS

Granadinas are the fandangos from Granada. Its verses sing the praises of this beautiful and ancient city. A guitar solo for granadinas is often played in the key of B Phrygian (with a major tonic chord) and is characterized by long passages of flowing arpeggios and tremolos. The following example includes the traditional opening: tremolo figures written as grace notes (small, quick ornamental notes) played *i–a–m–i* that are followed by thumb strokes; arpeggios on the II and I chords (C and B); a typical cadence with the slur/arpeggio technique we explored in Lesson 9 (page 173); and the characteristic slide up the 6th string from F♯ to B, which is the "signature" of toque por granadinas.

Notice that the Libre section at the end is unmeasured; there is no specific time signature. You will hear this rhythmic freedom on the CD.

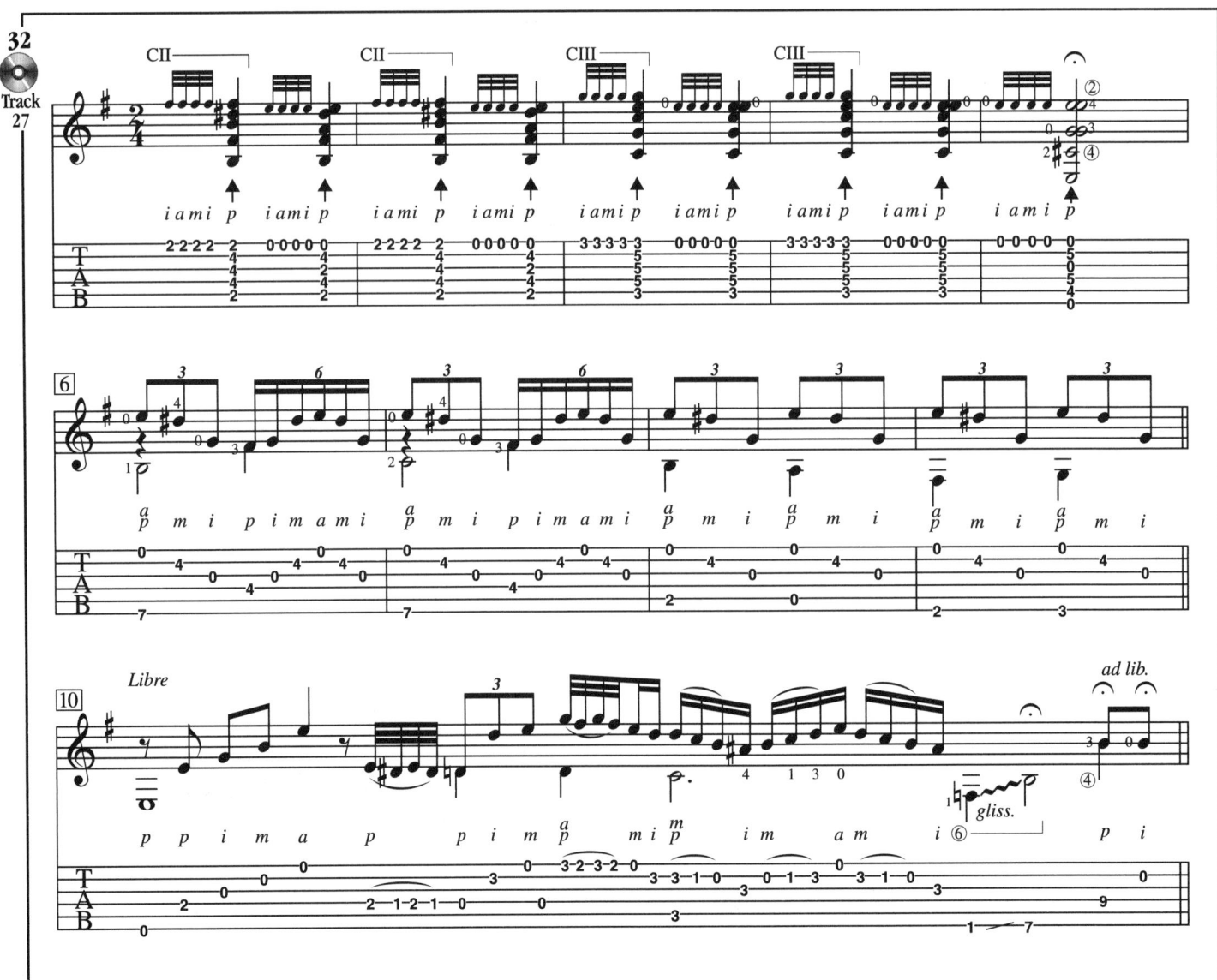

TARANTAS

Tarantas are among the darkest and most tragic flamenco expressions. The songs of the miners from the Linares region of Spain, the lyrics of tarantas describe the pain of young widows and the torture of a life deprived even of sunlight.

The anguish of the cante is reflected on the guitar with the use of the F♯ Phrygian mode. The open strings of the guitar clash with painful dissonance against the notes of the tonic F♯ Major chord. This short example demonstrates the extensive use of slurred passagework that is very characteristic of toque por tarantas. The desired effect here is not virtuoso display, but rather to have the guitar imitate the tortured wailing of the flamenco singer. These passages sound best when slurs are played as evenly as possible, allowing the notes of one string to overlap with the next. Because of the free nature of the taranta, no time signature is used.

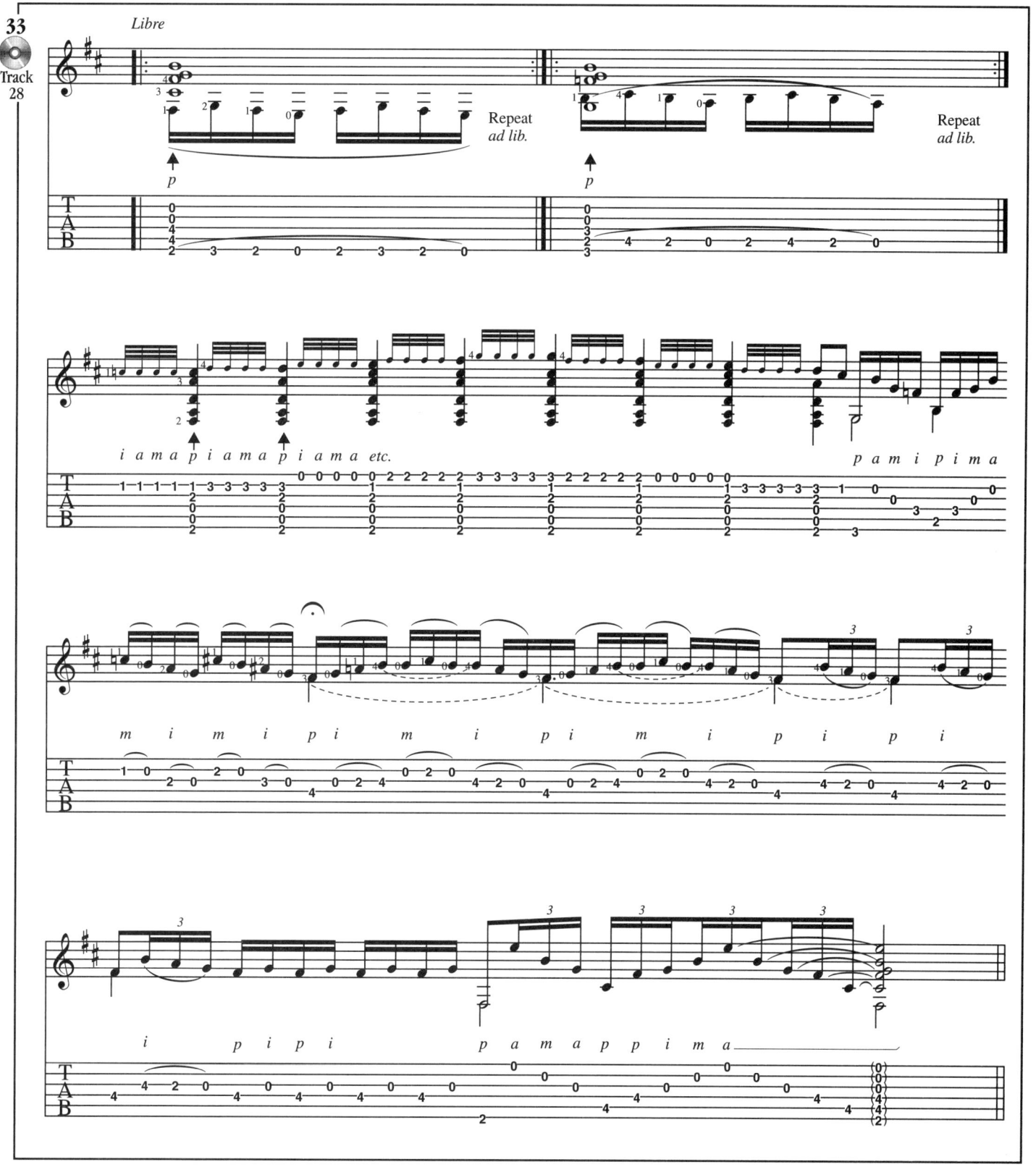

Chapter 3   CONCERT SOLOS

FINAL WORDS

As a reward for your hard work learning the material in this book, we now complete our study with three full-length solos that incorporate all the rhythms, techniques and falseta styles you have learned. Before we begin to discuss the pieces themselves, let's consider their style and place in concert guitar literature.

In recent years, I've been delighted to see such prominent classical guitarists as Pepe Romero and Elliot Fisk include flamenco solos in their concert performances. To me, this trend makes perfect sense, since flamenco solos in the style of Ramón Montoya, Sabicas, and Mario Escudero, while rooted in folk culture, were conceived for concert performance. They are exactly analogous to the folk-inspired concert guitar music of Villa-Lobos, Ponce, Barrios, and Lauro, as well as the nationalistic (quite often flamenco inspired) piano works of Albeniz and Granados.

Since concert flamenco solos are exciting, passionate, highly virtuosic, and often very serious pieces, I must frankly admit that I'm surprised more classical guitarists—who are open-minded musicians always in search of significant new repertoire—don't fully embrace and perform concert flamenco. Throughout my experience as a concert artist I've found that flamenco solos are taken very seriously by music lovers and critics alike, and that audiences just love these dramatic guitar pieces.

An additional benefit of the style is that concert flamenco solos offer far more freedom than most classical pieces. The rules of compás must always be followed, but you have complete freedom to choose the falsetas and rasgueado styles that best suit your technique and temperament, and structure them into a solo of your own design. Most professional flamenco guitarists know dozens, even hundreds, of falsetas for every flamenco form. In concert, they will often draw upon this arsenal and spontaneously create new pieces composed of many carefully rehearsed falsetas they may have been playing for years.

The most important goal in performing a concert flamenco solo is to communicate the essential aire—the emotional character—of the song or dance on which it is based. Thus, your soleares should sound serious and reflective, your alegrías joyous, and your bulerías firey and exciting. In the following solos, you will find much that is familiar, but always slightly changed from the original falsetas or compás patterns you encountered earlier in this book. If some falsetas seem too difficult for your technical level, feel free to use the easier versions you learned earlier. Also, feel free to change the order of the falsetas, delete, or add material at will. Then share the thrill of flamenco guitar with your friends and with your audiences.

SOLO POR SOLEARES

picado = Flamenco scale technique. Alternate *i* and *m*.

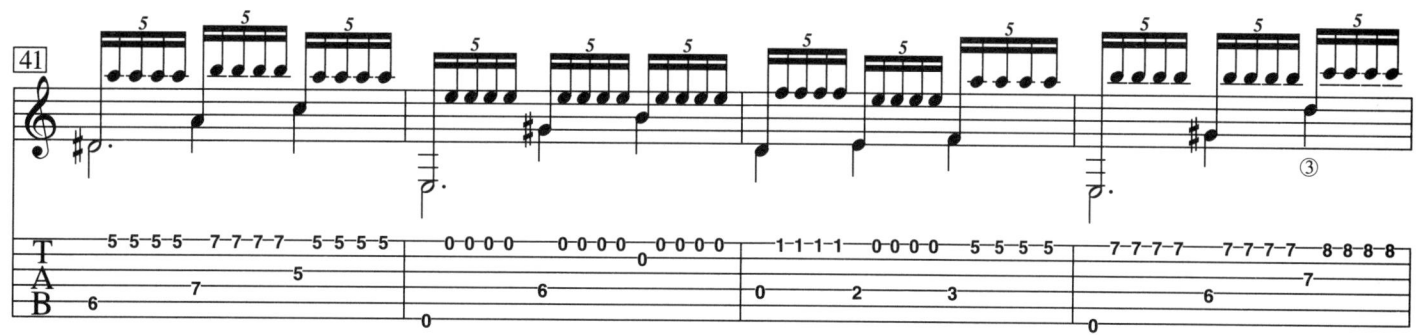
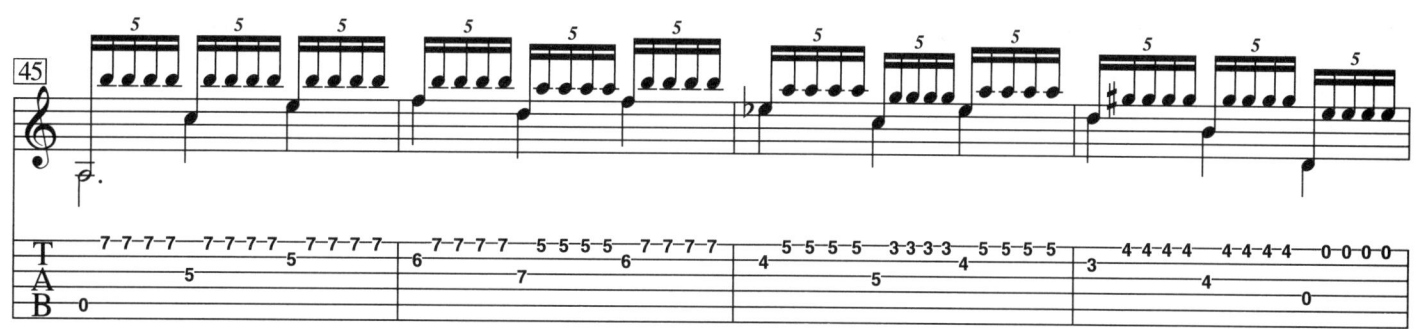
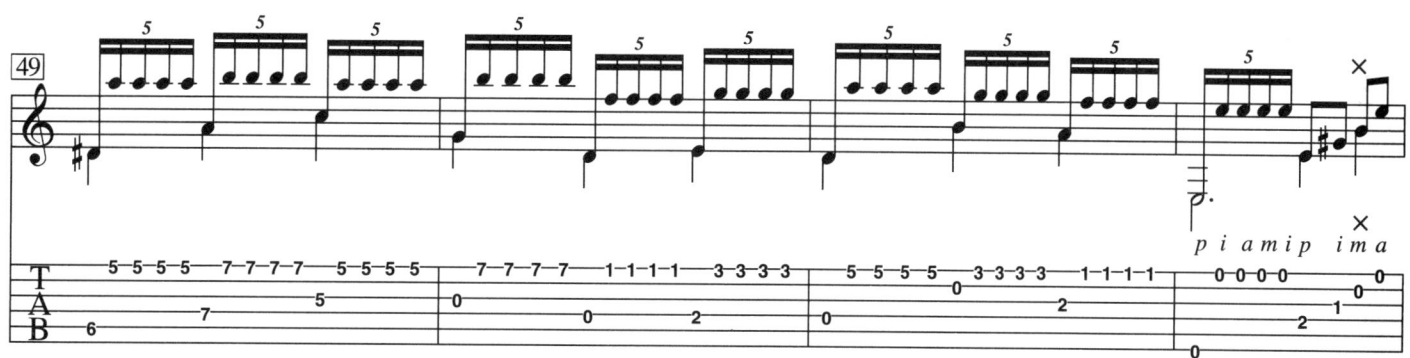

Guitar Atlas: Flamenco

SOLO POR ALEGRÍAS

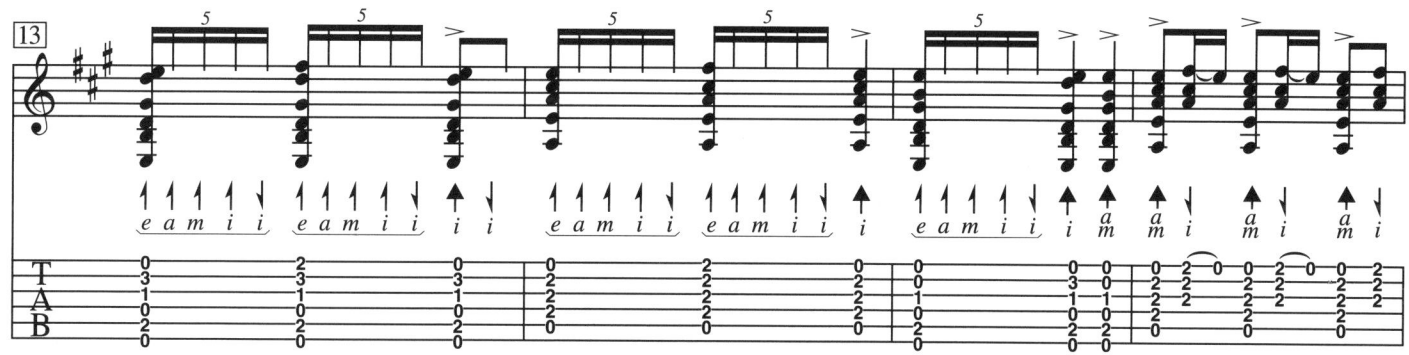
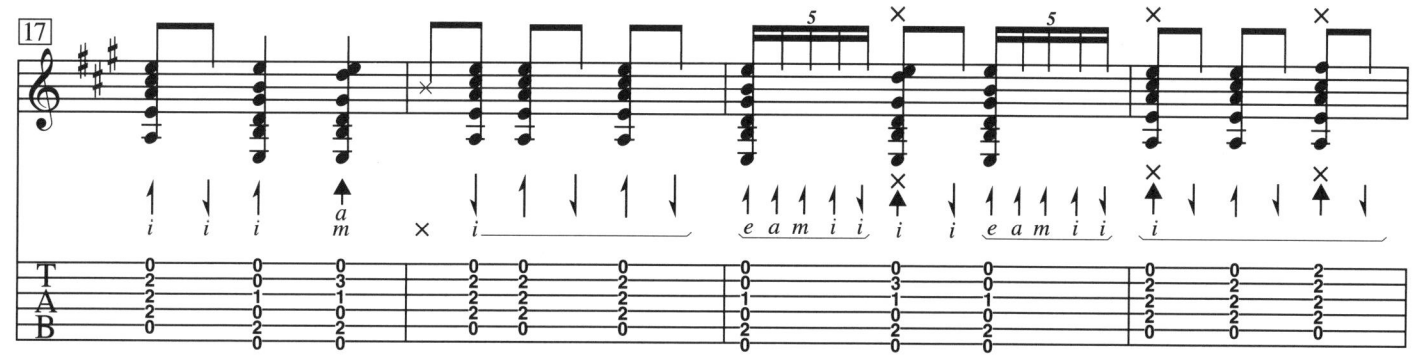

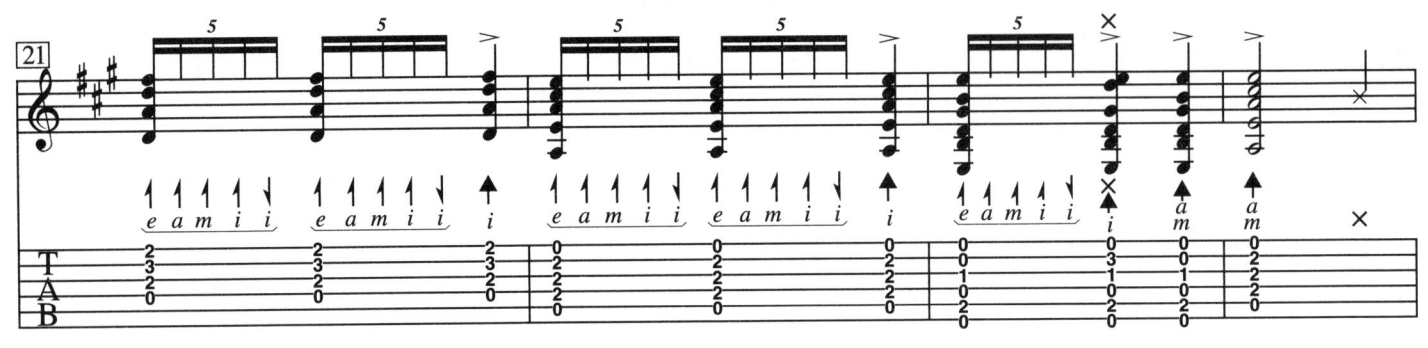

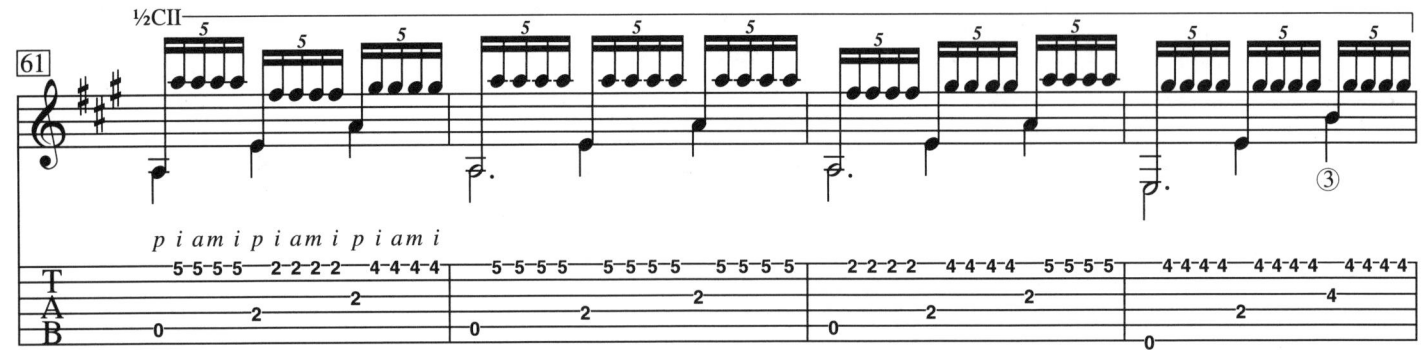
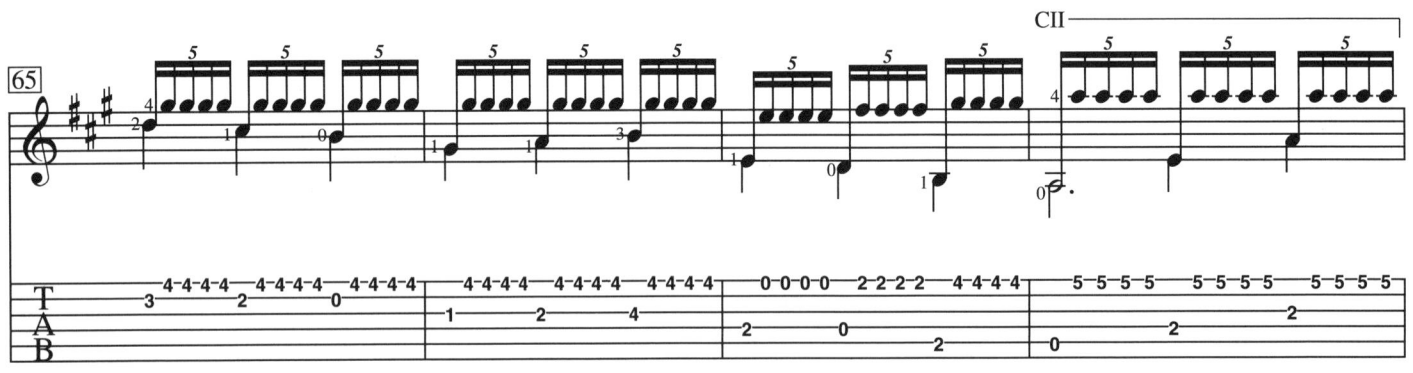
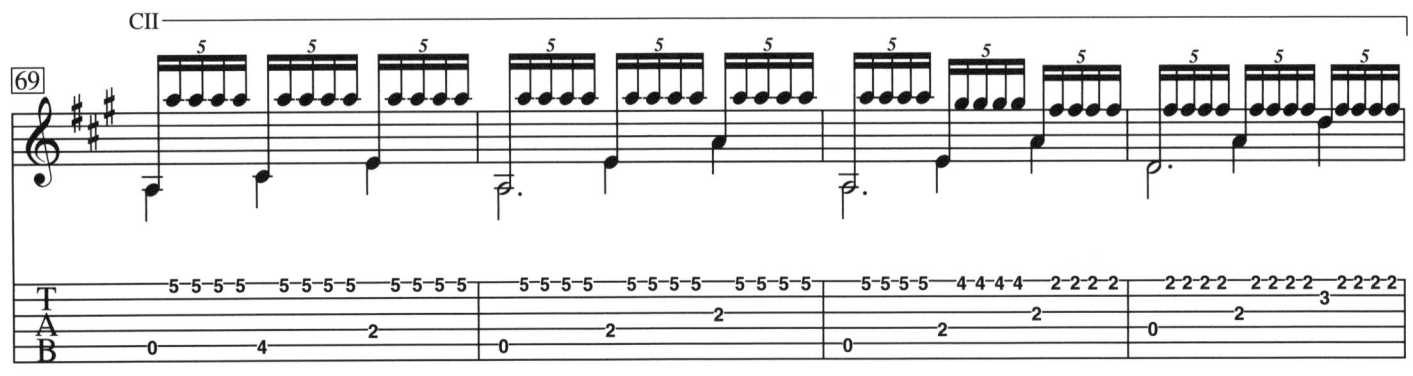
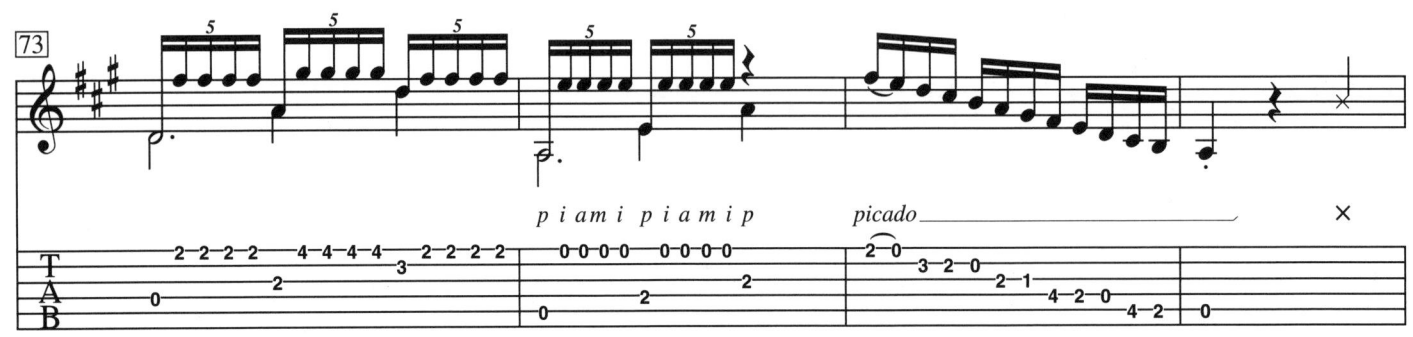

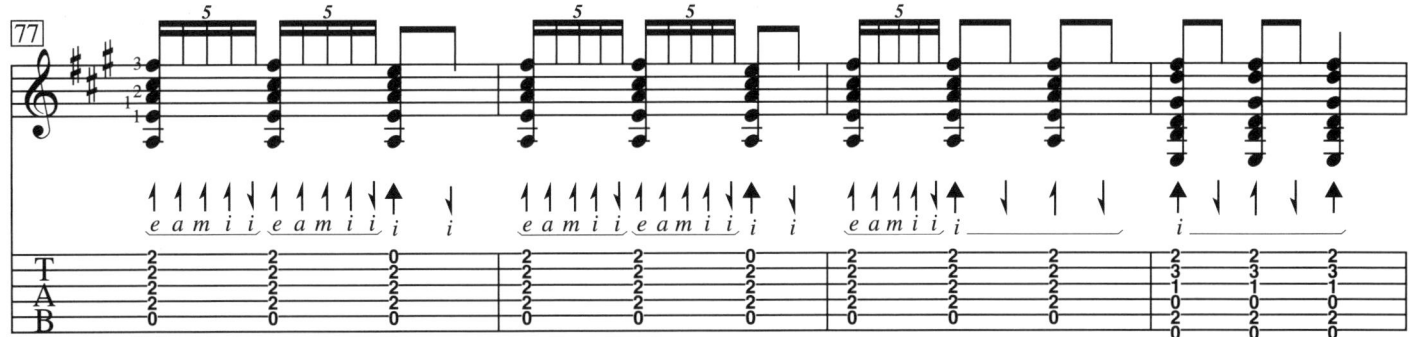
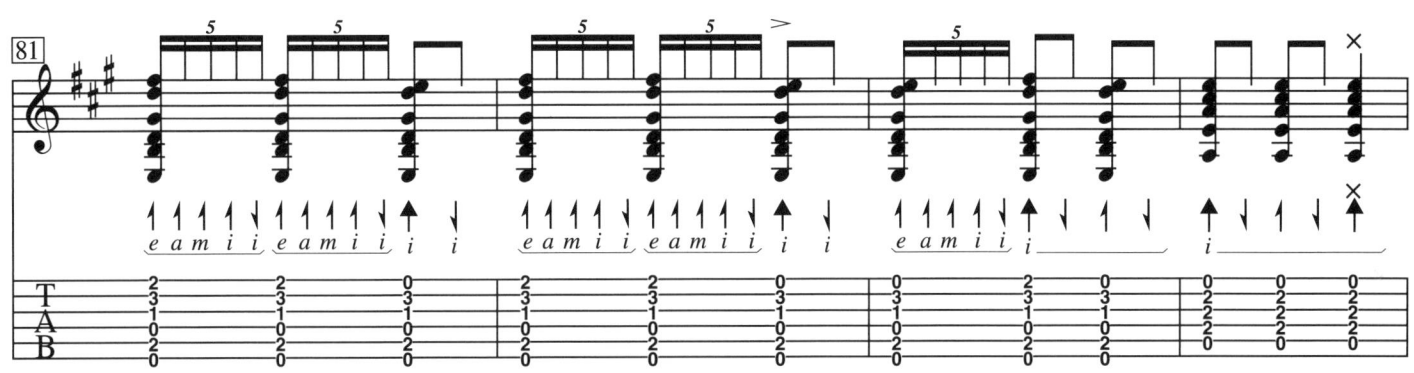
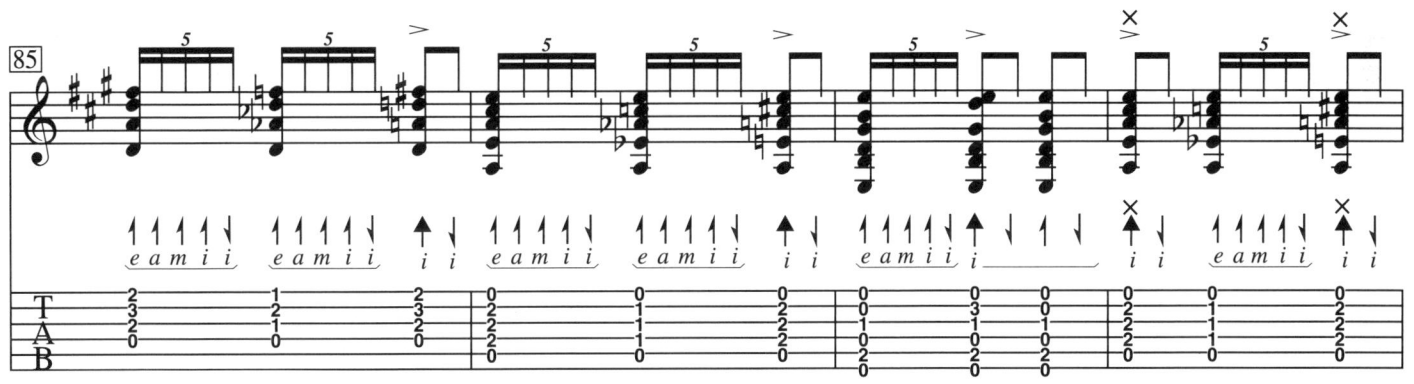
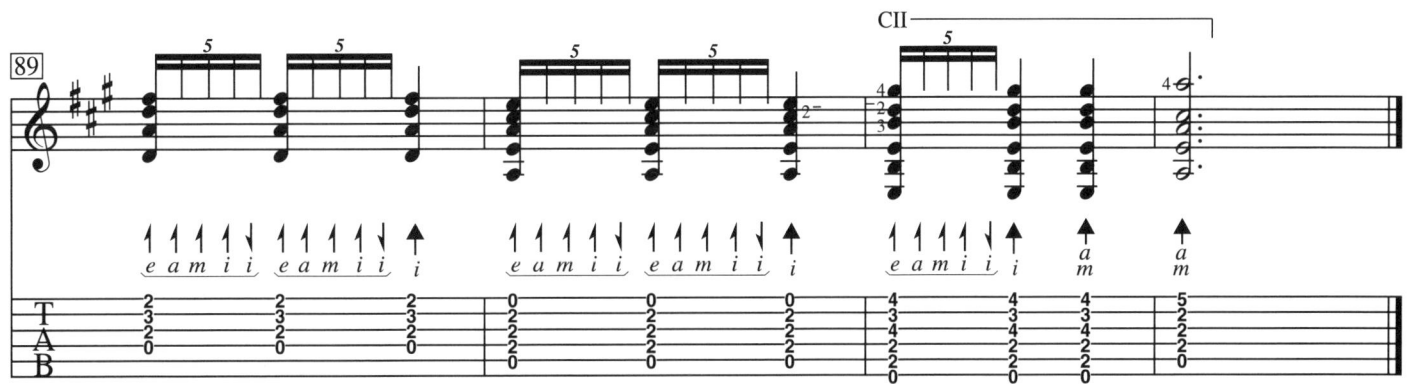

SOLO POR BULERÍAS

Track 31

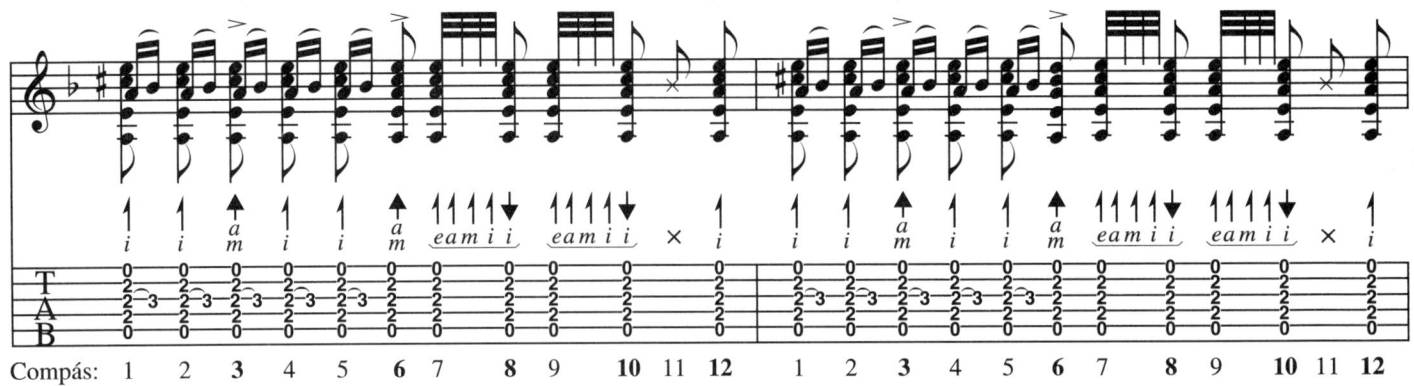

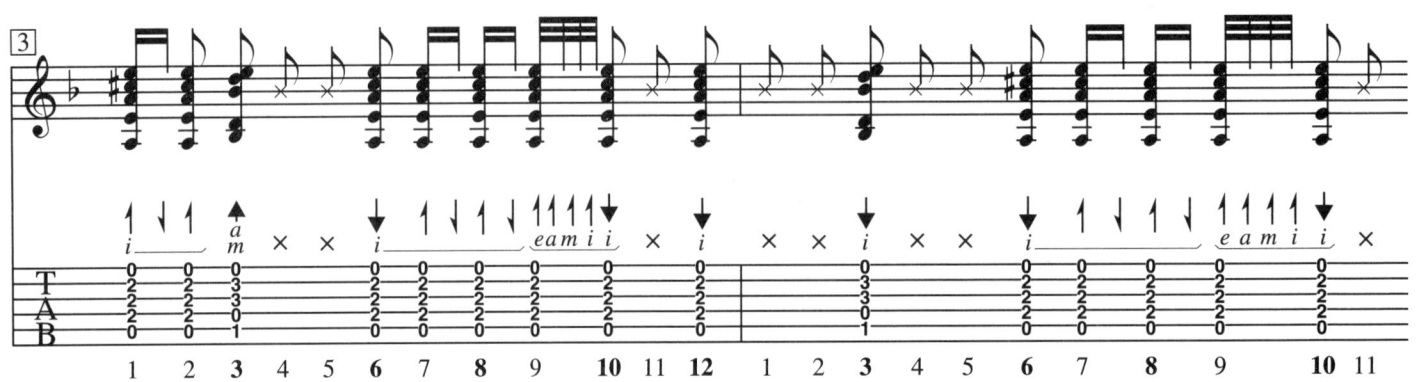

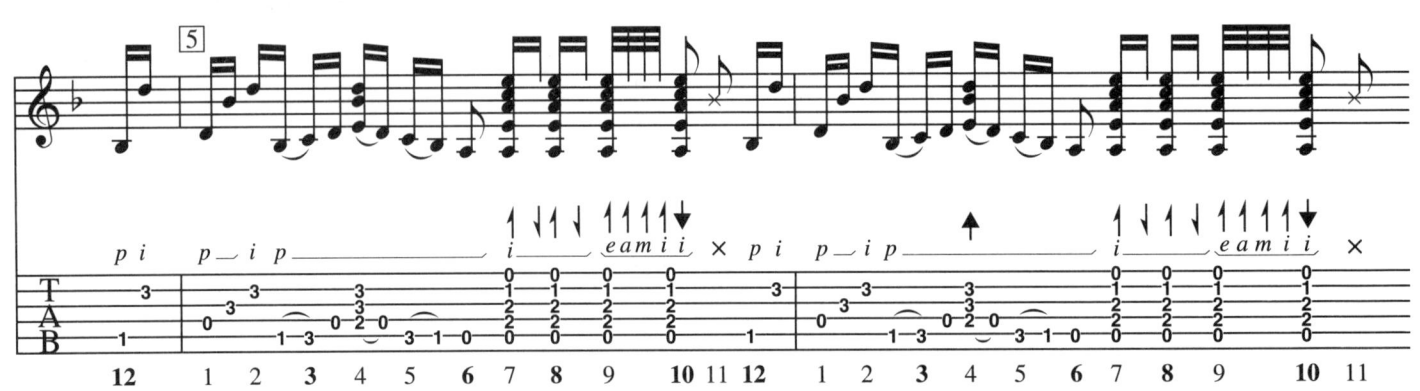

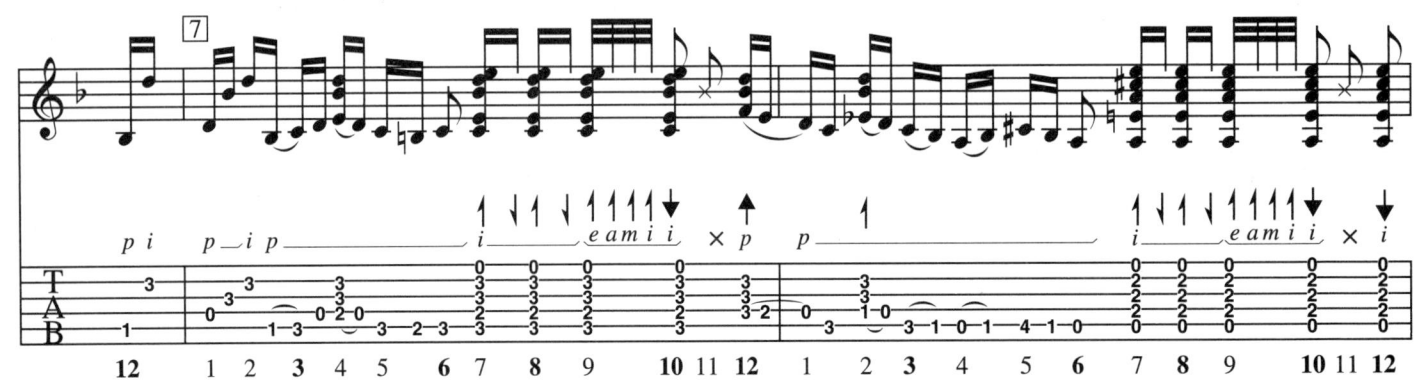

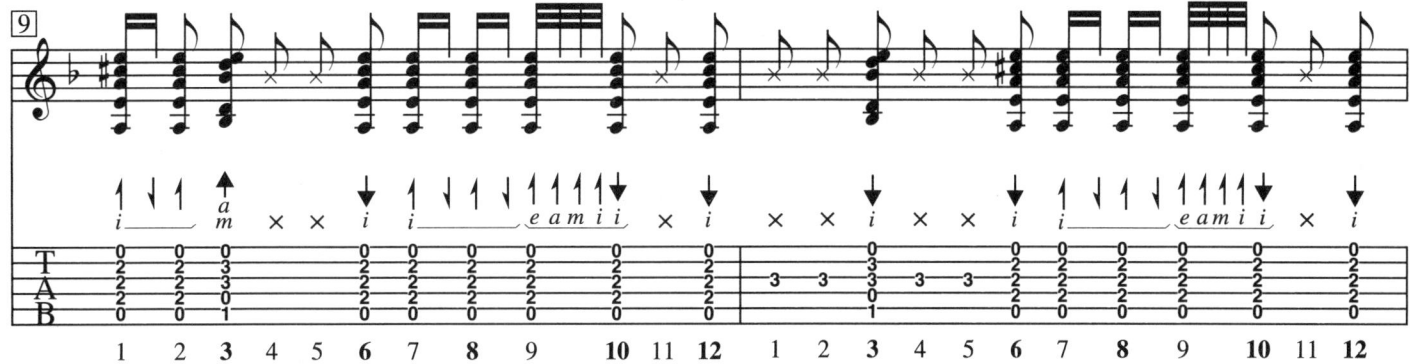
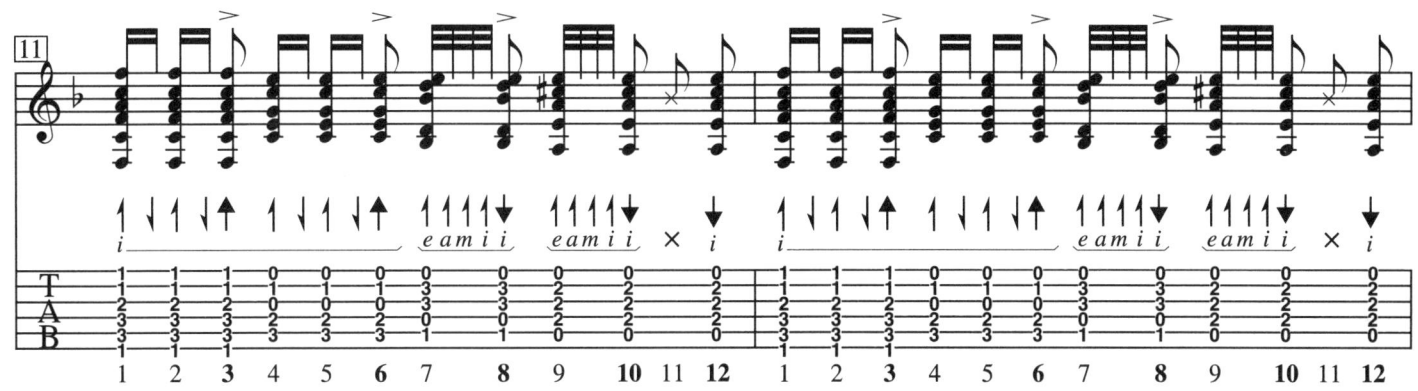
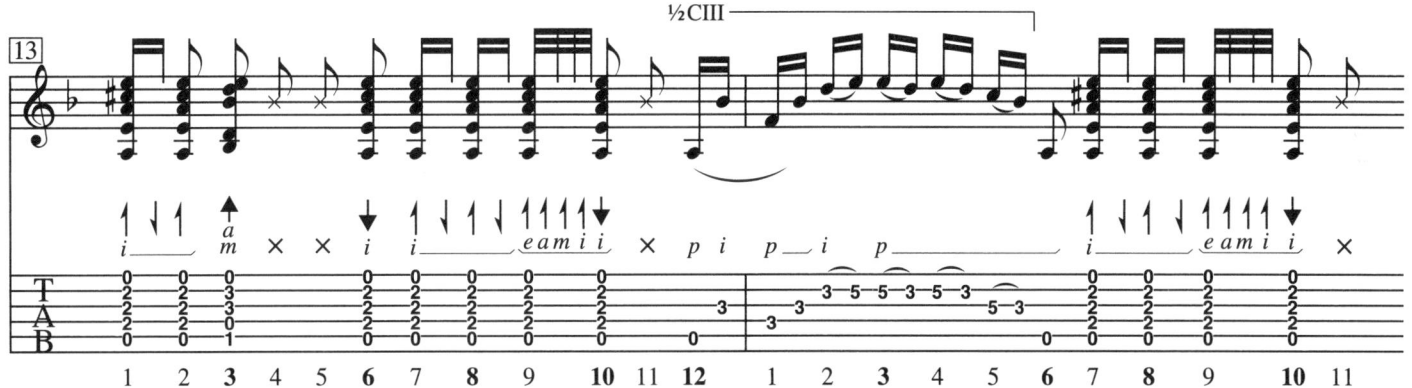
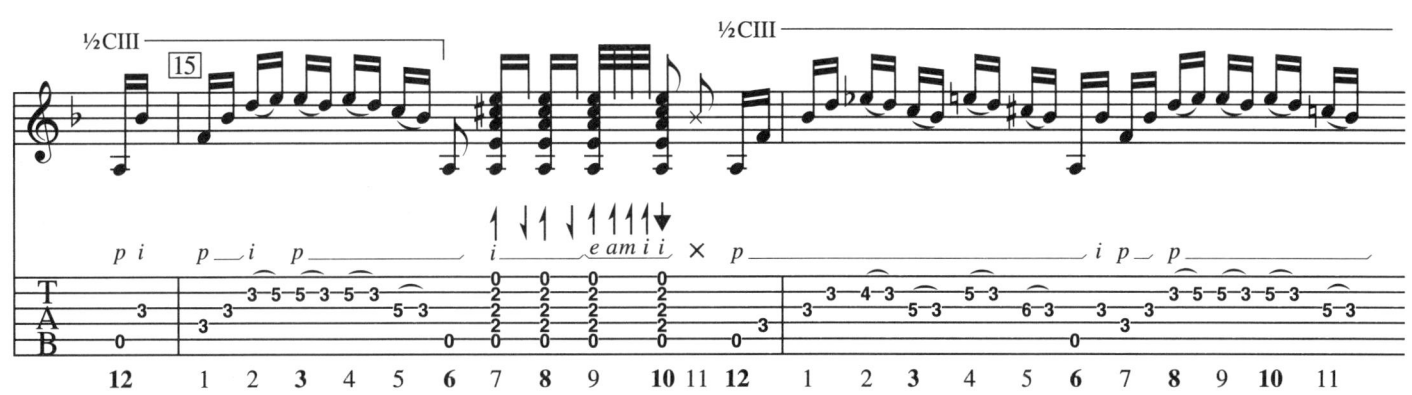

Guitar Atlas: Flamenco 191

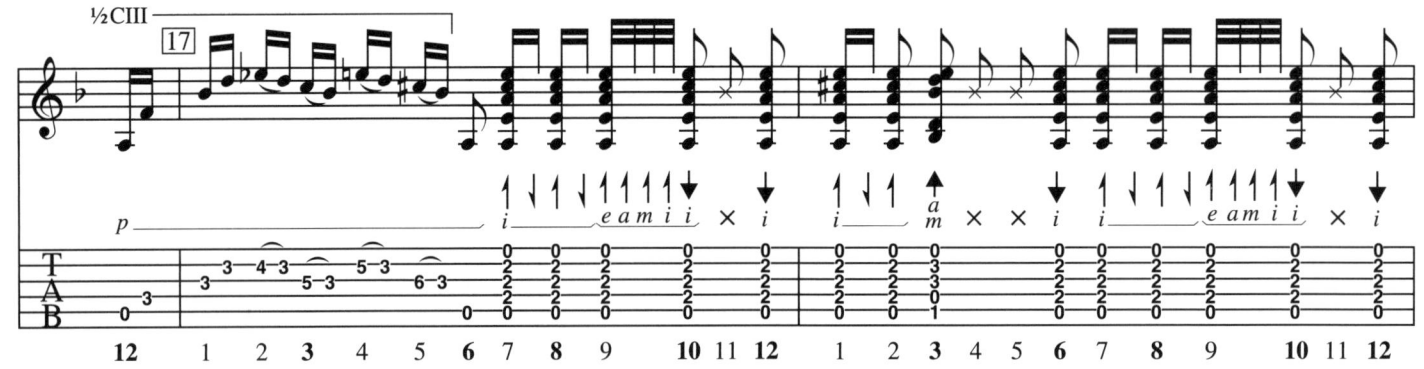
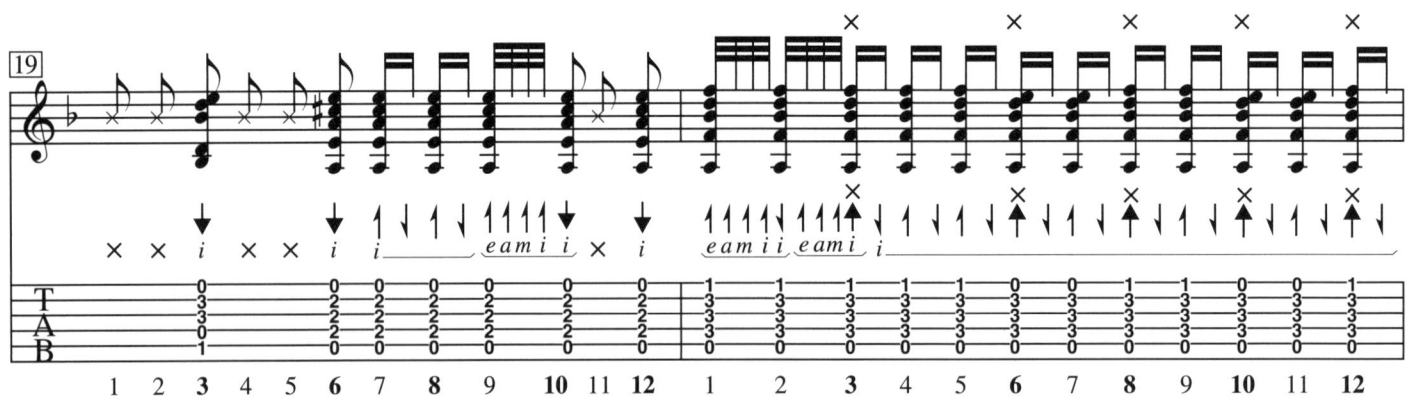
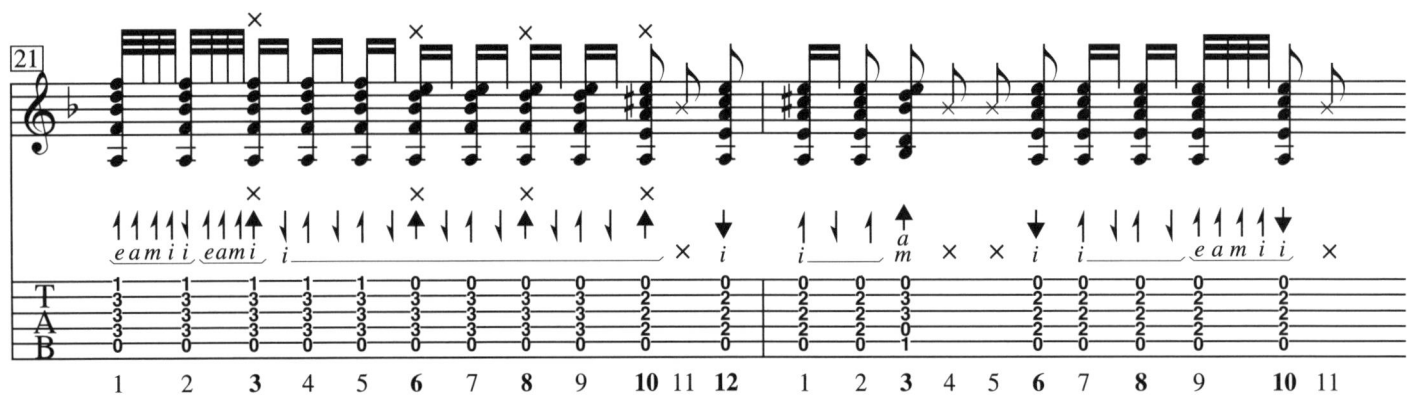

falseta de Sabicas:

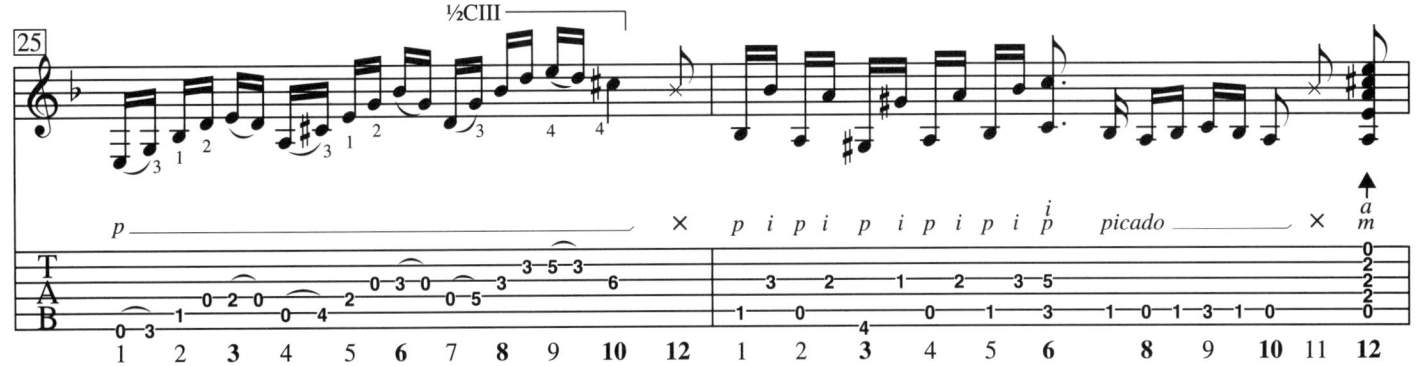
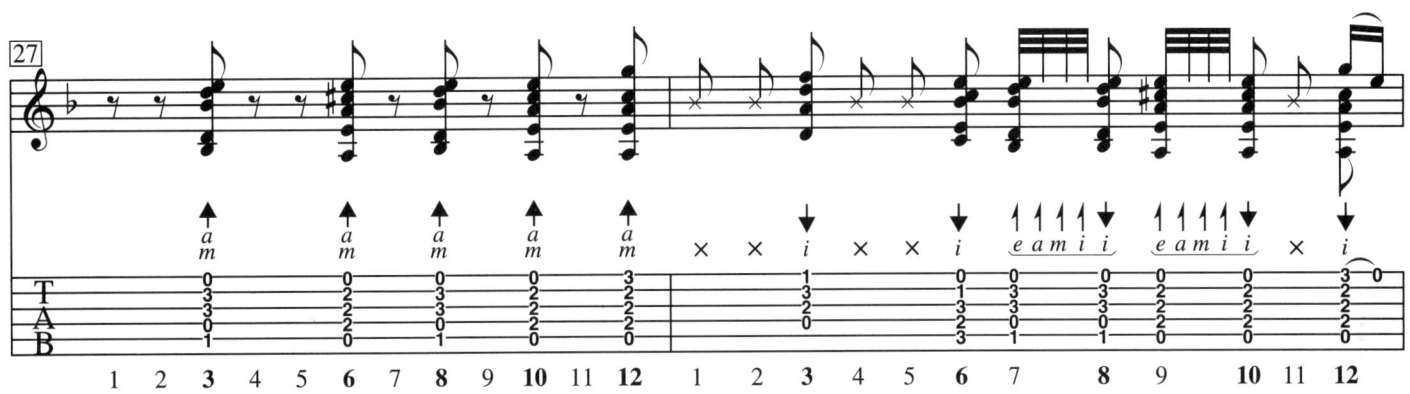
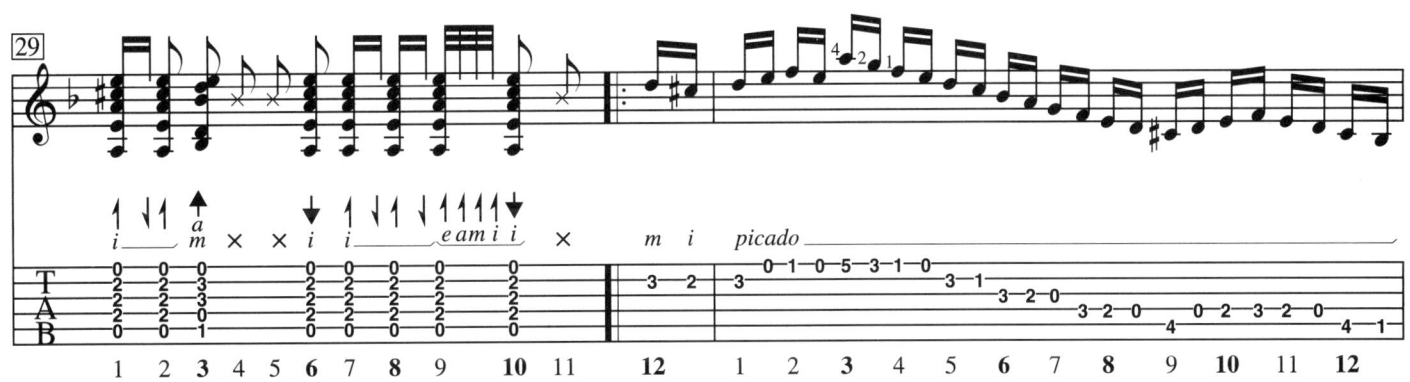
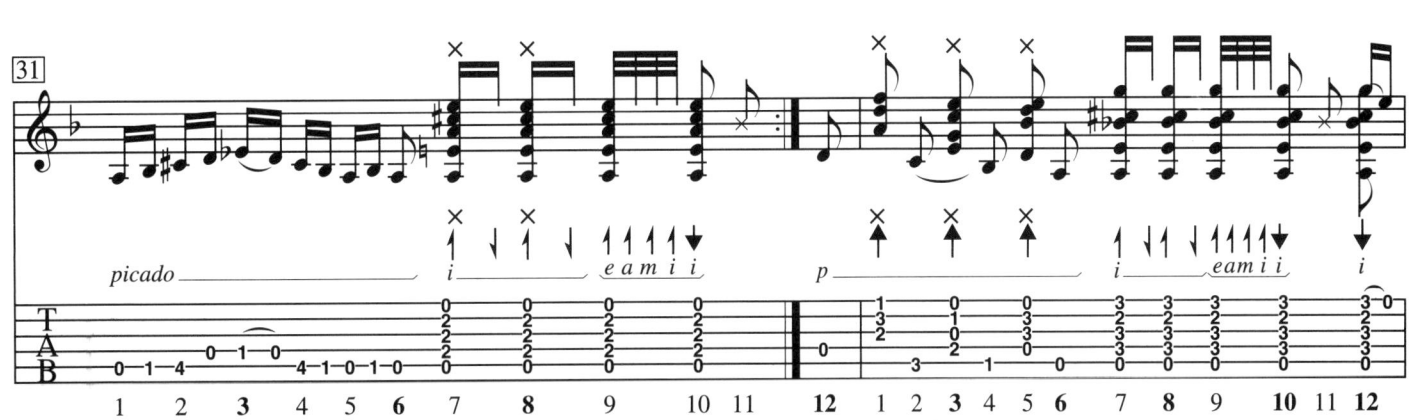

Guitar Atlas: Flamenco 193

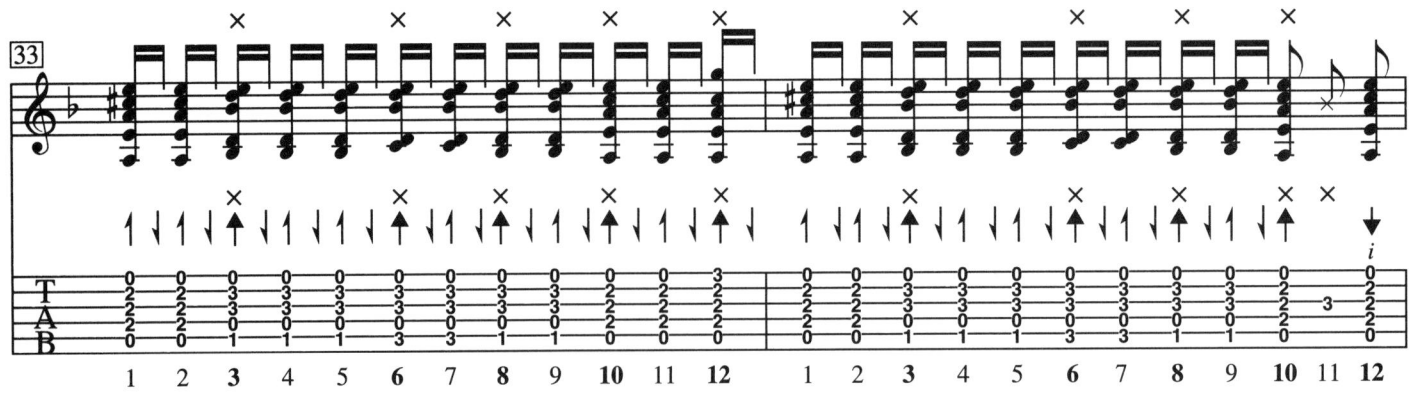
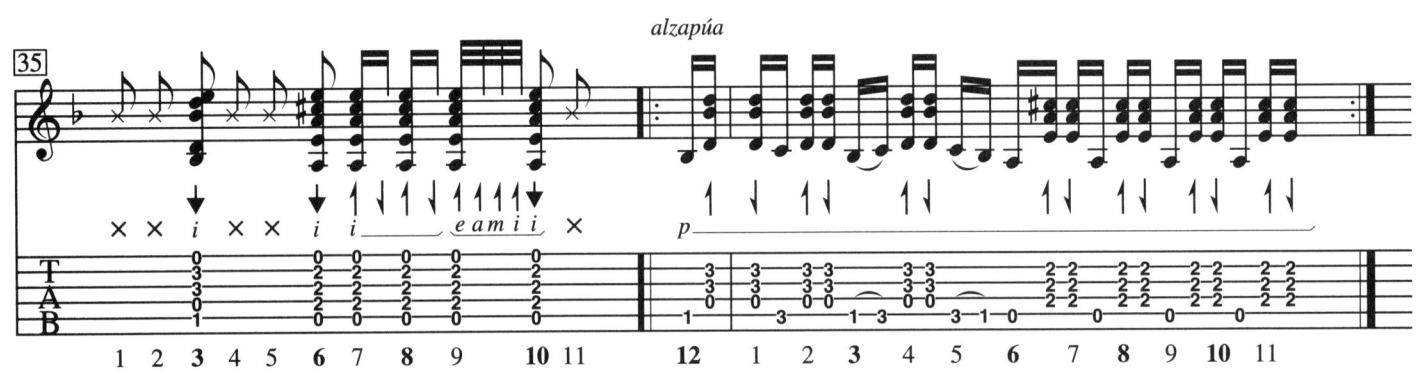
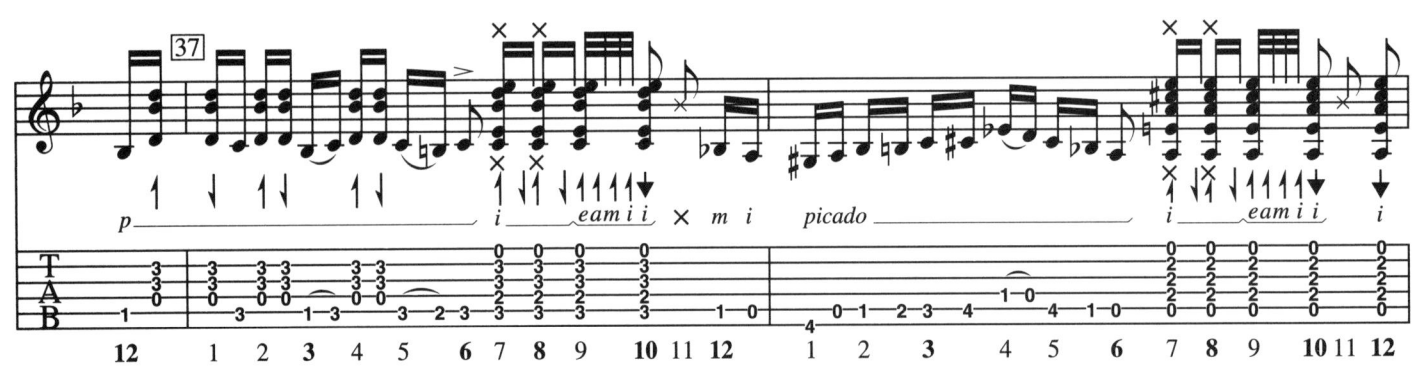
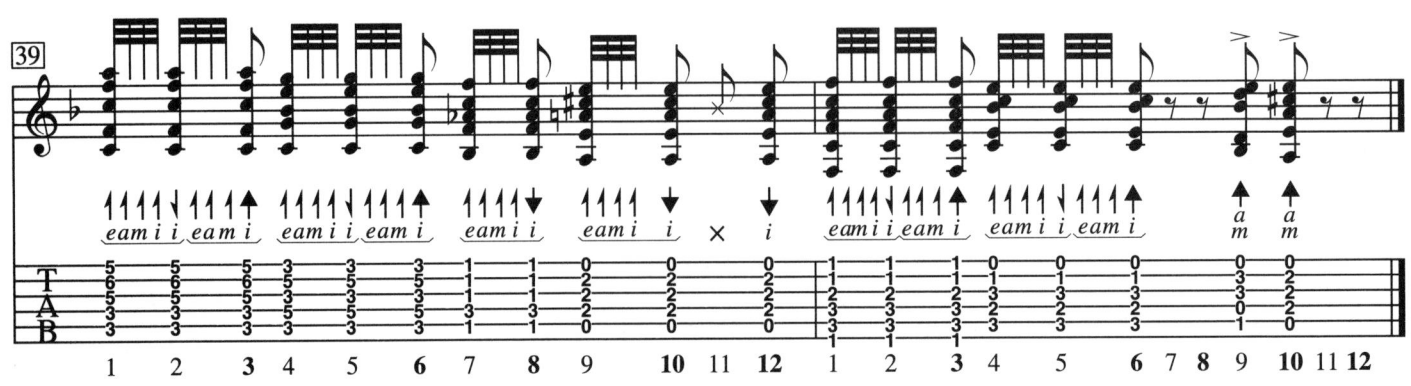

China

Jeff Roberts

*Guitar Styles
from Around the World*

This book was acquired, edited, and produced
by Workshop Arts, Inc., the publishing arm of
the National Guitar Workshop.
Nathaniel Gunod, acquisitions, managing editor
Burgess Speed, acquisitions, senior editor
Timothy Phelps, interior design
Ante Gelo, music typesetter
Barbara Smolover, interior illustrations
CD recorded by Jürgen Frenz at
Living Sound + Music (noise.now@gmail.com), Beijing, China
Jeff Roberts, (guitar)
Photograph on page 210 by Jeff Roberts

Contents

ABOUT THE AUTHOR 197
   Acknowledgements 197
   Notation Key 197

INTRODUCTION 198

CHAPTER 1—Chinese History 199

CHAPTER 2—Chinese Music Theory 201
   Scale Calculations and Ritual Music 201
   The Purging of Foreign Influences
      During the Ming Dynasty 202

CHAPTER 3—Instruments of China 203
   Metal 203
   Stone 204
   Clay 204
   Silk 204
   Bamboo 206
   Skin 206

CHAPTER 4—Blowing and Hitting Music 207
   "Wan Nian Huan"
      ("Ten Thousand Years of Happiness") 207
      Wan Nian Huan
        (Ten Thousand Years of Happiness) 208

CHAPTER 5—Silk and Bamboo Music 210
   Pipa: "Yue Er Gao" ("The Moon on High") ... 210
      Yue Er Gao (The Moon on High) 212
   Guzheng: "Chu Shui Lian" ("Lotus in Water") ... 214
      Chu Shui Lian (Lotus in Water) 214
   Dizi: "Tai Hu Chun" ("Tai Lake Spring") 216
      Tai Hu Chun (Tai Lake Spring) 216

**CHAPTER 6—Guqin and the Literati
   Scholar Tradition** 219
   "Ping Sha Luo Yan"
      ("Geese Descending on a Sandy Bank") 219
      Ping Sha Luo Yan
        (Geese Descending on a Sandy Bank) 220

CHAPTER 7—Chinese Opera 224
   Kun Opera Style and "Mu Dan Ting"
      ("The Peony Pavilion") 224
      Mu Dan Ting (The Peony Pavilion): Excerpt ... 225
   Peking Opera Style and "Ba Wang Bie Ji"
      ("Farewell My Concubine") 227
      Be Wang Bie Ji
        (Farewell My Concubine): Excerpt 228

CHAPTER 8—Ethnic Minority Music of China .. 230
   Yi Ethnicity of Yunnan 230
      Torch Festival Night 231
   Tibet 232
      Sodo Yala 233
   Xinjiang and the Uyghur Ethnicity 234
      Enjen (Sorrow) 234

FINAL WORD 235

APPENDIX A: Preparatory Exercises 236

APPENDIX B: Guitar Tunings 240

Track 0

A compact disc is included with this book. Using it with the book can make learning easier and more enjoyable. The symbol shown at the left appears next to every example that is on the CD. Use the CD to help ensure that you're capturing the feel of the examples and interpreting the rhythms correctly. Example numbers are above the symbol. The track number below the symbol corresponds directly to the example you want to hear. Tracks 20–25 will help you tune to this book.

About the Author

Jeff Roberts is a composer, guitarist, and guqin player, holding degrees in composition (PhD, Brandeis University) and improvisation (BM, New England Conservatory of Music). He also studied guqin performance with guqin master Li Xiangting at Beijing Central Conservatory of Music as a Fulbright Scholar in 2006–2007. Jeff's award-winning compositions have been performed in Europe, China, and the United States. He currently resides in Beijing where he composes, teaches, performs, and researches Han and ethnic minority Chinese music.

ACKNOWLEDGEMENTS

My deepest love and affection go to Xiaoting, for all of her love, sage advice, and support. I would also like to thank my guqin teacher in Beijing, the great guqin master Li Xiangting; through his guidance, I began to understand what Chinese traditional music truly means. I would also like to thank my advisors Eric Chasalow and David Rakowski at Brandeis University for supporting my work in China, as well as a big thank you to the Fulbright program for providing me with the opportunity to learn and explore the music of this vast and diverse country. Finally, but with no less significance, I would like to thank my family: Mom, Dad, Mike, and Elise. Their enthusiastic love and support (along with their tolerance of me living half a world away!) provides me with the strength to push outward and pursue the next great path in this adventure of life.

NOTATION KEY

H = Hammer-on.

P = Pull-off.

SL = Ascending slide.

SL = Descending slide.

½ 1 = Bend note the indicated steps.

= Bend and release to original pitch.

= Pre-bend and release to unbent pitch.

tr = *Trill.* Rapidly alternate between two notes.

= *Arpeggiate.* Quickly roll the chord with the right-hand fingers or thumb.

Harm. or ♦ = *Harmonic.* Notes of the harmonic series that are very pure and clear. In this book, written at the sounding pitch with a diamond shaped notehead. Touch the string lightly over the indicated fret and pluck, immediately removing the finger from the string.

p, i, m, a = The right-hand fingers starting with the thumb.

1, 2, 3, 4, 0 = The left-hand fingers starting with the index finger; 0 = open string. The left-hand fingers are indicated under the TAB.

rubato = Play in freer, less strict time.

rit. = Abbreviation for ritardando. Gradually slow down.

a tempo = Return to the original tempo.

p (*piano*) = soft.

pp (*pianissimo*) = very soft.

ppp (*pianississimo*) = very, very soft.

mp (*mezzo piano*) = somewhat soft.

f (*forte*) = loud.

mf (*mezzo forte*) = somewhat loud.

= *Crescendo.* Gradually increase volume.

= *Decrescendo.* Gradually decrease volume.

♩ = 185 = Tempo marking. In this case, there are 185 quarter notes, or beats, per minute. (If you have a metronome, set it to 185).

4x = Play four times.

①②③④⑤⑥ = The guitar strings, starting from the highest-pitched string, the 1st string, high E.

D.C. al Fine = *Da Capo al Fine.* Go back to the beginning of the piece and play to the **Fine**, which is the end of the piece.

= *Fermata.* Pause, or hold note longer than its indicated duration.

||: :|| = *Repeat signs.* Repeat music between the two symbols. When only the end repeat sign is present, repeat music from the beginning.

= *1st and 2nd endings.* Play to the repeat sign. Then, repeat as normal, skipping over the 1st ending and playing on from the 2nd ending.

Introduction

Welcome to *Guitar Atlas: China*. China is a country rich in history and ethnicity. Its history goes back some 5,000 years, and in addition to the *Han* majority (the ethnicity on which the foundations of Chinese society is based, making up 92% of the Chinese population), China is made up of 55 other ethnicities. Because of its long history and diversity, China has served as a cultural center in East Asia for thousands of years. In fact, much of the music and culture found in Japan and Korea has Chinese influence—no wonder the Chinese name for China is *Zhong Guo,* or "Middle Kingdom."

The musical traditions in China are plentiful. Han Chinese traditional music is what most people outside of China would identify as Chinese. This includes ancient guqin music (a guqin is a zither, often seen in period movies about China), the stone and bronze chimes of Confucian ritual music, and the extravagant face-painted singers of Peking Opera. However, ethnic minorities all over China have age-old folk music traditions as well. For example, in the southwest, there is the bamboo mouth organ music of the Yi, the far west has Tibetan folk music, the northwest has Muslim music of the Uyghurs, and the northeast has music played by the Mongolians of China's vast northern grasslands.

Regional and instrument-specific musical styles are communicated through idiomatic techniques used on each instrument. Sliding and pitch bending are two of the most prominent characteristics in Chinese traditional music. While they exist in the technical vocabulary of most Chinese instruments, each instrument executes these in their own way. Also, the nuances of these techniques are often communicated orally from teacher to student, and notation can only give an approximation. The music in this book takes care to incorporate the subtle technical nuances of Chinese instruments into the transcribed notation. When working with the music in this book, the guitarist should learn the notation first, then try to emulate the performance on the CD.

This book is intended for intermediate-to-advanced guitarists. "Easier" pieces like "Wan Nian Huan," "Torch Festival Night," "Sodo Yala," and "Enjen" may be a good starting point for intermediate guitarists. More challenging pieces include "Chu Shui Lian," "Tai Hu Chun," and "Ping Sha Luo Yan."

While most of the music in this book is intended to be played fingerstyle, there are pieces (such as "Ping Sha Luo Yan" and "Ba Wang Bie Ji") that can be performed using a pick. The aesthetic of Chinese traditional music favors natural acoustics, such as nylon- and steel-string guitars. However, the extensive sliding and single-string techniques can benefit improvising guitarists of any style.

Preparatory Exercises and Guitar Tunings

Most pieces in this book involve a significant amount of single-string playing, using combinations of slides, pitch bends, and grace notes. Because this style of playing may be new to the Western guitarist, Appendix A (page 236) provides a number of preparatory exercises. It is suggested that the guitarist practice the appropriate exercises before working on each new piece (the introductions to the pieces will direct you to the appropriate exercises). Also, Appendix B (page 240) includes the tunings used in this book, along with explanations.

We hope this music opens up a new stylistic world for your playing, and we invite you to sit back, relax, and enjoy the discovery process.

Chapter 1 — CHINESE HISTORY

Legendary Era and Xia Dynasty (27th–16th Centuries B.C.)
This is the earliest period of Chinese antiquity, where myth and legend meet recorded history. Ritual music was prominent and was played on ancient bronze bells and stone chimes. The emperor Huang Di's court established a 12-pitch tuning system, preceding the West by thousands of years.

Classical Era (16th–2nd Centuries B.C.)
This period encompasses two dynasties (*Shang* and *Zhou*) and several periods of unrest. The late Zhou Dynasty, also known as the "Spring and Autumn Period," yielded China's two foundational philosophies: Confucianism (based on the teachings of Confucius, 551–479) and Taoism (based on the teachings of Laozi). During this time, music became central to dynastic rule. Complex music theories arose, along with a government bureau to oversee the complex use of music in ritual practices.

Qin (B.C. 221–207) and Han (B.C. 206–A.D. 220) Dynasties
After generations of war and fractured rule, the emperor Shi Huangdi brought divisive feudal states under the rule of the Qin and declared himself emperor of all China. Shi Huangdi built the first Great Wall and during his brief reign, brought about the first standardization of written Chinese. The following Han Dynasty brought 400 years of prosperity and stability, out of which grew a gentry class that developed highly educated and refined scholars, who in turn produced China's first great era of poetry, painting, and music. Ritual music that dominated the earlier dynasties slowly took a back seat to new music traditions focused on entertainment and self-cultivation. This was also a period that began the establishment of distinctive northern and southern regional styles of music.

Sui Dynasty (581–618), Tang Dynasty (618–907), and Five Dynasties (907–960)
During these three dynasties, trade flourished with the Middle East, India, Central Asia, and kingdoms to the north of China. As a result, a tremendous amount of outside cultural influence poured into China. For example, in the Tang capital of Chang'an, 20 different types of music were performed at court, 10 of which were foreign. Through this foreign music, many instruments that are thought of today as essential Chinese instruments (such as *pipa* and *dizi*) were first introduced to China. The Tang Dynasty is also considered the golden age of Chinese poetry.

Song Dynasty (960–1127) and Yuan Dynasty (1271–1368)
The Song Dynasty was established 100 years after the fall of the Tang and was unstable from the start. The capital established in east-central China (in present day Kaifeng) was under constant threat from non-Chinese kingdoms in the north. This led first to a northern defeat and a shift of the Song court to the south, and eventually to a complete defeat by the Mongols of the north led by Kublai Khan. Kahn founded the Yuan Dynasty, the first time China was ruled by foreigners. Culturally, it was the southern Song Dynasty that flourished with new developments in music, drama, and painting.

Ming Dynasty (1368–1644) and Qing Dynasty (1644–1911)
The Ming Dynasty saw the return to Han Chinese rule, and, following the foreign-ruled Yuan Dynasty, a growing xenophobia among the Confucian elite. During the Ming, a conscious purging of foreign influence from the arts (including music) was undertaken.

For music, this purging meant the washing out of music modes, rhythms, and melodies brought into Chinese music during the Sui and Tang Dynasties. As a result, most Chinese music today uses just a *pentatonic* (five-tone) scale and transpositions of the pentatonic scale. Also, most of what we identify as "Chinese music" today comes from the Ming and Qing Dynasties. The last period of imperial China, the Qing Dynasty, saw a return to foreign rule under the Manchu people from modern northeast China. These foreign rulers preserved Chinese tradition, although the Han Chinese were pushed out of powerful court positions. By the mid-19th century, the dynasty grew weak, both morally and financially, and along with foreign invasion (beginning with the Opium Wars of 1840), would eventually see its demise in the early 20th century.

Regional music styles flourished and dominated the musical landscape. This is reflected in two distinct styles of instrumental music: the soft and melodic *silk and bamboo music (sizhu yinyue)* of southern China and the loud and intense *blowing and hitting music (chuida yinyue)* of northern China. Chinese opera, a deeply regional music genre, reached its zenith during the Ming and Qing Dynasties, first with *kun opera* in the Ming and then *Peking opera* during the Qing. Although Peking opera developed in northern China, it is considered a national style because of the influence it has experienced from other regional operas and because of its universal popularity all over China.

Modern China (1911–Present)

The fall of the Qing Dynasty in 1911 brought not only the end of dynastic rule, but also considerable foreign influence as Western nations forced China to open up. Republican China was established in 1911 but was weak and fell into disarray by the mid-1920s. During this period, Western influence brought the creation of Western style conservatories. This marked the beginning of the partial loss of regional styles because musicians were no longer just being trained in the local provinces. It also marked a new era of music "professionalism," contradictory to the "amateurism' of Chinese instrumental music, where the music existed for ceremonial function and self-cultivation.

In the first decades of the People's Republic of China (1949–present), the communist government used folk music to communicate communist propaganda to the Chinese people. The radicalism of the Cultural Revolution (1966–1976) sought to destroy links to China's feudal past, and this included the arts. At times, musicians had to bury their instruments and stop playing to avoid conflicts.

With the death of Mao Zedong in 1976, China entered into its current "opening-up" phase, where economic development has unfolded at a breakneck speed. Along with this development came a new wave of foreign influence. Western-style popular music made its way into China first from Taiwanese and Hong Kong pop music and later directly from the U.S. and Europe. By the mid-1980s, China saw its first outbreak of Chinese rock music *(yaogun yinyue)* in Beijing. Through the 1990s, jazz made its way into Beijing via cassette tapes brought by foreign embassy workers. Slowly, as Chinese musicians studied and emulated the jazz greats on these tapes, a jazz scene emerged in China. Western Classical music is thriving in China's many conservatories and promises to be a big part of China's future musical landscape.

With all of this foreign influence, the future of Chinese traditional music remains uncertain. But while regional flavors of the past may fade to greater or lesser extents, the Chinese people still remain tied to their cultural origins and continue to place value on their traditional arts.

Chapter 2 — CHINESE MUSIC THEORY

SCALE CALCULATIONS AND RITUAL MUSIC

Looking to find order in the vibrations of nature, Chinese music theorists and scholars organized musical systems according to the "unity of opposites." These opposites included *Yin* (negative)–*Yang* (positive), man–woman, earth–heaven, etc.

As early as the Shang Dynasty (16th–11th centuries B.C.), scholars investigated acoustics by cutting metal tubes in different proportional relationships. Chinese numerology, which symbolically represented earth with the number 2 and heaven with the number 3, used the proportional relationship 2:3 (symbolizing harmony between heaven and earth) to derive musical scales. The proportion 2:3 is also an acoustic property of two sound vibrations that are the distance of a perfect 5th apart: when a pipe is cut at 2/3rds of the length of another pipe, it will sound a perfect 5th higher. But in order to keep the pitches in close register with each other, pipes were cut in alternating longer and shorter lengths. Making a pipe longer by the ratio of 4:3 would produce the same pitch as 2:3, but an octave lower. For instance, Example 1 shows the pitches of the pipes cut in alternating lengths of 4/3 and 2/3.

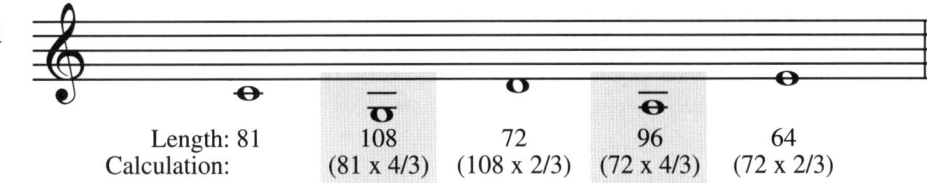

In Example 2, the G (108) and A (96) pitches from above are raised an octave. Then, all of the pitches are placed in succession to form the pentatonic scale.

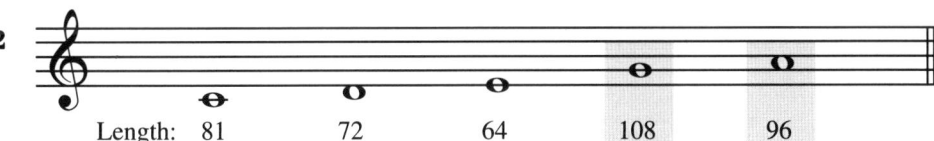

This method of acoustically generating a scale was first recorded in Chinese music history around 645 B.C. during the Zhou Dynasty, but may have existed earlier. By using intervals of successive 5ths and 4ths, the method obeys an acoustic principle of nature called the overtone series. This system of using 5ths and 4ths is also referred to as the "circle of 5ths." It is a system of scale construction and relationship that stands at the center of Western music, but Chinese use of these principles predated the West by some 1,700 years!

Eventually, Chinese scholars continued these calculations beyond five pitches and generated scales of more than five notes. For example, in the Zhou Dynasty, two more pitches were added to create a seven-note scale called *yidiaoshe*, or "esoteric scale." The pitches added were an F♯ and a B. This effectively creates a C Lydian scale:

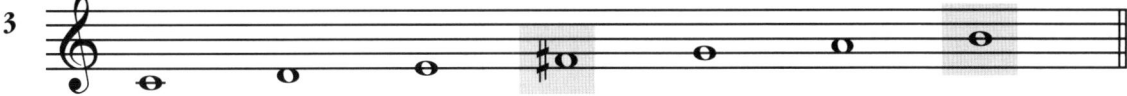

By applying the concepts discussed on the previous page, great sets of ritual bells *(bianzhong)* were tuned for use in ritual music during the Shang and Zhou Dynasties (16th–2nd centuries B.C.). Chinese theorists were concerned with the acoustic properties of the notes and how they resonated in the universe. Depending on their *cosmological* meaning, the various pitches would be assigned to particular rituals taking place at different times of the year ("cosmology" is the study of the natural order of the universe). For example, in one calculation, a whole tone scale was derived where each pitch was used as the basis for different types of seasonal rituals:

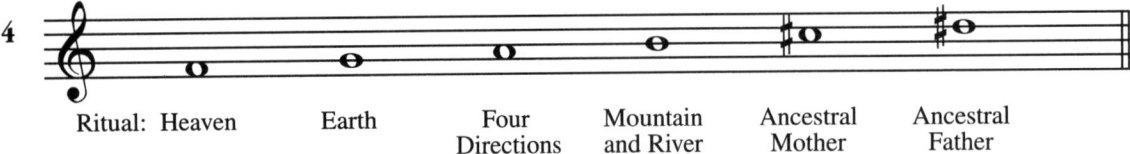

In the 3rd century, further calculations were carried out to arrive at 12 pitches within an octave, and eventually, a microtonal calculation was carried out producing 60 notes within the octave (the term "microtonal" refers to tones smaller then the semitone or half step). However, these scales did not enter the mainstream of Chinese folk or court music traditions.

THE PURGING OF FOREIGN INFLUENCES DURING THE MING DYNASTY

In addition to the basic pentatonic scale, other modes were introduced into Chinese music, coming mostly from foreign sources. Between the Qin and Tang Dynasties (2nd century B.C.–9th century A.D.), China came under enormous influence from cultures in Central Asia, northern nomadic tribes, and even cultures as far south as present day Vietnam. Some remaining fragments of information show scales and melodies derived from non-pentatonic modes. For example, one of the oldest surviving notations in Chinese music comes from the guqin piece "Youlan" ("Elegant Orchid") and contains both ♯4th and ♭7th scale degrees (the ♯1 was used more as embellishment rather than a scale tone):

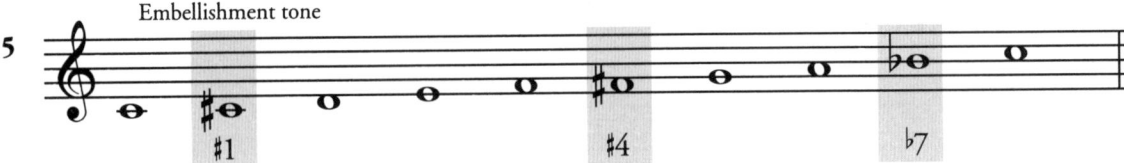

There are also a few surviving melodies from the Tang Dynasty that show a distinctly Central Asian or Middle Eastern flavor, including ♭3rds and ♮3rds along with other embellished half steps:

All in all, these examples reveal a certain richness of modes that once existed in ancient China. But the traditional Chinese music that survives today originates from periods following Tang Dynasty and is formed mostly around the pentatonic scale. This simplified modal foundation resulted largely from a purging of foreign influence during the Ming Dynasty. After having been overtaken and ruled by foreign Mongol tribes during the Yuan Dynasty, the Han-ruled Ming Dynasty wanted to rid itself of all foreign influence in music and return to an imagined time in Chinese history before foreign influence (i.e., Han Dynasty). Modes like the ones above were filtered out of the music and reconfigured to obey the "original" modes of Han culture some 1,200 years earlier. Needless to say, the purge robbed Chinese music that exists today of a richness in modal sound that had once existed.

Chapter 3 — INSTRUMENTS OF CHINA

The foundation of Chinese culture and philosophy rests on the idea of finding balance and harmony in the self, in society, and in the cosmos. Duality was a major concept in this belief system represented by the Chinese Yang (male, positive force, light) and Yin (female, negative force, dark). Ritual bell ringers from the Zhou Dynasty would ring the notes of their tuned bells, believing that the vibrations would contribute to a state of balance in the cosmos and human society. Vibration was more than just the pitch; it was also the vibrating material that produced this pitch. Thus, the Chinese classified their instruments according to the material that vibrated. This is called *bayin,* or "eight sounds," and this system groups instruments in eight categories: metal, stone, clay, silk, bamboo, wood, gourd, and skin.

Instruments made of particular materials were also tied to seasons. For example, instruments made of stone and metal would sound better in winter and were thus used in ritual during this time of the year. Bamboo instruments would become brittle and crack during the cold, dry winters, thus they were assigned to rituals in the warm and moist spring air. This special emphasis on the vibration of sound and instrument materials reveals a special value placed on musical *timbre,* or tone.

METAL

Bianzhong are the ancient bronze bells from the great period of bell tuning and ritual ensembles during the earliest era of Chinese history (Shang and Zhou Dynasties, 21st–3rd century B.C.). A number of these bell sets have been unearthed in different parts of central China. The Zheghouyi Bianzhong set, unearthed in Hubei Province, contains over 90 bells and has a range of over six octaves. The bells can produce two separate pitches by striking them in different locations.

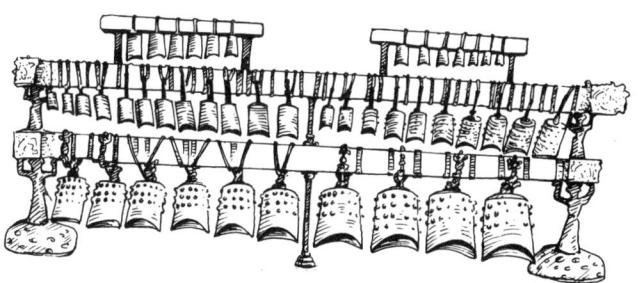
Bianzhong.

Bo are cymbals and are often tied to a specific genre of music. Perhaps the most recognizable cymbal is the bright, crashing sound of *jingbo* found in operatic genres such as Peking opera. There are also the *shuibo,* or "water cymbals," that have strong metallic sounds, and the light sound of *pengling* bells used in a variety of different ensemble contexts.

Shuibo.

Luo are gongs. The most recognizable gong is associated with Peking opera. This is the *xiaoluo,* with its characteristic rising tone that is produced when struck with a wooden stick. There are also the big resonant gongs, *daluo,* as well as the colorfully named *shiluo* ("lion gong") and *yunluo* ("cloud gongs") often seen in blowing and hitting ensembles of northern China.

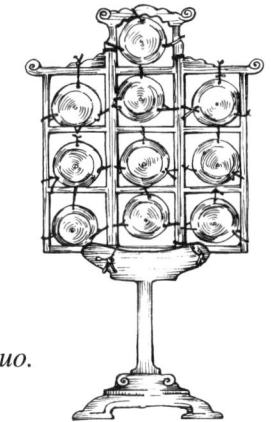
Yunluo.

STONE

Bianqing is a set of tuned, L-shaped, stone chimes hung by rope from a wood frame and played melodically. Usually in sets numbering around 12, the chimes were played alongside the bianzhong bronze bells in the court and ritual music of China.

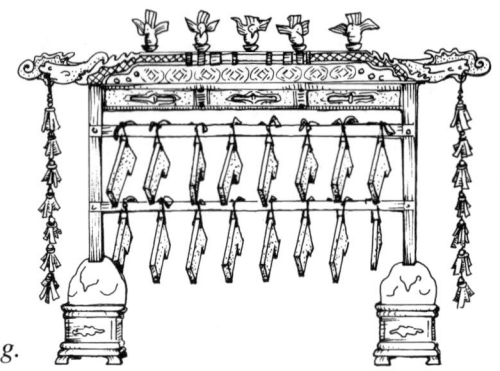

Bianqing.

CLAY

Xun is a vessel flute made of clay or ceramic and is one of China's oldest instruments. It was used in ritual music of the Shang and Zhou Dynasties alongside the bronze and stone chimes. The xun contained an open hole at its top to blow across and either two or four fingering holes that produced the pitches of a narrow-range pentatonic scale.

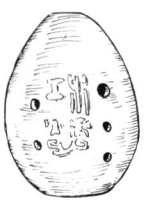

Xun.

SILK

The *guqin* is one of China's oldest and continuous instrument traditions, dating back to the early Zhou Dynasty (B.C. 1100–256). It was the instrument of the Chinese Literati Scholars, and Confucius himself played guqin. The guqin tradition is closely connected with Confucianism and Daoism, and from its Daoist influence, Guqin developed a spiritual practice where a scholar would play the guqin as a way to cultivate longevity and reconnect to the flow of the universe. The guqin has seven strings and lies flat on a special table or across the performer's lap. The instrument is tuned to one of several pentatonic modes, of which the two most common are presented here:

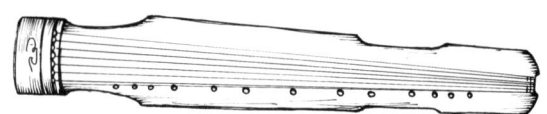

Guqin.

Zhonglü Tuning

Jinru Tuning

The right hand plucks the strings and the left hand either stops pitches on the fingerboard or gently touches locations on the string to produce harmonics. Guqin technique is complex and is oriented towards expressing a rich and subtle array of tone color. There are over 60 combined left- and right-hand techniques, each of which can produce a subtle difference in tone color. In guqin technique books, authors often used aesthetic words from Chinese painting and poetry, connected to a scene in nature, to create an emotional impression of the timbral quality of each technique. Guqin music has its own symbol notation that indicates left- and right-hand techniques, but contains no rhythmic notation.

The *guzheng* of today is a reformed version of an ancient instrument dating back almost as far as the guqin. The modern form of guzheng has 21 strings and consists of a large resonating box over which the strings are stretched. Each string has its own separate, adjustable bridge. Guzheng's pitches are preset, meaning, once the bridge is adjusted, the tone for each string is fixed. Thus the fixed pitches of the 21 strings are the only pitches used to play music. This is unlike guqin where pitches must be fingered on a fretless fingerboard. The larger resonating box of the guzheng makes it a louder instrument than the guqin and thus it was often used in classical silk and bamboo ensembles, playing with other instruments such as pipa, erhu, dizi, and sheng. The guzheng is tuned to the pentatonic scale and covers a range of several octaves. The guzheng player tapes small plastic *plectrums,* or picks, to his/her right-hand fingers and uses them to strum and pluck the strings. The left hand can also pluck strings but is mostly used for bending pitches by pressing strings down on the opposite side from where they are plucked. The most common tuning for guzheng's 21 strings is as follows:

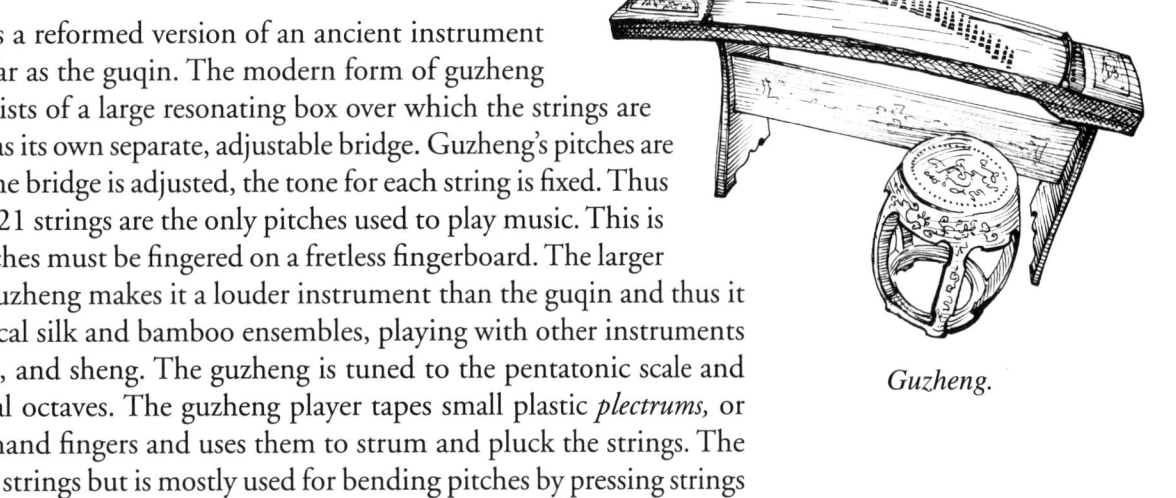

Guzheng.

While identified today as one of China's traditional instruments, the *pipa* is supposed to have been imported from nomadic tribes of Central Asia over 2,000 years ago. Its shape resembles a teardrop. Pipa thrived during China's international period and appears in the cave paintings in Dunhuang (a desert city on the Silk Road, the most important trade route of the pre-modern world). Unlike guqin, where some survive from before the 7th century and are still playable, there are no ancient pipas in existence today; perhaps the reason for this is that, at the time, pipa was a commonplace instrument, not to be buried with emperors or scholars. Historical pipas varied in their number of strings. Modern pipa has four strings. Following are the most common tunings.

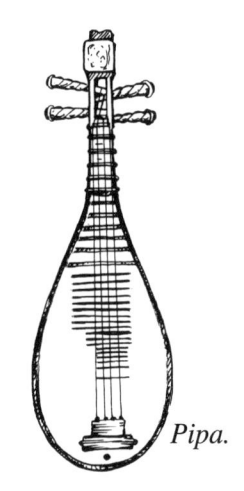

Pipa.

Zhendiao Tuning   Chidiao Tuning

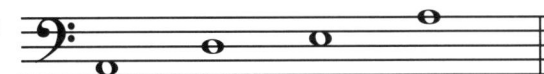   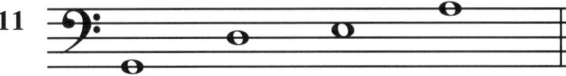

The pipa is held upright when performed. The player tapes small plectrums to his/her right hand. The left-hand fingers create pitches on a fretboard containing 25 scalloped frets, which allow for the player to produce deep bends by pressing down.

The *erhu* is a bowed string instrument first imported into China during the Tang Dynasty. It is actually one of many instruments from the *huqin* family of bowed stringed instruments. *Hu* originally meant "barbarian" and *qin* means "instrument," revealing its origins with the northern non-Han nomads. *Er,* meaning "two," refers to the instrument's secondary role to the *jinghu* (the primary bowed string instrument in Peking opera). The erhu consists of a body and neck across which two metal strings are tightly stretched. A horsehair bow is sandwiched between the two strings and can bow either. The left-hand fingers play notes on the strings without pressing against the fingerboard. The instrument is found in all types of music in China. The most common tuning of the erhu strings are the D and G above middle C.

Erhu.

BAMBOO

Dizi is a bamboo flute blown in a horizontal fashion, similar to the Western flute. Along its body, the dizi has holes that, by covering and uncovering them, produce different pitches. It is one of the oldest instrument traditions in China and its stories of origin range from the 2nd century B.C. to the 21st century B.C. and involve the famous semi-mythic emperor Huang Di. Dizi is found in all aspects of Chinese traditional music, but is perhaps most commonly associated with the silk and bamboo music traditions of southern China.

Dizi.

Xiao is a vertical, end-blown bamboo flute. With its unique, breathy timbre, it is much softer sounding than the dizi. One of China's most ancient instruments, the modern xiao dates back to the Ming Dynasty. Xiao is traditionally the only instrument that is played alongside guqin. To perform guqin and xiao together, the players must be able to perform both instruments. This reflects the great sensitivity and subtlety involved in performing both instruments, both solo and as a duo.

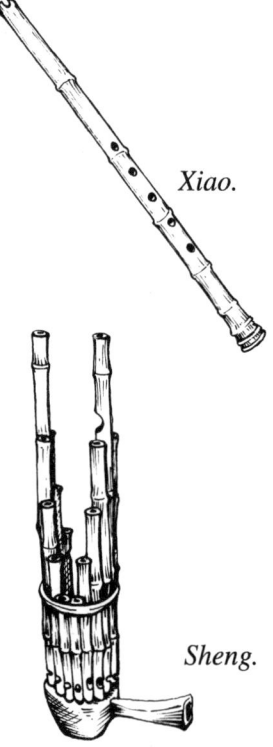
Xiao.

Sheng is a mouth organ dating back to the Zhou Dynasty and is one of China's oldest instruments. It has between 13 and 21 bamboo pipes standing upright from its base. The performer blows into a tube connected to the base. When different holes are closed, air is forced up the pipes and vibrates a bronze reed inside to produce a pitch. Similar to the Western harmonica, sound is created by either blowing air into the instrument or sucking air out of the instrument. Because many pipes can sound at once, it is possible to produce harmony. This is one of the only instruments that can produce harmony in Chinese music. Sheng was almost never used as a solo instrument (only in recent times) and was part of the court ritual ensembles during ancient times and part of the chuida music tradition of northern China in the past several hundred years.

Sheng.

The *suona* is a double-reed wind instrument with a bell-shaped body, similar in shape and design to the Western shawm. It is thought to have originated from instruments used in Central Asia. The instrument produces an intense and nasal pitch that can easily project itself over the loudest instrument in any traditional ensemble, including gongs, cymbals, or drums. It is most commonly seen in northern China chuida ensembles, where it is the primary melodic instrument backed by an array of drums, gongs, and cymbals. It is also occasionally used in Peking opera, but only in special scenes, where it is accompanied by a large drum.

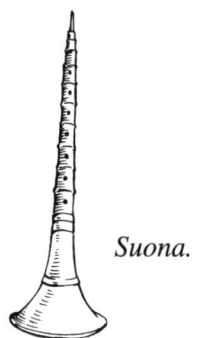
Suona.

SKIN

Dagu, or "large drum," is a category for different types of percussion that use a stretched membrane material to produce a sound. Some varieties of dagu are *huapengu*, or "flower pot drum," and the *yaogu*, or "waist drum." These drums are used in various types of Chinese music, but perhaps their sound is most familiar in a modern Chinese instrument orchestra, an ancient ritual orchestra, or in the ceremonial chuida music of northern China.

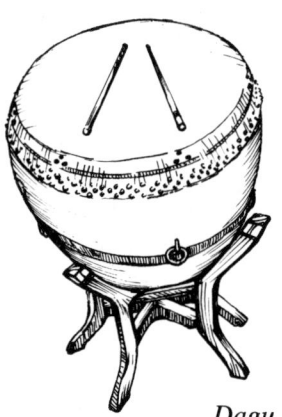
Dagu.

Chapter 4: Blowing and Hitting Music

Chuida yinyue, or blowing and hitting music, is a genre of instrumental folk music found mostly in the northern Chinese provinces of Hebei, Beijing, Tianjin, Liaoning, Shandong, Shanxi, and Shaanxi. It is called "blowing and hitting" music because the instruments used are wind instruments like the suona or dizi (hence, "blowing") and all varieties of drums, gongs, and cymbals (hence, "hitting"). The music is largely ceremonial and is usually performed for important life events. For example, local amateur groups will be asked to perform during certain parts of wedding ceremonies or in processions for funerals. Blowing and hitting ensembles also play for recurring events in a year's cycle, such as Chinese festival days. These include *Zhongqiujie* (Mid-Autumn Festival), *Chunjie* (Spring Festival, or Chinese New Year), *Yuanxiao Jie* (Lantern Festival), or *Qingming Jie* (Tomb Sweeping Festival). Often during these festivals, there are temple fairs, or *Miaohui*. These occur at Daoist temples, and along with food, different folk arts, and wares, chuida music is performed.

While chuida music has been associated with Daoist and Buddhist temples (the Daoist priests or Buddhist monks were often proficient in performing these instruments), modern chuida ceremonial music is not necessarily tied to just the temples. Today, professional performing groups may be hired to present a concert for entertainment rather than for ritual or ceremonial purposes.

The sound of chuida music varies from region to region, but the brazen sound of the suona, along with gongs, cymbals and drums, is vibrant, raw, and sometimes jolting for the non-Chinese ear. The music, while following a standard duple meter ($\frac{2}{4}$) is not always played by the instruments in perfect rhythmic synchronization. This *heterophonic* quality (multiple instruments simultaneously playing the same melody but in slightly different tempos) gives the music a rather loose, raw, and free feeling.

"WAN NIAN HUAN" ("TEN THOUSAND YEARS OF HAPPINESS")

"Wan Nian Huan" ("Ten Thousand Years of Happiness") is a well-known chuida piece often played at weddings and festivals.

The opening rubato section is usually performed by a dizi or suona and introduces the sound of the mode in which the piece is to be played. Afterwards, the entire ensemble enters and begins playing the music in a loose manner. Slowly, their rhythm becomes more established until, by the fifth complete measure, the tempo is established for the remainder of the piece. In the arrangement that follows, the melodies for both the suona and dizi are given. The upper line relates to the suona and the lower line is a combination of the dizi melody and some rhythms from the percussion.

Practice note: The triplet figure in measure 8 can be found in Exercises G1 and G2 (Appendix A, page 239).

WAN NIAN HUAN
(TEN THOUSAND YEARS OF HAPPINESS)

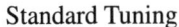

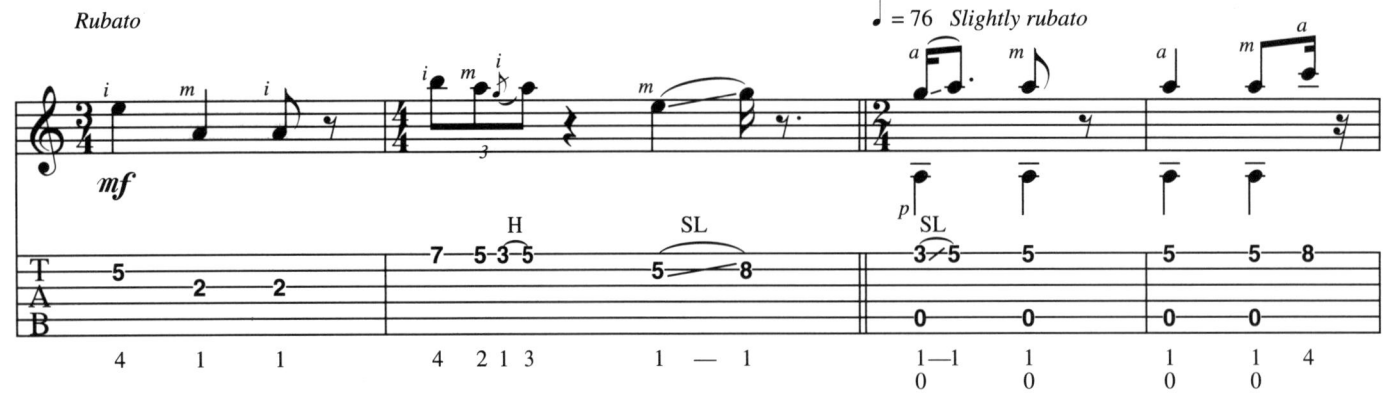

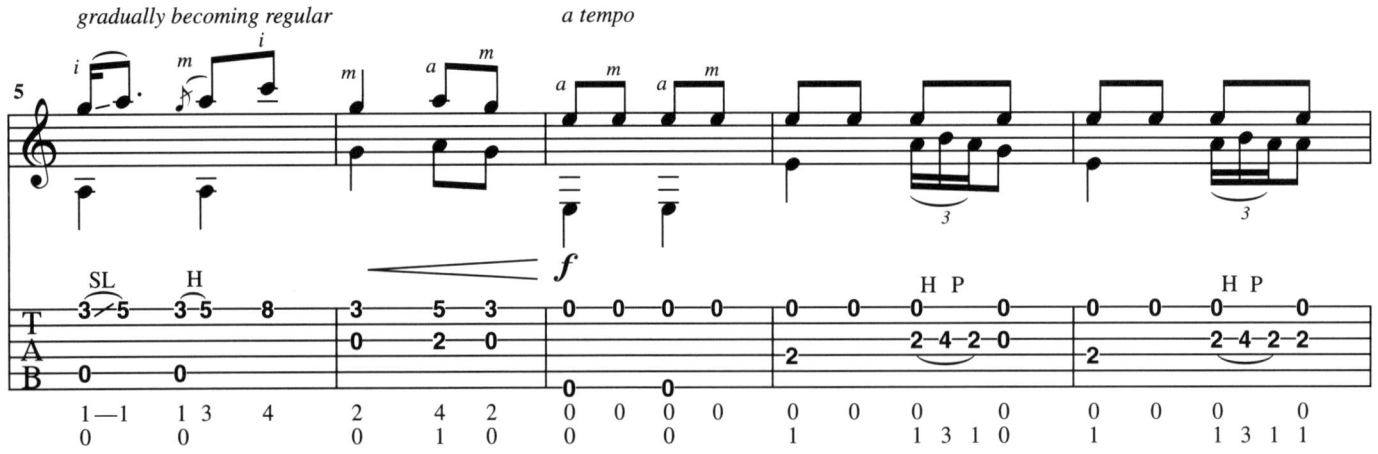

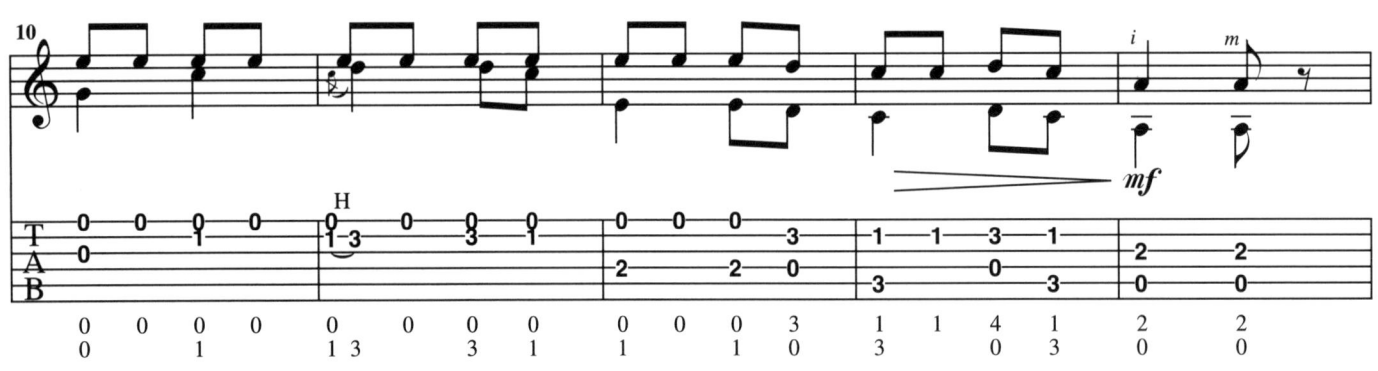

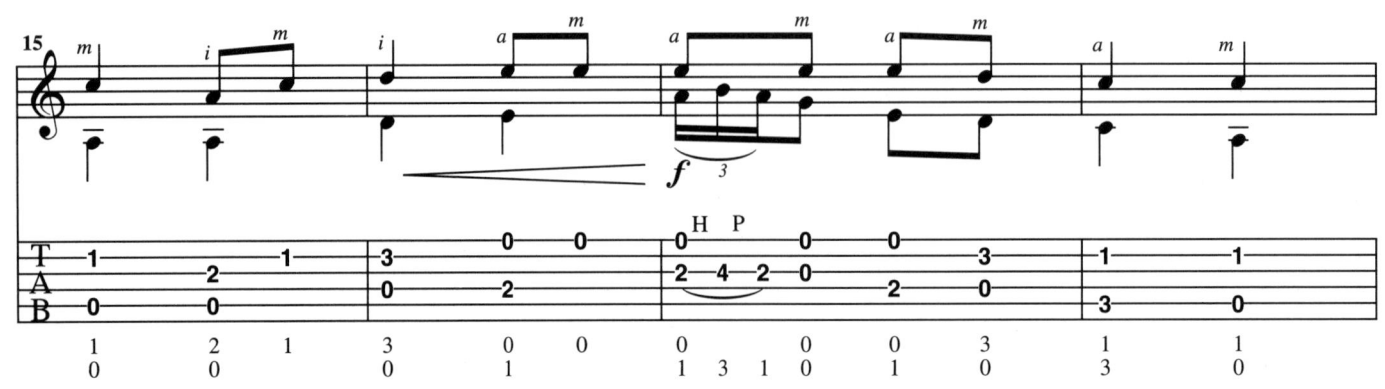

Chapter 5 SILK AND BAMBOO MUSIC

In the bayin system of instrument classification, a common combination of instruments is silk-stringed instruments (pipa, guzheng, erhu) and bamboo wind instruments (dizi, xiao). While these instruments are found in music all over China, southern China is home to a special style of regional music called *sizhu yinyue* ("silk and bamboo music"). Depending on the location in the south, this music has different local flavors and is called by different names: *jiangnan yinyue* ("south of the Yantze River music") or *nan yue* ("southern music"). Aside from ensemble music, the silk and bamboo instruments also have their own solo repertoires. This chapter presents some of the solo instrument pieces for the pipa, guzheng, and dizi.

PIPA: "YUE ER GAO" ("THE MOON ON HIGH")

The moon in Chinese culture has different meanings. Often, it has a connection with melancholy and homesickness (the moon that you see when traveling is the same moon you see in your hometown and viewing it makes you long to be home). "Yue Er Gao" ("The Moon on High") is a well-known pipa piece first written down during the 19th century, but probably existing in an oral tradition for sometime before this. It originates from around the Shanghai area and is seen in both the repertoires of the Shanghai and Zhejiang schools of pipa.

Pipa Techniques for Guitar

"Yue Er Gao" features several pipa techniques adapted for the guitar. Before playing the piece, let's look at these techniques.

Imitating pipa plectrum sound. Because pipa performers tape acrylic plectrums to their fingers, the sound of the attack is much stronger than the usual attack for Western fingerstyle guitarists. For this reason, the stronger thumb stroke should be used.

× = *Pluck string behind the nut.* In measure 65, where there is an "x" marked in the score, the guitarist should use the right hand to pluck the 1st string behind the nut (see photo below). This will make a percussive "click" sound, which is a special pipa technique.

Pluck string behind the nut.

※ = *Lun*. A tremolo on a single note performed by a rapid succession of right-hand finger plucks: *p–i–m–a*. One time through this finger sequence is referred to as a *lun cycle*. In Western notation, this is equivalent to four thirty-second notes (see Example 12 below).

Lun Cycle

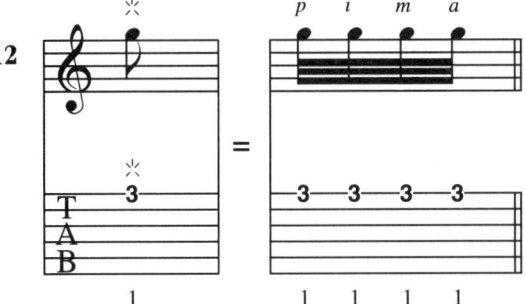

※··· = *Changlun*. Often, as is the case with longer notes, a tremolo must last for longer than one lun cycle. In this case, changlun, or "long lun," is used. Following are two examples of changlun: *single-string* and *double-string*. Where possible, double-string changlun is used because the *p* stroke is a bit easier to perform when isolated on its own string. The examples below are in pipa tuning.

Single-String Changlun

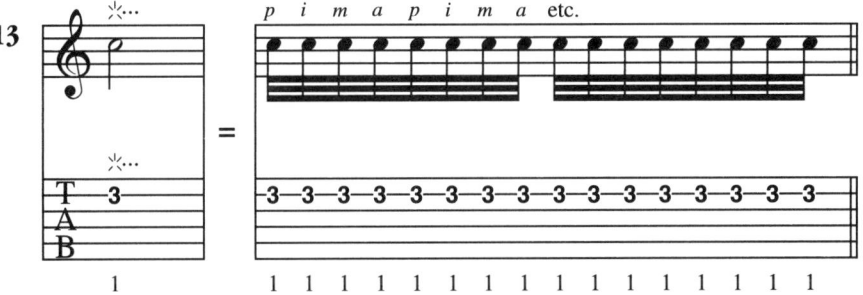

Double-String Changlun

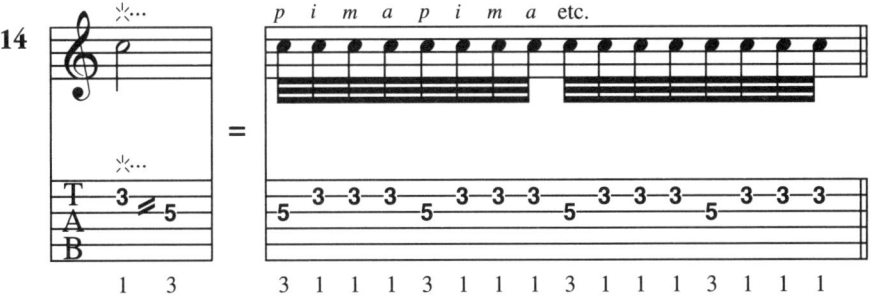

For guitarists using a pick, you can try a rapid alternate picking technique (down-up-down-up, etc.) to perform the lun or changlun techniques.

Practice notes: Focus first on playing the entire piece through, and then add the lun techniques. Depending on the technical facility of the guitarist, lun might take some time to build up the speed needed. It is suggested that the right-hand changlun technique be practiced separate from the piece. Also, to practice the bending techniques used in this piece, refer to Exercises F1 and F2 (the first two half-step bends) in Appendix A (page 238).

GUZHENG: "CHU SHUI LIAN" ("LOTUS IN WATER")

The composition "Chu Shui Lian" ("Lotus in Water") comes from southeast China where guzheng music was influenced by both local opera and folk music. The southern style was famous for the "breathing space" in its music and its classic style of simple, plain melody.

Guzheng Techniques for Guitar

Before playing "Chu Shui Lian," let's get acquainted with a couple of guzheng techniques adapted to the guitar.

Huazou (string sweeping). With guzheng's 21 strings tuned in a pentatonic scale, running the fingers up and down the strings has a very sonorous effect. For fingerstyle guitar, sweep downward with the right-hand finger indicated in the music. Examples of this technique can be seen in measures 1 and 3 below.

Huayin (string bending). Bending pitch on guzheng is done by pressing the string downward. This can bend a pitch as high as a minor 3rd (one and a half steps). On guitar, a major 2nd (one whole step) is the largest practical bend. For the type of bend seen in measure 4, bend a whole step and hold the bend until the lower note is plucked in the next measure. The descending half-step bend in measure 16 should be executed with a fast drop into the second sixteenth note. The long bend in measure 17 should be slow and unfold over the entire length of the measure. Refer to Exercises F1 and F2 (Appendix A, page 238) for bending technique practice.

DIZI: "TAI HU CHUN" ("TAI LAKE SPRING")

The composition "Tai Hu Chun" ("Tai Lake Spring") comes from the heart of the Jiangnan region of China, south of the cities of Shanghai and Hangzhou. Tai Hu, or Lake Tai, is a famous lake in this region. The immediate image evoked at the mention of its name is one of breathtaking forests alongside deep blue lakes. In the springtime, the landscape is engulfed in blossoming flowers. The dizi is closely tied to Jiangnan music, and its woody resonance and bright, high-pitched timbre evokes a lively and earthy sentiment.

Dizi Techniques for Guitar

"Tai Hu Chun" features several dizi techniques adapted to the guitar. Following are explanations of these techniques.

Trills and Grace Notes. The most common idiomatic features of the dizi are trills and grace notes. Trills are designated by the traditional notation (*tr*~) and, depending on the technical agility of the guitarist, can range from one hammer-on and pull-off to as many as two or three combinations. Trills usually occur within the duration of an eighth note, so the trill should fit within this rhythmic space and not disrupt the consistency of the established tempo. Where grace notes are notated, there only needs to be one hammer-on and pull-off sequence.

Slides. Slides are also a part of the dizi style and are usually notated as grace-note slides that should be performed very quickly on the beat, as a type of idiomatic note attack. Sometimes, as in measure 38, you will be sliding from an unspecified pitch; in most of these cases, you can start these slides from a couple of frets above or below the note to which you are sliding.

Chapter 6

GUQIN AND THE LITERATI SCHOLAR TRADITION

The great tradition of Chinese *Literati Scholars* began in the Han Dynasty, a couple of centuries before the turn of the millennia A.D. This period of dynastic history produced a new level of education, scholarship, and artistic refinement that would carry on for the next 2,000 years. The Literati Scholars were trained in reading, writing, and the arts via the Confucian doctrine. This was all in preparation for the official examinations that, if passed, would allow them to seek high positions in the government of the emperor.

In the Confucian context, the arts were as important as the doctrine itself, for excellence in poetry or painting exhibited the correct qualities befitting a *Junzi,* or a Confucian gentleman. While guqin was not part of this examination, it played a role in the scholar's life. Playing the guqin served as a reflective and meditative function—a way to cultivate these qualities. This was true of the other arts as well. Over the next two millennia, this practice continued. Daoism also played a fundamental role in the scholar's life. Where Confucianism advocated for harmony between men in society, Daoism searched for a connection and balance between the individual and the natural world. Guqin functioned to help the scholar reconnect with the Dao.

"PING SHA LUO YAN" ("GEESE DESCENDING ON A SANDY BANK")

"Ping Sha Luo Yan" ("Geese Descending on a Sandy Bank") is a guqin composition that embodies the noble, but sometimes melancholy, pursuits of the scholar. The imagery of geese quietly gliding onto a sandy bank in the dusk of late autumn creates an impression of a vast and timeless nature; an emotional landscape meant to evoke the Dao and the flow of the universe. But the impression can be tinged with a sense of melancholy, too. Depending on the political and social situations, scholars were sometimes banished from court. The cool feeling of an isolated landscape expressed the painful reality of isolation. But even while in isolation, the scholar still strove to achieve the highest moral levels.

Guqin Techniques for Guitar

Guqin is famous for its over 60 left- and right-hand techniques. These techniques produce nuanced timbres through a variety of vibratos, glissandi, right-hand plucks, and left-hand hammer-ons and pull-offs. Following are three sliding techniques in "Ping Sha Luo Yan." Because the music is transcribed for guitar, the symbols found in traditional guqin notation are not used. Rather, they are explained here with references to locations in the piece where they occur.

Jia (slide up), *gen* (slide down), and *fu* (return) are the basic sliding gestures of guqin technique. Jia and gen involve sliding away from a notated pitch. That is, the string is first plucked, and then the slide occurs. Sometimes these slides happen independently, and sometimes they combine with fu. An example of jia by itself is seen in measure 25, first beat, sliding up from A to C. Gen happens less frequently alone. The jia and gen are commonly used with fu. That is, after a gen slide away from a note, fu designates a return slide to the original note. A clear example of this can be seen in measure 24, A sliding down to G, then sliding back to A. When sliding through several notes with only one initial attack, the sound will fade out. This dying out of the sound is highly desirable in guqin music. It represents a Daoist aesthetic of "letting the sound take its natural course." These slides can be practiced in Exercises A and B (Appendix A, page 236).

Jiu is a quickly descending slide to the notated pitch right at the point of attack. Where the previous three sliding techniques have a definite starting note, the jiu is a quick slide from an indefinite starting point. It can be seen in measures 8, 11, 17, etc. The jiu slide can be practiced in Exercises C and D, Appendix A (page 237).

Rou, or "massage," means to move away slowly and return quickly to the original note. Because guqin has no frets, the movement is microtonal (less than a minor 2nd interval). Because microtonal slides are not possible, sliding away to and back from the next lowest fret will approximate the rou technique. The note should be held first and the slide should occur at the very end of the note's duration before moving to the next note. This is notated in the music as a line with a small dip and return at its end (⌒) and can be seen in measures 7, 10, 13, etc. The rou technique can be practiced in Exercises E1 and E2, Appendix A (page 237).

Daiqi, meaning to "lift up," is a common pull-off technique on guqin where a note from any location on the fretboard is pulled off to the open string. There is significant use of daiqi in measures 50–54. Daiqi can be practiced in Exercise D, Appendix A (page 237).

Practice tip: After working through the exercises in Appendix A, it is suggested to leave out the quick descending jiu slides until the jia, gen, and fu slides are mastered. This will make it easier to find fret locations. Jia can then be added afterwards to the longer slide combinations that you have mastered.

Note on timing: The constantly changing meter in "Ping Sha Luo Yan" is due in part to its transcription into Western-style notation. While the transcription does reflect a meter change that the guqin player would have to count, the player would not traditionally think of it in these terms. They would learn the music (via notation and their master's guidance) by remembering the overall flow of each phrase, not by counting Western-style measures. When performing this version, the guitarist should try to internalize the flow of the phrases as soon as possible and eventually discard the counting of Western-style meter.

220   *Guitar Atlas: Volume 2*

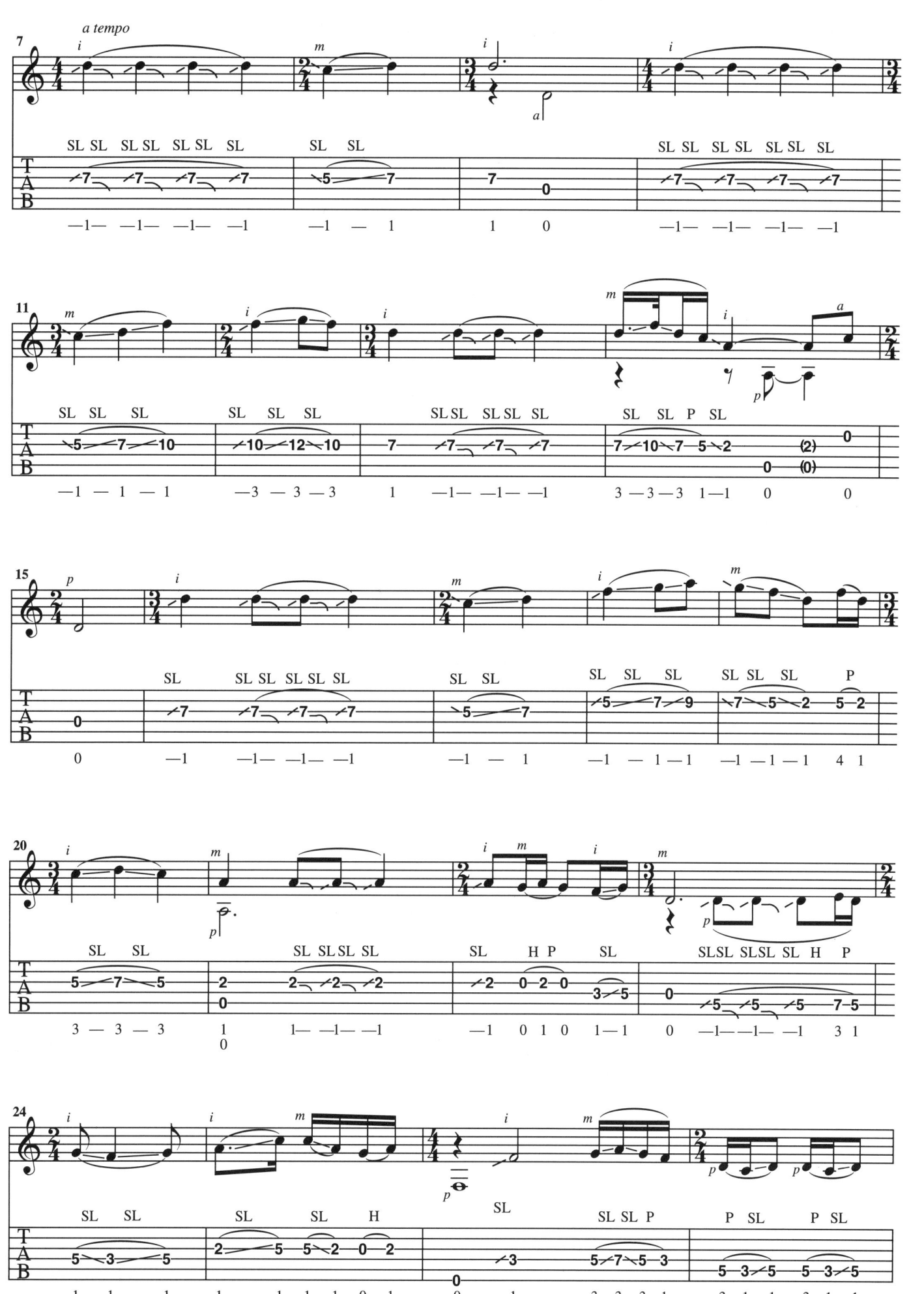

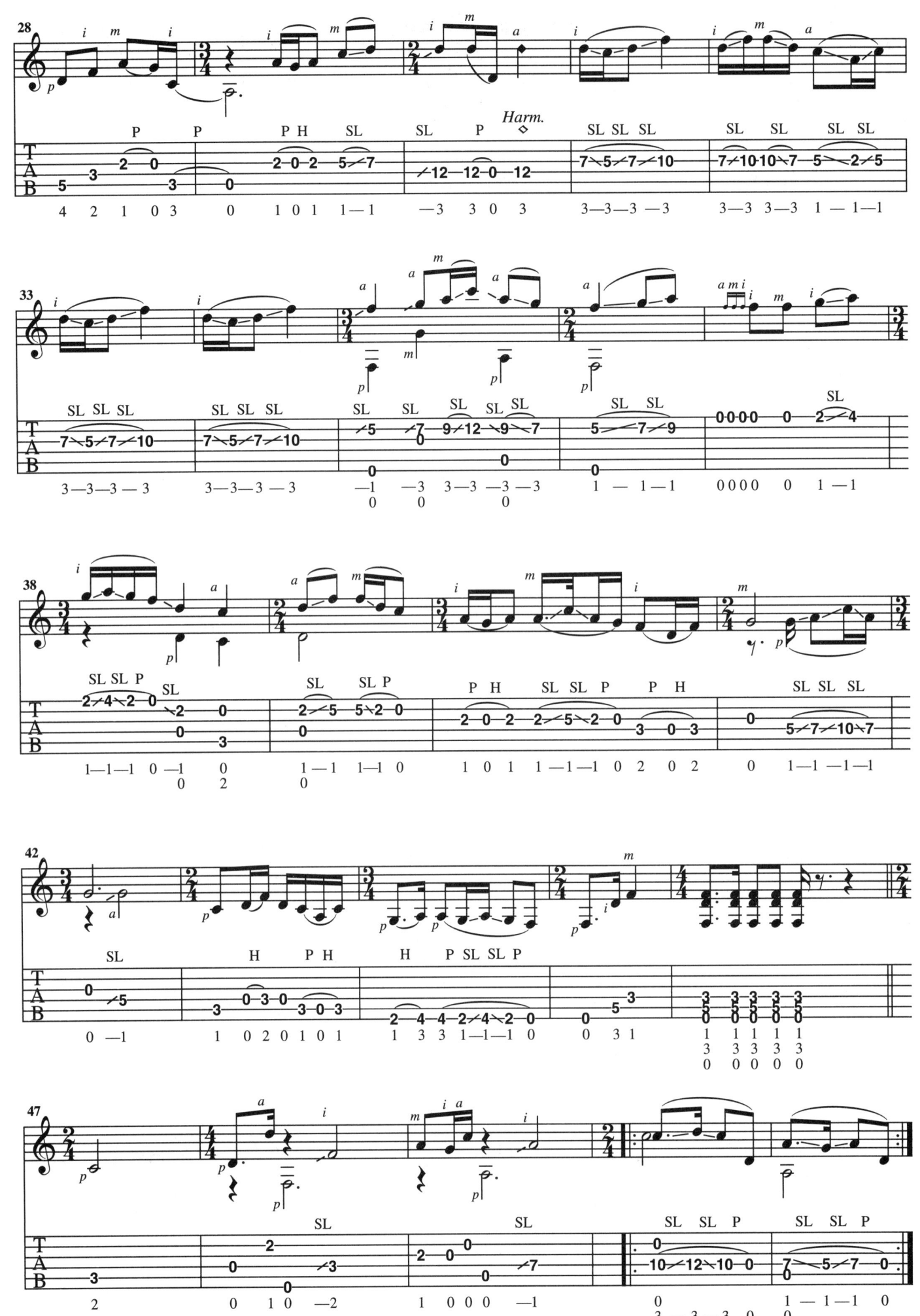

Chapter 7

CHINESE OPERA

Chinese opera has a history of over 700 years, stretching back to the Ming Dynasty. In the broader context of Chinese history, it can be considered a "modern" genre of Chinese music, reaching its peak of popularity in the 19th and early 20th centuries. The origins of Chinese opera can be traced back over 1,000 years with the gradual appearance and growth of various lyric song styles, narrative genres, and dramatic plays in the Tang Dynasty. For example, the *Chanjun* comic drama in the Tang Dynasty that eventually developed a character with a painted face and another character that played the comic role of a clown. Both of these characters are found in Chinese opera today.

Chinese opera, like other music of the past 1,000 years, is largely a regional phenomenon. That is, there is not just one type of opera in China, but many, built on local dialects, folk music, and folk tales. There is, for example, Cantonese opera in the south, Chuan opera in the western Sichuan province, and Xiang opera in the Hunan province.

The most famous opera styles in China are kun opera, which originated from around the Anhui province in eastern China, and Peking opera of northeastern China. Kun opera is considered China's classical opera and rose to prominence during the 16th–18th centuries. Kun opera faded in the 19th century at the time when China's famous Peking opera was on the rise. Peking opera is actually the only non-regional opera, as it incorporates elements from many different regional operas, including Kun opera. It is also the only opera to use the standardized dialect of Mandarin Chinese understood by people all over China. This is another reason for its national popularity.

KUN OPERA STYLE AND "MU DAN TING" ("THE PEONY PAVILION")

Kunqu, or kun opera, is a lyrical opera made of *quqiang* (arias) linked together. It is a lyrical style of singing where the craft of subtle embellishment of a *qupai* ("labeled tune": a common folk tune, identified by its title, that appears in many genres of Chinese music) is highly appreciated by connoisseurs. Embellishments around the central melody often reflect the tonal inflection of the Chinese word being sung. With the Chinese language containing four separate tones (flat, rising, dipping, and falling), an embellishment on a word spoken with the rising tone would add one note above the original pitch. A word with a falling tone would receive an embellishment of two descending scalar tones below the original note.

"Mu Dan Ting" ("The Peony Pavilion") is one of kunqu's most famous operas. The opera tells the story a girl who dreams of meeting the perfect man. When she wakes, she feels as if the dream is real, but falls into despair because she does not know where to find this man. She draws a picture of herself, asks her father to put it on her tomb, then dies of a broken heart. The father does as she asks and then evacuates his estate with his family, fleeing from an invading army. Some time later, a young man discovers the picture hanging on a tree, falls immediately in love with her (as if he knew her from a dream) and eventually finds that the girl is buried nearby. He comes to her grave to find that she has been given life again in order for her to fulfill her destiny of living out a life with her dreamed love.

Kunqu Vocal Style for Guitar

Southern-style embellishment notes. The following excerpt, from an aria in "Mu Dan Ting," reflects a southern singing style where most of the main notes of the melody receive an embellishment note. In this arrangement for guitar, these are designated sometimes as grace notes (measure 3, beat 2) or as thirty-second notes (measure 6). To emulate this vocal effect, the note is performed as a slide away from the original note and then back (or, to a new note). The introduction, played slightly rubato, has large interval slides of minor 3rds and perfect 4ths. These should be articulated in a long, languid, and graceful manner. The notated part below the vocal line is meant to loosely emulate the accompaniment provided by the kunqu instrumental ensemble, usually made up of the dizi flute, sanxian three-string lute, and the huqin fiddle. Sliding technique exercises for "Mu Dan Ting" can be found in Exercises E1 and E2 (the second and third slides), Appendix A (page 237).

PEKING OPERA STYLE AND "BA WANG BIE JI" ("FAREWELL MY CONCUBINE")

Whereas kun opera is based on a series of complete songs *quqiang* (songs), the music of Peking opera is based on *bianqiang*, or "beat-style," which consists of small, rhythmic-melodic fragments that repeat over and over again, either verbatim or in variation. While on the surface the music seems very repetitive, the repetitions (along with the percussive accompaniment and instrumental interludes) all have a type of coded meaning that communicates the emotional and dramatic content of the piece. Along with these musical characteristics, there is an intricate vocabulary of subtle and changing hand positions and facial expressions that symbolically represent the underlying emotional meaning expressed by the singer. The role of the young woman "Huadan" was brought to prominence worldwide in the early years of the 20th century by renowned singer Mei Lan Fang. He was famous both as a singer of kunqu (in which all Peking opera singers must first receive training) and Peking opera. His performances are considered exquisite and unparalleled in modern Peking opera history.

"Ba Wang Bie Ji" Transcribed for Guitar

While the following transcription does not present any new playing techniques, it does give the flavor of an exchange between the instrumental and vocal sections. The musical style of Peking opera is purely melodic, and the singer sings in tandem with the ever-present sound of the jinghu fiddle, whose role is to double the singer's melody. Other Chinese instruments such as the erhu ("second" fiddle) and the yueqin ("moon guitar") also play the melody, exactly or in an embellished manner, and are accompanied by a litany of drums, cymbals, and gongs. The following excerpt from "Ba Wang Bie Ji" begins with a fragment of an instrumental interlude. It is followed by the entrance of the singer, who sings three words of a seven-word poetic stanza, and concludes with another musical interlude. This interplay between jinghu and voice is an essential characteristic of Peking opera. Energy should be high and excited in the interpretation of this music, for not only is the rhythmic drive unceasingly strong, but the power of the singer's high and strong falsetto voice also brings an expressive energy to the music.

BA WANG BIE JI
(FAREWELL MY CONCUBINE)

Excerpt

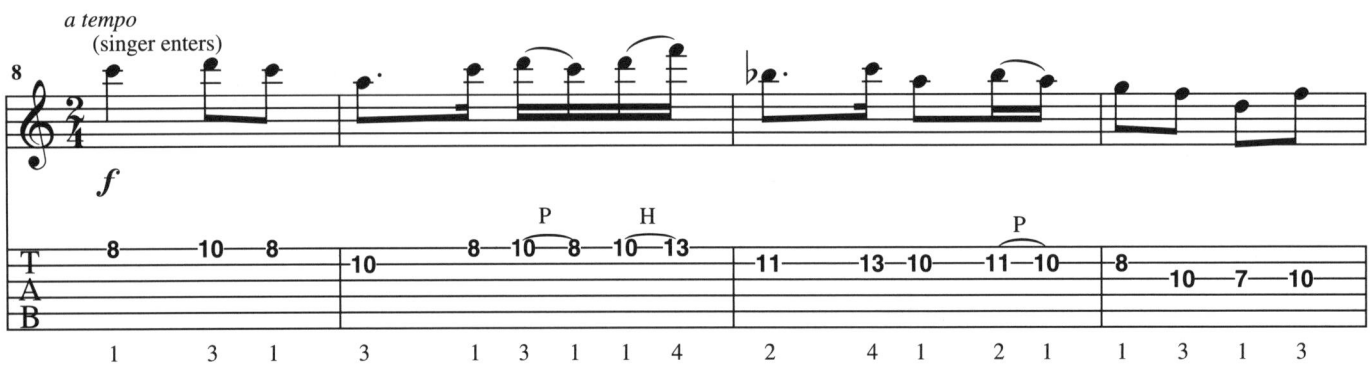

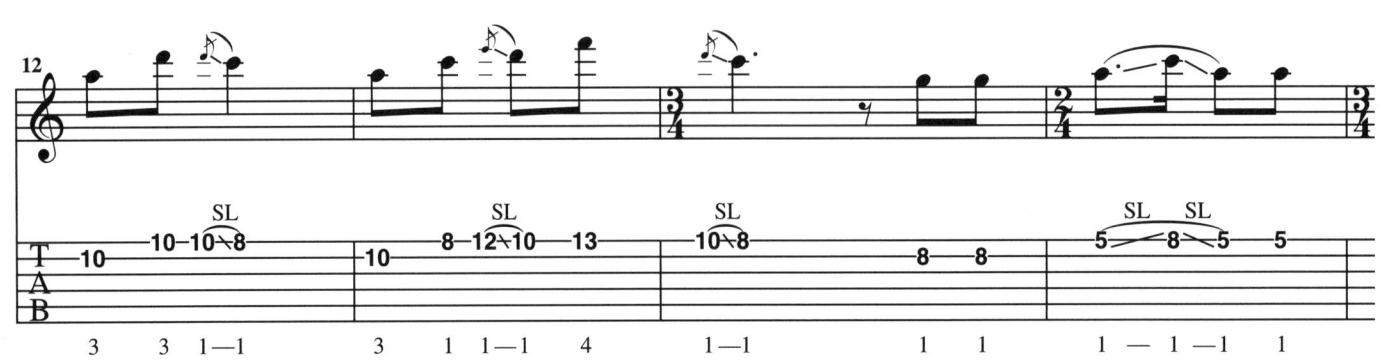

(opera ensemble)

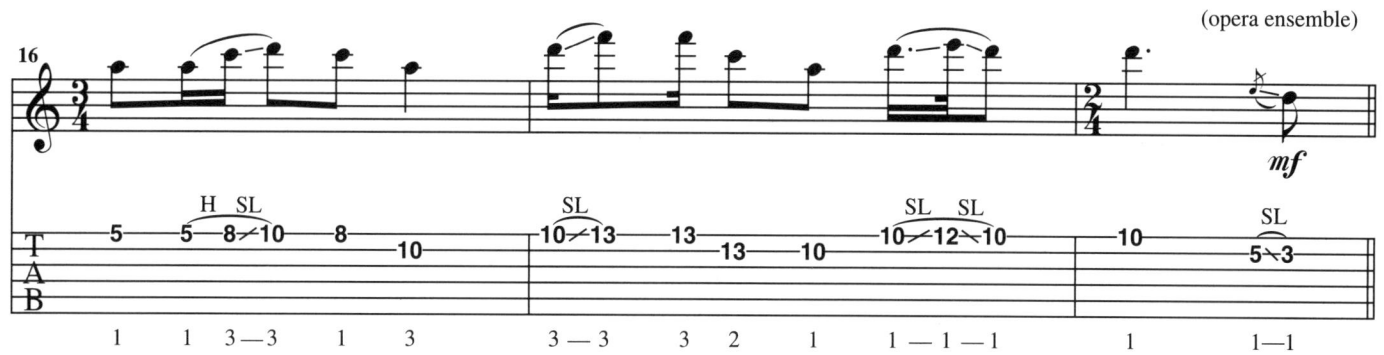

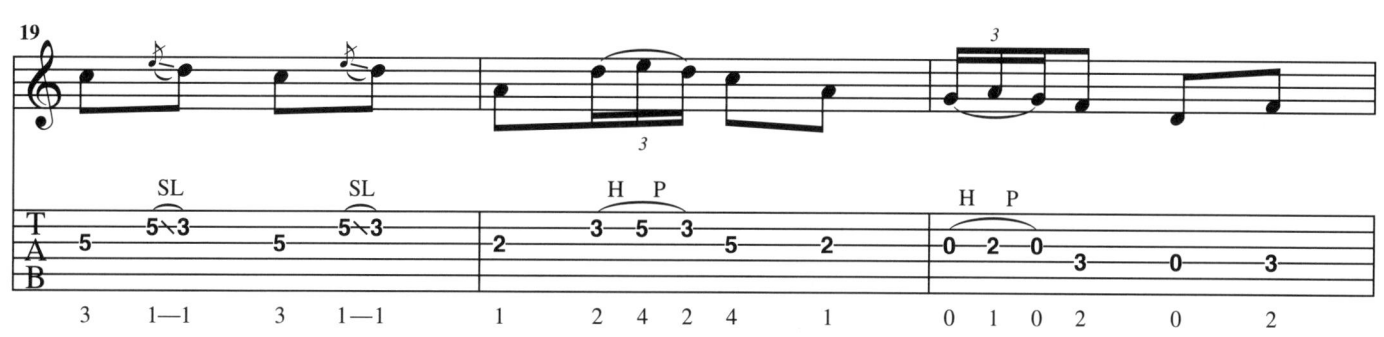

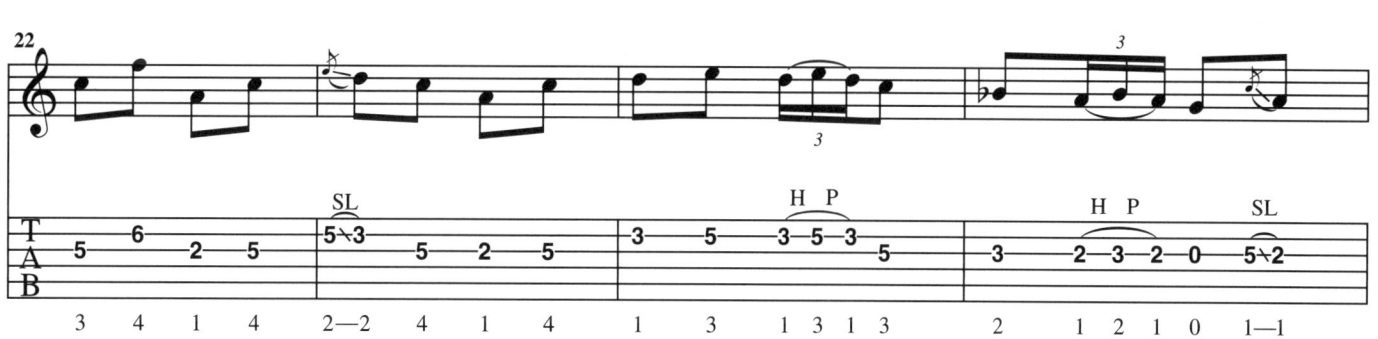

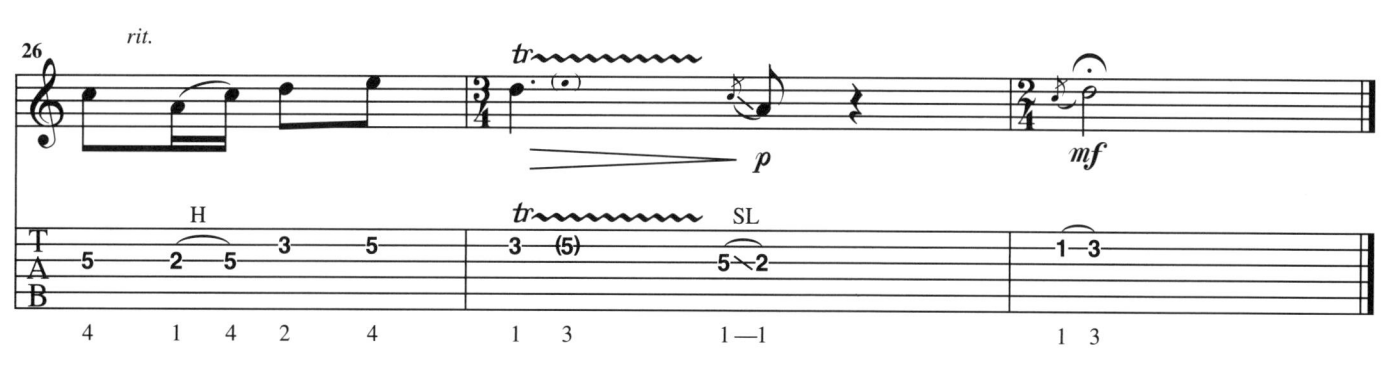

Guitar Atlas: China

Chapter 8: Ethnic Minority Music of China

All of the music we have looked at so far originates from the Han Chinese culture. While Han is by far the majority ethnicity in China (making up over 90% of China's population), there are dozens of other ethnicities that have resided in this region for hundreds, if not thousands, of years. Some of the most ethnically diverse regions of China are found in the western-most reaches of China. The southwest province of Yunnan ("South of the Clouds") alone contains 25 ethnic minorities including the Yi, Miao, Hani, Dai, Zhuang, and Bai. Further west are the great plateaus of Central Asia where Tibetan culture has thrived for thousands of years. To the northwest is the province of Xinjiang where the Muslim culture of the Uyghur ethnicity resides. Other parts of China also contain diverse ethnic groups. The northeast province of Inner Mongolia contains the Mongol ethnicity, and in the southeast are the indigenous ethnicities of the Min and Hakka people. These ethnicities (56 in all) collectively form a tapestry of cultural diversity across all of China and represent legacies of tradition stretching back to antiquity. The music that follows represents but a taste of this diversity.

YI ETHNICITY OF YUNNAN

The Yi ethnicity can be found in many different areas of western China, as well as Vietnam and Myanmar, but the largest population is found in the province of Yunnan. They can be found throughout the province but are largely concentrated in the mountain villages around the ancient city of Dali, in the west central part of Yunnan, close to the boarder with Myanmar. They were believed to be, in part, descendants of Tibetan tribes, and their language is rooted in the Tibetan-Burman language group.

Yi Music in Courtship and Festivals

Yi culture contains music and instruments for a variety of social functions. Two of the most significant are music for courtship and music that is played at annual festivals. In Yi culture, courtship involves music as a means to communicate and express feelings toward one another. While this music-courting process can happen at any time, it is most prominent during annual festivals. One such festival is the Torch Festival, held every year on the 24th day of the 6th lunar month. The Torch Festival is a yearly worship of the power of fire, thought in Yi culture to possess a strong spiritual presence. Festivals often provide opportunities for Yi men and women to find their prospective spouses. Different instruments are used in courtship, including a three-stringed instrument called *sanxian* (literally "three string"), a mouth harp. The following piece, "Torch Festival Night," is a typical melodic style of the mouth harp. The mouth harp, usually made of brass or bamboo, looks like a leaf with a vibrating reed carved out in its center. The leaf-shaped reed, called a *lamella,* is placed near the mouth and plucked. The player changes the shape of the opening of his mouth to produce various shades of buzzing timbre. While the instrument is limited to three or four pitches (depending on the number of lamellas used), the constant change of buzzing timbre, combined with the simple but varying melodic patterns, produces a mesmerizing music that is both hypnotic and invigorating at the same time.

Yi mouth harp.

TORCH FESTIVAL NIGHT

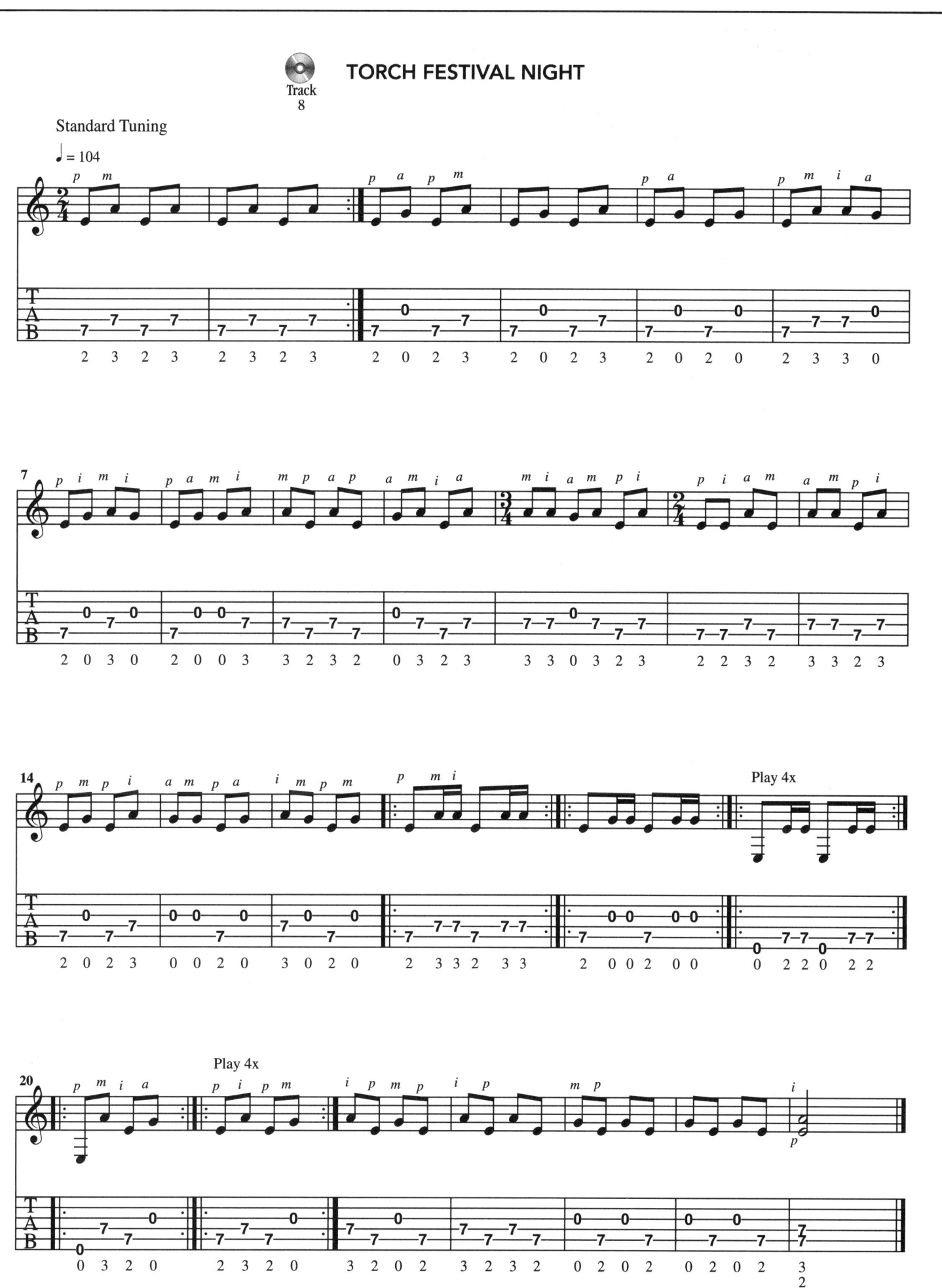

TIBET

Referred to in recent years as "The roof of the world," Tibet unfolds over the vast area of the Tibetan Plateau in Central Asia. It is a vast, expansive, and isolated land with some of the tallest mountain peaks in the world (e.g., Mount Everest). The mythical origins of Tibet stretch back to the 3rd century B.C. and the first supposed king Nyatri Tsenpo. However, documented history of Tibet begins in the 7th century A.D. and Songtsan Ganpo, who ruled over Tibet as a kingdom. Tibetan culture centers around two religious belief systems: the better-known Tibetan Buddhism, which came into Tibet originally as Vajrayana Buddhism, and Bön, an indigenous Tibetan religion predating Tibetan Buddhism and slowly marginalized by Buddhism over the last 1,500 years.

Tibetan Religious Music

Because Tibetan Buddhism is so central to Tibetan culture, much of Tibetan music is religious. Depending on the branch of Buddhism that a particular monastery might follow, it may have no musical instruments, or it may have an entire orchestra and dance troupe. An orchestra may consist of large brass instruments over 10 feet long, a piercing type of double-reed shawm instrument, cymbals and gongs, and on occasion, a flute made from a human thighbone! Singing and chanting occurs during the religious service, and the instrumental music is played between sections of chanting or at the beginning or ending of the service.

The function of sacred music in the Tibetan religious tradition centers on music as a path towards inner transformation—a process where the individual successively reaches a higher and purer state of mind called "Enlightenment." This is a stage where one can see the essence of all things and live in a constant state of wisdom and compassion.

Tibetan Folk Music

Tibetan folk music comes in many varieties and forms, depending on the location in Tibet and local dialects spoken. It serves a different function than religious music in that it provides music for everyday life, either in work, social ceremony, or general entertainment. Work music varies in style and tempo depending on the task being accomplished. A field song will have a different rhythm and character than a clothes-washing song. Other songs are not related to work or ceremony, but to aspects of culture or the surrounding natural environment. For instance, "Sodo Yala" (next page) is a folk song that might be sung by a traveler on a long and lonely journey across the expansive Tibetan Plateau.

SODO YALA

XINJIANG AND THE UYGHUR ETHNICITY

Of China's 56 ethnic minorities, the Uyghur population of Xinjiang province is the most culturally distant from the Han majority culture. Occupying China's vast northwest province of Xinjiang, the origins of the Uyghur population lie further westward, in the Turkic cultures of Central Asia. In the 8th to 9th centuries, the Uyghur's ruled a powerful empire in the area that today is part of Mongolia. With the fall of this empire, most Uyghurs migrated to their present location in Xinjiang. In the 15th century, Islamic religion came into Uyghur culture and produced something of a conflict. Islamic religion forbids most types of music, but in the Uyghur culture predating the Islamic influence, music and dance were fundamental. Over the centuries, a peaceful coexistence of the Uyghur music tradition alongside Islamic religion seemed to have worked itself out.

Uyghur music is centered on the *12 Mukam*. These are epic music pieces consisting of narrative poems, song and dance, and instrumental sections. Each Mukam is made up of many individual songs in a great variety of musical modes, meter, and performing styles.

Uyghur instruments originate from Turkic culture and therefore have no relation to Chinese traditional instruments. While wind instruments such as the flute or shawm are found in Uyghur music, plucked and bowed string instruments mostly dominate the music. The *dutar* and *tanbur* are the most well-known plucked instruments, while the *eijek* and *rawap* are the most popular bowed instruments. The *dap,* a small percussive hand drum, can be found in almost all Uyghur music, providing the rhythmic backbone.

"Enjen" ("Sorrow")

"Enjen" ("Sorrow") is an instrumental piece taken from one of the 12 Mukam. Struggle and sadness are a part of the fabric of Uyghur history, and often, their music is tinged with a melancholic sadness reflective of historic struggles. The minor mode and the solemn, trudging rhythmic and melodic character of "Enjen" express this sadness.

"Enjen" is usually performed by the tanbur with accompaniment provided by other bowed and stringed instruments. It would function as an introduction to a narrative, or song and dance, section of a Mukam. The music of "Enjen" is quite lengthy. After stating the initial melody, or "theme," variations follow, each time further embellishing the melody, becoming more and more elaborate while at the same time slowly increasing the tempo. This goes hand in hand with a spinning style of Uyghur dance, where the movements increase in intensity along with the music. This transcribed version, with its short form and slowly accelerating and decelerating rhythm, is just a small taste of the musical style found in the Uyghur Mukam.

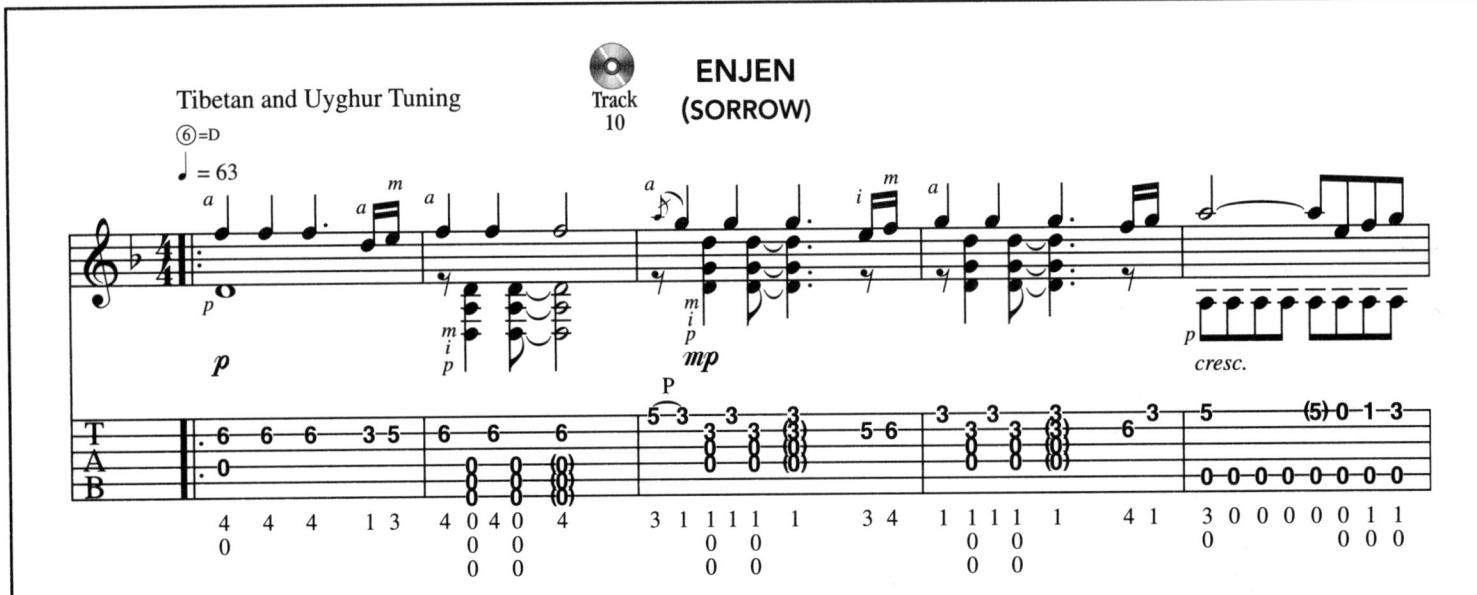

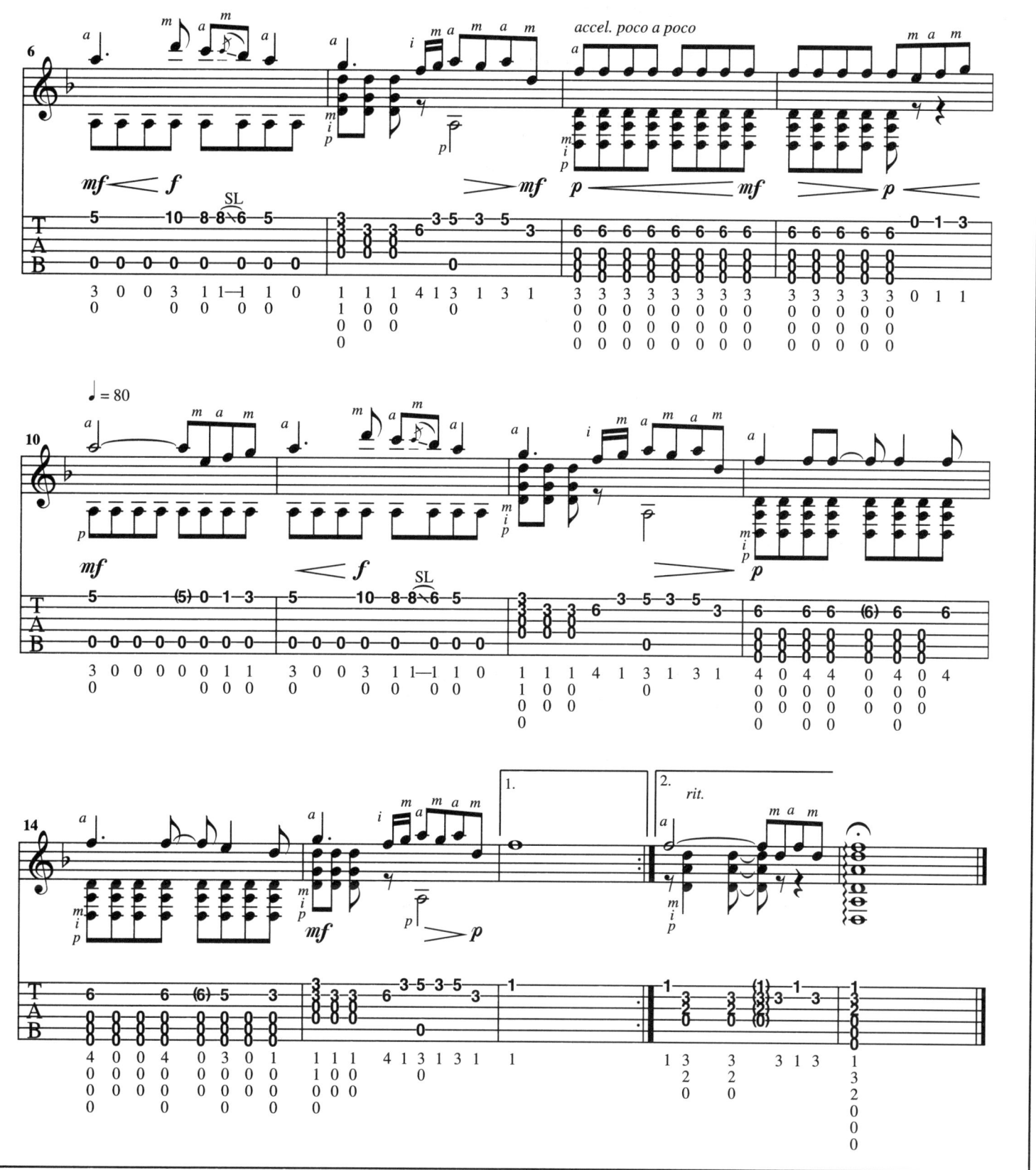

Final Word

I hope you have enjoyed your journey on guitar through the vast array of music that China has to offer. While this book was intended to give some depth to the music and history of China, it really only scratches the surface. I encourage you to explore more of China, both ancient and modern. While it is a culture with many differences from Western culture, the people of China are very warm and open, and would always welcome you into their home with a friendly smile. Thank you for your interest in this book, and enjoy your further explorations!

Appendix A

PREPARATORY EXERCISES

CHINA

Note: The following exercises are all in the guqin and guzheng tuning (see page 240).

These preparatory exercises address three major idiomatic techniques belonging to Chinese music: sliding, pitch bending, and trills/grace notes. Multiple techniques from different pieces can be found in each exercise. So, this appendix can be used for general preparation as well as practice for a technique related to a particular piece. When a technique is introduced in this book, reference is made to the appropriate exercise in this appendix.

It should be noted that, while a single technique shown here might be found in multiple pieces, the idiomatic style of the piece and the instrument from which it was taken should be considered carefully by listening to and imitating the CD. The technique may seem similar on paper, but in practice, each instrument has its own nuanced way of performing it.

Sliding Exercises

While Exercises A–D are closely related to guqin technique, they can provide general benefit for all pieces that contain single-string playing and sliding.

Exercise A: Quick slide up, slide away, return

Exercise B: Quick slide up, continue sliding up

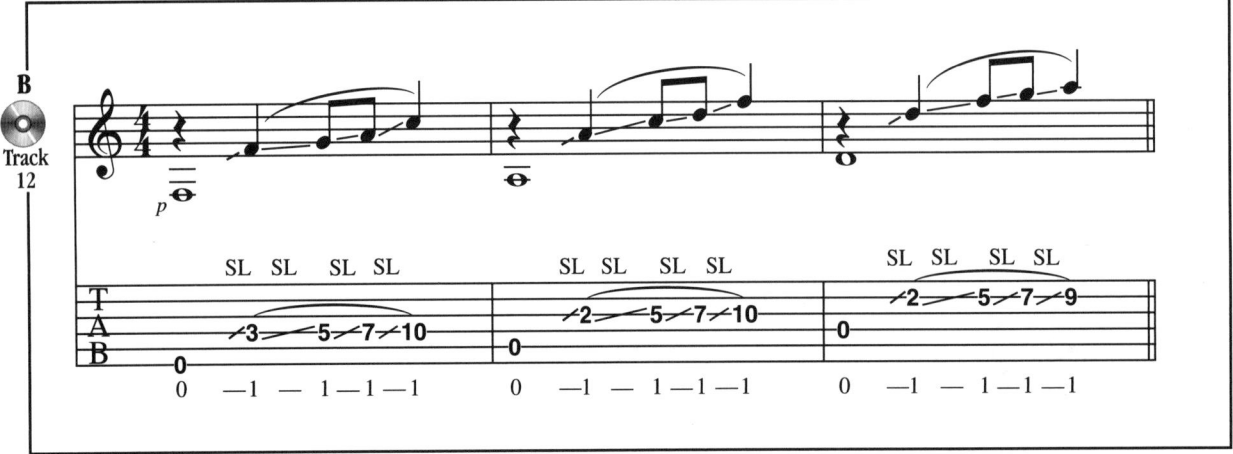

236   *Guitar Atlas: Volume 2*

Exercise C: Quick slide down, slide away, return

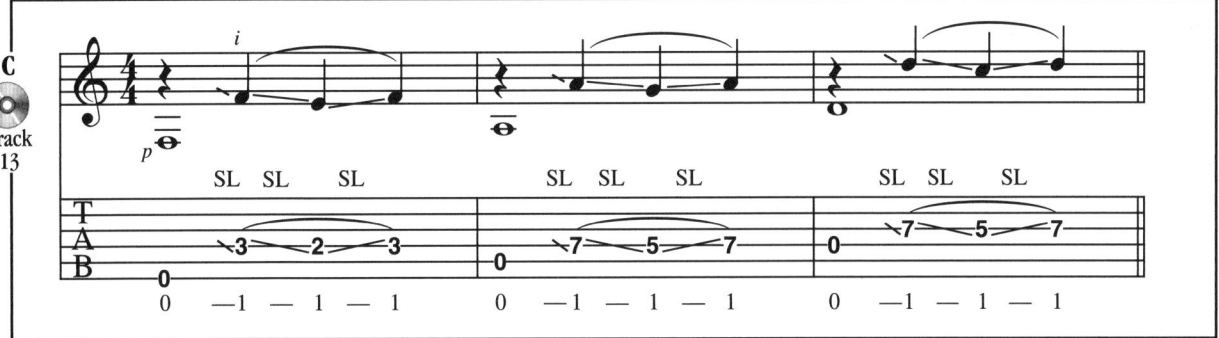

Exercise D: Sliding and pull-off combination

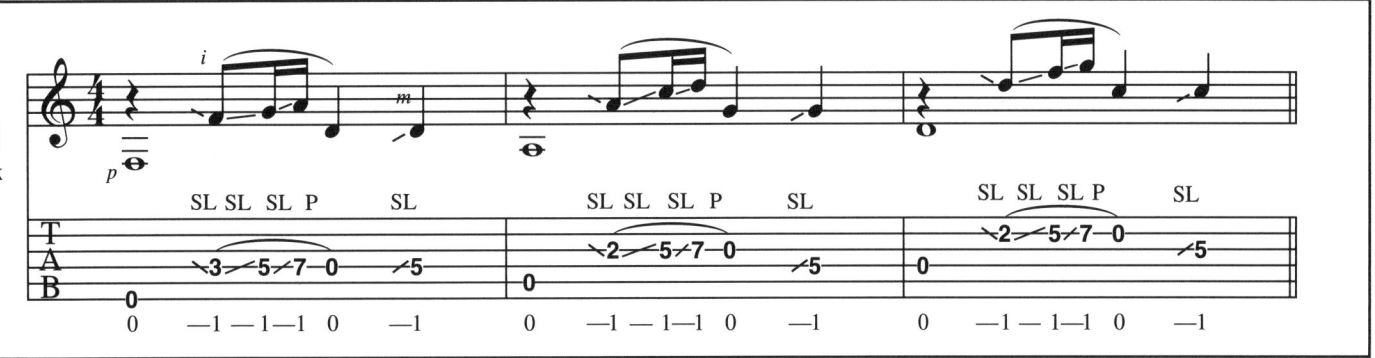

Practice note: The "quick slide down" (jiu technique in "Ping Sha Luo Yan," page 220) should be a very quick slide from an indefinite pitch. You can start the slide anywhere from 1 to 5 frets above the notated pitch to which you are sliding. In Exercise D, the pull-off technique is the daiqi technique in "Ping Sha Luo Yan."

Exercises E1 and E2: Quick return slides and the graceful slide

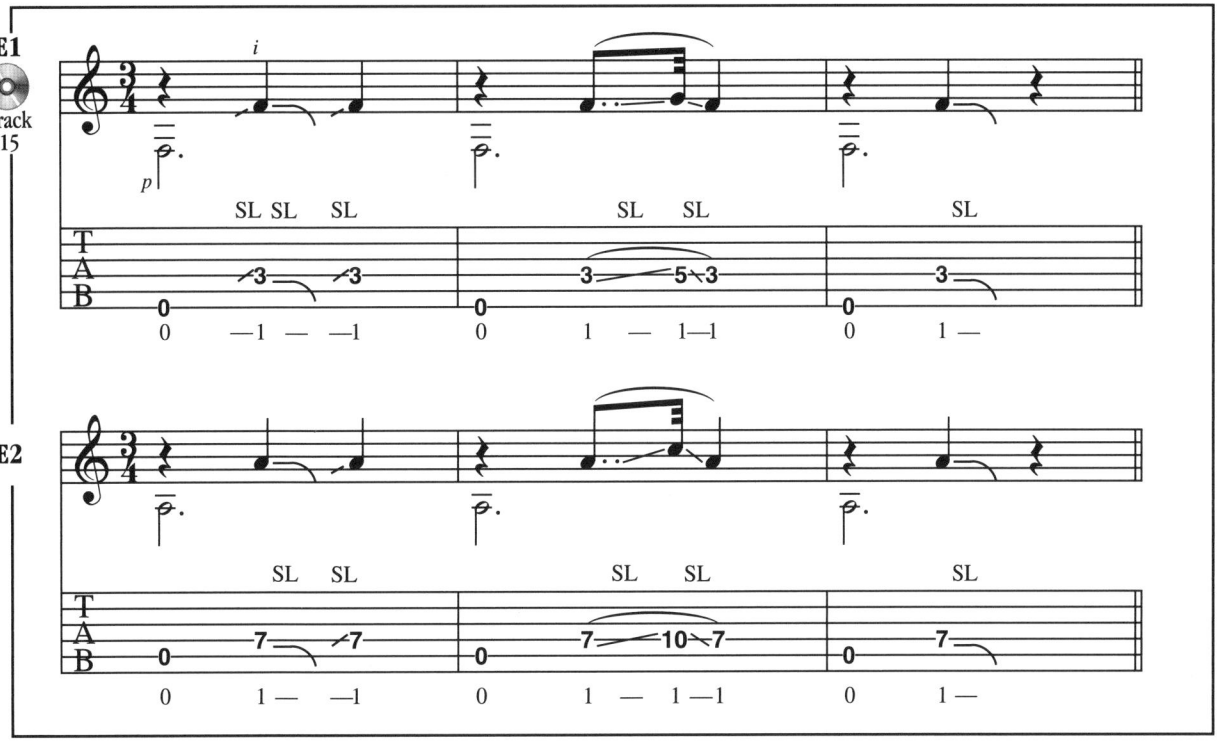

Practice note: The slide in the 1st measures of both Exercises E1 and E2 are related to the rou technique in "Ping Sha Luo Yan" (page 220). The slides in the 2nd and 3rd measures are found in "Mu Dan Ting" (page 225). The graceful slide in the 3rd measure should gradually slide down several frets before the sound dies out.

Guitar Atlas: China

Bending Exercises
Exercises F1 and F2: Quick half-step bends, slow whole-step bends

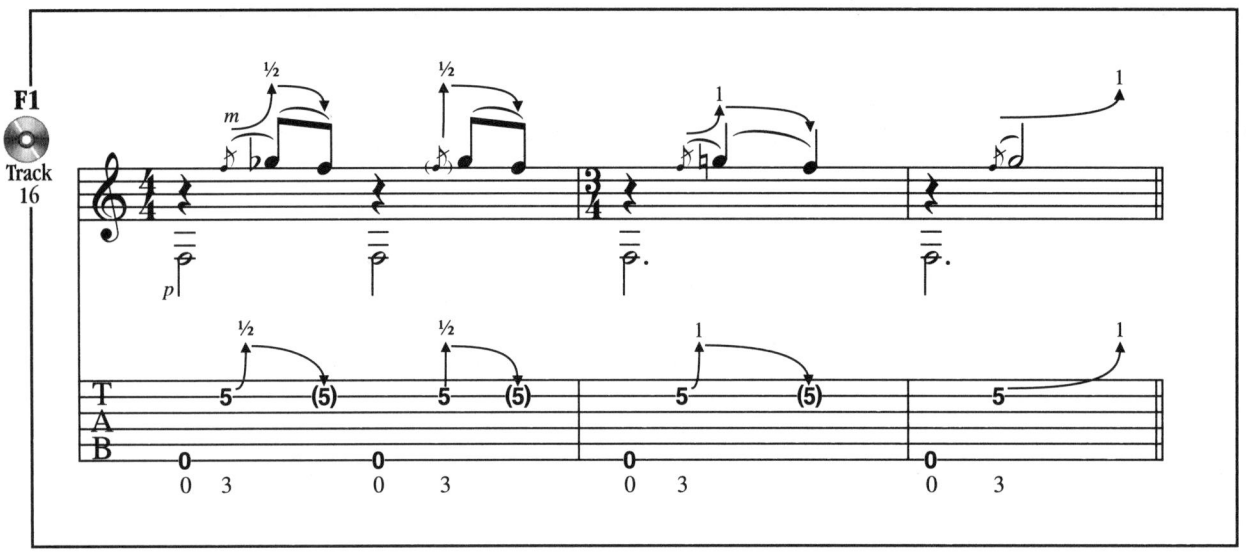

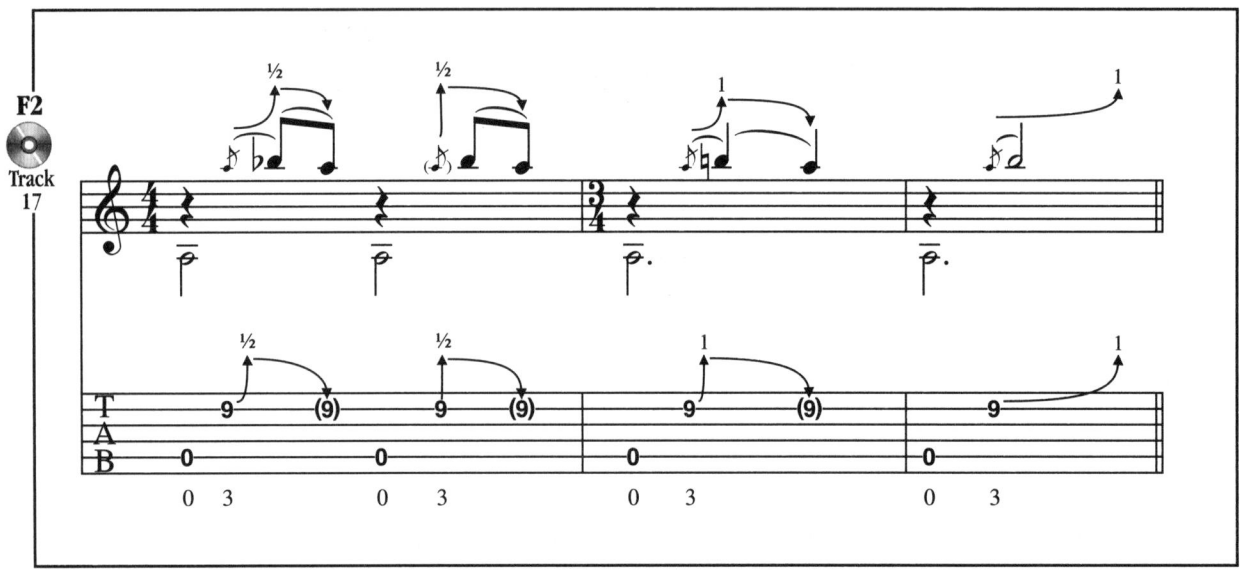

Practice note: The two half-step bends are found in "Yue Er Gao" (page 212). The half-step bend on beat 4 and the two whole-step bends are found in "Chu Shui Lian" (page 214). In theory, a whole-note bend is desirable, but in practice, a "greater-than-half-step, less-than-whole-step" bend is acceptable as well.

Trills and Grace-Note Hammer-On/Pull-Off Exercises
Exercises G1 and G2: Grace notes and trill figures

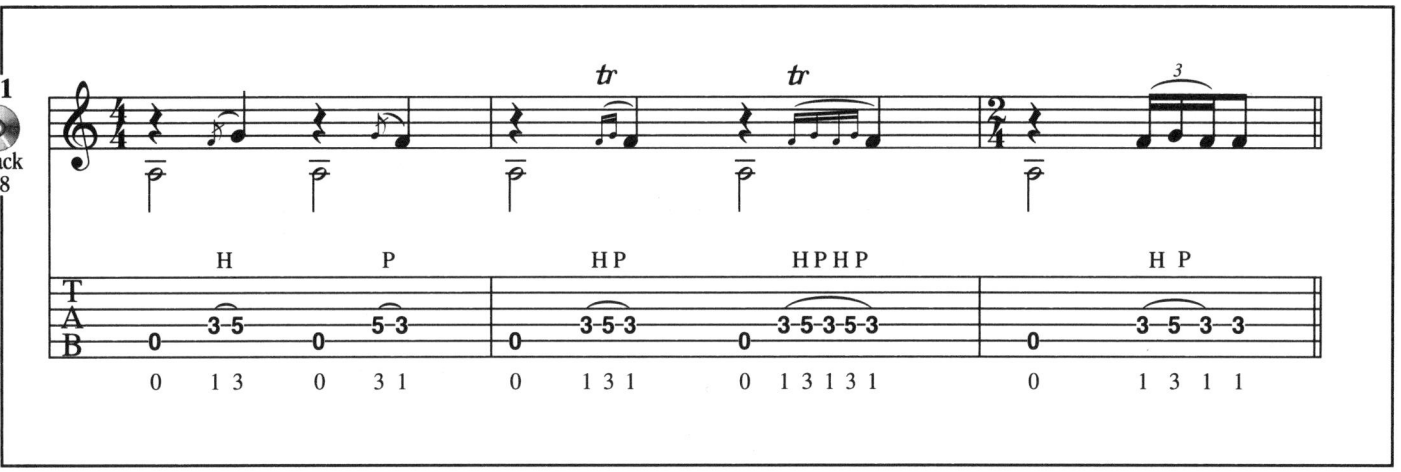

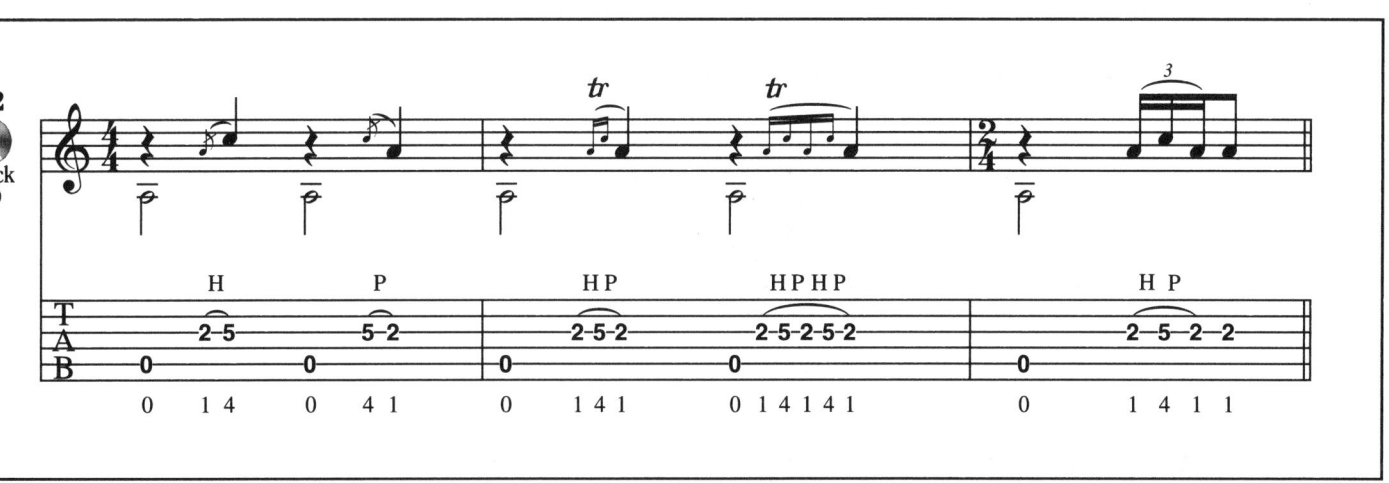

Practice note: The grace notes and trills in the first two measures are abundant in "Tai Hu Chun" (page 216). When *tr* is designated in the piece, as in measure 2 above, the guitarist can choose between the two trill figures. The triplet figure in the third measure is found in "Wan Nian Huan" (page 208) and "Ba Wang Bie Ji" (page 228).

Guitar Atlas: China

Appendix B — GUITAR TUNINGS

The variety of guitar tunings found in this book reflects the number of considerations that have to be made when transcribing Chinese music for guitar. These include: 1) the tunings of the Chinese instruments from which the music is transcribed, 2) the particular pentatonic scale used in the music, and 3) technical considerations of arranging the music for guitar. In reference to the last point, it is important to realize that virtually all of the idiomatic Chinese music techniques in this book are used for playing the melodies. Tunings were devised to provide maximum use of open strings; this minimizes complicated left-hand fingerings so that the technical aspects of performing the melodies can receive the most focus. Following are all of the tunings used in this book.

Track 20
⑥ = E   ③ = G
⑤ = A   ② = B
④ = D   ① = E

Standard Tuning
("Wan Nian Huan," "Ba Wang Bie Ji," "Torch Festival Night")
The three pieces above use standard tuning because the music is not related to the technique of a specific instrument and because the pentatonic mode that is used fits well with standard guitar tuning.

Track 21
⑥ = F   ③ = G
⑤ = A   ② = C
④ = D   ① = F

Guqin and Guzheng Tuning
("Chu Shui Lian," "Ping Sha Luo Yan")
This tuning approximates the open-string F Pentatonic scale tunings of both instruments. Guzheng only uses open strings to play its music and guqin makes ample use of unison pitches played between open and stopped strings.

Track 22
⑥ = E   ③ = G
⑤ = A   ② = A
④ = E   ① = E

Pipa Tuning ("Yue Er Gao")
This tuning emulates the flavor of the pipa tuning. While pipa has only four strings and the guitar has six, the predominance of perfect 5th intervals (A–E) is a typical feature of pipa tunings.

Track 23
⑥ = E   ③ = G
⑤ = A   ② = C
④ = E   ① = E

Dizi Tuning ("Tai Hu Chun")
This tuning provides open strings that fit in the mode. This allows more left-hand freedom to focus on the trill and slide techniques in the melody.

Track 24
⑥ = E   ③ = F♯
⑤ = B   ② = A
④ = D   ① = E

Kun Opera Tuning ("Mu Dan Ting")
This tuning is based on the D Pentatonic mode used in some kun operas.

Track 25
⑥ = D   ③ = G
⑤ = A   ② = B
④ = D   ① = E

Tibetan and Uyghur Tuning ("Sodo Yala," "Enjen")
The low D in this tuning is used to accommodate the modal nature of these two folk songs. Typically, stringed instruments in these traditions are tuned in 5ths, not 4ths. The D-A combination on the 6th and 5th strings accommodates this aspect of the music and allows the open strings to ring in the D Minor mode in which these pieces are written.

Russia

Frank Natter, Jr.

*Guitar Styles
from Around the World*

This book was acquired, edited, and produced
by Workshop Arts, Inc., the publishing arm of
the National Guitar Workshop.
Nathaniel Gunod, acquisitions, managing editor
Burgess Speed, acquisitions, senior editor
Timothy Phelps, interior design
Ante Gelo, music typesetter
Barbara Smolover, interior illustrations
CD recorded and mastered by Collin Tilton at Bar None Studio, Northford, CT
Frank Natter, Jr. (guitar)

Contents

ABOUT THE AUTHOR 243
   Acknowledgements..................................243
   Notation Guide..243

INTRODUCTION 244

CHAPTER 1—A Brief History of Russian Music.....245

CHAPTER 2—Traditional Instruments of Russia....246
   Balalaika..246
   Domra..247
   Gusli..248
   Garmon and Boyan...................................248
   Shepherd's Pipes......................................248
   Russian Percussion Instruments..............249
   The Russian Seven-String Guitar.............249

CHAPTER 3—The Tones, Popevki, and Kant........250
   The Tones..250
   The Gamut..250
   Popevki...250
      Znamenny Melody in Tone 1................254
   Kant..255
      Spiritual Kant..255

CHAPTER 4—Russian Orthodox Music................256
   Znamenny Chant......................................256
   Later Chant Styles....................................256
   Russian Hymns...257
   "Afonskoye" ("From Mount Athos")............258
      Afonskoye (From Mount Athos)............258
   Spiritual Verses...260
      A Dukhovnyi Stikh................................260

CHAPTER 5—Russian Village Music....................262
   Rhythm..263
   Melody..263
   Singing and Harmony..............................263
   Russian Folk Music Today........................263
   "Kamarinskaya"..264
      Kamarinskaya..264
   "Hey Ukhnem (Song of the Volga Boatmen)"......266
      Hey Ukhnem (Song of the Volga Boatmen)............266
   Svyatki...268
      Songs of Svyatki....................................268

CHAPTER 6—Russian Stage Music.....................270
   Russian Classical Music...........................270
   The Russian Folk Orchestra.....................270
   Other Stage Music....................................270
   "Moscow Nights"......................................271
      Moscow Nights......................................271
   "Evening Bells"...272
      Evening Bells...272
   "Kalinka"...274
      Kalinka...274

CHAPTER 7—Russian Romances........................276
   "Oochin Cyorni" ("Dark Eyes") and
      Russian Gypsies...................................276
      Oochin Cyorni (Dark Eyes)....................276

CHAPTER 8—The Bard Movement......................280
   Bulat Okudzhava......................................280
   Vladimir Vysotsky.....................................280
   Bard Chords in the Semistrunka Tuning....281
   Bard Guitar Styles.....................................282
      A Soldier's Song....................................282
      A March For Bulat.................................284

FINAL WORD 286
   References for Further Reading 286
   References for Further Listening...............286
   Web Links..286

APPENDIX—Alternate Guitar Tunings
Used in This Book 287

Track 1

A compact disc is included with this book. Using it with the book can make learning easier and more enjoyable. The symbol shown at the left appears next to every example that is on the CD. Use the CD to help ensure that you're capturing the feel of the examples and interpreting the rhythms correctly. The track number below the symbol corresponds directly to the example you want to hear. Track 1 will help you tune to this CD. Enjoy!

242   *Guitar Atlas: Volume 2*

About the Author

Frank Natter, Jr., an accomplished guitarist, composer, and teacher, has performed in various folk rock, blues, and contemporary ensembles across the United States. He is the author of *The Total Acoustic Guitarist* (#24426), *No Reading Required: Chords and Strums for Acoustic Guitar* (#26058), and *The Blues Guitar Experience* (#32650), all published by Alfred/National Guitar Workshop. Frank received a B.A. in Music Theory and Composition from Central Connecticut State University. In 2002, Frank had the fortunate opportunity to visit Russia. This trip fostered his interest in Russian culture and music, and led to the writing of this book. Frank continues to draw on this experience when composing original music and when teaching at his music store/studio, Face Arts Music, located in Deep River, Connecticut.

PHOTO BY TIMOTHY PHELPS

ACKNOWLEDGEMENTS

Thank you, Mom, Dad, Malissa, and Hillyn, for your support and help. Thank you, Burgess, for the opportunity to continue my exploration of this music. Thank you, Rolande Duprey and Alex Kuzma, for pointing me in the right direction. Thank you, Masha Marth, for your help and confirmations. A very special thank you goes to Valentina S. Tuchina, Valeriy N. Tuchin, Nikolai V. Tuchin, Maria V. Tuchina, Irina G. Kutyrina, and Vladimir A. Kutyrin, for such a warm and welcoming stay in Russia.

NOTATION GUIDE

H = Hammer-on.

P = Pull-off.

SL = Ascending slide.

SL = Descending slide.

⌒ = *Fermata*. Pause, or hold note longer than its indicated duration.

\> = *Accent*. Emphasize the note or chord.

♩. = *Staccato*. Make note shorter than its indicated duration.

✗ = *Chuck*. Muted, percussive, unpitched note.

①②③④⑤⑥ = The guitar strings, starting from the highest-pitched string, the 1st string, high E.

p, i, m, a = The right-hand fingers starting with the thumb.

1, 2, 3, 4, 0 = The left-hand fingers starting with the index finger; 0 = open string. The left-hand fingers are indicated under the TAB.

rit. = Abbreviation for *ritardando*. Become gradually slower.

p (piano) = soft.
f (forte) = loud.
mf (mezzo forte) = somewhat loud.

⟨ = *Crescendo*. Gradually increase volume.

⟩ = *Decrescendo*. Gradually decrease volume.

Harm. or ♦ = *Harmonic*. Notes of the harmonic series that are very pure and clear. In this book, written at the sounding pitch with a diamond-shaped notehead. Touch the string lightly over the indicated fret and pluck, immediately removing the finger from the string.

Capo VII = Place the capo at the 7th fret. Standard music notation and TAB are written as if in open position. In other words, for easier reading, *true* pitch is not indicated.

grad. accelerando = Become gradually faster.

rubato = Play in freer, less strict time.

≋ = *Tremolo*. Rapidly strum the chord, alternating between downstrokes and upstrokes for the indicated duration.

⦚ = *Arpeggiate*. Quickly roll the chord with the right-hand fingers or thumb.

↑ = Downward strum using a right-hand finger.

↓ = Upward strum using a right-hand finger.

BV = Barre all six strings at the 5th fret.

BV₃ = In this example, barre three strings at the 5th fret.

♩ = 185 = Tempo marking. In this case, there are 185 quarter notes, or beats, per minute. (If you have a metronome, set it to 185).

D.C. al Fine = *Da Capo al Fine*. Go back to the beginning of the piece and play to the *Fine*, which is the end of the piece.

‖: :‖ = *Repeat signs*. Repeat music between the two symbols. When only the end repeat sign is present, repeat music from the beginning.

Introduction

Russia is the largest country in the world, extending across northern Asia and into eastern Europe. Though 80 percent of Russia is actually in Asia, the country was founded by Slavic and Norse tribes of eastern Europe. Due to Russia's enormous land mass and ethnic diversity, there are many types of traditional Russian music. However, there is a common element in all traditional Russian genres: the words, whether sung, chanted, or recited, define the structure of the music. Ancient folk traditions of epic poetry and ritual dance songs furnished Russia with a unique foundation of rhythms and melodies that were passed on to Russian religious and stage music. During the 17th century, social reforms put Russian musicians in close contact with western European music theory. Russian music, however, retained its individuality through a continued connection with folk music traditions.

Even though the seven-string guitar (page 249) was a popular 19th century instrument in Russia, some music in this book was not originally played on guitar. These pieces are arranged to capture the nuances and beauty of music originally performed on traditional Russian instruments like the balalaika and domra (pages 246 and 247), or sung unaccompanied by instruments (page 263). Many pieces use alternate tunings (see page 287) to emulate the techniques of traditional folk instruments and Russian village singing. One piece, "Kalinka" (page 274), calls for the use of a capo to bring the pitch of the guitar up to that of the balalaika. "Kalinka" also uses *tremolo* (page 246), a technique essential to the sound of the balalaika and domra. All but five arrangements are fingerstyle. The five pick-style pieces—"A Dukhovnyi Stikh" (page 260), "Kamarinskaya" (page 264), "Songs of Svyatki" (page 268), "Evening Bells" (page 272), and "Kalinka" (page 274)—use alternate tunings to evoke the character of Russian village harmony and the nuances of the instruments on which the music was originally performed.

This book is intended for intermediate to advanced guitarists who can read standard music notation or tablature (TAB) and who know a fair amount of technique and music theory. (The Notation Guide on page 243 should help you with any unfamiliar notation.) Even if you can't read standard music notation, you can still get a lot out of this book. Just read the TAB, and listen to the examples and pieces on the accompanying CD. You can also just relax, read the book, and listen to the CD; you'll find an insightful overview of the important songs and major developments in Russian music. However you choose to approach the material in this book, we hope you enjoy the journey.

Chapter 1

A BRIEF HISTORY OF RUSSIAN MUSIC

Let's get started by looking at events that have influenced Russia's music history.

Early Rus' (10th Century and Prior)
The mingling of ancient Slavic peoples and Norse tribes (called *Rus'*) fostered traditions of epic poetry and seasonal rituals of dance and song that honored heroes and celebrated seasons. By the year 862 A.D., these peoples united under the state called *Kievan Rus'* (the medieval ancestor of Russia, Ukraine, and Belarus).

Old Russia (988 A.D.–Mid-17th Century)
Old Russia refers to a time that began around the year 988 A.D. when Prince Vladimir of Kievan Rus' adopted Byzantine* Christianity (known today as Eastern Orthodox). During the century that followed, Byzantine religious texts were translated into *Old Church Slavonic* (the first literary Slavic language) and a particularly Russian type of religious chant music was born. This music, called *znamenny*, or "sign" chant, was written using special symbols called *neumes*. It was constructed by combining short musical patterns that were influenced by village music. Though church music was always restricted to vocal music, instruments remained an important part of village life and were used by traveling minstrels called *skomorki* (page 262) to accompany singing of spiritual verses and epic poems.

Westernization (Mid-17th Century–18th Century)
In the 17th century, Western music theory found its way to Russia. A Polish invasion exposed the Russian people to the Roman Catholic practice of using orchestras and church organs during services. Though instruments continued to be banned in Orthodox church services, European-style *harmony* (the blending of notes or simultaneous musical lines) was accepted. Early styles of harmony, called *strochnoie penie* (line-singing) and *kant* (page 255), found their way into Russian church and secular music. Soon, new types of chant emerged with simple melodies that were ideal for adding harmony. Despite the Western model, Russian harmony demonstrated unique *dissonances* (unresolved, clashing notes) because of its link to village music.

Urban Culture (19th–20th Century)
During this period, urban folk music developed, as songbooks, called *pesenniki*, circulated in the cities. Pesenniki contained harmonized versions of village songs and songs belonging to a new genre called the *Russian romance*. These songs were performed in the homes of amateur musicians as well as on the concert stage by professional artists. In the 1880s, song collector Vasily Andreyev (see page 270), created a Russian folk "orchestra" that performed folk music along with well-known classical pieces. Andreyev's format was first sponsored by imperial Russia and later used by the Soviet government to promote a "national" Russian image. Beginning in the 1960s, as an alternative to mainstream state-sponsored stage music, singer-songwriters known as *bards* circulated original tunes called *author's songs* (page 280). Bards sang their songs with simple guitar accompaniment, fusing older folk and city genres into a new, unique style.

---

* "Byzantine" refers to the Byzantine Empire of the Middle Ages. The capital of the Byzantine Empire was Constantinople (present-day Instanbul).

Chapter 2

TRADITIONAL INSTRUMENTS OF RUSSIA

RUSSIA

In Russia, it is common to find traditional instruments in the homes of villagers and city folk, as well as on the concert stage. Historic accounts of Russian string instruments date back to the Kievan Rus' period when they were commonly used by skomorki minstrels. Though many instruments considered "traditional" are actually modern reconstructed versions of Old Russia's instruments, some wind and percussion instruments of ancient origin survive in villages today.

BALALAIKA

The *balalaika*, a three-stringed guitar-like instrument with a triangular sound box, is the most popular Russian instrument. Its three strings are often doubled like mandolin strings. Mention of the balalaika can be traced back to skomorki minstrels, however, the balalaika in use today was standardized in the 1880s by Vasily Andreyev. His modern version comes in various sizes. From highest in pitch to lowest, these are: *piccolo, prima, seconda, alto, bass,* and *contrabass*. Modern *balalaika orchestras* (the first was founded by Andreyev himself) use Andreyev's balalaika designs. In these groups, the balalaikas function much like orchestral string instruments (i.e., violin, viola, cello, and contrabass).

Technique

The prima balalaika is the most common type and is used as a solo instrument as well as in small groups and large orchestras. The balalaika is usually played fingerstyle but some players use a pick (especially bass balalaika players). Players use all five fingers of the left hand (including the thumb) to fret notes and chords.

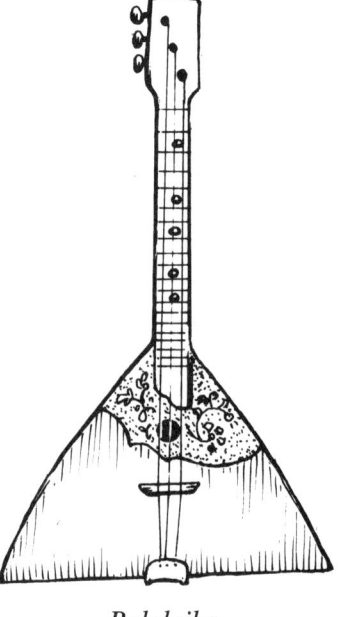

Balalaika.

The balalaika is well known for a special technique called *tremolo*, which is a very fast strumming or plucking of notes or chords. The effect is created by alternating the strumming hand (or pick) in a rapid down-up motion across one or more strings (see "Kalinka" on page 274). Players also *roll* chords by quickly moving individual right-hand fingers across the strings.

Tunings

Two common tunings for the prima balalaika are *balaechnyi* and *gitarnyi*.

Balaechnyi is the traditional prima balalaika tuning. The two lower strings are tuned to the same E note and the top string is tuned a 4th higher (four letter names up from E) to an A note. In this book, the balalaika tuning found in the Appendix (page 287) simulates the balaechnyi tuning.

Balaechnyi Tuning

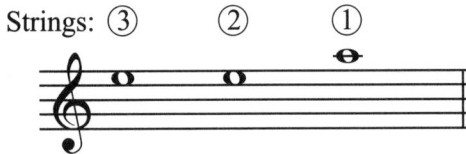

Gitarnyi means "like the guitar." In this tuning, the balalaika is tuned to a G Major chord (G–B–D), matching the top three strings of the Russian seven-string guitar.

Gitarnyi Tuning

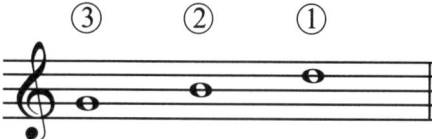

The bass balalaika and contrabass balalaika are tuned similar to the bottom strings of the electric bass guitar (E–A–D, an octave lower than the 4th, 5th, and 6th strings of the guitar). These very large, low-tuned balalaikas are found in many small groups, but were designed to function like the double bass in a classical orchestra.

Bass Balalaika Tuning

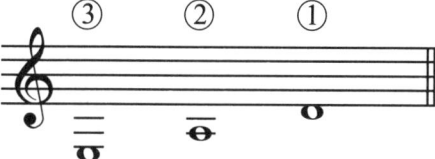

DOMRA

The Russian *domra* is a three-string, round-back, mandolin-type instrument. Unlike the mandolin, its strings are not doubled. Skomorki minstrels are thought to have used this instrument when performing epic poems. Although many historic accounts mention the domra, no one knew exactly how one looked until an instrument, thought to be a domra, was found in the 19th century. This domra made its way to Vasily Andreyev, who used it as a model for a family of modern domra (piccolo, prima, alto, etc.), which he included in his balalaika orchestra. The prima domra is tuned to the notes E, A, and D (from the lowest to highest strings). Domra players use a pick and often take the lead melody in ensembles. Like balalaika styles, domra playing incorporates tremolo.

Domra Tuning

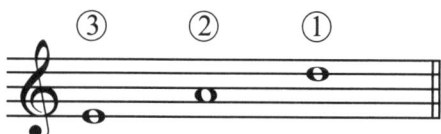

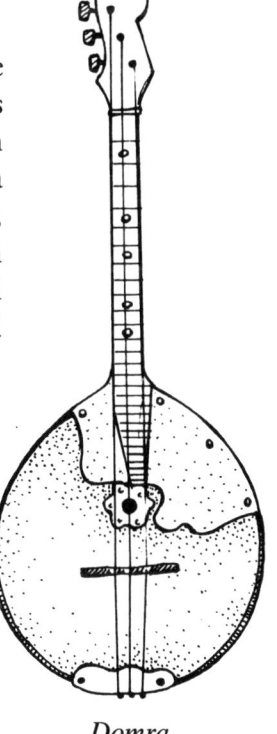

Domra.

GUSLI

The *gusli* is a plucked, harp-like instrument whose strings are stretched across a flat, wing-shaped sounding board. It is a relative of the medieval psaltry and hammer dulcimer. A performer typically holds the gusli upright in the lap and mutes unwanted strings with the left hand while plucking or strumming with both the right and left hands. Today, one can find guslis in various tunings with different numbers of strings. Sometimes, they are equipped with pitch-changing levers that allow them to be played in any key. A large type of gusli (resting on a stand and including a keyboard) exists today in balalaika orchestras.

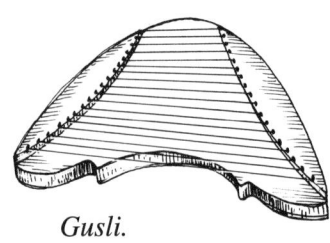
Gusli.

GARMON AND BOYAN

The *garmon* and *boyan* are accordions used in Russian folk music. They differ from western European accordions because they do not have a piano keyboard; they are *button accordions,* which are played by pushing buttons with both hands. The garmon was widespread by the mid-19th century and extremely popular from the 1860s to the 1880s. Like many harmonicas, the garmon is *diatonic,* or tuned to a specific key.

The boyan is the modern Russian accordion (designed in 1905). It is fully *chromatic*, which means it can play all 12 notes of the octave like the piano. (Therefore, it can be played in any key.) Many European tunes came to Russia through accordion music, and the accordion is commonly used in Russian ensembles (including balalaika orchestras).

Garmon.

Boyan.

SHEPHERD'S PIPES

The *rozhok*, *sopel*, and *zhalaika* are three ancient Russian wind instruments that can still be found in villages as well as on performance stages. Like the garmon, these wind instruments are diatonic. *Rozhok* are wooden trumpets of various sizes with five finger-holes and one thumb-hole. Shepherds used them to call animals and other shepherds when herding livestock. In villages of the Vladimir and Yaroslavl districts, large rozhok "choruses" were said to "sing" with their horns. Another wind instrument, the *sopel*, is an end-blown, flute-type instrument much like the Irish pennywhistle. The most popular Russian folk wind instrument, however, is the *zhalaika,* a single-reed, clarinet-like instrument.

Interestingly, shepherd's pipes are often played in pairs by a single performer who can play two simultaneous melodies. These instruments continue to make appearances in small Russian folk ensembles as well in large balalaika orchestras.

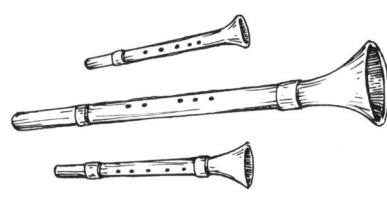
Rozhok.

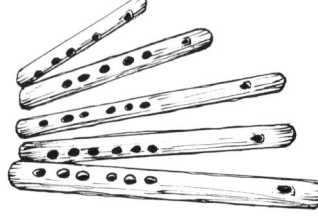
Sopel.

Zhalaika.

RUSSIAN PERCUSSION INSTRUMENTS

A number of percussion instruments from the Old Russia period survive today in popular folk music. Some, like the wooden spoons, or *lozhki*, have even become worldwide symbols of Russian folk culture. Russian spoon players hold (at least) two spoons in one hand and use another spoon, held in the other hand, to create intricate rhythms. Another popular Russian percussion instrument is the *treshchotka*, or rattle. This is a set of flat boards, strung on a wire, that are "clapped" together. The larger the boards, the louder they clap. Usually, in large folk orchestras, a mechanical version of the treshchotka replaces the traditional instrument. Yet another percussion instrument, called the *buben*, or Russian tambourine, once associated with the performances of skomorki minstrels, is still heard in modern Russian folk ensembles.

Lozhki.

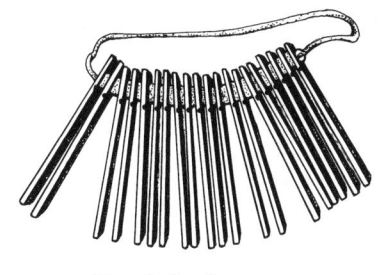

Treshchotka.

Treshchotka (mechanical).

Buben.

THE RUSSIAN SEVEN-STRING GUITAR

The Russian seven-string guitar, or *semistrunka*, has a vibrant history that began in the 19th century and continues to this day. In "standard" tuning, its strings are tuned to a G chord (the notes G–B–D). From the 7th string to the 1st, the tuning is D–G–B–D–G–B–D. Ignoring its 5th string, the semistrunka's standard tuning is the same as the open G tuning of a regular six-string guitar (see below). Normally played fingerstyle, the Russian seven-string has a strong classical tradition and was often used to accompany stage performances of Russian and Gypsy *romances* (see page 276). Before the 1917 revolution (and later disapproval of the guitar by the Soviet Union Government), the seven-string was the prominent guitar of Russia. In 1926, Spanish guitarist Andrés Segovia toured Russia playing the six-string guitar. This attracted many Russian classical guitarists to the six-string guitar. Consequently, seven-string guitars were less available in the 20th century. However, Russian Gypsies and, later, Russian bards, kept the seven-string's popularity alive. Let's compare the standard tuning of the semistrunka to the open G tuning of a six-string guitar.

Russian Seven-String Standard Tuning

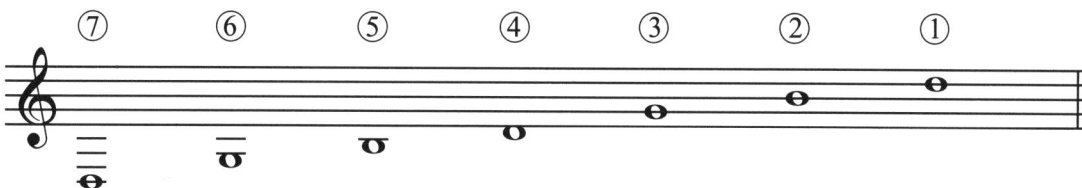

Six-String Open G Tuning

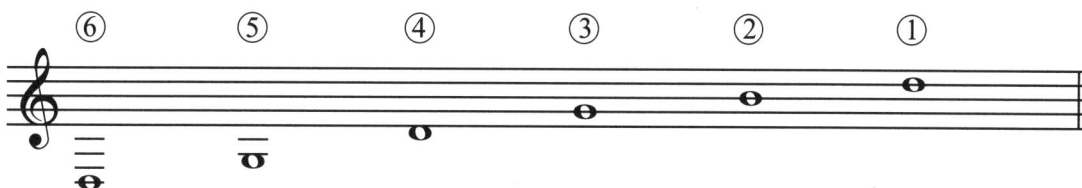

Chapter 3: The Tones, Popevki, and Kant

In this chapter, we'll look into some music theory concepts that have contributed to the unique character of both Russian church music and folk music. In Russian song, there is an underlying connection between melody and lyrics. In traditional Orthodox church singing, the meanings of prayers, hymns, and psalms are carefully punctuated by melodies created within a system of eight *tones*, or scales. Church music from the Old Russia era, called *znamenny* chant, inherited this system from the Byzantine Church. Over time, the Russian tones evolved into eight sets of melodic patterns, or *motives*, called *popevki*. Because these patterns were based on one scale (called the *gamut*) and incorporated Slavic village melodies, the Russian tones developed into something unique and different from their Byzantine origins. Today, Russian church choirs apply "classical" harmony to melodies based on these tones.

THE TONES

The tones are both scales and strict guidelines for creating melodies. Each of the eight tones calls for the distinct treatment of notes in relation to the words of a hymn, such as a specific final note or special notes for resting points (at commas and periods). In Orthodox Church traditions, the tones are used over an eight-week church cycle. Each week, a different tone is designated for the singing of the week's psalms, hymns, and responses.

THE GAMUT

The Russian tones are derived from the *gamut*, which is a specific pattern of *whole steps* (W) and *half steps* (H). (On the guitar, a whole step is the distance of two frets, and a half step is the distance of one fret.) As shown below, a W–W–H pattern is repeated across a 12-note scale ranging from G to D (a 5th past the octave of G). These 12 notes are further arranged into four *tonal ranges*. The majority of Russian chant stays in the middle-two tonal ranges. Traditionally, the pitches indicated in chant notation are relative to the first note sung by those chanting; they are not exact pitches as suggested by standard music notation.

The Gamut

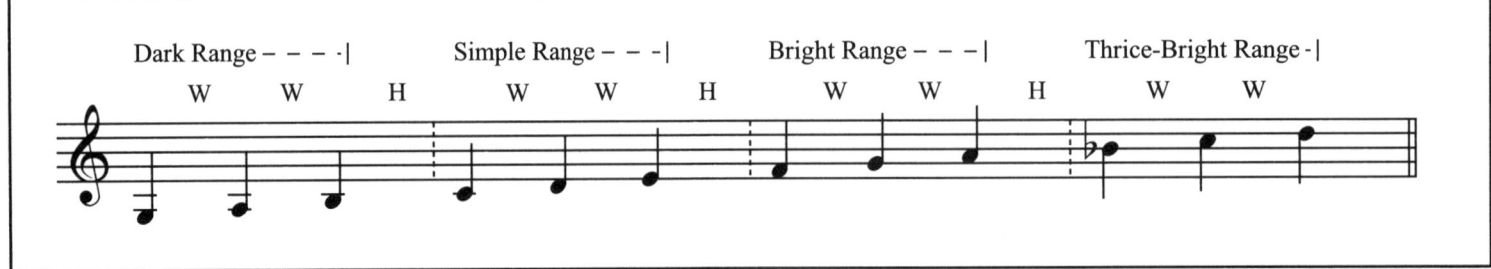

POPEVKI

Each Russian tone consists of a set of musical patterns, called *popevki*, which are derived from the gamut. Popevki are very short melodies (actually melodic fragments, or motives) that combine like mosaic pieces to create larger melodies. A masterful chanter could freely combine hundreds of memorized patterns.

Following are some examples of the more than 500 popevki patterns belonging to Russian znamenny chant. Since volumes have been written describing the complex and ancient art of combining popevki patterns with text, it is beyond the scope of this book to list all the patterns and the rules that dictate their use. Instead, the patterns presented here (numbered as they appear in *kokizniki*, or medieval handbooks of Russian music theory) are meant to illustrate popevki's general qualities. You'll notice that these patterns do not fall into consistent time signatures, nor do they clearly outline major or minor keys. These qualities are characteristic of many Russian melodies. As mentioned on the previous page, each tone consists of many different melodic patterns. We'll start by looking at some representative patterns belonging to Tone 1.

TONE 1

No. 3

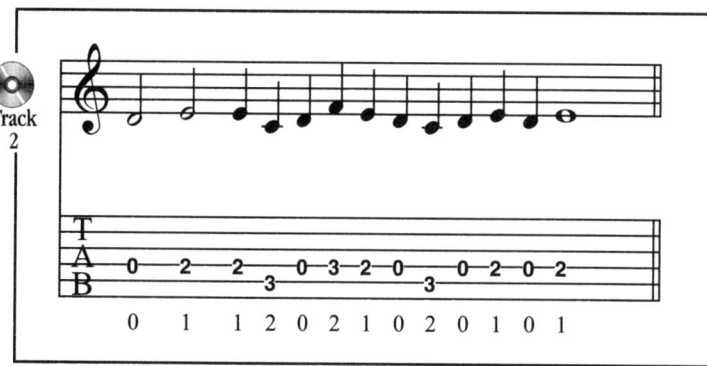

No. 10

No. 16

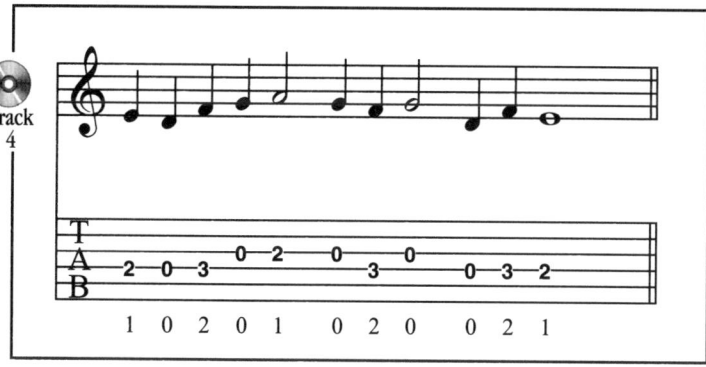

No. 25

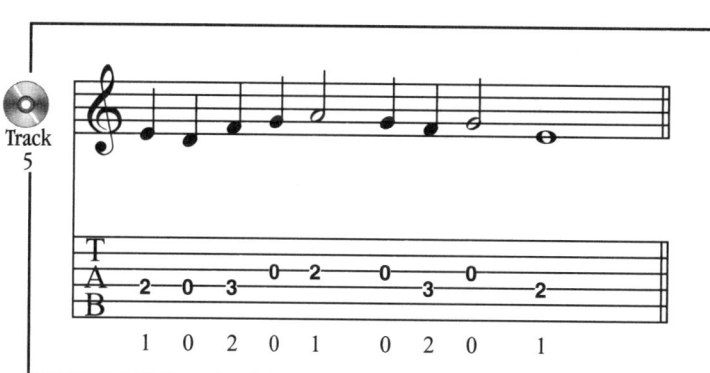

No. 68

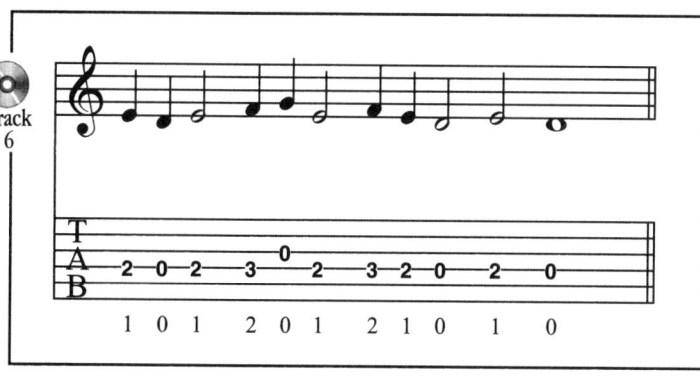

No. 69

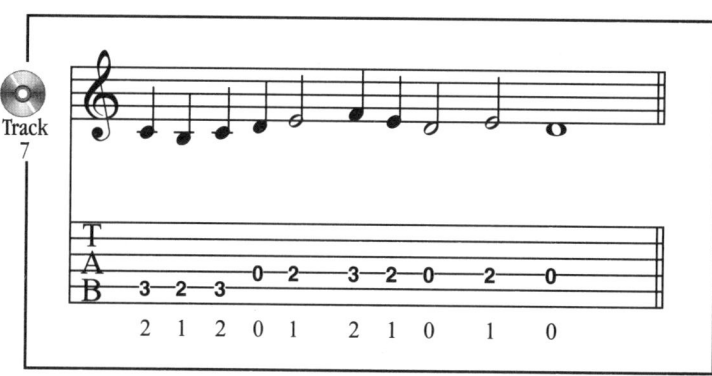

Guitar Atlas: Russia

TONE 2

No. 8

No. 41
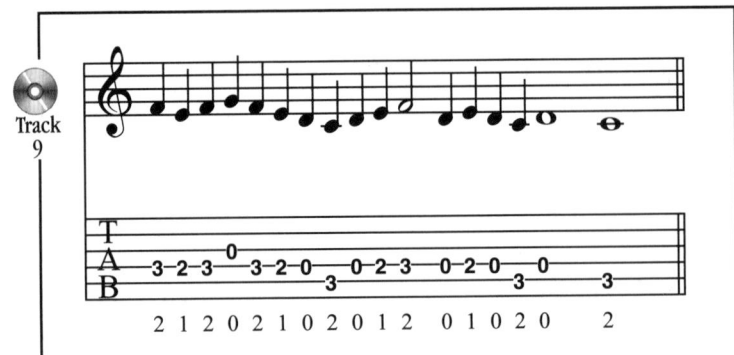

No. 52
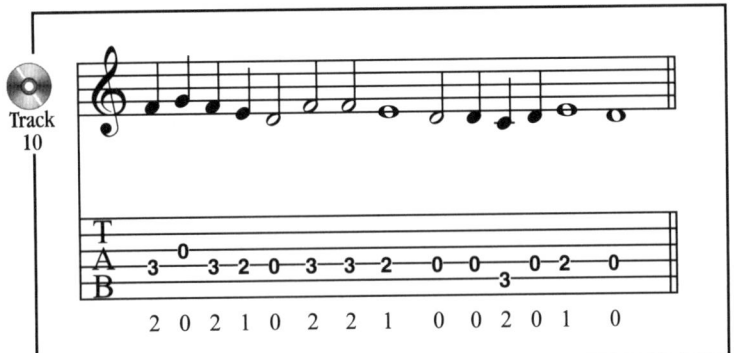

No. 59

TONE 3

No. 4
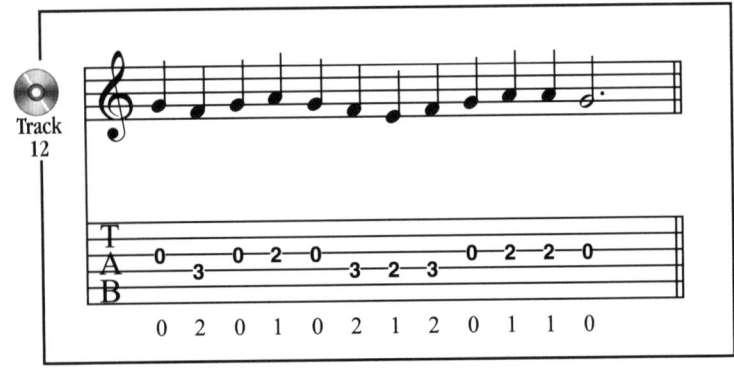

No. 11
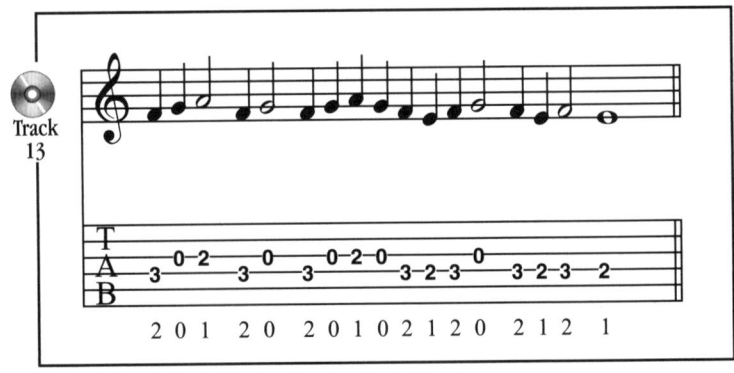

No. 27
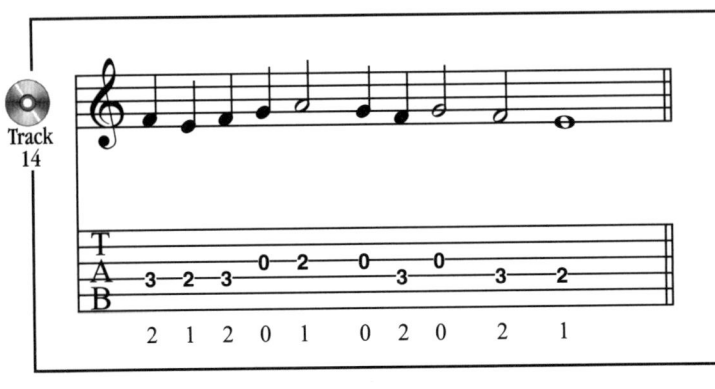

No. 30

TONE 4

No. 2

No. 57
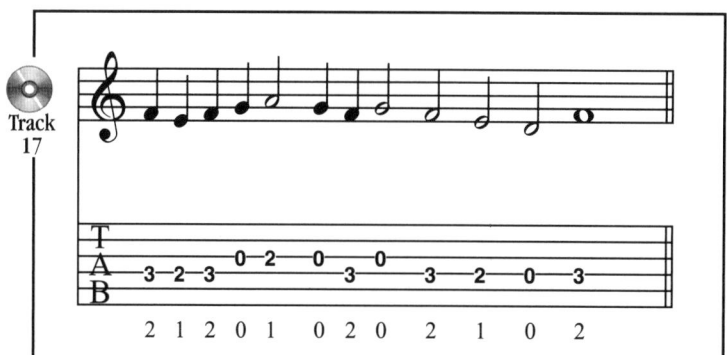

TONE 5

No. 9

No. 33

TONE 6

No. 1
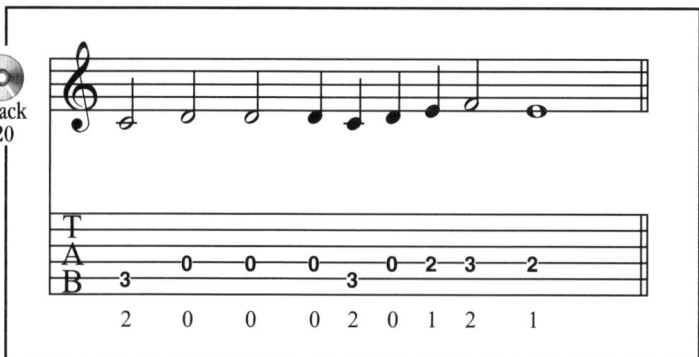

No. 2
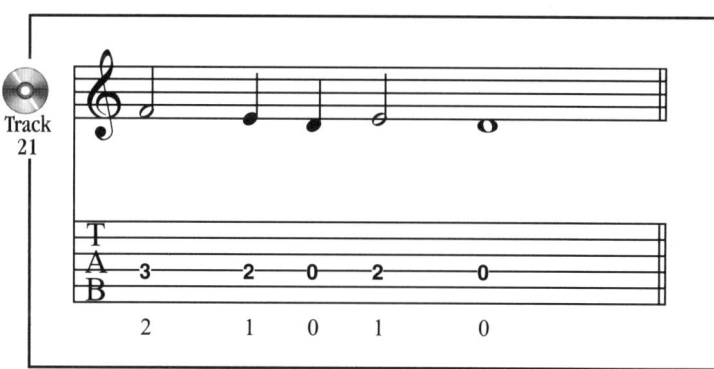

TONE 7

No. 29
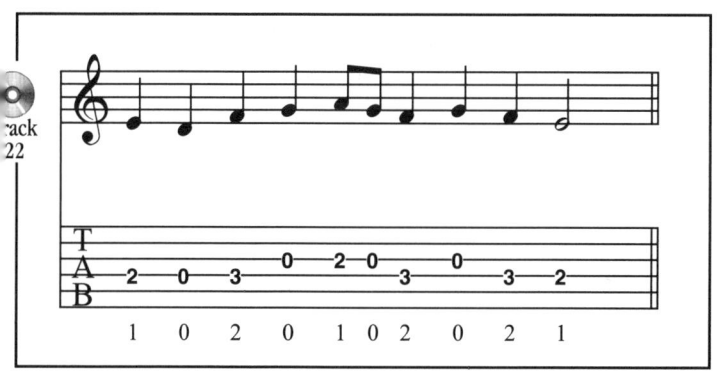

No. 38

Following is a guitar arrangement using popevki patterns from Tone 1 (page 251). The patterns (which are separated by dotted barlines) are written in octaves to imitate the wider sound created by many voices of a choir chanting the same melody. The piece is easiest played fingerstyle, with your thumb *(p)* on the lower notes and index *(i)* or middle finger *(m)* on the upper notes. Notice no time signatures or key signatures are given, since a znamenny melody does not define a key in the traditional sense, nor does it pulse in a consistent time signature (such as 4/4 or 3/4). The fluidity and asymmetry found in many Russian songs can be traced back to znamenny roots. Remember (page 250), popevki patterns combine to support and convey the meaning of religious texts. This short example cannot encompass all possibilities and considerations involved in popevki use, but its approach may inspire your own creative process.

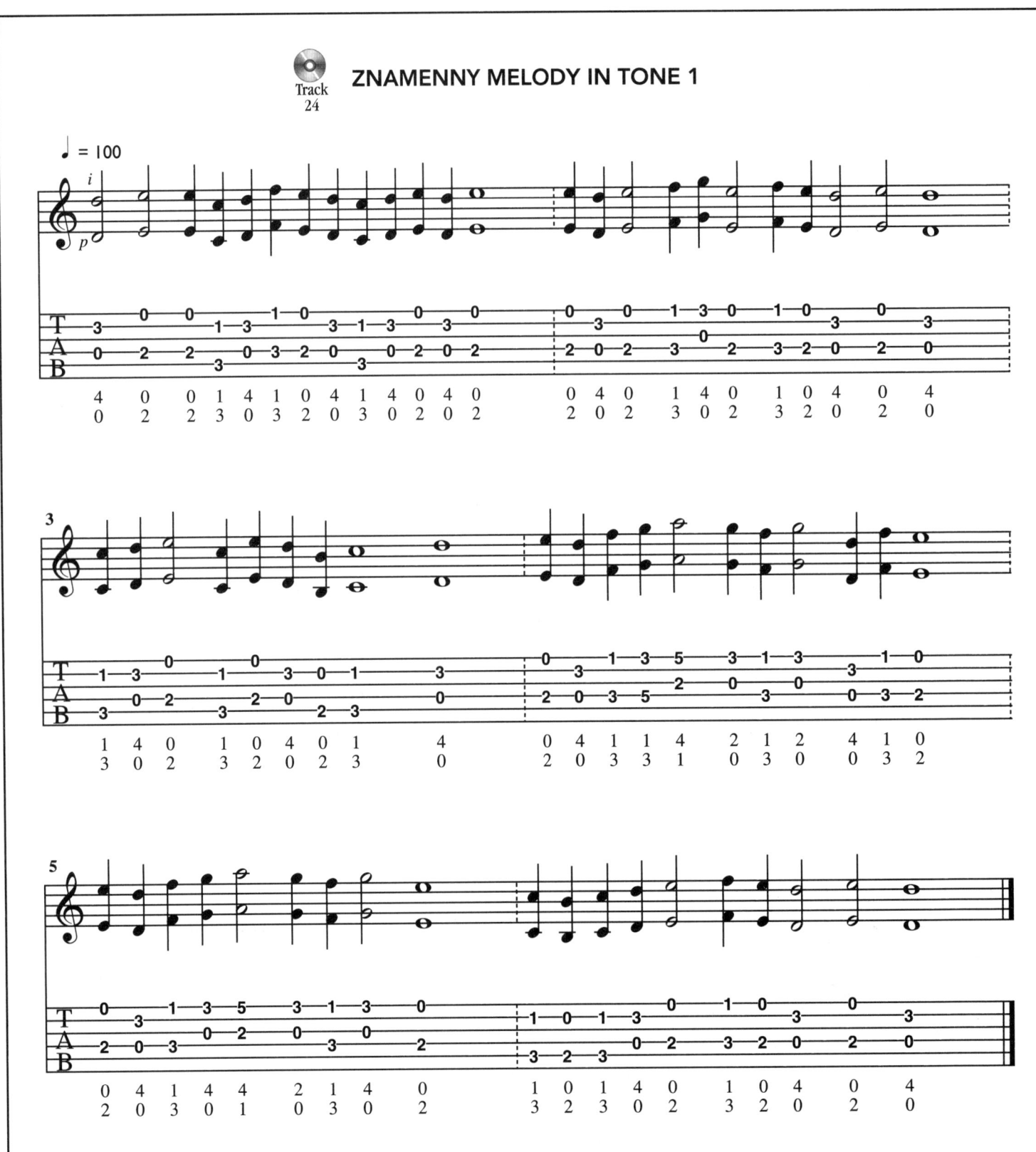

KANT

During the 17th century, Russian church music began to adopt the Western style of singing multiple lines to harmonize melodies. Eventually, a three-part style known as *kant* became popular for harmonizing religious songs as well as folk songs. These harmonized songs set the stage for the popular Russian romance songs of the 19th and 20th centuries (see page 276). In the kant style, two upper voices move together in 3rds while a lower voice sings a counter-melody that outlines the chord changes.

Below is a kant harmonization in the style of a 17th-century hymn honoring a church forefather. This piece is best played fingerstyle. You'll notice that for variety (in measures 11–14) the upper voices stray a bit from strict harmony in 3rds. Although the even four-bar phrases in $\frac{4}{4}$ time reveal Western influence, the hymn's slow pace and long resting notes are reminiscent of popevki melodies.

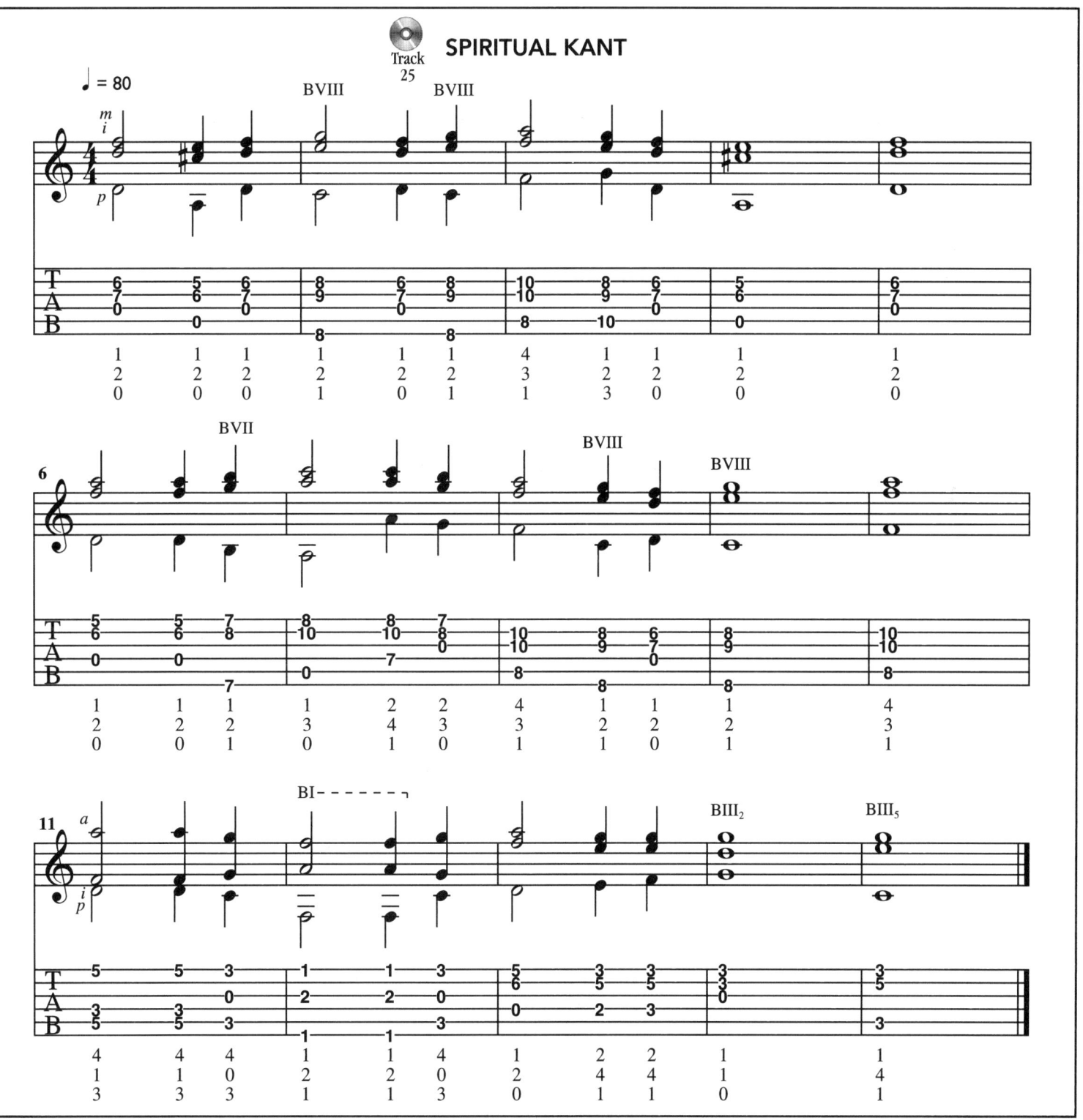

Chapter 4: Russian Orthodox Music

In this chapter, we'll look at different styles of Russian Orthodox chant music and the relationship between Russian religious music and folk music.

ZNAMENNY CHANT

As we discussed in Chapter 3, Russian religious music stands out from other Orthodox Church traditions because, in Russia, village melodies were incorporated into church melodies (through popevki patterns). To convey the meaning of the text, Russian church singers developed special rules for combining popevki patterns. This became the basis of znamenny chant. Znamenny melodies, which were initially influenced by folk songs, later inspired folk genres like the *spiritual verse* (page 260).

Originally, znamenny chant did not include singing of simultaneous musical lines or harmony of any sort. Singers would sing the same melody together in unison. After social and church reforms in the 17th century introduced Russia to western European music theory, Russian church singing gradually developed into its current familiar style, in which znamenny and other Russian chant melodies are decorated by the harmony of choral ensembles. Yet, unlike Western church practices, Russian Orthodox church music remains strictly a vocal art with a unique structure inherited from znamenny roots.

LATER CHANT STYLES

Three other chant types, stemming from znamenny chant, emerged in the 17th century: *Kievan chant, Bulgarian chant,* and *Greek chant.* These used more straightforward melodies that were ideal for harmonizing in the Western style.

Kievan Chant

Kievan chant is thought to be a Ukrainian variation of znamenny chant that became popular in Russia. The appearance of Kievan chant was accompanied by *Kievan square notation,* an early form of standard music notation that used square noteheads and a five-line staff. Although it is similar to znamenny in many ways, Kievan chant focused on shorter, "tuneful" melodies, which were more apt to fall into major and minor keys.

Bulgarian Chant

Bulgarian chant came to Russia through Ukrainian chant books, but the exact origin of this chant type is a mystery. (It is not directly connected to chant music of the Bulgarian Orthodox Church.) Ukrainian and Russian composers may have marked chant melodies with the "Bulgarian" label to suggest an air of Byzantine "legitimacy," since Bulgaria is near Greece and Turkey, and the Bulgarian Orthodox Church is slightly older than the Russian Orthodox Church. Bulgarian chant melodies often fall into major and minor keys, like Kievan chant, but Bulgarian chant is more symmetrical with repeating musical phrases (see "Afonskoye," page 258).

Greek Chant

The so-called "Greek" chant originated in southwestern Russia. Greek chant adapted and simplified older Byzantine chant melodies. Although the relationship of Greek chant to the Greek Church is still a subject of debate, it does resemble other Eastern Orthodox Church chant styles (like Romanian Church chant).

RUSSIAN HYMNS

In the century that followed Russia's conversion to Orthodox Christianity, the Russian Church translated the original Byzantine religious texts into Old Church Slavonic. The differences in the natural pulse of languages encouraged Russian church composers to write new hymns (non-biblical religious songs) in the Russian language to ease the composition process. These hymns used Slavic village melodies and contributed to a unique Russian style of Orthodox Church music. *Stichera* and *troparia* are two types of hymns common among all Eastern Orthodox traditions, yet they take on a noticeably new character in Russian chant styles.

Stichera

Stichera (whose singular form is *sticheron*) are hymns devoted to a specific saint or occasion. They are usually inserted between psalms (biblical poems of praise). A sticheron's position in the eight-week church cycle determines the tone in which it is sung. Some stichera stand alone, such as the "Stichera after Psalm 50." This is sung during morning church services *(Matins)* of the 12 great feasts. The feasts are yearly celebrations and include the "Feast of Feasts," also known as *Pascha*, or Easter. Another important stichera, called *theotokia,* honors the *Theotokos* (literally, "God-bearer," the Orthodox name for Mary).

Troparia

A troparion (whose plural form is *troparia*) was originally a short *refrain*, or recurring set of words, that a congregation inserted between psalm verses sung by a lead chanter. Many troparia still function in this call-and-response manner today, but some have developed into longer self-standing hymns. Three of the most common self-standing troparia are the dismissal troparia, troparia of the feast, and the troparia of the day. These hymns highlight the main theme of a given worship day, and some are sung in the "tone of the week." Remember (page 250), each week, a different tone is designated for the singing of the week's psalms, hymns, and responses.

"AFONSKOYE" ("FROM MOUNT ATHOS")

The following arrangement is in the style of a choral piece written by composer Dmitry Yaichkov (1869–1953). His tune, "It Is Truly Fitting," is a sticheron glorifying the Theotokos. It is based on a Bulgarian chant melody in Tone 1 known as "Afonskoye," or "from Mount Athos." Mount Athos, located in northern Greece, is known as the "Holy Mountain," and is home to 20 Orthodox monasteries. In the guitar arrangement below, the chant melody is present in the octave figures in the first and fifth systems (highlighted); otherwise, the melody is harmonized in the kant style. Instead of a time signature and conventional measures, dotted barlines indicate suggested phrase separations. This piece is played fingerstyle. Also, to allow wider separation between the bass and upper parts, this arrangement calls for the drop D tuning (page 287).

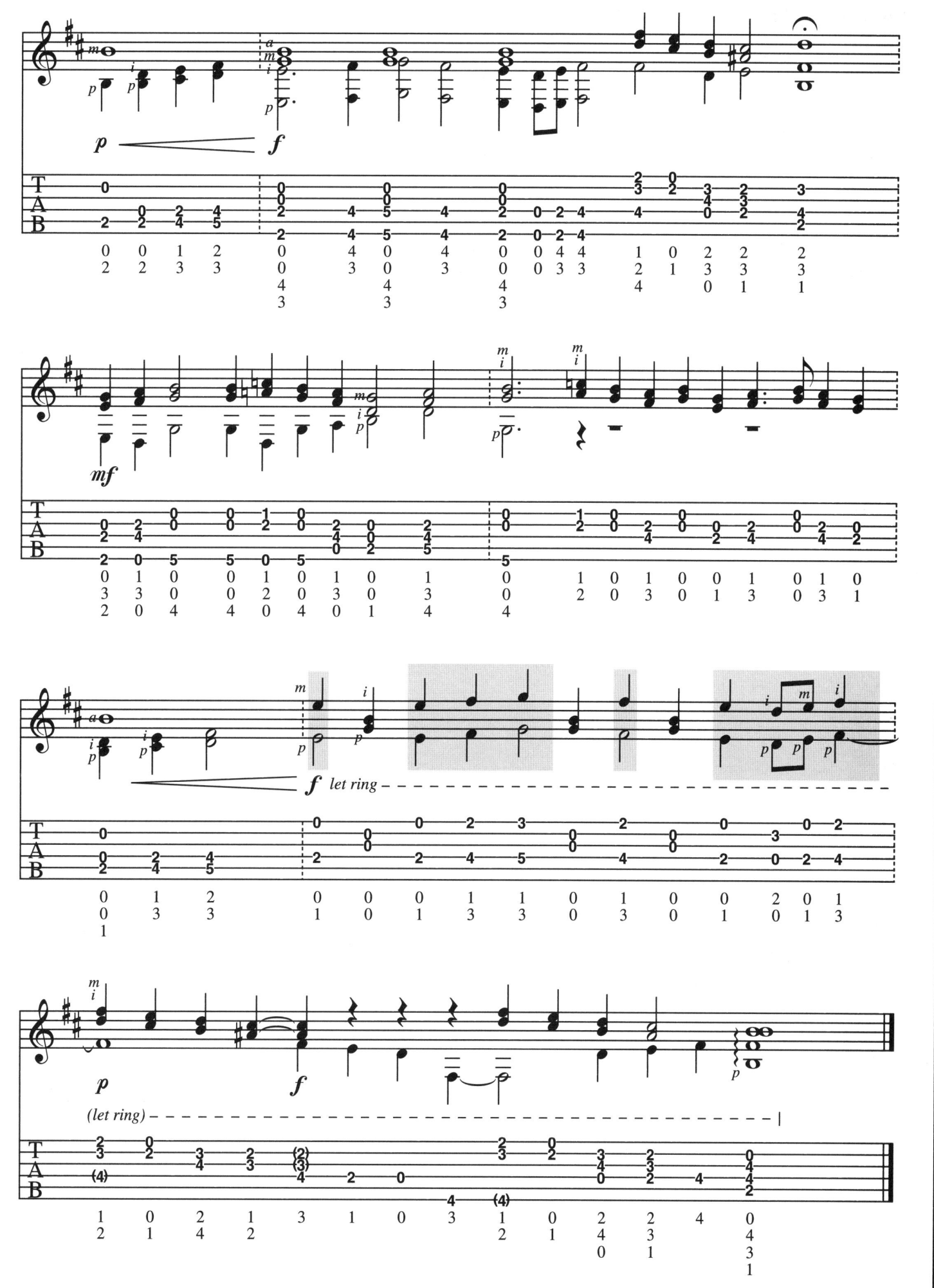

SPIRITUAL VERSES

Another type of Russian religious song is the "spiritual verse," or *dukhovnyi stikh*. These old sacred songs are sung not in church, but at social gatherings. Drawing on the common roots of Russian folk and church music, spiritual verses relate Biblical events and re-tell old myths with added Christian heroes. Many of these songs have been preserved by a group of people known as *Starovery*, or "Old Believers," who fled abroad, or to frontier regions, in protest of religious and social changes in the 17th century. Centuries of separation has allowed the Old Believers to maintain many traditions from the Old Russia period, including chant practices and village songs.

"A Dukhovnyi Stikh" is based on a spiritual verse remembered by the *Nekrasovtsy*, a group of Old Believers who lived in Turkey until their return to Russia in 1962. You can play this one with a pick. Just watch out for the muted 4th string (indicated with an "x") in measures 14, 19, and 21. To mute the 4th string, you must allow the pad of your left-hand 2nd finger to muffle the 4th string as the fingertip frets the note on the 5th string. This arrangement uses the balalaika tuning (see Appendix, page 287) to blend qualities of church chant and village song (discussed in the next chapter).

Chapter 5 RUSSIAN VILLAGE MUSIC

In this chapter, we'll take a look at Russian village music. Across rural Russia, villagers keep (or can be asked to recall) local song customs that accompany births, marriages, burials, parties, season changes, work, and other occasions. The term "Russian folk music" embraces a wide variety of regional styles that differ from village to village. Still, Russian folk songs can be arranged into some general categories based on the occasion of their use:

- **Calendar Songs.** These songs were originally sung during rituals linked to the agricultural calendar. Festive, lively, and making frequent use of repeated melodic motives, they are one of the oldest types of Russian folk song. *Kolyadas* are calendar songs that are still sung by children during *Svyatki* (Yuletide).

- **Epic Songs.** These songs, called *bylina,* meaning "what it was," come from old Kievan Rus' song tradition. Once performed by medieval skomorki minstrels, they are elaborate poems (as long as 2,000 lines) that glorify heroes and recount historic events and ancient myths. A living tradition of epics has survived in the north and also among the Old Believers.

- **Lyric Songs.** This genre encompasses songs that reflect on love and other personal subjects. It includes *protyazhnayas,* or "long-protracted songs." These are slow songs with long, emotional (often sorrowful) phrases. Rich in poetry, the lyric song genre evolved into the Russian romance of the 19th and 20th centuries (page 276).

- **Dance Songs.** Included in this category are round-dance songs, called *khorovods.* These are festive songs that incorporate movement and games. Also included are *plyaskas,* elaborate dance solos performed with choral accompaniment or instrumental accompaniment on the balalaika, domra, garmon, or shepherd's pipes (see "Kamarinskaya," page 264).

- **Lament Songs.** These are songs of sorrow (called *keening* songs) traditionally sung at funerals for departed loved ones, and at weddings, as a bride grieves leaving her family and her family grieves giving her away.

- **Work Songs.** Barge haulers, timber loggers, and other hard laborers originally sang these songs to accompany and coordinate work. Some work songs like the famous "Hey Ukhnem" ("Song of the Volga Boatmen," page 266) have become popular Russian folk songs. Work songs tend to use evenly phrased, repeated melodies that incorporate the *pripevka,* an exclamation sung on the interval of a 4th, meant to signal an "all-together" movement.

Now, let's consider general characteristics that apply to Russian village music. Then we'll look at pieces demonstrating some of these folk song genres.

RHYTHM

Russian people say that they "tell" a song. This reveals the influence words have over rhythm and structure in Russian music. Putting the rhythm of poetry first, traditional village songs often use *asymmetrical meter*, or time signatures such as $\frac{5}{4}$ or $\frac{7}{4}$ that group odd and even numbers of beats. (For example, $\frac{7}{4}$ can be understood as a measure of $\frac{3}{4}$ followed by a measure of $\frac{4}{4}$.) Further, when conforming to poetry, musical phrases may be organized into uneven numbers of measures. (Although, some dance and game songs take a more even approach to rhythm and phrasing.)

MELODY

Russian folk melodies are related to the popevki patterns also used in Russian church chant (page 250). The oldest calendar songs demonstrate short, repeated patterns within a three- or four-note range. These persistent repeated patterns contributed to the creation of popevki, which, strung together in chains, form the basis of many later Russian folk and church melodies.

SINGING AND HARMONY

In village group singing, a lead singer introduces each song with a solo, called a *zapev*, after which the other voices, or *podgolosok*, enter. The exact way a chorus blends voices to create harmony differs from region to region. In north and west Russia, an entire chorus may sing a single melody embellished differently by each singer (an approach called *heterophony*). In central Russia, many villages take a two-part approach, in which the lower voices sing the melody and a solo singer improvises an upper part. In central and south Russia, three-part singing exists. In this style, a low bass melody is accompanied by shrill voices of two or more women (in heterophony with the bass) and a wordless *drone*, or unchanging note. Sometimes, different songs are sung simultaneously at weddings and during laments, embracing great amounts of contrasting sound. Overall, traditional Russian village music contains much dissonance, which may sound foreign to a new listener.

RUSSIAN FOLK MUSIC TODAY

During the 20th century, mass media and stage performance promoted the general popularity of Russian folk music. Radio exposed rural villagers to urban "folk" songs, which they adopted into their local traditions. Many of these urban songs were first written for the concert stage and arranged in the classical format. During the Soviet era under Joseph Stalin, the "official" folk music was stage music that attempted to promote a national Russian image. Under Soviet influence, large folk choirs and folk instrument orchestras popularized new and traditional folk tunes. In reaction to Stalin-era folk music, a folk revival began in the 1960s. Led by musicologists like Dmitry Pokrovsky, the movement produced thousands of ensembles comprised of amateur, professional, and academic musicians who traveled to remote villages to learn authentic folk songs. Recordings of these ensembles were not widely distributed. The folk revival did encourage a group of singer-songwriters to circulate homemade cassette recordings of a new folk style called *bard music*. Bard music did not model itself after Russian village music, but, instead, was a fresh urban take on the oral tradition of folk music.

"KAMARINSKAYA"

"Kamarinskaya" is a plyaska (see page 262), a popular Russian folk dance. The song is thought to have originated in the Kamarinskaya province among fugitive serfs (peasant slaves), who danced and sang the song with a furious, reckless energy. Its rhythmic pattern is based on an 11-syllable phrase with an accent (>) on the final syllable. In the arrangement below, a zapev-like solo introduces the basic phrase (found in the first 11 notes of measures 1–4). Each time the phrase is repeated, it is embellished differently. A second voice (the down-stemmed notes) joins in at measure 7. It adds a loose harmony that frequently doubles the first voice, creating unison. "Kamarinskaya" is often danced to instrumental accompaniment on the balalaika, garmon, or rozhok. Improvised dance steps and instrumental embellishment are important features of this dance song.

This arrangement uses the balalaika tuning. As you play it, notice how clashing dissonances in measure 19 contribute to the captivating quality of this Russian village dance song.

"HEY UKHNEM (SONG OF THE VOLGA BOATMEN)"

"Hey Ukhnem (Song of the Volga Boatmen)" is a work song that originated from the *burlaks*. These were Russian serfs who harnessed together, in groups of 50 to 125, to pull barges and ships up rivers from along the riverbanks. So grueling and sorrowful was their work that they sang to urge each other on and to avoid collapsing from weariness. The word *ukhnem* comes from the guttural sound, "ukh," that they made as they heaved together. A pripevka (the sung interval of a 4th) cued each synchronized tug.

In the arrangement below, a pripevka exclamation occurs on beats 2 and 3 during the song's refrain. (This does not occur in measures 3 and 7.) The notes falling on these beats, A and E, create the pripevka's perfect 4th interval. Notice that a rest follows each pripevka. Haulers would fill this space with the sound "ukh" as they tugged together. At measure 9, the song moves into a gentler verse. The verse coincided with a short break from work where a single hauler would sing to console and urge the group on. The group would sing only on the refrains as the work resumed. The "Song of the Volga Boatmen" became such a well-known folk song that in the 20th century, long after the steamboat replaced the harsh work of the burlaks, their song was still frequently performed on the professional stage. The fingerstyle arrangement below is harmonized in the popular stage format.

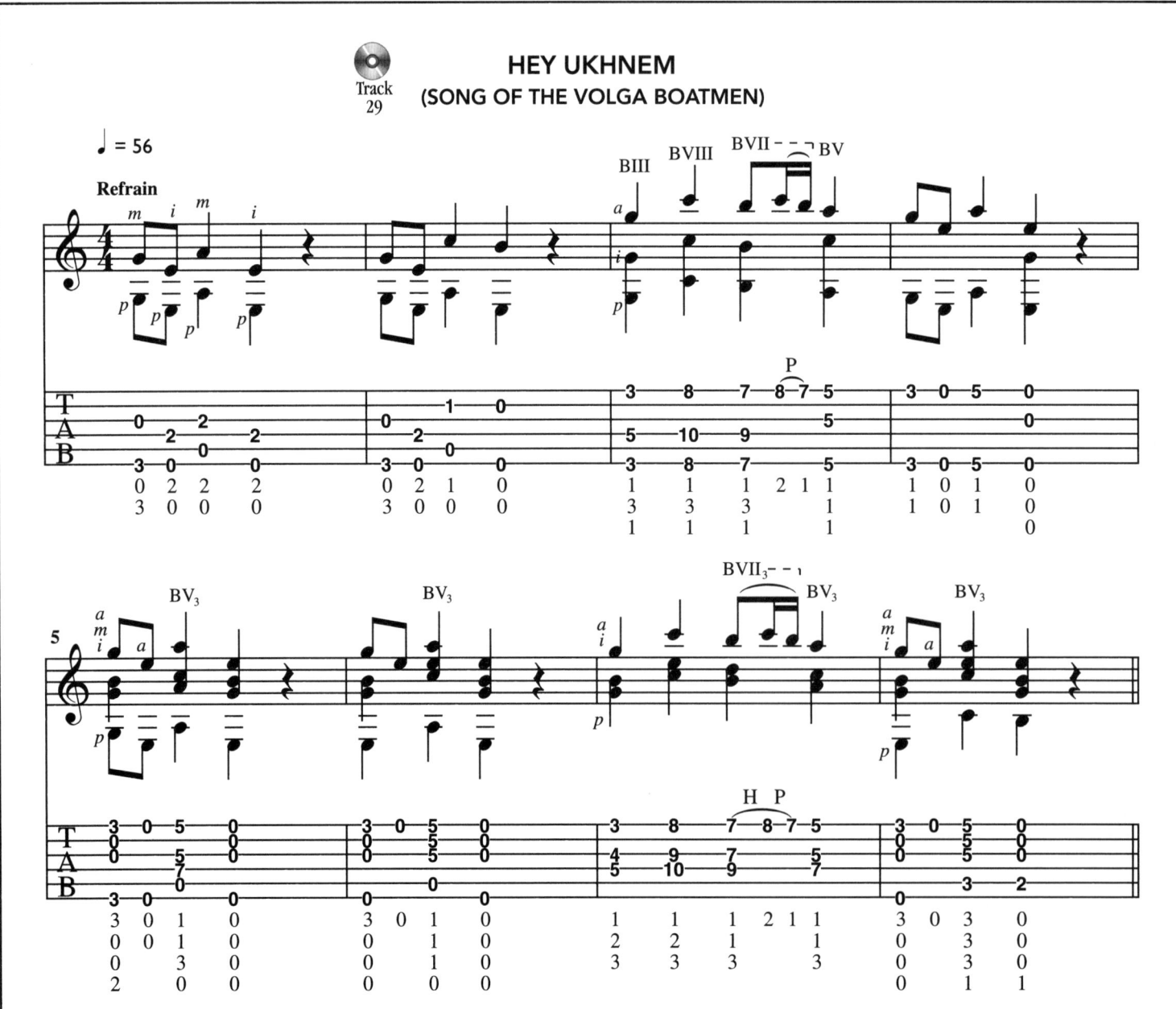

The painting **Burlaks on the Volga** ***by Ilya Yefimovich Repin (1844–1930).***
The gruesome sorrow captured in this painting inspired composer Mily Balakirev to arrange the now famous "Song of the Volga Boatmen," which was once sung by barge haulers, called "burlaks."

SVYATKI

Svyatki (Yuletide) was once linked to rituals of the winter solstice. People gathered during this time to play games, dance, and sing songs. Many, dressed as animals (such as bears and goats), played the wooden spoons or balalaika and engaged in comical mock fighting. Children went from house to house singing short songs called kolyadas. With these songs, children would praise the owners of the house, then demand gifts. After receiving gifts, they would sing praise again, or, if the owners were not generous, the children would mock and curse them in song. Young women sang *podblyudayas,* fortune-telling carols. The words of these songs were meant to predict their marriage and foretell their riches. The melodies and character of podblyudayas are related to religious songs.

"Songs of Svyatki" is an arrangement in the balalaika tuning. It begins and ends with a podblyudaya melody (measures 1–6 and 19–22). Compare the pacing of this melody to that of "Afonskoye" (page 258). Measures 7–18 demonstrate the playful character of a children's kolyada. Play this one with the pick.

Chapter 6 — RUSSIAN STAGE MUSIC

Folk music became very popular in Russian theaters and concert halls in the late 1800s. Since then, staged folk music has greatly influenced the way people view and play Russian folk music. This chapter provides arrangements of some of the most popular tunes continually performed by Russian professional concert artists.

RUSSIAN CLASSICAL MUSIC

During the 19th century, a feeling of nationalism swept across many European countries, including Russia. In this spirit, Russian composers such as Mikhail Glinka (1804–1857), Mily Balakirev (1837–1910), Modest Mussorgsky (1839–1881), and Nikolai Rimsky-Korsakov (1844–1908) used Russian folk melodies as building blocks for operas and symphonic works. These and other Russian composers published many arrangements of folk songs based on melodies that had been circulating in pesenniki songbooks since the time of Catherine the Great (1762–1796), Empress of Russia. Eventually, classical arrangements of folk songs became popular stage performance pieces in Russia.

THE RUSSIAN FOLK ORCHESTRA

Vasily Vasilievich Andreyev (1861–1918), who we learned about earlier (pages 245–247), founded the Russian *folk orchestra*. He was a Russian landowner who was inspired by nationalism and a fondness for Russian folklore. After collecting various traditional instruments in markets and villages, Andreyev set out to rebuild the balalaika and domra in various sizes (from soprano to bass), modeling his designs after the instrument families of the symphony orchestra. He combined his instruments into an ensemble called The Great Russian Orchestra of Folk Instruments. From the 1880s into the early 20th century, Andreyev's ensemble played in St. Petersburg halls and toured Russia. His orchestra, and the many so-called *balalaika orchestras* that followed, popularized original compositions and folk tune arrangements by Andreyev and other professional musicians. They also performed Russian "classics" by composers like Glinka and Pyotr Ilyich Tchaikovsky (1840–1893).

Today's full balalaika orchestra includes various sized balalaikas, domras, and gusli, as well as shepherd's pipes and traditional Russian percussion instruments like the lozhki and buben (see Chapter 2). It performs Russian folk instrumentals, well-known "classical" pieces, and often accompanies famous vocalists and traditional dancers.

OTHER STAGE MUSIC

Other staged folk music performances of the 20th century include Russian and Gypsy choirs, solo and duo accordionists, and small ensembles consisting of balalaika players, domra players, singers, and accordionists. These combos also often included dancers who acted out the words of the folk songs.

"MOSCOW NIGHTS"

"Moscow Nights" (or better translated as "Evenings Near Moscow") is a Russian song that was written in the 1950s by composer Vasily Solovyov-Sedoy and poet Mikhail Matusovsky. This popular song is performed on the Russian stage by small ensembles, choirs, and large balalaika orchestras and is widely known across the globe. Here, it is arranged for fingerstyle guitar. Try bringing out the accents in measure 3.

"EVENING BELLS"

The poem "Evening Bells," written by Ivan Kozlov in 1827, was based on an English poem by Thomas Moore called "Those Evening Bells." Kozlov's version, with its melancholy expression of personal emotion, attracted Russian composer Alexander Alyabyev (1787–1851) who set it to music. It is uncertain if Alyabyev's work was the inspiration for the better-known folk song called "Evening Bells" (which uses only the first verse of Kozlov's poem). There are distinct differences between the two. For example, Alyabyev's romantic song is in a minor key and full of anxiety, whereas the folk song is in a major key with a rising, uplifting melody.

The arrangement below is in open G tuning and is best played with a pick. It is modeled after the popular folk song, and uses *natural harmonics* to simulate the tranquil sounds of ringing bells. To produce clear natural harmonics (the notes with diamond-shaped noteheads), lightly touch the strings directly above the fretwire as you strike the strings with the pick. Play accented notes (>) slightly louder than unaccented notes. This will bring the "Evening Bells" melody to the forefront. In measure 7, there is a *shift slide*. When executing a shift slide, both notes are picked. Overall, play this piece slowly and with a gentle touch.

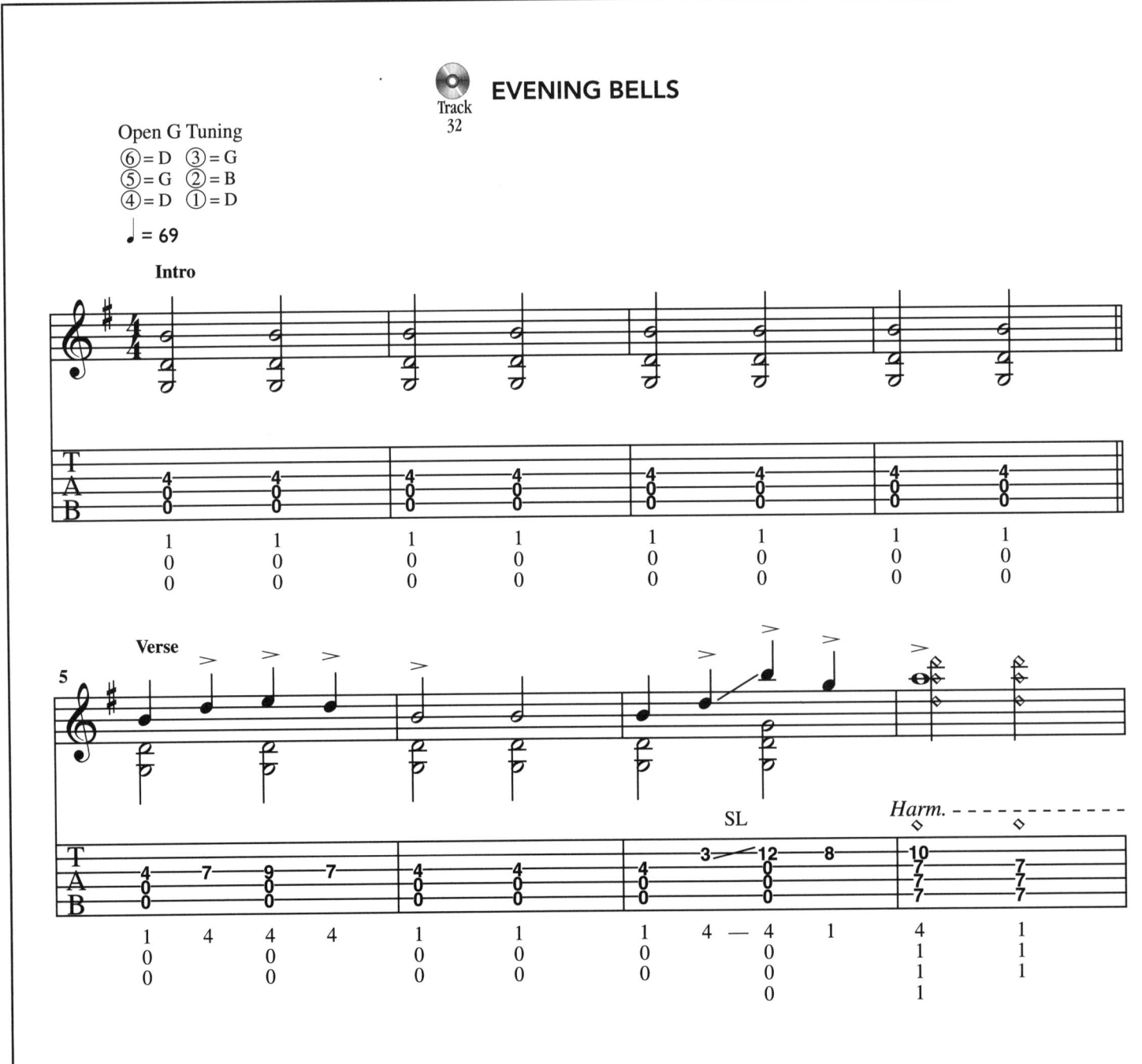

272   *Guitar Atlas: Volume 2*

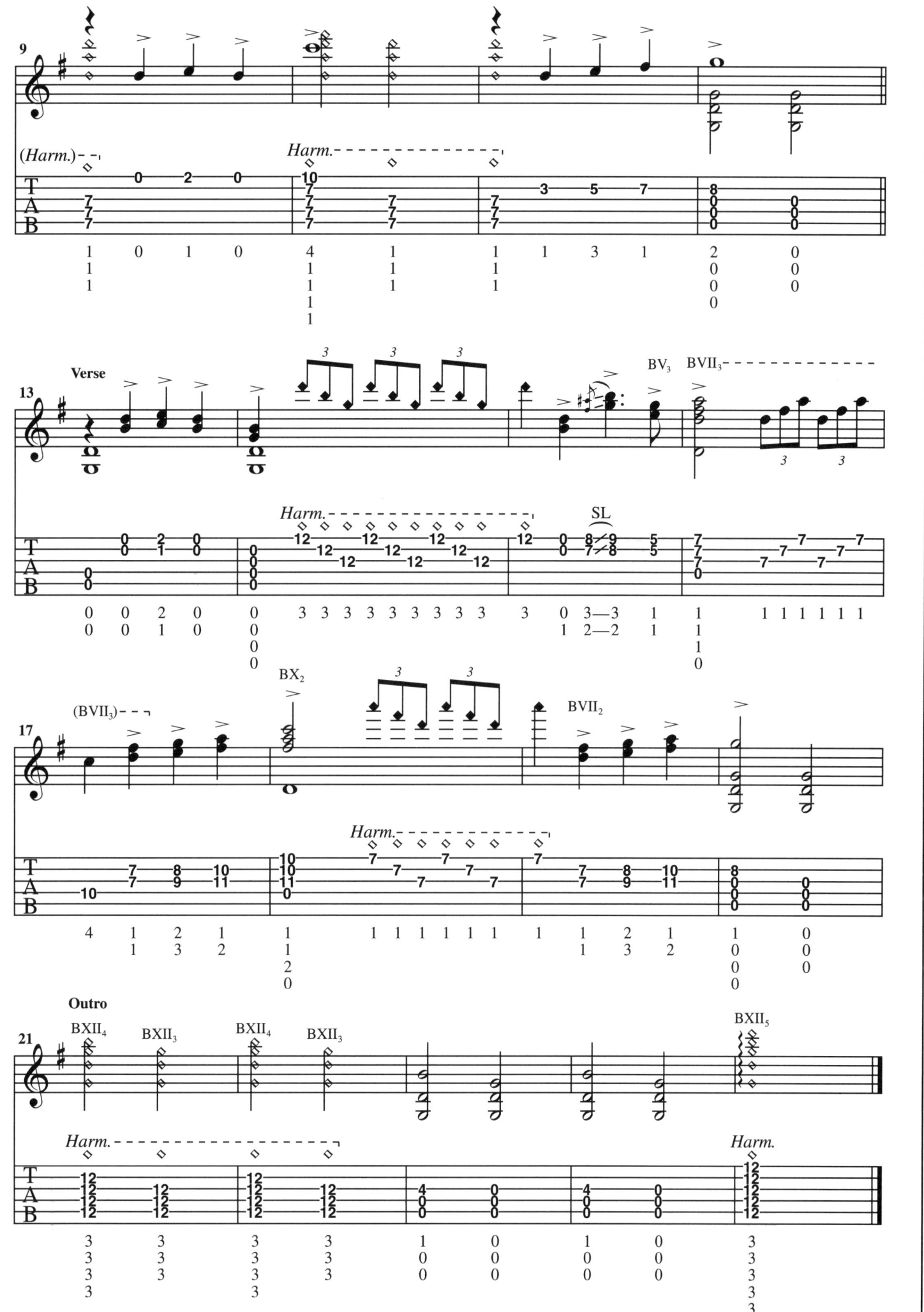

"KALINKA"

"Kalinka," like "Moscow Nights," is a Russian song that is popular across the globe. It is a favorite stage piece of small and large balalaika ensembles. "Kalinka" evolved from an old dance form in which dancers would speed up the steps until everything whirled with fiery energy. This musical effect, called *accelerando*, is common in Russian dance songs and Russian Gypsy music. In "Kalinka," the accelerando occurs over a repeating refrain, and is contrasted against a slower, gentler verse. To enhance the song's dramatic flare, balalaika and domra players incorporate the tremolo technique (page 246). The arrangement below is in the balalaika tuning and should be played with the pick. Watch out for *staccato* (short, detached) notes (indicated by a dot above noteheads). You achieve this detached sound by resting the heel of your right hand on the strings quickly after striking staccato notes. Place a capo at the 7th fret to bring the pitch of the guitar up to the balalaika. If you don't have a cutaway, this may make some of the higher notes difficult to reach. To compensate, you could place the capo at the 5th fret, or play the piece without a capo.

274 *Guitar Atlas: Volume 2*

Chapter 7 — RUSSIAN ROMANCES

The Russian romance is a lyrical type of song that dwells on love and emotional sentiment. Transcending the barriers of city and village life, it plays a special role in the history of Russian music, because it exists both as a professional art and as an oral tradition. First emerging in Russia as short pieces between opera acts that set famous Russian poems to folk melodies, the romance soon spread across Russia in circulating songbooks. By the 19th century, this sort of urban song was commonly known to village musicians and consequently entered into the oral folk tradition.

"OOCHIN CYORNI" ("DARK EYES") AND RUSSIAN GYPSIES

The intense emotive character of *Romani,* or Gypsy, music deeply intrigued composers of Russian romances, who wrote many songs in the Gypsy style. Beginning in the 19th century, Gypsies themselves toured Russia promoting the Russian "Gypsy" romance. In fact, it was the Gypsies who became known as the virtuosos of the genre, complementing their infectious singing with flashy seven-string guitar and violin licks. "Oochin Cyorni" ("Dark Eyes") is perhaps the most famous Russian Gypsy romance (even though it was written by a 19th century Ukrainian poet and a German composer). Performers tend to play this tune with *rubato,* or loose timing. They freely speed up, slow down, and linger on notes to enhance the song's emotional impact; be sure to listen to the CD to acquaint yourself with the rubato effect. This song should be played fingerstyle.

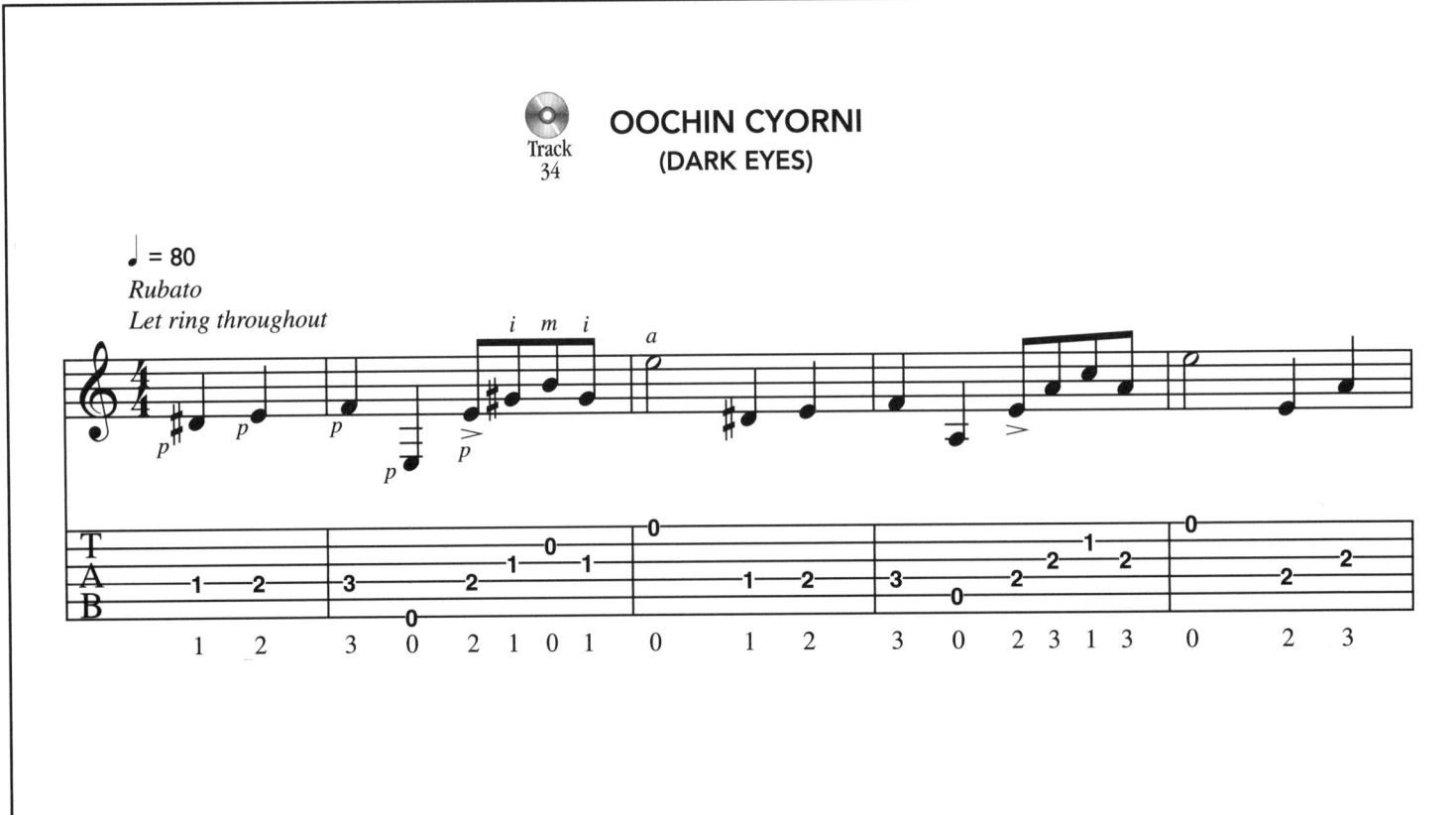

276 *Guitar Atlas: Volume 2*

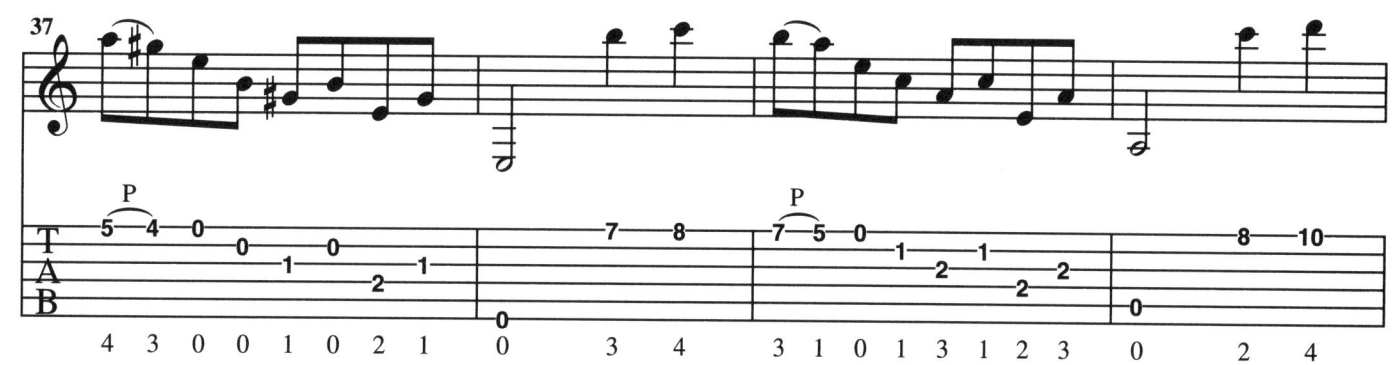
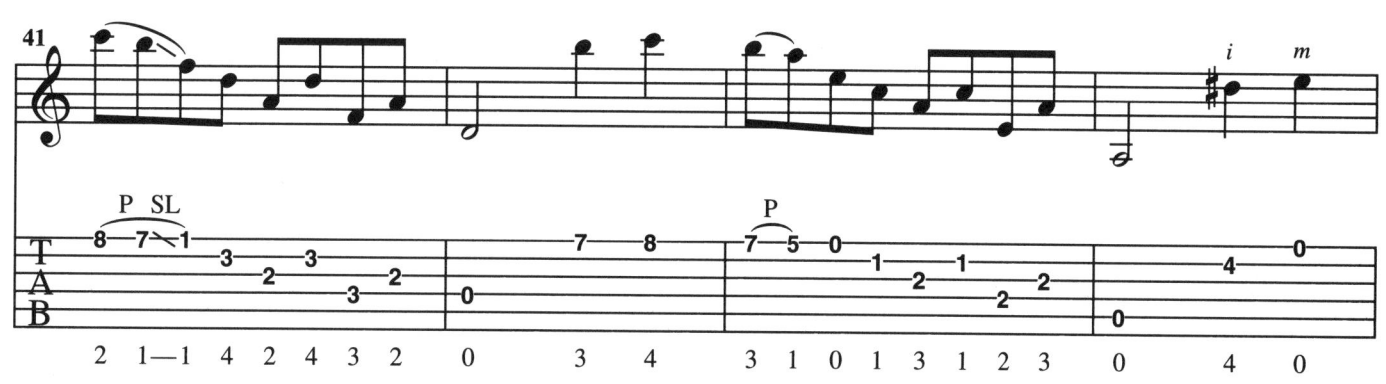
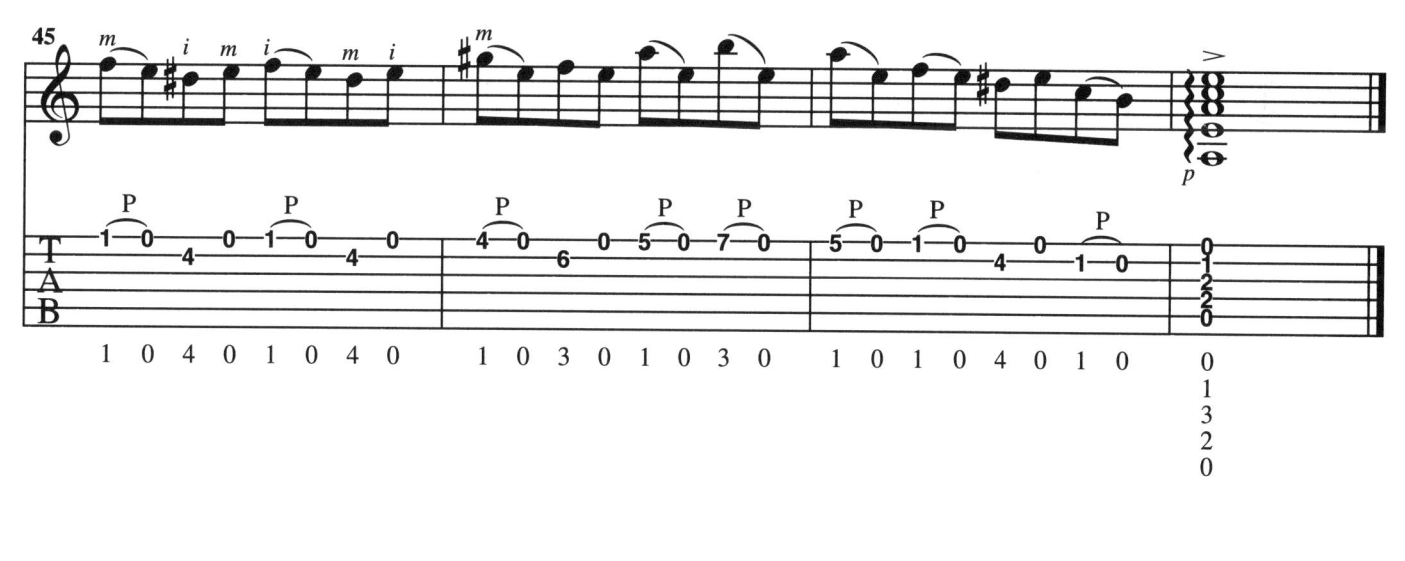

Chapter 8

THE BARD MOVEMENT

RUSSIA

Post-Stalin Russia of the 1960s experienced a folk revival as musicologists, taking a closer look into village life, re-examined the national "folk" image promoted by state-sponsored orchestras and choruses. At the same time, urban youth embraced the nostalgic idea that folk music is not a written tradition but one that is passed orally from musician to musician through performance and listening. This sentiment fostered a singer-songwriter movement known as the *bard movement*. Bards were poets who sang their own poetry to simple, seven-string guitar accompaniment. Their music, called *avtorskie pensi*, or "author's song," was circulated on homemade cassettes and drew young people to "unofficial" gatherings and city venues. Bard music was hardly related to village music, but its foremost feature, the poetry, tended to borrow from folk genres like criminal songs and soldier's songs (two urban lyric song genres that, like the Russian romance, found their way into village folk tradition). Today, bard festivals held in Russia and in the United States draw thousands of enthusiasts who gather to listen, sing, learn, and share songs.

Now, let's look at two of the most influential figures of the bard movement. Then, we'll explore chords and techniques these bards used to support their poetry.

BULAT OKUDZHAVA

Bulat Okudzhava (1924–1997) is considered the father of the author's song. He was not a trained musician and considered himself more of a poet than a guitarist. His songs focused on honest verses about war, peace, and love. Like most bards, he used only three to five chords to support his melodies. His approach was influenced by labor camp songs, Gypsy romances, soldier's songs, *chastushki* (short humorous ditties), and other folk-related genres. He accompanied himself on the Russian semistrunka (page 249) for most of his career, switching to the six-string only in the 1990s, which he tuned to open G to imitate the standard tuning of the Russian guitar.

VLADIMIR VYSOTSKY

Vladimir Vysotsky (1938–1980) is a well-remembered author's song artist, although he did not consider himself a bard. In fact, his first career was as an actor who appeared in films, performed leading Shakespearean roles, and starred in a popular television series. While Vysotsky's talent and success as an actor was acknowledged, his secondary musical career remained largely unrecognized by the official state music publisher due to his poetry's cynicism and social commentary. Heavy circulation of his music during the bard movement made his works so widely known that in the 1970s, some of his songs were officially published. Like Okudzhava, Vysotsky also used the Russian seven-string to accompany his over 600 songs, usually tuning it down a whole step (or more) to match his deep, gruff vocal style. He sang most of his songs as first-person monologues from the point of view of the many characters he created, including soldiers, outlaws, average folk, and even inanimate objects.

BARD CHORDS IN THE SEMISTRUNKA TUNING

Chapter 2 discussed the similarity between the semistrunka's standard tuning (D–G–B–D–G–B–D) and the open G tuning of the six-string guitar (D–G–D–G–B–D). Both tunings outline a G Major chord, but in the hands of Russian bards the seven-string is often used to play songs in minor keys. These songs may be humorous or melancholy, but they are always poetic and thought provoking. Many bards also lower their strings a step or more for a deeper, darker sound.

Bards are primarily poets and do not generally consider their guitar work extravagant. But that doesn't mean the guitar parts are not challenging. Their chord fingerings often leap around the neck. The poetry is supported with many different techniques, such as march-like *chucking* (slightly muted strokes), *arpeggios* (chord notes played in succession), strumming, plucking, and snapping. These techniques are never meant to steal the show but rather to support the story being sung, or "told." As a general rule, bards play fingerstyle.

Following are some chord shapes (arranged for the 6-string guitar in open G tuning: D–G–D–G–B–D) used by bards like Bulat Okudzhava and Vladimir Vysotsky. The first chord below, Amin, calls for muting the 4th string. To do this, allow the pad of your 2nd finger to muffle the 4th string while it frets the note on the 5th string. Also, note that since the 4th and 6th strings are both tuned to a D note, you may vary the bass by placing any given 4th-string note below on the 6th string instead. The pieces on pages 282–285 will give you a taste of the different ways bards use these chords to accompany their voice.

Semistrunka Chords

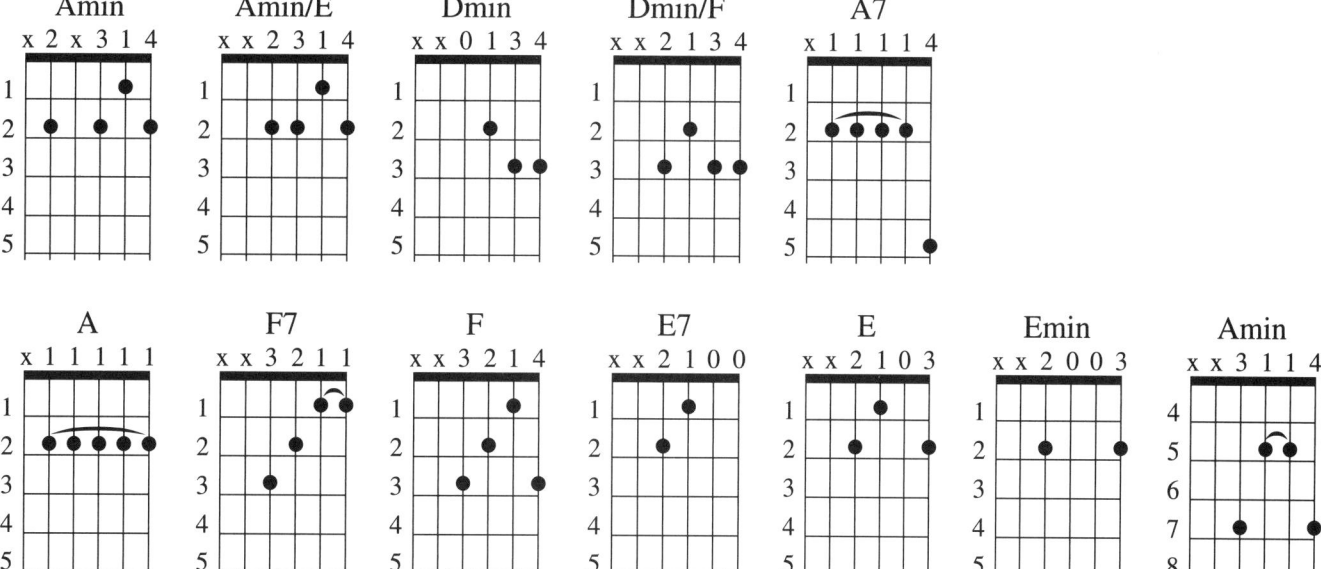

Guitar Atlas: Russia

BARD GUITAR STYLES

"A Soldier's Song" and "A March for Bulat" (page 284) display guitar styles used by bard singer-songwriters. "A Soldier's Song" demonstrates a Gypsy-influenced accompaniment style with a moving bass line. It is best played fingerstyle (though it is possible to play with a pick). Play all bass notes (the notes on the 4th, 5th, and 6th strings) with your thumb and the top three strings with an alternating strum using your index finger. "A March for Bulat" evokes a military feel using the chuck effect. This is executed with constant downstrokes of the thumb. Each stroke is played staccato by resting the pad of your right hand across the strings after each stroke. (It is possible to play "A March for Bulat" with a pick as well.) In both pieces, the chord diagrams that do not have chord symbols above them are "color" chords. They are not integral to the overall harmony of the tune, but make the basic chords more colorful and provide smoother transitions between chords.

282 *Guitar Atlas: Volume 2*

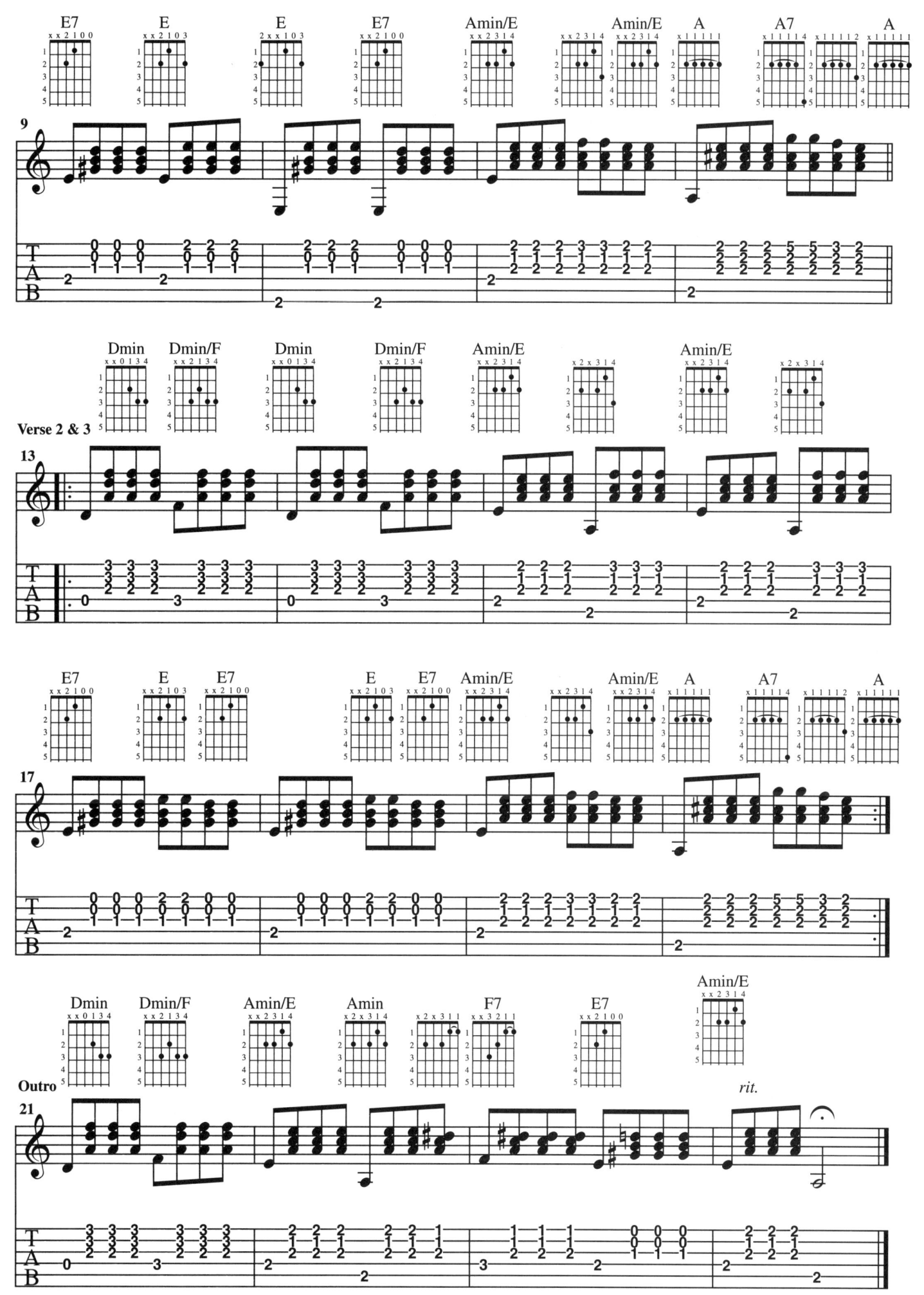

In "A March for Bulat," many of the chord fingerings presented on page 281 are located at different positions on the fretboard and, therefore, they have different letter names. For example, if you move the first fingering from page 281 up two frets, you get a Bmin chord instead of an Amin chord. As in "A Dukhovnyi Stikh" (page 260), there are instances in this piece when you must mute the 4th string with the pad of your 2nd finger as you strum across the strings.

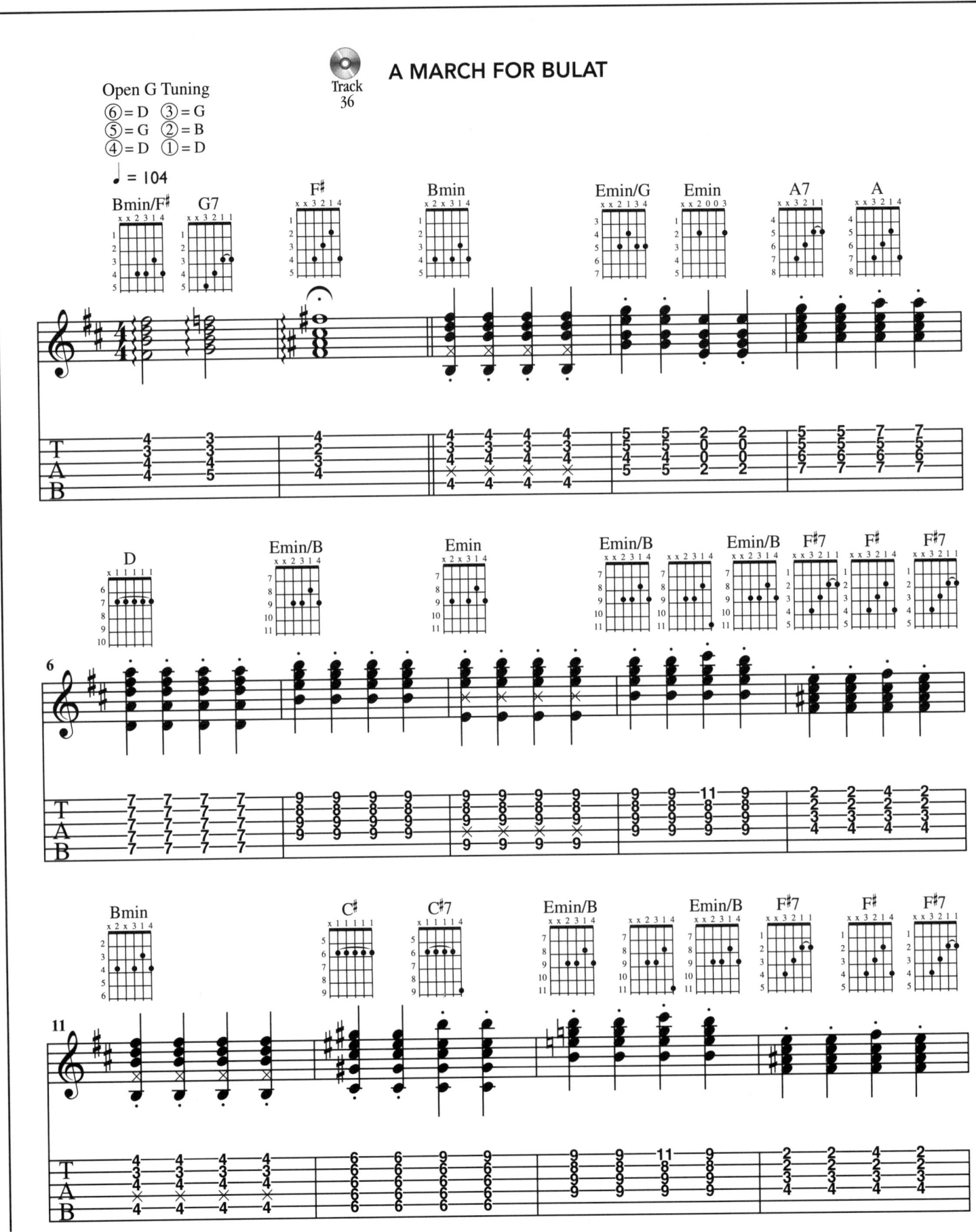

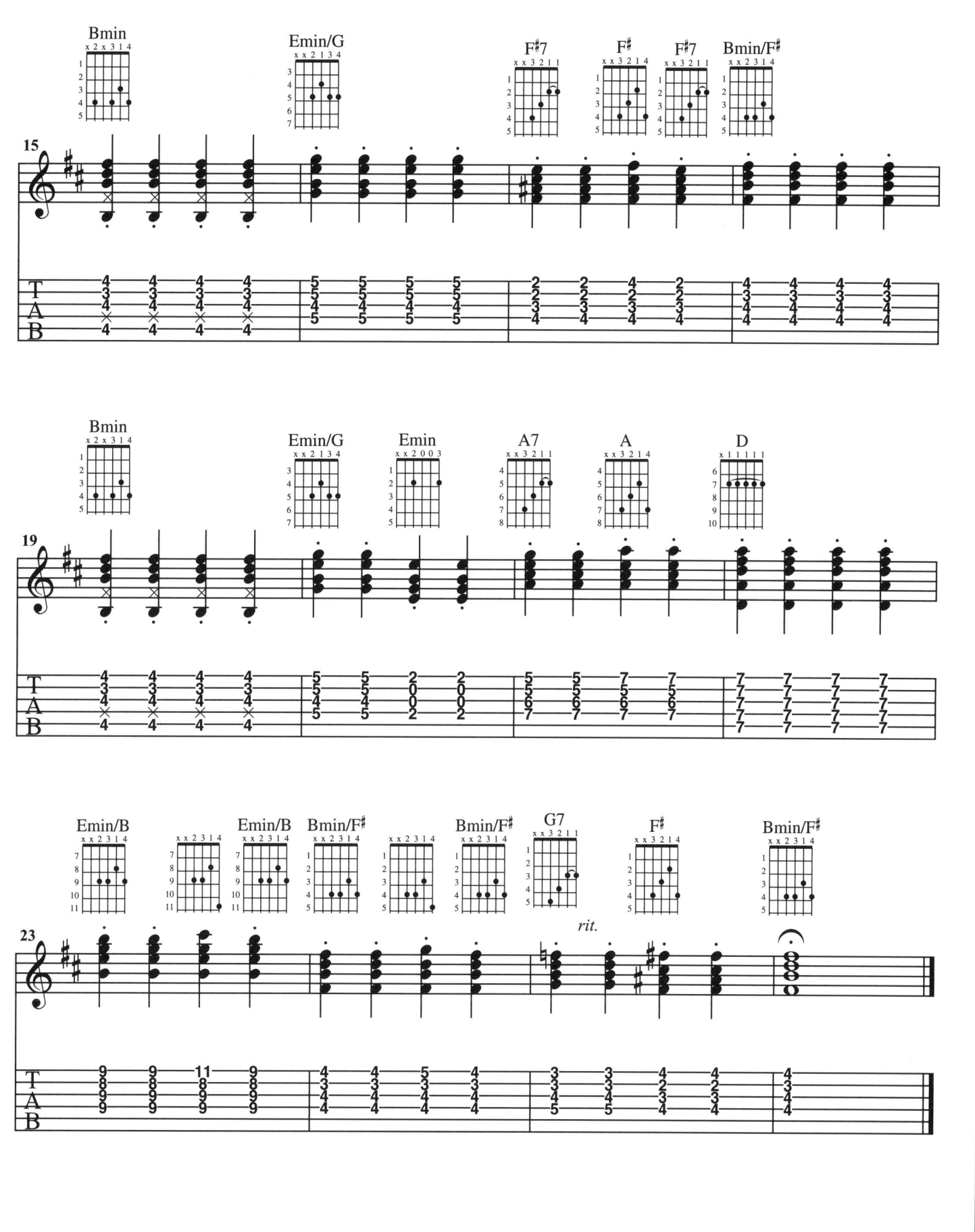

Final Word

RUSSIA

Thank you for taking the time to read through this book. I greatly enjoyed writing it. Russian music is deeply rooted in the traditions of the Russian people. At family gatherings, weddings, and funerals, Russian life is accompanied by song. This truth is evident in the work of modern Russian musicians who continue to incorporate elements of folk music into contemporary rock, pop, and classical contexts. Through the pages of *Guitar Atlas: Russia,* you have embarked on your own exploration into the rich content of Russian music. Now, with the insight you've gained, you are equipped to continue your journey. Following is a list of books, recordings, and websites to aid you on your way. Enjoy!

(If you have any questions or comments, write to: franknatterjr@faceartsstudio.com.)

REFERENCES FOR FURTHER READING

Olson, Laura. *Performing Russia: Folk Revival and Russian Identity.* New York: Routledge/Curzon, 2004.

Prokhorov, Vadim. *Russian Folk Songs.* Lanham: Scarecrow Press, Inc., 2002.

Morosan, Vladimir. *One Thousand Years of Russian Church Music.* Washington, DC: Musica Russica, 1991.

Swan, Alfred J. *Russian Music and its Sources in Chant and Folk Song.* New York: W.W. Norton & Co., Inc., 1973.

Zemtsovsky, Izaly. *The Garland Encyclopedia of World Music.* 2000 ed.

REFERENCES FOR FURTHER LISTENING

Musics of the Soviet Union. Smithsonian Folkways (SFW 40002), 1989.
Old Believers: Songs of the Nekrasov Cossacks. Smithsonian Folkways (SFW 40462), 1995.
The Rough Guide to the Music of Russia. World Music Network, 2002.
The Russian Holy Easter: Selected Festal Hymns of the Trinity-St. Sergius Lavra. Melodiya, 1999 (recorded 1978).
The Very Best of Russia. ARC Music Productions, 2006.
The World's a Stage: Music of Russia. Artemis Strategic Marketing, 2006.

WEB LINKS

To see Vladimir Vysotsky perform his song "Fastidious Horses":
http://www.youtube.com/watch?v=hWEOaosGDi0&feature=related

For online reading about Russian Orthodox Church Music:
http://www.liturgica.com/html/litEOLitMusDev5.jsp

For online articles about Russian music:
http://www.russia-ic.com/culture_art/music/description/

Appendix

ALTERNATE GUITAR TUNINGS USED IN THIS BOOK

RUSSIA

Following are the three *alternate tunings* used in this book. An alternate tuning is any tuning other than *standard tuning* (E–A–D–G–B–E). *Open G tuning* (common in American blues and folk styles) is used in this book to emulate the tuning of the Russian seven-string guitar (page 249). The *balalaika tuning* is derived from the tuning of the prima balalaika (page 246). Notice in this tuning that the 2nd and 3rd strings are tuned in *unison,* or to the same note. Also, if you place a capo at the 7th fret, the top three strings will exactly match the pitches of the balalaika strings. *Drop D tuning* allows for deeper bass notes by lowering (or "dropping") the 6th string down a whole step (from E to D). The CD includes tuning tracks for these tunings, so you can be sure the pitches are correct.

Open G Tuning

D G D G B D

Balalaika Tuning

E A D A A D

Drop D Tuning

D A D G B E

Guitar Atlas: Russia   287

If you love this book, you'll love our schools!

Online...

WORKSHOPLIVE

The next generation of music education from the founders of the National Guitar Workshop

Take a FREE online lesson today.
workshoplive.com

...or Near You!

N·G·W
National Guitar Workshop

LOCATIONS: Connecticut, Florida, Seattle, Nashville, Los Angeles, Texas, San Francisco, Virginia ...every summer!

1-800-234-6479
guitarworkshop.com